W9-DAD-235

DISCARD

RIGHT-WING EXTREMISM IN THE TWENTY-FIRST CENTURY

CASS SERIES ON POLITICAL VIOLENCE
ISSN 1365-0580

Series Editors: David C. Rapoport, University of California, Los Angeles
Paul Wilkinson, University of St Andrews, Scotland

1. *Terror from the Extreme Right,* edited by Tore Bjørgo

2. *Millennialism and Violence,* edited by Michael Barkun

3. *Religious Radicalism in the Greater Middle East,* edited by Bruce Maddy-Weitzmann and Efraim Inbar

4. *The Revival of Right-Wing Extremism in the Nineties,* edited by Peter H. Merkl and Leonard Weinberg

5. *Violence in Southern Africa,* edited by William Guttereidge and J. E. Spence

6. *Aviation Terrorism and Security,* edited by Paul Wilkinson and Brian M. Jenkins

7. *The IRA, 1968–2000: Analysis of a Secret Army,* J. Bowyer Bell

8. *Terrorism Today,* Christopher C. Harmon

9. *Terrorism and Liberal Democracy: The Problem of Response,* Paul Wilkinson

Right-Wing Extremism
in the
Twenty-First Century

Editors
PETER H. MERKL
LEONARD WEINBERG

FRANK CASS
LONDON • PORTLAND, OR

First published in 2003 in Great Britain by
FRANK CASS PUBLISHERS
Crown House, 47 Chase Side, Southgate
London N14 5BP

and in the United States of America by
FRANK CASS PUBLISHERS
c/o ISBS, 5824 N.E. Hassalo Street
Portland, Oregon, 97213-3644

Website: www.frankcass.com

British Library Cataloguing in Publication Data

Right-wing extremism in the twenty-first century. – 2nd
rev. ed. – (Cass series on political violence; no. 4)
1. Right-wing extremists – Europe 2. Radicalism – Europe
I. Merkl, Peter H. (Peter Hans) II. Weinberg, Leonard III. The
revival of right-wing extremism in the nineties

320.5'3'094'0905

ISBN 0-7146-5182-6 (cloth)
ISBN 0-7146-8188-1 (paper)
ISSN 1365-0580

Library of Congress Cataloging-in-Publication Data

Right-wing extremism in the twenty-first century / editors, Peter Merkl, Leonard
Weinberg. – 2nd rev. ed.
   p. cm. – (Cass series on political violence)
Rev. ed. of: The revival of right-wing extremism in the nineties.
Includes bibliographical references and index.
ISBN 0-7146-5182-6 (cloth) – ISBN 0-7146-8188-1 (pbk.)
   1. Right-wing extremists. 2. Radicalism. I. Merkl, Peter H. II. Weinberg, Leonard,
1939–   III. Revival of right-wing extremism in the nineties. IV. Series.

HN17.5 .R49 2003
320.5'09'05–dc21

                                                                    2002035008

Typeset in 11/13pt Bembo by Vitaset, Paddock Wood, Kent
Printed in Great Britain by
MPG Books Ltd, Victoria Square, Bodmin, Cornwall

Contents

List of Tables and Figures and Appendices   vii

List of Abbreviations and Glossary   ix

Notes on Contributors   xiii

Preface   David Rapoport   xvii

Introduction   Peter H. Merkl   1

Part 1 The Extreme Right in the Ascendancy

1. Stronger than Ever   Peter H. Merkl   23

2. Ten Theories of the Extreme Right   Roger Eatwell   47

3. The Growing Threat of the Radical Right   Hans-Georg Betz   74

Part 2 Comparing Public Opinion Indicators

4. Racism and the Political Right: European Perspectives   Charles Westin   97

5. Explaining National Variations in Support for Far Right Political Parties in Western Europe, 1990–2000   Allen Wilcox, Leonard Weinberg, William Eubank   126

6. The Development of the Extreme Right at the End of the Century   Piero Ignazi   143

Part 3 Changing National Contexts

7. The Front National in Context: French and European Dimensions   Michael Minkenberg, Martin Schain   161

8. The FPÖ: From Populist Protest to Incumbency   Kurt Richard Luther   191

9. Right-Wing Extremism and
   Xenophobia in Germany: Escalation,
   Exaggeration, or What?   Ekkart Zimmermann   220

10. Right-Wing Extremism in Russia:
    The Dynamics of the 1990s   Vera Tolz   251

11. Patterns of Response to the Extreme
    Right in Western Europe   Jaap van Donselaar   272

Conclusion   Leonard Weinberg   293

Index   303

List of Tables and Figures and Appendices

TABLES

4.1   Options for integration or assimilation   100
4.2   Self-declared 'racism' in the 1997 Eurobarometer survey across   102
      EU member-states
4.3   Trust in public institutions and political establishments   103
4.4   Awareness of discrimination in the labour market and   105
      acceptance of (more) minority groups
4.5   The Nordic states and international memberships   109
4.6   Distribution of tolerant/intolerant attitudes in Europe   114
4.7   Percentage of respondents that agree with statements   116
      concerning: (1) anti-discrimination; (2) diversity-management;
      (3) equal opportunities; (4) participation
4.8   Acceptance of migrants from different regions and for different   117
      reasons
4.9   Country differences   121
4.10 Protest parties and extremist organizations in the EU   124
5.1   Far-right voting in Western Europe: 1990–2000   128
5.2   Correlates of far-right voting   134
5.3   Relationships between standard deviations of values and far-   135
      right voting
5.4   Relationships between economic variables and far-right voting   136
5.5   Relationships between political variables and far-right voting   137
6.1   Electoral trend of the extreme right parties by country   144
      (1980–99)
7.1   Dominant actors in the French radical right-wing family (post-   165
      1965)
7.2   Support for the Front National by percentage of North   172
      Africans and Turks in *départements*
7.3   Party support and the presence of immigrants at the commune   173
      level in 1996
7.4   The motivations of voters: 1984–97   178

7.5   Public opinion on immigration: 1966–91   179
7.6   Comparing Front National loyalists with new FN voters in   180
      1997
7.7   Loyal Front National voters in 1997 compared with 1988   181
8.1   Freedom Party vote within selected social groups (1986 and   195
      1999)
8.2   Development of the Freiheitliche Partei Österreichs'   205
      membership: 1986–2000

FIGURES

8.1   Freiheitliche Partei Österreichs shares of the vote at Austrian   194
      general elections: 1945–99
8.2   Freiheitliche Partei Österreichs party membership: 1956–99   202
8.3   Freiheitliche Partei Österreichs vote and membership density   203
      during its four periods of development: 1956–99

APPENDICES

5.1   Far-right parties c. 1990 and 2000   139
5.2   Number of times each nation registers among the top three   140
      nations in the far-right direction across the 28 variables and
      among the top three in the non-far-right direction

List of Abbreviations and Glossary

Anders Lange Party – Far-right Norwegian party, now the Norwegian Progress Party (FRPn).

AN – Alleanza Nazionale: successor to the neo-fascist MSI (Italy).

BKA – German Federal Criminal Office.

Black Hundred – Violent anti-Semitic bands in late-nineteenth-century Russia.

BNP – British National Party.

BVS – Office for the Protection of the Constitution (Germany).

CCS – Comités Chrétienté-Solidarité (Christianity-Solidarity Committee).

CD – Centrumdemocraten (Centre Democrats), a far-right party (the Netherlands).

CDU – Christian Democrat Party (Germany).

CEVIPOF – Centre d'étude de la vie politique française (France).

CP – Centrumpartij (Centre Party): far-right Dutch party.

CPRF – Communist Party of the Russian Federation.

CPSU – Communist Party of the Soviet Union.

CRIDA – Centre de Recherche d'Information et de Documentation Antiraciste (France).

CSU – Christian Social Union: Bavarian affiliate of the CDU (Germany).

DC – Christian Democrats (Italy).

DF – Dansk Folkeparti: Danish People's Party, extremist right party led by Pia Kjaersgaard.

DPA – Movement in Support of the Army (Russia).

DRP – German Rightist Party (Germany).

DVU – German People's Union (Germany).

EMU – European Monetary Union.

ENEP – Effective Number of Electoral Parties.

EPEN – Ethniki Politiki Enosis National (National Political Union) (Greece).

EUMC – European Monitoring Centre on Racism and Xenophobia.

FANE – Fédération Action Nationale Européenne (Federation of National European Action).

FAP – Free Workers' Party (Germany).

FDVP – Freiheitliche Deutsche Volkspartei (Germany).

FN – Front National: French right-wing party.

FNB – Front Nouveau de Belgique/Front Nieuw België.

FNE – Faisceaux nationalistes européens (European National Fascists).

FNJ – Front national de jeunesse (France).

Forza Italia – Right-wing Italian party.

FPÖ – Freiheitliche Partei Österreichs (Austrian Freedom Party).

FRG – Federal Republic of Germany.

FRPd – Fremskridtspartiet: Danish Progress Party, far-right party.

FRPn – Norwegian Progress Party (formerly the Anders Lange Party).

GDR – German Democratic Republic (formerly East Germany).

GRECE – Groupement de recherche et d'études pour la civilisation européenne (France).

GUD – Groupe Union Defense (Union Defence Group).

IPSA – International Political Science Association.

JN – Junge Nationaldemokraten (Young National Democrats) (Germany).

KEPRU – Keele European Parties Research Unit (UK).

KP – Kommunistische Partij –Vlaanderen, a Communist/militant Trotskyist party (Belgium).

KPD – German Communist Party.

LDPR – Liberal Democratic Party of Russia, far-right party.

LIF – Liberales Forum, centre-left (Austria).

LN – Lega Nord: far-right Italian party..

MNR – Mouvement National Républicain (France), far-right party.

MSI – Movimento Sociale Italiano., neo-fascist Italian precursor of AN.

MSIFT – Movimento Sociale Italia Fiamma Tricolore, neo-fascist Italian party.

NATO – North Atlantic Treaty Organization.

NBP – National Bolshevik Party (Russia).

NCIS – National Crime Intelligence Service (UK).

NF – National Front (UK).

NPD – National Democratic Party, neo-fascist German party.

NVU – Nederlands Volksunie (Dutch People's Union).

NyD – New Democracy, far-right Swedish party.

OECD – Organization for Economic Cooperation and Development.

ONP – One Nation Party: far-right Australian party.

ÖVP – Österreichische Volkspartei: Austrian People's Party.

Pamiat – Russian far-right movement.

PCF – Parti Communiste Française (France).

PDS – Party of Democratic Socialism, successor to East German state communist party.

PDS – Party of the Democratic Left, successor of the Italian communist party.

PR – proportional representation.

PRM – Greater Romania Party.

PS – Parti Socialiste (France).

PUNR – Party of Romanian National Unity.

RAF – Red Army Fraktion (Germany).

REP – Republican Party (Republikaner): far-right German party.

RF – Russian Federation.

RFB – Rotfront, German communist youth of Weimar republic.

RNU – Russian National Unity Party.

ROS – Russian Public Union.

RPR – Rassemblement pour la République: French Gaullist party.

RSFSR – Russian Federation of Socialist Republics.

SA – Nazi storm-troopers (Germany).

SCALP – Sections carrément Anti-Le Pen, anti-fascist movement (France).

SD – Schweizer Demokraten (Swiss Democratic Party) (Switzerland).

SED – Socialist Unity Party, Communist (GDR).

SORA – Institute for Social Research and Analysis (Austria).

SPD – Social Democrat Party (Germany).

SPÖ – Sozial Demokratische Partei Österreichs, Austrian Social Democratic Party.

SRP – Socialist Reich Party, German neo-fascists of the 1950s.

SVP – Swiss People's Party, far-right Swiss party.

UDF – Union pour la démocratie française, right-wing party (France).

UDR – Union of Democrats for the Republic, predecessor of RPR (France).

USSR – Union of Soviet Socialist Republics (Soviet Union): dissolved in 1992.

VB –Vlaams Blok (Flemish Block): far-right Belgian party.

VdU –Austrian far-right party of the 1950s.

VMO – Flemish militant order, far-right movement (Belgium).

VTsIOM – All-Russian Centre for the Study of Public Opinion (Russia).

VVD – Dutch right-wing party.

Notes on Contributors

Hans-Georg Betz is an Associate Professor of Political Science at the Canadian Centre of German and European Studies, York University; and he is currently a Visiting Professor at the Université de Genève, Geneva, Switzerland. He is the author of numerous publications dealing with radical right-wing populism in Europe.

Roger Eatwell is Professor of European Politics at the University of Bath, UK. His main field of research covers the ideology of, and support for, classical fascism and the contemporary extreme right, and related issues such as charismatic leadership. His books include: *Fascism: A History* (1995); and *Fascismo: verso un Modello Generale* (1999); he has also contributed over 30 articles to journals and books on related topics.

William Eubank is an Associate Professor at the University of Nevada, USA. Besides his continuing interest in political violence, he is also interested in choice theory, voting and electoral behaviour, and social science research methods. At present he is engaged in a study of the evolution of terrorist organisations.

Piero Ignazi is Professor of Comparative Politics at the University of Bologna, Italy. He has worked extensively on the comparative study of political parties, with a particular emphasis on the European extreme right.

Kurt Richard Luther is Senior Lecturer in Politics at Keele University, UK. He is Convenor of the Keele European Parties Research Unit (KEPRU), which is commencing a major research project on the Europeanization of national political parties. He has published widely on Austrian party politics, and his most recent publications (as co-editor) include: *Fifty Years of the Second Republic* (1998); *Austria Consociational Democracy* (1999); and *Political Parties in the New Europe: Political and Analytical Challenges* (2002).

Peter Merkl is Professor at the University of California, Santa Barbara. His recent books include: *A Coup Attempt in Washington?*; *The Federal Republic of Germany at Fifty*; and, with Leonard Weinberg, *The Revival of Right-Wing Extremism in the Nineties*. He is currently co-editing essays, with Kay Lawson, on party systems, *When Parties Prosper*.

Michael Minkenberg is Professor of Political Science at the Europa-Universität Viadrina, Frankfurt (Oder), Germany. He received his MA in 1984 at Georgetown University, USA, and his PhD in 1989 at the University of Heidelberg. He is the author of *Die neue radikale Rechte im Vergleich: USA, Frankreich, Deutschland* (1998); and the co-editor of *Religion und Politik: Zwischen Universalismus und Partikularismus* (2000).

Martin Schain is Professor of Politics, and Director of the Center for European Studies, New York University. In addition to numerous publications concerning contemporary French politics, Professor Schain is the Chair of the European Community Studies Association, and the co-editor of a new transatlantic journal, *Comparative European Politics*.

Vera Tolz is Professor of Contemporary History and Deputy Director of the European Studies Research Institute at the University of Salford, UK. She has published widely on various aspects of Russian history and politics. Her books include: *The USSR's Emerging Multiparty System* (1990); *Russian Academicians and the Revolution: Between Professionalism and Politics* (1997); and *Russia: Inventing the Nation* (2001).

Jaap van Donselaar is a researcher at Leiden University, the Netherlands, and at the Anne Frank House. His publications include: 'De staat paraat?', a comparative analysis of state responses to racism and right-wing extremism.

Leonard Weinberg is Foundation Professor of Political Science at University of Nevada, Reno. His recent publications include: *Political Parties and Terrorist Groups* (co-edited with A. Pedahzur); *The Democratic Experience and Political Violence* (co-edited with David Rapoport); and *The Emergence of a Euro-American Radical Right* (co-edited with J. Kaplan). His articles have appeared in such journals as: *Comparative Politics*; *The British Journal of Political Science*; *Party Politics* and *Terrorism and Political Violence*.

Charles Westin is Professor of Migration and Ethnicity Studies at Stockholm University and Director of the Centre for Research in International Migration and Ethnic Relations, Sweden. He has edited: *Racism, Ideology and Political Organization* (1998); and *Racism Xenophobia and the Academic Response*

(2001); and has co-edited *Nationalism and Internationalism in the Post-Cold War Era* (2002).

Allen Wilcox is a Professor at the University of Nevada, USA. His major interests and current research are in the areas of public opinion, political psychology, and radical political movements.

Ekkart Zimmerman is a Professor of Macrosociology at the Dresden University of Technology. From 1981 until 1992, he taught at the University of the Federal Armed Forces in Munich. He is currently finishing two book-length manuscripts: 'Development, Change and Globalization'; and 'System Transformation: East Germany in Comparative Perspective'.

Introduction

B RADFORD WAS the fourth northern English city to be racked by violence involving whites, South Asian immigrants and police in late May and early July of 2001. At the height of the clashes, several hundred youths – some say over a thousand – erected burning barricades, set cars on fire, and showered police with Molotov cocktails, bricks, bottles and other debris. They attacked each other, and the police, with bats, knives and other lethal weapons. Police helicopters were hovering overhead. Dozens of paddy wagons with officers in riot gear tried to patrol the streets of central Bradford. About 200 police officers were reported to have been injured by mobs of white, Pakistani, Indian, Sri Lankan and Bangladeshi youths. Nineteen civilians had injuries too on first count. Thirty-six rioters were arrested, two-thirds of them South Asians. In earlier years of English racial violence, South Asians had tended to be mostly at the receiving end of 'Paki-bashing'.

Bradford is an industrial city with a population of about half a million, around one-fifth of South Asian origin. It is a part of the rustbelt north – a pocket of poverty and neglect in prosperous England. The confrontation began – as earlier in Oldham, Aylesbury (a town in Buckinghamshire), Leeds and Burnley, and later in Stoke-on-Trent – with ultra-right agitation by members of the National Front (NF) and the British National Party (BNP). In Oldham, a gritty, declining mill town with 10 per cent unemployment and a largely segregated population half of Bradford's size, it had been the mugging of a 76-year-old man, allegedly by Asian youths, that had brought in the ultra-right agents and set off four nights of rioting and destruction. Thirty-three whites and 16 South Asians were arrested. The decline and stagnation of Oldham's main industry hit everyone hard, but particularly the young South Asians whose unemployment rate is much higher and who hang around in the town's centre in large idle groups, divided by ethnic origin, region, caste and by the corresponding youth gangs they form. More than half of the 572 racial attacks reported by Oldham police for the year 2000 were attributed to such Asian gangs. White skinhead and neo-Nazi gangs, by contrast, show up in force on weekends in the town centre to accost the Asians, in defiance of a three-month ban on all political marches issued by the Home Secretary who is well aware of the rising tensions in northern England. The clashes were preceded by racially tinged skirmishes at a school in a white neighbourhood and, on a Saturday (26 May 2001), a scuffle between two 15-year-olds in front of a fish-and-chip shop brought out mobs of hundreds. There were fears also that the violence might spread to an impending cricket test-match between England and Pakistan in Manchester ten miles away. The media have long suspected a linkage between racially flavoured soccer violence and right-wing agitation, especially after the Eurocup riots of 2000 on the continent.

The Oldham riots took place during Prime Minister Tony Blair's re-election campaign – the general election was on 7 June – and caused considerable embarrassment to the government. William Hague, the leader of the Conservative opposition, had stated at the outset of the campaign that Britain was becoming 'a foreign land' under the pro-European policies of the Labour party, and that the country was too easy on the flood of 'bogus asylum-seekers' trying to come in. Most of the Asian immigrants of northern England, of course, had already arrived in the 1960s and 1970s in response to very real labour shortages. Hague was accused of pandering to xenophobic and racist sentiments while another Conservative representative, John Townend, added his own invective about immigrants undermining Britain's 'homogeneous Anglo-Saxon society'.

The recriminations among the major parties finally produced a pledge not to exploit racial issues for electoral gain. The ultra-right fringe parties, of course, felt no such restraint – two BNP candidates were running for the House of Commons in this area – nor did the establishment's assurances calm the fears of the white residents. The media reported that Asians have little confidence in the overwhelmingly white police force and what they view as an indifferent and often hostile local officialdom. In Oldham, they said, many Asian victims of hate crimes tend not to report the attacks on them. A series of recent violent assaults on Asian cab drivers did not even make the local newspapers which are another target of Asian criticisms. Amnesty International, in a recent report, pilloried the biases of British police, judges and prison authorities towards people of colour and warned of worse to come if government failed to investigate the charges of discrimination and abuse. Among the more glaring cases were instances of ill-treatment by police, deaths in custody and failure to investigate alleged racial abuse by police officials, according to Amnesty's report to the UN World Conference against Racism in August 2001.

In Bradford, where there had been earlier clashes in April, considerable tension arose again in early July. Following a demonstration of the Anti-Nazi

League, hundreds of Asian youths had gathered for a peaceful rally when they found themselves taunted by groups of whites emerging from downtown pubs and shouting racial epithets at them. Next evening, after the riot had run its course, a gang of about 30 white youths were still smashing the windows of an Indian restaurant and an Asian-owned gas station on the [white] outskirts of the city. The re-elected Prime Minister Tony Blair called the Bradford riots a result of 'thuggery', and added: 'There may initially have been an element of provocation from the far right at some point during Saturday, but first evidence is that this is simply thuggery and local people determined to have a go at the police and, in the process of doing that, destroying their own community.' The editor of the *Bradford Telegraph and Argus* estimated that 'there was a hardcore element of 150–200 youths who were just set on violence and thuggery, and racism is just an excuse'.[1]

Bradford residents blamed the tensions building over BNP rallies that claimed they were defending the 'rights of white Britons'. The BNP had put up 33 candidates nationwide in the last general elections and polled 4.6 per cent of the vote in North Bradford, 11.4 per cent in Burnley, and 16.4 per cent in Oldham-West. Under the first-past-the-post electoral system, of course, this did not elect anyone to the Commons, but under the proportional representation systems common on the Continent, some might have been elected to the national legislature. In Bradford, moreover, the neo-Nazi NF threatened to challenge the Anti-Nazi League gathering with a march of its own.[2] And when the police denied it a permit, belligerent NF members evidently gathered in the pubs surrounding the Anti-Nazi League rally and shouted at the Asian youths. A week after Bradford, it was the rumours of a march of the BNP or NF, again, that triggered a riot in the Midlands town of Stoke-on-Trent. Hundreds of Asians gathered in response. The police appeared in order to control the crowds and ended up arresting 50 people, 31 of them white, after bricks and paving stones began to be thrown.

Britain's problems with xenophobia and right-wing violence have their equivalents all over the Continent, from Antwerp to Vienna. I could just as easily have begun this book with descriptions of the right-wing street terror of the East German university towns of Jena and Erfurt, or the widespread surmises – probably untrue – behind the soccer hooligan violence of the European Cup in 2000. Or the right-wing electoral surges that occurred from Romania to the German state of Saxony-Anhalt. Or the racist prejudice and violence visited upon asylum-seekers and immigrants in places as far apart as Paris and Budapest. A host of extreme right-wing phenomena – though hardly anything resembling the fascist and Nazi upsurge of the 1920s and 1930s – are on the march all over Europe.

APPROACHES TO RIGHT-WING EXTREMISM

Where did it come from, all of a sudden, this renewed threat of the radical right in Europe? What motivates the revival of right-wing extremism in so many Western countries since the 1980s? Is it really just an ideological conflict over values and ideas, as some observers see it, or a reflection of new socioeconomic pressures – for example of the information revolution or economic globalization – on the least-educated, most vulnerable sections of the working class? Obviously, it takes both elements and several additional factors to give rise to social movements – not to mention political parties – as social movement theory has pointed out since the 1970s. We have only the space and resources to skim the surface of evolving phenomena in Europe rather than being able to go into great depths regarding any one movement or aiming at a comprehensive theory to explain a political reality that is still in transition and showing us new faces every day. The nature of right-wing extremism has not quite jelled and experienced analysts still disagree on categorization, labels and boundaries between its different manifestations. Except for some journalistic flights of fancy, at least there seems to be a consensus now that very little of it still relates to the fascist era of the first half of the last century. Does it reflect deep-rooted changes in Western societies, perhaps in the very structures of individual and family life, among the primary relationships that guide the process of growing up? Is it a new kind of street violence that arises from the fashions and music of skinhead youth gangs, their laboured substitute for the primordial dimensions of a lost tribal sense of belonging?

SUBCULTURES, SOCIAL MOVEMENTS AND POLITICAL PARTIES

In the first chapters of this book, some of the contributors spell out their perceptions of the new radical right, some more in terms of values and slogans, others more empirically. But we need to remember that we are still far from a universally agreed and detailed template of right-wing extremism, and that it would be highly misleading to generalize from any one country's experience to all the others. The very nature of these different ultra-nationalisms, to name the most prominent feature, militates against universalizing the striking diversities. With each national movement asserting its uniqueness so desperately, how dare we claim they are all the same? Having said this, and in the face of the various subjective visions of this book, we still need at least a rough framework of methodological assumptions to order the competing interpretations in a preliminary way. Let us distinguish, first of all, between subcultures of the extreme right – which produce its basic values and ideas – its social movements and, highest on the food chain (in a manner of speaking), its political parties.

A right-wing subculture is a rather stable social world in itself that may derive its specifically right-wing views from an antecedent subculture, profound reactions to a historical crisis, the anomie of war and destruction, the dragon seed of struggles against cruel antagonists and rivals, or the walking wounded of horrible massacres of the past, or of painful social changes. To give an example, right-wing recruits may grow up amidst the socialization processes of Italian, German or Spanish families, once identified closely with the regimes of Mussolini, Hitler or Franco, bitterly remembering their families' reactions to their downfall and subsequent purges. Or they may have grown up in families associated one way or another with former colonial empires, with prejudicial views towards their erstwhile colonial subjects – especially when the latter become immigrants or asylum-seekers in the mother countries. Or they may grow up in otherwise stable settings of middle-class or working-class families that find themselves increasingly impoverished or displaced by major economic changes over which they have no control. People may also be socialized into these subcultural attitudes and never become political activists of the extreme right, merely sympathizers.

By way of contrast, a right-wing social movement is the dynamic product of a right-wing subculture and exhibits some degree of organization, for example as an association devoted to the defence of certain salient issues, or the tribe's identity, or against threatened measures of antagonists or government agencies. There may be several, even antagonistic, social movements within the same subculture. There often are also wider circles of sympathizers, or occasional collaborators within the subculture who may prefer not to get involved more deeply or share only some but not all of the issue positions of the organized movement. Social movements have a discernible point in time of origin, may undergo splits and transformations, and eventually fade away.

A right-wing party, finally, like all political parties, is a highly specialized organization for electing representatives, or defeating opponents, and participating in legislation and administration at any level. Whether and how members of a social movement form a party depends mostly on the opportunities afforded by the existing political system and the electoral market place. Unless there is a gap among the competing parties, possibly due to the decline of a more moderate party, the extreme right may have a hard time breaking through. Successful parties are highly dependent on financial and other resources, the entrepreneurial skills of their leaders, and the engagement of their activists. It is very common that some members of the subculture and even of the social movement have serious misgivings about 'their party' and its activities. It is the specialized activities that define the party and this may often attract certain specialists, for example in campaign management, public relations and fund-raising, who may have little commitment to the values of the subculture or the social movement.

In a similar fashion, the nature of its activities defines the violent fringe of the extreme right. In a well-established system, political violence is proscribed as an illegitimate instrument of competition and the pursuit of power. There can of course be some members of a subculture or social movement who in the heat of the political battle commit violent transgressions against the other side. But this violent minority is often distinguished from the rest of the faithful by a violent predisposition, or a criminal record, by psychopathology rather than only the beliefs and values of the extreme right. But we need not go far towards extremes of political violence to arrive at the 'thuggery' – with 'racism just an excuse' – that Blair and the local press saw at work in Bradford. Once violent confrontations have begun, persons of a violent predisposition may well be swept away to react to such situations in their most violent way.

In the context of organized violence, moreover, for example of the street violence of Nazi stormtroopers and young Communists in Weimar Berlin, specialists of violence such as military veterans trained in the use of explosives and weapons, or amateur boxers and wrestlers play a far bigger role than ideological hotheads.[3] Rather than looking solely into the motivations of violence, social researchers have often found it more meaningful to examine the incidence of it over time, or to speak with Clifford Geertz, to explore 'thick descriptions' of what actually takes place. In some countries even law-enforcement carefully separates mere thuggery from ideological protest that may be understandable, even excusable, up to a point.[4] Social psychologists have also studied the genesis of violent dispositions in individuals, beginning with their childhood and the factors that may have made a child into a violent teenager or adult.[5] It is no accident that violent skinheads often have long records of earlier violent encounters unrelated to their recent political targets or prejudices.

THE EXTREME RIGHT: STRONGER THAN EVER

The selection of topics for this book has been shaped by current events and the preoccupations of scholars in the field. Chapter 1, by Peter Merkl, highlights recent extreme right-wing developments in Europe. The chapter starts with the meteoric rise of the Greater Romania Party (PRM) of

Corneliu Vadim Tudor and the Austrian Freedom party (Freiheitliche Partei Österreichs, or FPÖ) of Jörg Haider in recent elections. These two provide an intriguing contrast between an East European, 1930s-style, nativist kind of integral nationalism and racial imperialism and a slick, media-savvy West European right-wing populism that feeds on hostility to immigrants and asylum-seekers.

Merkl goes on to explore the issue of unwanted immigration as a trigger of xenophobic reactions all around the rim of the embattled Fortress Europe, evident now even in the tolerant Netherlands, in Ireland, Spain, Italy and, of course, in its old battlegrounds in Austria and Germany, Switzerland, Belgium and France. Without the irritant of immigration and asylum-seekers, West European right-wing extremism would probably have remained a *quantité négligeable*, a concern of only a small number of eccentrics and racist cranks and no threat to Western European democracy.

While Western European racism may still be alive and well in many parts of Europe, in the form of prejudicial reactions and discrimination against people of colour and from Third World countries, it appears to lack the organized force to be a dynamic factor in the politics of, say, Germany and France. This is not to say that it does not still play a defensive role in slowing down or stopping the integration and assimilation of immigrants from outside the European Union (EU).[6] In Eastern Europe and Russia, by contrast, it is not always easy to draw a line between racism and the integral nationalism of the nativist radical right, as the example of Vadim's PRM demonstrates (see also Chapter 10 of this volume, by Vera Tolz, on Russia) which has long turned its wrath upon imaginary domestic enemies such as the Hungarian and Roma (gypsy) minorities or the Jews. Anti-Semitism, in particular, is still deeply rooted among Russians, Ukrainians, Poles, Czechs, Hungarians and Austrians. It can also be found in the form of so-called secondary anti-Semitism – that is a new resentment against reminders of the Holocaust and Jewish wartime labour, and organized Jewish efforts to obtain compensation for survivors and surviving family members.[7]

A special case of popular racism in today's Western Europe are the attitudes displayed by soccer hooligans, coaches, players and the public towards foreign teams and players of colour at prominent soccer games. Since the players of the major teams are often foreigners or men of colour, such expressions of racist or xenophobic prejudice are not limited to international matches. The ease of travelling to other cities and abroad with the team, furthermore, has encouraged a large volume of soccer camp-follower tourism and, increasingly, of hooligan violence that, in recent years, has come to challenge and almost overwhelm the capacity of domestic police forces to control it. Since extreme right-wing movements in most countries known for soccer hooliganism – for example in Britain, Germany, Belgium and Turkey – have always sought to recruit some of the more violent and racist hooligans for their respective movements, various observers in the media have long suspected that the racist propaganda and violence at big soccer matches were not only inspired but organized by the extreme right.

Merkl also examines the extent to which the German extreme right, after nearly a decade of relative eclipse, appears to be once again on the upswing. Throughout the 1990s, in spite of a tidal wave of asylum-seekers – half a million in 1992 alone – and widely reported anti-foreign violence, radical right parties such as the German Republicans had been unable to take advantage of the situation.[8] The long-delayed change in the asylum article of the German constitution (article 16) finally curbed the influx of alien refugees and made Germany's neighbours intercept most of them.[9] But now one of the lesser-known extreme right parties, the German People's Union (DVU) has scored breakthroughs in some East German states, most notably Saxony-Anhalt. The rising curve of German extreme right sentiment is also evident in the public atmosphere in the streets and schools of a number of East German cities where right-wing skinheads have imposed a veritable regime of terror on foreigners and left-wing youth. East German authorities and the media largely tolerate or ignore incidents of intimidation and violence. This right-wing youth terror, of course, resembles more the impact of the BNP or NF on South Asian immigrants of northern England than the Nazi movement of old. The German Office of Constitutional Protection regularly publishes reports on the membership of various extremist organizations as well as on their hate crimes, so that one can track their rising or falling curves over the decades.

Chapter 2, by Roger Eatwell, discusses ten theories to explain right-wing success at the polls. Among these are interpretations of the radical right as single-issue movements, a protest or 'anti-political' vote, as the result of social breakdown, or of national traditions, or as the product of charismatic leadership. This chapter also emphasizes the different levels, macro, meso and micro, at which the extreme right can be observed and analysed against the background of a crisis of democracy. Skinhead violence is obviously generated and has an impact at a very different level than do the 'respectable' extreme right parties and nationally elected representatives.

Hans-Georg Betz, in Chapter 3, also emphasizes ideology and theory. The author of a widely quoted book on right-wing populism, Betz defines this 'exclusionary populism' as 'the mobilization of diffuse anxieties and resentments … and a nativist agenda of exclusion that focuses on the defense of the socio-economic gains and socio-cultural integrity of nationals in liberal democracies'.[10] Betz distinguishes at least three kinds of current movements of right-wing extremism: (1) the old New Right standby of ethnopluralism – a radical nativist populism that has been surging across Europe and beyond, from the Swiss People's Party (SVP), the Austrian Freedom Party (FPÖ), and the Norwegian Progress Party (FRPn, formerly the Anders Lange Party) to Australia's One Nation Party down under; (2) *Völkisch* socialism (with socialist overtones, as in 'exclusionary welfarism'); and (3) White Resistance, an all-out attack on immigration from the Third World and on the rights of people of colour. These three types, of course, overlap in some instances. *Völkisch* socialism can be found mostly in Germany in the National Democratic Party (NPD) and the German People's Union (DVU) and among the hard-line Italian neo-fascists of the Italian Social Movement/Fiamma Tricolore (MSIFT). White Resistance has its precedents and parallels in the United States – branches were established as far away as Sweden – and is characteristic of the BNP. Underlying the political formations are the economic dynamics, such as global competition, and the cultural trends that marginalize and deeply alienate the working class clientele of the radical right. Its mostly young male and under-educated recruits feel helpless and vulnerable in the face of complex, powerful changes in the structures and role models that apply to them. By joining militant groups they can lash out at their fate.

COMPARING PUBLIC OPINION INDICATORS

One way of plumbing the dimensions of developments on the right is by comparing the support of the extreme right in various European countries on the basis of major cross-national public opinion surveys. While the study of radical right movements cannot but stress the subjective particulars of each ultra-nationalist variant, objective scales may put the findings in comparative perspective. To this end Charles Westin in Chapter 4 examines patterns of racist opinion in the 1997 and 2000 polls of 15 EU countries in the Euro-barometer and Institute for Social Research and Analysis (SORA) surveys. His findings indicate not only that those new waves of immigration appeared to trigger new waves of racism – by whatever definition – but that democratic beliefs are not necessarily incompatible with expressions of prejudice. Large majorities with strong democratic commitments overlap with majorities of self-declared racists. In some European countries, moreover, for example Denmark, popular views on immigration and race are remarkably polarized.

In sum, his analysis points to three regional clusters of opinion on this subject. One is the 'integrationist' cluster of Scandinavia (without Norway), Britain and the Netherlands where majorities believe that the immigrants should be integrated in society.[11] (These are mostly liberal democratic and

Protestant societies.) A second cluster is formed by countries where the plurality of integrationists over those preferring assimilation – requiring that immigrants shed some or all of their culture before they can be fully accepted by the natives – is much weaker, say between 40–45 per cent integrationists to 20–30 per cent assimilationists, as in Luxembourg, Germany and France. Westin also included Belgium and Austria in this group even though, in his comparative table, Belgium has an assimilationist plurality and, in Austria, a plurality of 40 per cent disagrees with both integration and assimilation. As the author points out, these countries have all had guest-worker programmes and currently have either large right-wing parties, such as the Vlaams Blok (VB), the Front National (FN), and the FPÖ, or refuse to consider themselves 'countries of immigration' (Germany).

Finally, there is a group in which those disagreeing with both integration and assimilation make up a plurality (Greece and Portugal) or even a majority (Ireland, Spain and Italy). These are countries which, according to Westin, have only just begun to make immigration and incorporation subjects of public discussion, even though Third World immigrants are now pressing at their gates. This group also scored rather well in exhibiting little or no prejudice, or rather they appear not to have the large numbers of self-declared racists found in countries that have gone through such contentious debates – which may not be quite the same as being low in prejudice.[12] As a hint of the complexity of polling people on such emotional and subjective questions, we should note that the Eurobarometer survey of 2000 was bedevilled by an extraordinarily high rate of refusals: in nine of the 15 EU states, more than 40 per cent of respondents (75 per cent in the Netherlands) did not cooperate with the interviewers and answer questions regarding their views on racism or xenophobia. Such high rates of refusal suggest that these respondents consider this a shameful subject, and that none of the responses may be very reliable.

The conflicting attitudes of the extreme right subculture may also be characterized succinctly in the Ruud Koopmans thesis that suggests that the incidence of xenophobic or racist violence is in inverse proportion to the size of the radical right party present in a country. The right-wing subculture may not change but it expresses itself either in violent explosions or in the degree of political organization, but rarely both.[13]

Allen Wilcox, Leonard Weinberg and William Eubank in Chapter 5 discuss their research of the World Value Survey and other sources which permit an assessment of the European national cultures that seem most hospitable to the views and values of voters of the radical right. Right-wing voters typically are dissatisfied, distrustful and extra-punitive, and they feel they have little control over their lives. They are comparatively religious – as compared to the mostly secular urban cultures of Europe – and believe in the virtues of hard work and discipline. They dislike sharing jobs or anything else with immigrants, the elderly and the handicapped and are averse to having neighbours of different racial, religious or national backgrounds. Countries where the extreme right flourishes also stand out as having high levels of disagreement over basic values, self-control and life satisfactions. Where have European societies corresponded most closely to these polarized attitudes? In Austria, France, Belgium and Italy, all countries where the radical right grew by leaps and bounds in the 1990s and where trust in public institutions is at very low levels. At the other end of the scale, Norway, Sweden and Switzerland have also seen a substantial right-wing vote, though perhaps of a different shade of brown.

This survey research is further expanded in Chapter 6, by Piero Ignazi, a frequent contributor to this debate. With the help of an analysis of voting patterns, Ignazi presents an encompassing explanation of the rise and transformation of the European extreme right since the 1980s. Before that watershed, he writes, the radical right consisted mostly of traditional neo-fascist parties feeding off the subcultures left behind by the fascist movements and regimes of the interwar period and World War II. Most of these old parties either shrank into insignificance or dramatically had to change their spots. An example of the latter route is the Italian neo-fascist MSI (Italian Social Movement) which shed some of its traditional marks such as the emphasis on overthrowing democracy, state corporatism, authoritarianism and the devotion to violence.

The newer parties of the extreme right, beginning with the French FN were made of different stuff. The impact of post-industrialism and the decline of class conflict in favour of value-based conflicts produced not only the familiar post-materialist New Left but also a neo-conservative New Right deeply alienated from the democratic politicians and parties of Western governments. Their 'silent counter-revolution' battened upon issues of crime, law and order, leadership, the corruption and inefficacy of democratic governments, and the flood of immigrants that appeared to threaten the right-wingers' ideal of an ethnically homogenous national community. Radicalized, polarized, and proletarianized, such preoccupations could be stretched into their right radical extremes by charismatic leaders and their young, male and working-class following: xenophobia, integral nationalism and racism. The intractable challenges of globalization and the socioeconomic dynamics of the information revolution pushed many working-class families into radical right positions, because they could no longer control their own fate, nor rely on sympathetic governments to defend them against having to share their entitlements with the foreign hordes.

CHANGING NATIONAL SETTINGS

How does this new right-wing extremism manifest itself in different and everchanging European contexts? In Chapter 7, Michael Minkenberg and Martin Schain look at the growth and development of the FN in France. There, the challenge of the restructuring of the labour force and the symbolic devaluation of national identity came early with the Europeanization and, ultimately, with the beginnings of globalization of social and economic life. It was, at least initially, a radical right reaction to the individual and group emancipation of the 1960s and 1970s and an attempt to return to the roles of individuals in the romanticized national community. The authors also draw distinctions between different strains of the radical right. There is the old French authoritarian-fascist variant, the classic racist (also colonialist) perspective, the xenophobia of the ethnocentric reaction, especially to the immigrants from North Africa, and finally the anti-Islamic/religious-fundamentalist strain.

In the late 1970s, the new waves of immigration gave the FN its big break as a political party that has since occupied a hegemonic position under the experienced hands of Jean-Marie Le Pen in its right-wing niche of the French system of political cleavages. Its expansion in the 1980s went hand in glove with a redirection of its programme in tribute to the era of Ronald Reagan and Margaret Thatcher, until the Gulf War of 1991 and the EU agreement at Maastricht once more turned the FN around, this time against the New World Order of President Bush (Senior) and a tighter development of the EU. Le Pen called the White House 'a Trojan horse of globalization' and his second-in-command and eventual rival – in the FN split of 2000 – Bruno Megrét, said: 'The EU of Maastricht is a tool of Americanization'. From its 1984 electoral breakthrough, the FN had reached a reported membership of 70,000 and laid claim to the vote of about 15 per cent of the French electorate when the party broke up into the Le Penist and Megrétist Mouvement national républicain (MNR) wings in 2000.

While the party or parties of the radical right thus seem to have suffered a painful loss of stature, the extreme right subculture is alive and well: sweeping majorities still express strong anti-immigrant views or say, with resignation, that 'one can no longer truly feel at home in France'. But the 'ideas of Le Pen' or Megrét now only command the support of one out of five French adults. The authors make clear that this should not deceive us regarding the very considerable leverage the FN and MNR still wield through coalitions and local representatives in the south, in particular regarding immigration policies. Nor should it leave any doubt that an attempt to ban the FN outright would have much credibility with the average French voter whose trust in a manipulative government is already at the lowest level. The deficits of democracy, whether in France or the EU, cannot be cured by undemocratic restrictions. This can only be achieved by expanding democratic political freedoms and trusting the ultimate judgement of the voters.

In Chapter 8 Kurt Richard Luther analyses the spectacular rise of the Austrian Freedom Party (FPÖ) along the lines of traditional party theory – rather than with the usual emphasis on the strident statements of its leader, Jörg Haider. Luther's chapter provides an intriguing glimpse of the nuts and bolts of the development of an extreme right party and of the internal repercussions of entry into governmental responsibility of a rambunctious populist protest movement. In its first 30 years, since 1956, the FPÖ was rather on the margins of Austrian politics, sidelined by the presence of two large, dominant and well-disciplined mass membership parties, the Austrian Social Democratic Party (SPÖ) and the Catholic-conservative Österreichische Volkspartei (ÖVP), or Austrian People's Party. In 1983, to be sure, under its right-wing liberal leader Norbert Steger, it had briefly joined the ÖVP in the national government. But this experiment so unbalanced this radical right party of the *deutsch-national* (German nationalist) *Lager* that the leadership lost control of the rank and file and Haider was able to take it over and turn it into a vehicle for right-wing populist agitation and his own advancement. Since 1986, under his demagogic leadership, the FPÖ has grown tremendously in the electorate, especially among young, male blue-collar workers, a development that coincides with the relative decline in popular following of both major Austrian parties, especially the SPÖ. Like other European conservative parties, the FPÖ's present partner in the national government, the ÖVP, also suffered the disorienting consequences of the collapse of communism, its favourite *Feindbild* and excuse for political hegemony in the country. The weakening long-time hegemons of Austrian politics also had little to offer in the face of rising popular discontent over the large waves of post-communist immigration.

The FPÖ's entry as a junior partner into the ÖVP government in February 2000 triggered the hostility and sanctions of most of the other EU member governments. But, as in the Waldheim affair some time ago, such outside pressures have tended to help rather than hinder FPÖ popularity, as many an Austrian patriot rallied to its defence. This surface reaction, however, also masked the noticeable impact of sharing governmental responsibility on a party that had prospered for more than a decade precisely because of its irresponsible stridency and aggressiveness on a broad range of issues, from law and order, government corruption – not to mention undisguised praise for aspects of the Nazi regime of Austrian-born Adolf Hitler – to the 'threat of foreignization (*Überfremdung*)' and 'EU arrogance'. The organizational and internal dynamics of the party's growth and triumph in them are producing the seeds of its rising difficulties and internal conflicts, as the author shows rather persuasively. Its resources increasingly stretched, and short of enough plausible candidates – or with careerists in its team who will not please the true believers at the base – the FPÖ is likely to pay a high price for power. As Luther puts it: 'The longer the party remains in government, the more likely it is to deradicalize.'

Is the German extreme right in escalation, or has it all been a matter of exaggerations by the media and the *Ausland*? asks Ekkart Zimmermann in Chapter 9. There is no doubt that acts of right-wing violence and so-called propaganda offences (like swastika graffiti) and racist incitement (*Volksverhetzung*) have been surging tremendously since 1998 and this especially in East German Thuringia, Brandenburg and Mecklenburg-Pomerania. Curiously, such offences have decreased precisely in East German states such as Saxony and Saxony-Anhalt where the radical right scored electoral successes – extremist violence and political organization seem indeed to be mutually exclusive manifestations. The smallest but most virulent extreme right party, the NPD, has demonstrated a new mobilization technique, the penetration of the youth scene in distressed, economically marginal towns and rural areas where the NPD *Kameradschaften* are creating their own 'liberated zones' by taking over public, communal spaces (streets and squares, public transport) and terrorizing dissenters and foreigners – shades of Oldham in the north of England and perhaps also of the last days of the Weimar Republic when the 'collapse of intermediate structures' (to quote Kornhauser) and services (local government and police) signalled the imminent death of Weimar democracy. The usurpation of Max Weber's concept of the state monopoly of violence and other local services by skinhead *Kameradschaften* is the most convincing evidence of the growing anomie and anarchy of these neglected areas where the legitimacy of the communist state, and now of its successor, has vanished.

Zimmermann is quite critical of the habit of recent analysts to ignore the riches of the older explanatory theories of the radical right, such as those of Seymour Martin Lipset and William Kornhauser, which also supply a plausible basis for understanding the commonly observed welfare chauvinism of the followers of the extreme right. Jean-Marie Le Pen and Jörg Haider alike have warned that 'natives come first' and many natives indeed feel, quite rationally, that foreigners should not be entitled to the benefits of a national welfare state to which they have not contributed while the natives have. Ignoring the protestations of the latter, especially in the midst of a major economic crisis or while facing a tidal wave of immigrants – as Germany did in 1992 with nearly a million asylum-seekers and repatriated German ethnics from Eastern Europe – is tantamount to squandering the legitimacy of that state. Beyond the threatening escalation and the blatant exaggerations about the German extreme right, the author sketches its immediate future and suggests likely measures to control it. He expects little increase in radical right voting unless they can overcome their fragmentation and lack of charismatic leadership. But the incidence of political street violence may well increase, and this especially if the extreme left is also rising – which seems to be the case – making right–left clashes as in the streets of Weimar Berlin in 1929–33 inevitable.[14] But fortunately, East German law enforcement by now has learned to be quicker and more effective in responding than it used to be. Local authorities are less tolerant of the young toughs, and the German media may begin to understand and avoid the disastrous mistakes of the past.

Perhaps no greater contrast can be found among contemporary movements of the European radical right than that between Western and Eastern Europe, particularly Russia. In Chapter 10, Vera Tolz explains that the Russian right of today really originated in the 1960s and 1970s, and surfaced as a larger phenomenon on the new playing fields created by Gorbachev's *perestroika* (restructuring) and *glasnost* (transparency) in the mid 1980s. Observers noted with surprise that the old subcultural heritage of the Black Hundreds and paranoid tales of the Judeo-Masonic conspiracy that was said to have brought on the Russian Revolution were still alive in many places, including Pamiat (Memory), a literary and historical society[15] frequently accused of anti-Semitic agitation and plots. Add to this, the Russian and European (see Alain de Benoist) elements of the New Right which believed in ethnopluralism but were opposed to New Left ideas and to the communist welfare state. This far-flung subcultural world rejected both communism and American liberalism and passionately defended the Soviet Union of Stalin, or at least the pan-Russian parts of it: Russia, Belarus and Ukraine. Its first political parties and candidates, in 1989/1990, were unable to attract much of the vote.

The demise of the Soviet Union in 1992, the 30 million Russians trapped in various newly independent states, severe economic crisis and intermittent regional struggles in the south gave radical right politicians a new political lease of life. Vladimir Zhirinovskii's Liberal Democrats and Aleksandr Barkashov's Russian National Unity party (RNU) were part of the crest of the extreme right wave in the 1993 elections and the military confrontation between Russian President Boris Yeltsin and parliament. It was a turbulent, xenophobic time, marked by street violence against people from the Caucasus, Central Asia and Africa, and assaults on Jewish cemeteries and synagogues. As recently as after the terroristic attacks on New York and Washington in September 2001, the Moscow Choral Synagogue was vandalized by 'hooligans', even though Russian Jews have otherwise enjoyed substantially better opportunities since the demise of the Soviet Union. Judaism has now been given equal status, along with Orthodox Christianity and Islam, as one of the three 'traditional religions' of Russia. From their 1993 combined plurality of 23 per cent, however, the extreme right vote drifted down again to 6 per cent in 1999 and seems unlikely to rebound in the foreseeable future. Professor Tolz now considers even Zhirinovskii's movement – in spite of its imperialistic tenor, violent language, virulent anti-Semitism and xenophobia – a tame, mainstream party along with the similarly tame, if verbally abusive, Russian Public Union (ROS) of Sergei Baburin and the Communist Party of the Russian Federation (CPRF).[16] There are other aggressive imperialists such as Aleksandr Dugin's neo-Eurasians – who lay claim to the entire Eurasian continent from Dublin to Vladivostok – and Barkashov's swastika-adorned, national socialist RNU which excludes Jews, gypsies and people from the Caucasus and Central Asia. Numerous smaller but violent groups, including skinheads and religious (anti-Islamic) fundamentalists, round out the picture of a large if fragmented subculture of the extreme right.

Given the vast popularity of the war against Chechnya, I also wonder about its impact on the role of the Russian radical right. Popular wars often drown out the nationalistic rantings of right-wing extremism. Professor Tolz also details the desultory efforts of the Russian state to enforce some of its own laws against flagrant offences by the radical right groups. She concludes that, even though there are similarities in the factors of the post-1968 transition in East and West, the 'social, economic and political changes in Russia' have been so cataclysmic as to make 'racial intolerance and … a paranoid world view' much more popularly acceptable there.

We chose not to include as much coverage of East European movements of the radical right this time,[17] but can easily extrapolate the parallels to Russia from our old 1997 data. In *The Revival of Right-wing Extremism in the Nineties* we concluded:

> After nearly half a century of communist internationalism and deliberate repression of nationalistic politics [in Eastern Europe], ultranationalist feelings and movements are back with a vengeance, like genies from the bottles in which they were long confined … There are once again nationalist, even fascist groups and parties which do indeed resemble their interwar predecessors even though their class-specific context has changed profoundly.

In place of the interwar 'class struggle *au rebourse*' of bourgeoisie, nobility and the military against *bolsheviki* and labour movements, today's East European right-wing supporters are more likely working-class and filled with hatred against the new tycoons and against minorities that seem to 'forget their place' or to thrive by crime or the drug trade. All the East European states, indeed, have minorities and ready scapegoats such as the Jews or the gypsies. And, even though none share the Russian fate of an imploded empire, they all have major border problems of one sort or another so that their xenophobia and paranoid fear can easily focus on allegedly aggressive neighbours and, in some cases, an irredenta of coethnics oppressed by them.

On the other hand, post-communist Eastern Europeans such as the Czechs, Poles, Slovaks and Hungarians have in recent public opinion studies shown a substantially more positive attitude towards democracy and human rights than have the Russians, Belarusians and Ukrainians whose support for democracy has been at best ambiguous and tentative. A firm grasp of democracy and its requirements and a widespread commitment to a democratic future for the whole country is the antithesis of extreme right, often culture-pessimistic convictions. There is a gradation of popular acceptance of democracy that runs from the most democratic Czechs (comparable to the Germans and Italians) via the Poles, Slovaks, Hungarians, the Baltic states and Romania, to the Russian–Belarusian–Ukrainian bloc where democracy seems to be understood and favoured by only the smallest of minorities.[18] This is not to deny the presence of ultra-nationalist and neo-fascist groups even in the Czech Republic, and of course also in Western Europe. But chances are good that the more democratic political systems will keep their right-wing radicals at bay, or at least that they will not be taken over by them. At the other end of the democratic gradient, on the other hand, little would stand in the way of a well-organized right-wing extremist movement (or communist/right-wing alliance) that set out to storm the ramparts of their shaky democracies.

The reader may well wonder what can be done, or what is being done, about the right-wing extreme threat. In Chapter 11 Jaap van Donselaar offers a comprehensive survey of the range of governmental measures against right-wing extremism in five European countries: Britain, France, Germany, the Netherlands and Belgium. The government responses have run the gamut from efforts to educate and influence public opinion – for example towards tolerance of minorities – to addressing the presumable 'causes' of racist and extreme right agitation, to various ways of suppressing its manifestations. Attacking the alleged causes may be the most costly and least effective of these responses because it assumes, I believe, that they are rational causes and that the problem will simply go away once the government modifies its minority and urban policies to suit the right-wing protesters, or if more jobs are made available to them, or to the unemployed for whom they claim to speak. By comparison, 'repressive government action [against extreme right organisations], threatened or actual, has a profound effect on the phenomenon of right extremism.'

While they may have had less impact on the ethnically based Vlaams Blok (VB: Flemish Block), international conventions and national legislation like the British Race Relations Act of 1965 have, in general, noticeably curbed racist propaganda and supplied a ready basis for the suppression of violent activities. Indirect barriers, such as the British and French single-member electoral districts or the insistence of the German Law on Political Parties on internal party democracy and programmatic concordance with the 'free and democratic constitutional order' have often hamstrung the politicians of the radical right. They also find themselves caught between the proverbial rock and a hard place, namely the necessity to adjust to the 'repressive' rules of the government on the one side and the need to maintain their extreme profile so as not to lose their extremist following.

NOTES

1. *Los Angeles Times*, 10 July 2001.
2. As Sven Reichardt has pointed out, confronting each other's violence-prone marches and rallies was a recurrent cause of major street battles between the Nazi storm-troopers (SA) and young Communists (RFB) in Weimar Berlin three-quarters of a century ago. 'Formen faschistischer Gewalt: Faschistische Kampfbünde in Italien und Deutschland nach dem Ersten Weltkrieg', *Sociologus*, 51.1/2 (2001), pp. 55–88. See also Peter Merkl, *The Making of a Stormtrooper* (Princeton, NJ: Princeton University Press, 1980), Ch. 3.
3. See also the essays of Harold Lasswell and others on the Nazi Führerlexikon of 1934, a classic forerunner of quantitative elite studies.
4. German criminal law, for example, separates '*niedrige Beweggründe*' ('lower motives', such as personal enrichment or thuggery) from higher motives such as ideological or religious convictions in sentencing offenders.
5. See for example Wolfgang Kühnel, 'Gewalt im Jugendalter', *Humboldtspektrum*, 4.1 (1997), pp. 38–43 and the sources cited there. Also Helmut Willems, *Fremdenfeindliche Gewalt* (Opladen: Leske & Budrich, 1993).
6. See Peter Merkl, 'Racism, New and Old: Changing Aspects and Approaches', in Charles Westin (ed.), *Racism, Ideology, and Political Organisation* (Edsbruck: CEIFO, 1998), pp. 7–50.
7. Werner Bergmann and Rainer Erb, *Anti-Semitism in Germany: The Post-Nazi Epoch since 1945* (New Brunswick: Transaction, 1997).
8. See Peter Merkl, 'Are the Old Nazis Coming Back?', in Peter Merkl (ed.), *The Federal Republic of Germany at Forty-Five* (London: Macmillan, 1995), pp. 427–83.
9. See William M. Chandler, 'Integration and Identity in German Politics', in Peter Merkl (ed.), *The Federal Republic at Fifty* (London: Macmillan, 1999), pp. 58–71.
10. In his article in *Politik* (Newsletter of the Conference Group on German Politics), Summer 2001.
11. In Britain, only 45 per cent preferred this option and we could probably put Britain just as easily into the second bloc.
12. The inclusion of Italy in this category brings to mind the debates over Albanian 'boat people' who, after finding Italians rather hospitable upon the fall of Albanian communism

a decade earlier, in the late 1990s found themselves hunted down and expelled as unwelcome, 'dirty' illegals.

13. Ruud Koopmans, 'A Burning Question: Explaining the Rise of Racist and Extreme Right Violence in Western Europe', Berlin: Wissenschaftszentrum Discussion Papers, FS III, pp. 95–101.

14. See Merkl, *The Making of a Stormtrooper*, Ch. 2.

15. See Vladislav Krasnov, 'Pamiat: Russian Right-Wing Radicalism', in Peter Merkl and Leonard Weinberg (eds), *Encounters with the Contemporary Radical Right* (Boulder, CO: Westview Press, 1993), pp. 111–31.

16. In addition to the incendiary writings of CPFR party leader Gennadii Ziuganov, there is also a General Albert Makashov, CPFR-member, who is known for his outrageous anti-Semitic statements.

17. In *The Revival of Right-wing Extremism in the Nineties*, we also covered Poland, the Czech and Slovak republics, Hungary, Romania, Belarus and Ukraine.

18. See also Peter Merkl, 'The Russian Prospect: Hope and Despair' and 'Postcommunist Democratization and Economic Reforms', in M. Donald Hancock and John Logue (eds), *Transitions to Capitalism and Democracy in Russia and Eastern Europe: Achievements, Problems, Prospects* (Westport, CT: Praeger, 2000), pp. 95–113 and 259–84.

Part 1
The Extreme Right in the Ascendancy

CHAPTER ONE

Stronger than Ever

Peter H. Merkl

'WHY ARE They so Strong Now?' was the title of my essay in *The Revival of Right-Wing Extremism in the Nineties* published only five years ago. The answers by the editors and contributors were ambiguous. We were rather sceptical of the widespread stereotypes that had characterized the contemporary radical right in the perception of the public and the media. We found most comparisons of today's right-wing extremism with interwar fascist movements and Nazism rather wanting, and emphasized instead the diversity of contemporary manifestations, cultural and social trends, movements, skinheads and radical right parties. Instead of the old right-wing causes of 50–75 years ago – even of 30 years ago – a whole range of new confrontations, social problems and issues now appear to trigger responses on the radical right. There are new elements that are often hardly susceptible to the strong-arm solutions of yesteryear. Many of the new problems, in fact, may have no solutions at all, or at least few governmental ones that would not place democracy itself at risk.

Typical among the new confrontations was the 1960s and 1970s challenge of the New Left, of the 1968 youth rebellion and its issues from anti-authoritarianism to feminism, pacifism and racial (or minority group) equality.[1] Another major factor that did not play an appreciable role in the interwar period are the nativist reactions to migrations of refugees, really a manifestation of the inequalities among nations, in particular between north and south. The ever-swelling ranks of the oppressed, hungry and under-employed of the world that are pushing their way into the small minority of developed societies on earth have triggered extreme and violent responses on the far right of the political spectrum, and considerable hostility from the moderate right. This is quite different from the effect of migrations of the early twentieth century, say in 1917 or 1935, when the flight from communist or fascist takeovers spread the polarization between extreme left and right throughout the West. Finally, the advanced democratic societies have undergone tremendous social change in the last 30 years that obliterated the significance of important old divisions, such as the class struggle, and replaced them with new ones and new problems such as the 'new individualism', the information revolution, and the 'digital divide'. Contemporary movements of the extreme right that draw heavily upon unskilled working-class youth and on young unemployed obviously owe much to these new experiences of helplessness and alienation. The forces of economic and cultural globalization reinforce the rage of being left behind.

STRONGER THAN EVER

The first decade of the new century and millennium finds several of the radical right movements and trends we observed earlier stronger than ever. The largest of them in percentage terms is the Romanian PRM of Corneliu Vadim Tudor which towards the end of 2000 won 33 per cent of the popular vote in the presidential run-off elections. Born of a newspaper of the same name, Greater Romania, the ultranationalist PRM is about a decade old and some of its leaders, particularly 'Vadim', have a revealing national communist background with the media of the old communist regime. Vadim and Eugen Barbu, among other things, are former editors of the extreme communist culture weekly, *Saptamana*, in which Vadim praised the Ceauşescu regime as Romania's 'years of light'.[2] Now revealed as rabidly anti-Semitic and anti-Hungarian, in 1990 Vadim was close to the Securitate and to Ceauşescu's nemesis, Ion Iliescu, who narrowly defeated him and his PRM in 2000. The PRM advocates imperial expansion at the expense of Bulgaria and Moldova, and is anti-Hungarian, anti-gypsy and anti-Semitic. It is now the leading opposition in a rather fragmented parliament.

Another frontrunner in the radical right of today is Austria's Jörg Haider whose FPÖ is analysed below by Richard Luther and others. Although he and his movement have been around for some time,[3] many Americans and Europeans became alarmed about Haider only in February 2000 when his party entered the Austrian conservative government of Wolfgang Schüssel (leader of the ÖVP). Haider himself remained in Carinthia province where he has been governor. A flamboyant demagogue, Haider 'needs scandals and tumults as Narcissus required a mirror', according to Werner Perger writing in *Die Zeit*.[4] He likes to present a youthful, dynamic image as a skier, marathon runner, mountain climber and bungee-jumper, but has also been a dictator and the agent of ruthless purges in his own, centralized party. Among his eyebrow-raising contacts in recent years was a visit to Muammar Gadafy, one to the Pope, and past connections to right-wing politicians in France and Germany who often speak of him with disdain and – especially after his recent electoral triumphs – with envy. The entry of the FPÖ into the national government drew massive protest demonstrations throughout the country – involving at least 300,000 protesters at Vienna's Heldenplatz – and in some other European cities. Chancellor Schüssel, who was blamed by many for lending respectability to FPÖ, responded to the demonstrations by attributing them to 'the far left, the hippie generation, the youth, and the Internet crowd'. Haider claimed the protesters were paid as much as 1,800 schillings (about $130) a day, but retreated somewhat from the soapbox by turning over his party chairmanship to Susanne Riess-Passer, which may have been merely a preliminary manœuvre prior to campaigning for chancellor himself.

In the European Union, a hard-line anti-Austrian faction was formed by Portugal, France and Belgium – Britain, Denmark and Greece expressed a fear of isolating Austria. The EU along with the United States eventually agreed to impose diplomatic sanctions on Austria. The downgrading of diplomatic relations by the other 14 EU nations and the United States was supposed to pillory Austria until the FPÖ would step down. Some countries recalled their ambassadors to Vienna and the Austrian representatives in EU councils often found themselves cast in pariah roles. As Italian Prime Minister Massimo D'Alema put it, Austria had ignored the 'common standards of values underlying European unity' by entertaining a government coalition with the extreme right. He neglected to mention that the Berlusconi governments of 1994 (and 2001) did the same thing by bringing Gianfranco Fini's Alleanza Nazionale (AN), the successor to the neo-fascist MSI, into the Italian national government.

By September 2000, after half a year of weak sanctions and strong words, however, at least six EU members were already trying to retreat from their position of severity even though emissaries of the European Court of Human Rights were still searching for concrete violations of the human rights of immigrants and asylum-seekers by Austria. Hardnosed press assessments of the EU stance began to call it a case of the pot calling the kettle black. Several of the other EU governments have also featured occasional collaboration between moderate and radical right parties, for example of local French Gaullists (RPR) with the FN or the German Christian Democrat Party (CDU) with right-wing dissidents from its midst. In the United States, of course, the inclusion of radical right figures and issues, e.g. of the religious right, in Republican administrations is not unheard of. And almost all the governments of the EU and the United States have experimented with the various curbs on immigration and asylum-seeking of which they now accuse the Schüssel-Haider government. While the exclusion of radical elements may be a noble goal, it is clearly not enough for ostracizing a member from the EU. Short of concrete findings of violations of common laws and policies, such efforts at controlling the internal politics of member states run the risk of blunting the weapon of sanctions and of crying wolf once too often.

Haider and his FPÖ are not entirely defenceless in this all-European purge attempt. In August of 2000 the Austrian government passed an 18-point plan to achieve the lifting of the EU sanctions, including an Austrian plebiscite on them.[5] If such a popular referendum did pass with the expected majority, however, it could backfire disastrously among the EU partners who had just been treated to the spectacle of another typical FPÖ national convention (1 May 2000) at which all internal dissent and discussion were stifled and Haider's allegedly surrendered leadership was reasserted in a manner reminiscent of the rhythmically clapping parliament of Ceauşescu's heyday.

Another prop of Haider's strength is the curious foreign aid package – 25 million dollars – from Libya with which the Carinthian governor, for example, arranged for on-the-spot discounts on Libyan gasoline for his citizenry. Gadafy has long been known for distributing his largesse to neo-fascist and terrorist groups. Haider's Libyan contact apparently dates back to 1988 when the FPÖ had its first modest electoral success. The party also has a faithful paladin in Gadafy's son, Saif al-Islam, who lives in an exclusive Vienna suburb with his two pet Bengal tigers.[6] Finally, we should mention the ambiguous light cast on Haider by his December 2000 visit to the Pope for the purpose of bringing the Vatican an 81-foot fir tree for a Christmas display on St Peter's Square. Large crowds of anti-fascist demonstrators had to be held back while John Paul II granted a half-hour audience and graciously accepted the tree. A papal aide gave Haider a copy of the Holy Father's recent World Peace Message which included a denunciation of racist nationalism, among other things. Haider is a devoted Catholic and the Vatican, whatever it may think of him privately, is reluctant to offend Austrian Catholics.

How seriously neo-Nazi is the Haider movement? Austrian President Thomas Klestil made the Schüssel government pledge to accept collective responsibility for the 'monstrous crimes of the national socialist regime', which is more than current French governments have ever admitted about their own collaborationist Vichy period. Provincial governor Haider, who is a member of the 'coalition coordinating committee' that meets every month in Vienna, has described himself as 'a modernizer, a national populist of the free market persuasion'. He obviously knows his Austrians well, of whom over 50 per cent in surveys expressed the belief that Jews were responsible for their own persecution and 37 per cent are 'not sure' they could shake hands with a Jew.[7] Haider has also praised the 'honorable veterans of the Waffen-SS', and calls both Churchill and Hitler 'war criminals'. On German TV, the 50-year old said: 'If Jews receive reparations for their sufferings under Nazism, then Germans expelled from Czechoslovakia and former Austrian

POWs in the Soviet Union should be similarly compensated.' But he simply denies the relevance of any of this to the present: 'I am a child of postwar Austria. Why should I take upon myself the problems of the past?'[8] In neighbouring Switzerland, almost a carbon copy of the FPÖ has arisen with the SVP. Once the smallest of the four 'cartel parties' of the consociational establishment, the SVP doubled its share of the vote under the demagogic Christoph Blocher to 23 per cent in 1999 which made it the largest of all the Swiss parties. Blocher hews closely to the Haider line but is prone to putting his foot in his mouth as for example, when he endorsed a booklet, *The Decline and Fall of Swiss Freedom* by Jürgen Graf who turned out to be a notorious denier of the Holocaust.

IMMIGRATION: THE UNIVERSAL IRRITANT

Austrian National Socialism (Nazism) in the earlier half of the twentieth century had many causes: the imperial collapse of Habsburg, the powerful socialist and labour upsurge after World War I, multi-ethnic competition and others. The hostilities generated by refugees and immigration played a minor role. Today, however, immigration appears to be the mighty irritant that stirs up right-wing protest from Austria to California, and even Australia. Haider's following is clearly energized by it when he speaks of '*Überfremdung*' (being overrun by foreigners and foreign culture), and claims that the Austrian welfare state coddles immigrants and encourages them to have large families which may eventually bring about a 'degeneration of the Austrian nation'. These are typical stereotypes of 'welfare chauvinism' and xenophobic anti-immigrant propaganda everywhere. They can also be heard from the Belgian VB of Filip Dewinter, the Danish People's Party (Dansk Folkparti, DF) of Pia Kjaersgaard, the Norwegian Progress Party (FRPn), the Swedish Democrats, the French FN, the Italian AN, the British BNP, several German radical right parties, and from the extreme right movements of such prospective EU member countries as Poland, the Czech and Slovak republics, Hungary and Turkey. Eurobarometer and other polls give depressing evidence of the receptiveness to the appeal of such messages of a significant percentage of the population in all these countries.

There are a number of recent examples of European countries that in the past seemed to be more or less free of the disease of immigrant- and minority-bashing but have since come down with it. One of them is the Netherlands where the Ministry of the Interior commissioned a study at the University of Leiden, 'Monitor – Racism and Right-Wing Extremism'. The disquieting report by, among others, Jaap van Donselaar (a contributor to this book), revealed that the Dutch police routinely failed to disclose the full extent of Dutch aggression and violence against foreigners and especially asylum-seekers. For 1998, for example, the police reported only 22 of 313 such incidents with full identification of the perpetrators. Dutch prosecutors pursued only about half the known cases of discrimination and dropped one fourth of the lawsuits against right-wing extremists. Ostensibly out of a fear of copycat crimes, the Dutch media are reluctant to speak about domestic right-wing violence, while always eager to report such incidents abroad, especially in neighbouring Germany. There is also a great deal of uncertainty about the definition of racist violence. In fact, Interior Minister Claas de Vries himself characterized a recent firebomb attack on an asylum-seekers' hostel as perhaps merely 'a display of youthful exuberance'. Racist offences are actually on the increase in the Netherlands, even though right-wing groups like the Dutch Popular Militia, White Power and the Anti-Islamic Front have declined in importance.[9]

As the coming invasion force from the Third World and Eastern Europe gathers around the prosperous 'Fortress Europe', another new example of right-wing reactions has been Ireland, the Celtic Tiger, whose economy has given it the highest growth and lowest unemployment rate (3.6 per cent) in the EU. Immigrants and refugees (also returnees) of all races and creeds have followed the allure of this once homogeneous white and Catholic island. A small, outspoken group, the Immigration Control Platform formed and called upon the government to withdraw from the 1951 Geneva Convention on Refugees. Physical and verbal attacks on people of colour have mushroomed and there are widespread complaints about discrimination. The Irish parliament passed a Prohibition on Incitement to Hatred Act and, in 2000, the first offender, a Dublin bus driver, was convicted of verbally abusing a Gambian passenger. So far the number of immigrants and returning Irish emigrants is still small, but the government expects it to rise to 340,000 more in the next five years – almost one-tenth of the population of the Irish Republic – and the percentage of asylum-seekers among them is rising. Teenagers and Irish youth in general are particularly reluctant to accept the need for the skills of these immigrants. Estimates of the level of industrial need for them have been in the neighbourhood of 200,000 over the next five years. Law enforcement has been slow to prosecute racist violence. There are laws against all kinds of discrimination, but they are unevenly enforced. Furthermore, even the most ebullient economic expansion will eventually cool down, and when it does, many of the natives may come to blame immigrants and asylum-seekers for the recession.[10]

In Spain, which is all too accessible to small boats from North Africa, a tough new law now threatens illegal immigrants with immediate expulsion.

The law denies them housing, schooling for their children, legal aid and the right to join trade unions, hold public assemblies, or to go on strike. It has been the cause of massive pro-immigrant demonstrations in Barcelona and elsewhere, following a two-week hunger strike by 700 immigrants protesting the summary rejection of 34,000 visa applications. If the popular reaction in Spain looks like welcome relief from the depressing climate of European anti-foreign prejudice, neighbouring Portugal has gone one better with a recent immigration law that is now widely admired across the Continent. The law allows illegal immigrants and migrants on tourist visas to take employment which extends their stay in one-year increments and eventually lets them legalize their status and become citizens. In the last decade, rising Portuguese prosperity has turned the once large emigration surplus into one of immigration (361,100 more immigrants than emigrants in the 1990s). More than half of these legalized immigrants are from Eastern Europe, Russia, Ukraine, Moldova and Romania, rather than from such traditional Portuguese-speaking sources as Brazil and the former African colonies of Portugal.

Another seemingly peaceful country, bucolic Switzerland, has long been a covert battleground for anti-immigrant agitation (see also Hans-Georg Betz, Chapter 3). Since 1965, in fact, there have been seven popular initiatives to limit the percentage of foreigners in the country. One of the most draconian, the 1970 Schwarzenbach Initiative, postulated a 10 per cent ceiling and received approval from 46 per cent of the citizenry. The most recent initiative, in 2000, tried to reduce the percentage of foreign residents from the current 19.3 per cent to 18 per cent which would have meant the expulsion of 100,000 and considerable international embarrassment for the country. Two recent bilateral treaties of Switzerland with the EU about the free movement of persons hung in the balance, and such a mass expulsion would probably have violated the UN refugee convention. Half of the targeted 'foreigners' were actually born in Switzerland or had lived there for at least 15 years. The resistance to this latest initiative enjoyed the support of the government, industry, trade unions, churches, the media, and of all established parties except for the SVP. Swiss decentralization further aggravates the conflict by assigning local communities the right to decide the acquisition of Swiss citizenship. In the Lucerne suburb of Emmen, for example, the personal dossiers of 56 applicants were circulated for approval among the 27,000 citizens, complete with family photographs, income, savings, tax status and personal background, even hobbies. In bigger cities such as Bern and Zurich, the SVP and radical right groups are now proposing another initiative, an echo of the Haider movement of neighbouring Austria.

In France, the longtime leader of the immigrant-bashing FN, Jean-Marie

Le Pen, was stripped by a court of all representative posts to punish him for a 1997 campaign incident, a physical attack on the socialist mayor of Mantes-la-Ville. His party was weakened by the 1999 exodus of his second-in-command, Bruno Megret, which attracted many of Le Pen's old comrades and some defectors from the conservative RPR. But the broader shadow of the anti-immigrant sentiments on which the FN capitalized for so long has by no means faded away. In 2000, a national *Sofres* survey showed that 31 per cent of a national sample still believes that 'there are too many immigrants in France'. Another 28 per cent 'rather agree' with that sweeping statement. Even among socialists and young respondents, such anti-immigrant attitudes are only barely topped by their opposites. Nearly half of all respondents (24 per cent strongly and 23 per cent rather) expressed the belief that 'one can no longer truly feel at home in France'. Nevertheless, four out of five French adults rejected 'the ideas of Le Pen' or Megret, although both the FN and MNR now seem less of a menace to them.[11]

The question of ostracizing the FN is, of course, a very sensitive point in the context of the breakdown of the taboos against coalitions with the FN/MNR. In recent years, as many as five conservative RPR presidents of administrative regions have been elected with FN support, after accepting some issues dear to the FN and in spite of the strong condemnation of the FN as 'racist and xenophobic' by President Jacques Chirac. Two more presidents of the moderate right resigned upon learning that they owed their election to FN support. Le Pen himself hoped, in vain, for moderate conservative backing for his own bid for the presidency of the Provence-Alpes-Côte d'Azur region. The moderate right is clearly split in its attitude towards collaboration with the radical right.

In addition to the pattern of prejudice towards the Muslim minority, France and Belgium also suffer from the reverberations of Middle East crises which frequently produce anger and violence between their large Jewish and Muslim communities. In October 2000, for example, there was a wave of bombings and arson attacks against five synagogues in France, fortunately without causing injuries or worse. Anti-Semitic graffiti was commonplace.[12] In Belgium, at about the same time, a destructive rampage by 200 militants that spun off from a pro-Palestinian, anti-Israeli demonstration caused considerable damage to property. On the other hand, the anti-immigrant VB achieved considerable gains in the municipal and provincial elections of October 2000. In the large port city of Antwerp, for instance, it received 33 per cent of the vote and it did well also in rural Flanders. VB leader, Filip Dewinter, expressed the hope that Belgium's moderate conservatives might follow the example of the FPÖ and invite the VB into the national government.[13] The example of Austria and, earlier, Italy unfortunately set a mark for respectability of the radical right that calls for emulation by other extreme right parties.

In Italy itself, the messages from the right have been as confusing as ever. Even aside from the relations between the Vatican and Haider, the moderate right hand often does not seem to know what the radical right hand of the same party is doing. In the city of Verona, for example, right-wing rowdies assaulted a Catholic theologian of Jewish origin, Luis Marsiglia, with crow-bars, which led to an outpouring of local and also right-wing expressions of sympathy. The chief of the Lega Nord (or LN, which has its own ties of sympathy with Haider), Umberto Bossi, declared: 'The Lega is a friend of the Jews', but complained about 'the Left which has opened the borders to immigrants and homosexuals'. Marsiglia originally came from Argentina where he converted to Catholicism. Gianfranco Fini, the longtime leader of the neo-fascist MSI and now of the AN, expressed his 'full solidarity' with the injured Marsiglia.

With the exception of Friuli-Venezia Giulia, Northern Italy is otherwise not exactly the area of the AN's greatest support. The party achieved its highest percentages in recent elections in Lazio (Rome) and further south, especially in Puglia, Campania, Abbruzzi, Calabria and Basilicata, in that order. It is a mass membership party, moreover, whose reported total of 324,000 was topped only by the East German communist Party of Democratic Socialism (PDS). There is a small but growing fringe of violent groups – often called 'Nazi skins' – in Rome and in the north to whom violent attacks are frequently attributed. Among recent right-wing bombings was one at the Rome memorial to the wartime massacre of Jewish hostages at the Adreatine Caves and another in front of a theatre that was showing a documentary about Adolf Eichmann, the 'shipping clerk' of the Holocaust. Several hundred right-wing activists also demonstrated against globalization at an international meeting at Cernobbia on Lake Como. On the internet, a website 'Holy War' listed 10,000 names of Italian Jews, including Marsiglia. And at soccer stadiums, banners have been reported that read 'Auschwitz is your home'.

RACISM AMONG SOCCER ROWDIES

The escalation of racism and violence at international soccer matches in recent years once more raises the question to what extent groups of the radical right might be involved in these shocking clashes. I have written about this repeatedly[14] and, by now, there is a large literature on soccer hooliganism in many countries. British soccer rowdies, in particular, have a long tradition, beginning in the mid 1970s when Leeds United and Manchester United were excluded from European competitions because of the mayhem perpetrated by their camp followers on the Continent.[15] The 1980s witnessed new flare-ups and, once again, British teams found themselves barred, this time until 1990, even though they had their domestic soccer donnybrooks, for example at the 1988 match between Scotland and England, when 90 were injured, and the Hillsborough Stadium (Sheffield) tragedy of 1989 when collapsing bleachers killed 95 before the semi-final between Liverpool and Nottingham Forest. In 1990, 200 British 'hoolies' were expelled from the World Cup in Italy and, two years later, about 1,000 were arrested at the World Cup in Holland.[16]

If the foregoing has left the impression that soccer violence is a British monopoly, the '*mal anglais*', we need to broaden the perspective to the 'hoolies' of other European nations. But it is true that, to quote the *Sunday Mirror*[17] on the occasion of the World Cup embarrassment of 2000 when nearly 400 were arrested in Brussels: 'We British have become a nation of drunk, tattooed and skin-headed hooligans.' But this time, German hoolies were involved as well who had already distinguished themselves with rioting and the near-fatal beating of a French policeman in Lens the previous year. There are soccer hooligans all over Europe by now, and French and Tunisian ones who, along with the British, had clashed with the police before the 1998 World Cup in Marseilles where 16 people were injured. But by any measure, the year 2000 was the worst, beginning with a disturbance in February after an English team played Galatasaray in Istanbul. Two Leeds hooligans were killed by Turkish hoolies and there were further disturbances at a rematch in Copenhagen.

Several of the governments involved had prepared themselves for the European Cup games in Charleroi, Belgium. The British government created a football division in the National Crime Intelligence Service (NCIS) as early as 1998, and in 1998/99 alone, as many as 3,341 hooligans were arrested in Britain. The 1999 Football Offences and Disorder Act permitted law officers to arrest known hooligans on their way to international meets – a seemingly effective way of forestalling trouble. The hooligans of 2000, however, are not as easily recognized as the skinheads of the 1980s – for a start, many of them now avoid tell-tale haircuts and insignia. As German police learned the hard way, moreover, some of the most violent offenders, such as the killers of Lens, may have no prior record of violence and therefore slip right through their hands, especially since the Schengen Accord eliminated most border checks.[18]

Another line of defence was established at the football stadium in

Charleroi on the advice of the ninth commission (since 1945) on stadium security: the suppression of chants and shouted racist insults, of invasions of the playing field by the hooligans – for example at half-time or before or after the game – and strict control of resale of tickets which have sometimes opened the floodgates to mobs of hoolies. At Charleroi, 5,000–10,000 eager fans showed up without tickets and often drunk at the gates. A new, fast-track system of magistrate officers allowed the Belgians to detain hundreds of unruly persons on the spot, expel half of them from the country, and keep some of them in jail for the duration of the games.[19] The final results for Charleroi were a devastated downtown area, 921 arrests of what the French and French-speaking Belgians call '*les croquemitaines*', 464 deportations, and the likelihood that England would lose its opportunity to host the Eurocup games of 2006.

There is much discussion, of course, of the motives of soccer rowdies, in particular a widespread suspicion that their excesses are instigated by radical right groups. There is no doubt about the frequent displays of racism among the hooligans, especially with the growing numbers of black players in recent years. Most of the big teams in any case include players from foreign countries who often command star salaries but have to endure more than their share of insults and envy. In the lower leagues, black or brown players are often 'put down' and insulted without the compensation of high incomes. Richie Moran, 'a black ex-professional footballer', has told appalling stories of verbal and physical abuse of Jamaican, African and Asian players by opponents and their fans, by coaches, managers, and especially by the public at large – and of the frequent failure of police, managers and sports associations to act on their complaints.[20] 'Without doubt', wrote the *Economist* (24 June 2000), 'England's travelling supporters included some members of the far right whose presence was signalled by their repeated chanting of [the slogan] "no surrender to the IRA", a curious sentiment to express before a football match against Portugal or Germany.' There is a surprising note of nationalism and 'defence of local turf' in hooliganism, says *Le Figaro*, 20 June 2000. Some observers have also read anti-EU sentiment into its outbreaks, another issue dear to the far right (*Le Monde*, 21 June 2000). There may also be anti-Muslim prejudice on display in the clashes between British and Turkish hoolies.

But the vast police apparatus of the host countries ought to be able to keep violent right-wingers from taking advantage of the attractions of the big games. At Charleroi, the police had 3,000 men (out of a force of 18,000 national gendarmes and 20,000 local police), 120 horses, two helicopters, 30 water cannons and 45 dog-handlers with dogs ready. Against them, aside from the Brits, Germany could mobilize at most 2,500 hooligans for its national team.[21] Belgium and the Netherlands have perhaps a hundred hoolies for each major team. Figures for the Turkish hoolies are hard to come by. Although most of them probably cannot afford the trip, many are already living in Western Europe. Only about a thousand were expected from Britain which has an estimated 5–15,000 fans, not necessarily all hooligans. And why are the Brits such soccer chauvinists? As a letter-writer to the *Economist* (1 July 2000) put it: 'Where else do xenophobic tabloids enjoy daily circulations of several millions and regularly publish frankly racist articles directed for the most part at England's close neighbours?'

So the answer to the often-asked question of 2000 about radical right conspiracies behind the spectacular eruption of hooliganism comes down to this: as the same letter-writer, Michael Green, continued somewhat simplistically:[22] 'English football hooliganism is the extreme physical demonstration of an English culture of prejudice which ranges from a general feeling of dislike and distrust of "foreigners" to the more excessive expressions of xenophobia found in tabloid newspapers or in pub talk across England on any Saturday night.' Lots of racism, primitive nationalism and rude juvenile behaviour indeed, but no noteworthy conspiracies, even though radical right parties would of course love to take advantage of the seemingly endless opportunities to recruit tough-fisted members who, at least superficially, appear to agree with them. This is not to say that there have not been many individual hoolies, small groups, and sporadic incidents of hooliganism associated with the BNP, NF, Combat 18, and other groups in the past. In fact, Jon Garland documents a whole table full of efforts of radical right groups like the NF trying to muscle in on the games and, sometimes, orchestrating the chanting or showing their banners.[23] Journalists and some scholars perhaps tend to overrate the importance of these incidents, and to interpret them as signs of radical right success in taking over soccer hooliganism.

And what is to be done about it, other than what is already being done? Perhaps it would make sense to deny them the media coverage they crave, although televising their stadium excesses by close-circuit TV has already proved a valuable tool for identification and conviction for the use of the police and a deterrent in some documented cases. Football authorities should denounce hooliganism in no uncertain terms, especially 'The racist chanting and the booing of foreign anthems inside [stadiums] ... General loutishness [usually] precedes an outbreak of violence. Fans who shout racist abuse or give fascist salutes are committing offences, ranging from breach of the peace to threatening behaviour' (*Economist*, 1 July 2000). Last but not least there is the proposal of J. Garland and M. Rowe to use football as 'a vehicle for anti-racist education and youthwork in a more general setting', such as the schools.

GERMANY: IS THE WAVE CRESTING AGAIN?

The last big wave of right-wing and anti-foreign violence in Germany crested in 1991/92, along with the sudden arrival of nearly half a million foreign asylum-seekers – and hundreds of thousands of German ethnic repatriates from Eastern Europe (*Umsiedler*) – whom government authorities housed temporarily in hostels and camps all over smalltown and rural Germany.There they became the targets of racist violence, arson attacks and hate crimes by local skinheads and mostly unaffiliated groups, that are unconnected to any known right-wing extremist parties. This occurred particularly in East Germany where youth unemployment has been extremely high, and the disorientation following the fall of communism even higher. Curiously, the radical right parties, such as the Republican Party (REP),[24] the then seemingly moribund National Democratic Party (NPD), and the German People's Union (DVU) had not received much benefit from the opening up of post-communist East Germany, or from the arrival of the asylum-seekers, at least not in membership or in votes at the time. Their membership, as compared to West Germany, was miniscule and in no proportion to the number of violent anti-foreign incidents. In 1993 the two major parties in Bonn, Christian Democrats (CDU/CSU) and Social Democrats (SPD), joined forces to tighten the extremely permissive constitutional clause relating to asylum (article 16), and this reduced the influx of asylum-seekers and the anti-foreigner excesses to manageable proportions.[25] Hundreds of thousands of anti-racist demonstrators in 'chains of light', marched for tolerance all over Germany.Violent incidents decreased, or at least they were no longer the object of intense media attention.

Since the dramatic decline of the mid-1990s, however, the number of anti-foreign incidents has gone up again and appears to be approaching a record high, once more concentrated in East Germany. According to Manfred Klink, the director of the German Federal Criminal Office (BKA), about 15,000 political extremist offences were committed in 1999 in Germany, about two-thirds of them by right-wing activists and about 15 per cent violent in character. Left-wing groups also contributed their share of this violent action, but much of that was specifically aimed at anti-fascist action against the right wing.[26] A large part of the right-wing extremist offences involves agitation and the (illegal) production and distribution of neo-Nazi propaganda. One recent law-enforcement coup was the extradition from Denmark of Gary Laucks, an American who for many years had exported his Nazi propaganda material to Germany from a safe haven in Lincoln, Nebraska. Since his activities were illegal not only in Germany but in most other European countries, he was arrested, extradited and jailed for several years in Germany. The interventions against right-wing and anti-foreign propaganda also include 'hate websites' and the purveyors and distributors of skinhead rock music, again much of it from off-shore.[27] The German government had already banned neo-Nazi rock music – advocating racism, anti-foreign violence, and genocide – at the height of the 1992 wave of incidents. As a result, its production went abroad from where the compact disks may still be imported. In the meantime, the efforts at suppression also involve Internet distribution and trade in hate literature, although the nature of cyberspace frustrates efforts at control.

A report by Klaus-Dieter Fritsche of the Federal Office of Constitutional Protection (*Verfassungsschutz*) supplies the latest update on right-wing extremist membership and activities. Since 1990, the membership of different organizations has nearly doubled from 32,300 to 51,400. Of this number the DVU, which is known for its recent East German electoral victories, its Holocaust denial and elaborate apologias for the Third Reich, now has 17,000 members. The three right-wing parties learned from their 1997 election débâcle in the state of Hamburg where they split their votes in such a way – the DVU had 4.9 per cent, the REP 1.8 per cent, and the NPD 0.1 per cent – that no single right-wing party succeeded in surpassing the 5 per cent minimum for representation in the Hamburg *Bürgerschaft* (state legislature).[28] So, in 1999 the REP agreed to stay out of the Brandenburg elections while the DVU agreed in turn promised not to compete for the Berlin *Abgeordneten Haus* (House of State Deputies). At this point the DVU still had to create a district organization for Brandenburg, where it only had 200 members. It finally put up a general slate of 16 candidates, mostly unknowns (and no direct candidates), a clear sign of it still being an under-developed party in that state. The previous year, the DVU had already surprised everyone with a vote of 12.9 per cent in neighbouring Saxony-Anhalt, and now it sought to make up for its obvious weakness with the media power and the financial resources of its well-established weekly, *Deutsche National-zeitung* and its owner, DVU leader Gerhard Frey. Its only remaining rival, the youthful, skinhead NPD was better established locally, but unlikely to match that power.[29] The politics of Brandenburg had been in flux as Minister President Manfred Stolpe (SPD) found himself challenged by a resurgent CDU. This transition and the low turnout (54.4 per cent) offered a window of opportunity to the radical right. The DVU garnered 5.3 per cent of the vote and five seats, the NPD 0.7 per cent. A percentage of 5.3 may not seem much by American or British standards, but under a modified proportional election system it was a rare achievement for an extremist party. At the federal level, no single right extreme party seems capable of surpassing the 5 per cent minimal hurdle, but all three of them combined have scored 5 per cent in public opinion polls.

The REP has had less success in recent East German elections as a result of their internal squabbles and their past inability to harmonize their relations to other parties of their ilk. In West German Baden-Württemberg they did obtain 9.1 per cent in the state elections of 1996. Their original leader, TV chat show host Franz Schönhuber, was overthrown and reinstated repeatedly for trivial reasons, most recently because he had proposed precisely the kind of electoral agreement with the DVU that made for the 1999 success of the latter in Brandenburg. Nationwide, the REP now has 14,000 members and there is some evidence of their secret collusion with right-wing fringe groups. The NPD, with 6,000 members, has made efforts to woo the clientele of the successor party (PDS) of the old state communist party (SED) with slogans of an 'anticapitalist alternative' (to the regime in Berlin), 'people-oriented socialism', and stating that 'the [old communist] German Democratic Republic was the better Germany'. Its new East German recruits are increasingly replacing the older West German comrades' traditional aim of struggling for the 'control of the streets', like the stormtroopers of old,[30] with the familiar slogans of xenophobia and welfare chauvinism. As Michael Minkenberg put it:'We are not dealing with a backward-looking, right-wing–radical segment of the public intent on returning to the Nazi past but rather with reactions to the radical transformation of East German politics, society, and economy.' For that purpose, they also try to work with local neo-Nazi and skinhead groups in campaigns of 'national resistance'. Recent examples are their common demonstrations against the Berlin Holocaust Memorial and marching through the Brandenburg Gate (29 January 2000).

The smaller neo-Nazi groups, as far as they are known to the Constitutional Protection service, have about 2,200 members. Many of those groups have been suppressed in recent years. Aside from their decentralized condition of autonomous 'comrade groups', they also stand out for their attempts to use the Internet and 'national info-telephones' to remain in touch with each other. Their chief preoccupation has been with counteracting left-wing, antifascist actions, especially with lists of their political enemies, including members of the Bundestag, published addresses of Jewish institutions, and a 1999 brochure of White Aryan Resistance. There has been a steep rise in extreme right-wing home pages on the net – a tenfold increase between 1996 and 1999 alone, and as many as 400 today. In addition to these groups there are about 10,000 violent right-wingers today, mostly skinheads and over half in East Germany (which holds only one-fifth of the population of Germany). Repeatedly, caches of arms and explosives have been found with them. In fact, they bombed the Berlin grave of Heinz Galinski, the former head of the Central Council of Jews in Germany in December 1998, and the travelling exhibit 'War of Annihilation: Wehrmacht Crimes, 1941–

1944' in Saarbrücken (March 1999). Would-be bombers can download the instructions for making a bomb from the Internet, for example from '*Der kleine Sprengmeister* [The Little Bomb Master]'. Gun-nuts and would-be bombers are often attracted to the extreme right, in Germany as elsewhere.

Why do they commit these violent acts? According to the Constitutional Protection Office, the motives are complex. Their marginal economic and social situation is often a cause, especially in East Germany where more than half of the violent anti-foreign and anti-leftish (anti-antifascist) incidents take place, even though the percentage of foreigners per population is only one-fifth (1.8 per cent) of that of Germany (9 per cent) as a whole. Young males also fear the high unemployment rate and suffer from what Fritsche called 'a lack of orientation', a sense of having 'no future'. The typical skinhead perpetrator is not a member of a larger right-wing organization, but nevertheless exhibits a 'diffuse right extremist ideology'. His violence is often triggered by extensive alcohol abuse and after skinhead rock concerts with intense racist, neo-Nazi and hate lyrics that glorify violence and give it a patina of pseudo-patriotism and victimology, with the Germans as victims. Neo-Nazi and extremist parties not only supply the ideological overtones and music but usually recruit skinhead guards and goons for particular local actions and events.[31]

At a 1997 international convention in Seoul, Klaus Wasmund, an authority on the political socialization of political activists reported on interviews with social workers and teachers, and an analysis of underground magazines (fanzines), neo-Nazi rock lyrics and biographical background data for clues to the motives of violent skinheads. He found that German neo-Nazi skinheads were distinguished by their low educational levels – often having dropped out of school altogether – and working-class or lower-middle-class backgrounds. He estimated about one-third to be under eighteen,[32] and characterized their common social–psychological backgrounds with major 'emotional deficits' in the family, particularly a 'bad emotional atmosphere', weak or absent fathers, domineering mothers and authoritarian childhoods. They exhibit a lack of autonomy in making their own decisions and have frequently suffered corporal punishment, or other humiliation routines, as punishment. Their protest orientation is 'diffuse and unreflected' (meaning not aimed at practical political goals or constructive conflict resolution) and extremely violence-prone.

They seek to escape from 'boring' home lives, schools, or vocational training into the 'real comradeship' of the skinhead group whose acceptance they crave. Like gangs in the United States, these groups are not held together by shared interests or hobbies, only by their beery conviviality and resentful attitudes. The group has shared views of sorts, a sense of ethnic identity, and a saviour complex about saving the country, particularly German women, from imagined dangers and real aliens. Its slogans, often invoked by neo-Nazi music and propaganda, sharply separate friend and foe. They pillory the 'racial contamination of the white race', international Zionism and the alleged enslavement of the German people. There is the familiar primitive national-ism (or racism), social Darwinism, a totalitarian authoritarianism and a pronounced tendency to believe in scapegoats and conspiracy theories – typical Nazi attitudes that make a revisionist defence of the Third Reich (as far as historic national socialism is understood) all but inevitable. The crimes of the old Nazis, of course, are never admitted. The skinheads may collaborate with extreme right parties – for example as paid guards or bouncers – but they are loath to submit to their discipline and commitment.[33] Wasmund succinctly connects the sociopsychological atmosphere of youth under the communist system of the GDR – for instance the friend–foe propaganda and the parent-less, collectivist *Kinderkrippen* (government childcare) socialization from age three – with skinhead attitudes in the decade-and-a-half since.

WHY COMPARE EXTREME RIGHT MOVEMENTS?

There is something about right-wing extremism in any country that tends to get under the skin of well-intentioned natives. It is only natural that they should ask themselves: Why us? Why is this happening here? Since right-wing politics usually fastens upon national identity and factors unique to one culture, moreover, it provokes every coethnic – even those who are violently opposed to it – and yet it also makes it seemingly harder to compare one country's right-wingers to those of another.[34] They themselves usually do not recognize themselves in their equivalents abroad. It would never occur to a German or French xenophobe that he might have a lot in common with the ethnocentric among the minorities he hates, say a German neo-Nazi skinhead with a Turkish Grey Wolf, or an American racist with a black nationalist and vice versa. And yet we compare because we all hope to benefit in various ways from the comparison in spite of the apparent (and relative) lack of commonalities. It is important, however, first to set aside the easy stereotypes of perpetual national character – such as that France, Germany and Italy all had mighty fascist movements some 60 years ago – and that, perhaps, they are inclined in that direction. Today, the situation is very different: the threat no longer comes from a terrorist, even genocidal, and imperialist government making war upon its minorities and neighbours, but from right-wing, racist vigilantes and, perhaps, a rather passive police force and judiciary.

The cultures supporting right-wing movements in various countries do matter and we do well to keep track of attitudes and cultural trends among youth. For example, the German media in the summer of 2000 gave intensive coverage to the new eruption of right-wing radicalism and xenophobia in their country, especially in East Germany. In a supplement addressed particularly to young people, for example, the *Süddeutsche Zeitung* of Munich (2 October 2000) took the pulse of current youth trends by interviewing four young anti-fascists aged 16–25 and a 47-year-old resident foreigner of colour about everyday life with right-wing radicalism in the city of Jena, Thuringia. One of them was a 23-year-old leftish soccer fan who no longer attends the games of his favourite regional team, because, already on the streetcar *en route* to the stadium, armed neo-Nazi skinhead gangs (not with guns but with knives and brass knuckle-dusters) start searching for people who 'look like left-wingers'. During the game, a chorus of rowdy fans, many no older than fifteen or sixteen, shout slogans like 'out with the foreigners' or 'out with the kanaks', and chant songs like 'We are building a subway to Auschwitz', or something about Hitler. The stadium security guards make no effort to control the chanting, nor do the football club's coaches intervene at outings of the junior team to which the respondent belongs.

At his place of work, a hospital, the nurses talk in xenophobic terms about the 'Fijis' (Vietnamese), and the doctors tolerate it. The nurses also defend the right-wing shenanigans of their teenage children as 'normal for that age'. Once, at a pick-up soccer game, when the respondent had joined the outspoken pro-foreigner youth pastor of the town, black-clad vigilantes of the *Heimatschutz Thuringia* (Protective Association of Thuringia) showed up to videotape each of them, a familiar quasi-police action of intimidation. The Heimatschutz website includes the pictures of local left-wingers and the caption: 'We have your names and addresses. There'll be no forgiving or forgetting.' This left-winger also has reason to distrust the police which have shown a pronounced prejudice in favour of the right, he believes. Another 23-year old anti-fascist told how he avoids the town's market place after dark, because the neo-Nazis usually take it over to listen to their hate music. They accost whoever they think is 'leftish' and physical attacks are frequent. This is obviously street terror of the worst kind, and it is racist and Nazi talk, but the scenario is quite different – possibly worse – than the organized street-fighting of old Nazis and communists in the Weimar Republic.

A third respondent, aged 16 and also an anti-fascist, was careful not to give out his unlisted telephone number, name and address to casual acquaintances. When he still wore dreadlocks (a typical left-wing fashion), he was beaten up twice. He now hides a gas pistol on his person. His friends had similar experiences, and they also suffered vandalism against their property. He too has stopped playing goalie in his soccer club because the rest of the team were hostile right-wingers: 'In Jena it is normal to be on the extreme right.' As one moves towards the suburbs and the environs of the city, the extreme right subculture becomes ever more inescapable: children simply grow into it. A young woman, aged 23, the fourth respondent, said that the university town of Jena 'compares favourably with the right-wing street terror of Gera and Erfurt (where a synagogue was attacked in 2000)' or in Fürstenwalde and Wurzen – all smalltown locations of recent major anti-foreign incidents – where 'there is nobody [young] left that is not of the radical right'. She added that, in spite of her dreadlocks, she herself is 'considered too old' to have to anticipate physical attack. Then she told of a 16-year-old couple of which the boy was beaten up by six men in black and the girl threatened with mayhem if she went to the police: 'We have your name, your address, your wanted poster.' The girl was in such a fright it took a lot of persuasion to make her go to the police.

The last interviewee, a Congolese journalist writing reports for the university, laughed out loud at the question whether 'he was sometimes insulted or accosted'. 'Sometimes? Always!' The first four of his seven years in Jena he was left alone but, more recently, he has been seriously assaulted three times, once in front of his door and once in the tram on the way home. His assailants always carried gas pistols, knives, or baseball bats. Since his last mugging – the police showed up but let the skinheads go because 'they carried no identification' – he is afraid for his life. The police would have dropped the case but for his insistence on following it up. Now he no longer dares sleep in his own flat, go out after dark, or even follow the invitation of friends who promise to accompany him home. He feels safe, more or less, only in daytime and in the centre of Jena. The *Süddeutsche Zeitung* concluded:

> In some parts of [East] Germany, meanwhile, xenophobia has become so much a matter of everyday life that, if you don't share it, you soon run into problems ... Unlike notorious centers of right-wing radicalism, the town of Jena ... is considered comparatively harmless and 'normal'. Now we see what 'normal' means these days.[35]

We can also see what is meant by the neo-Nazi 'liberation' of whole towns and rural areas into a condition of near-anarchy (see Zimmermann, below).

This theme was echoed in other media reports, for example on the 'normality' of xenophobia in many East German schools where 13–15-year-olds have a wildly exaggerated idea of the presence of foreigners, for instance in Saxony. When journalists asked one class of teenagers how many foreigners they thought were in Saxony, the students' estimates varied from 8 to 40 per cent of the population – the real percentage is only 2.3 per cent.[36] The intolerance and readiness to excuse anti-foreign violence of the East German teenagers is striking, and this has also been confirmed in youth surveys.

In an interview with journalists of the weekly *Die Zeit*, Wolfgang Thierse, the most prominent East German Social Democratic politician, called East German xenophobia 'a part of everyday opinion that is almost taken for granted. It is alarming that people are not at all ashamed of it.' Thierse was alarmed also about the ubiquitous fear of young democrats and leftists of the threats of physical violence and about 'the mixture of blindness, denial, whitewash, and helplessness' regarding right-wing extremist manifestations among local police and politicians. He attributed the public propensity of East Germans for scapegoating foreigners to the complex 'social fears and insecurities, and the moral deracination of German unification'. The authoritarianism of the communist GDR swept anti-Semitism and xenophobia under the rug and never prepared the people for dealing in a civil manner with their everyday social conflicts. 'Sometimes I am ashamed of this country when I see how anti-capitalist rhetoric and nationalist resentment are joined [like in the Third Reich]', said Thierse. 'I never thought that this brew … would ever surface again.'[37] The Social Democratic leader also saw striking differences between the right-wing extremist phenomenon in East Germany and its manifestation, say, among skinheads and Turks in West German suburbs. In the East, which is still smarting from the real and imagined humiliations and inequalities of German unification, skinheads find almost no foreigners to serve as a likely scapegoat, someone they can rationally blame for their misfortunes, but this seems to infuriate them even more. There are none of the very real problems of integration and multicultural coexistence which challenge the West German scene. Like the proverbial anti-Semitism without Jews, the objectless East German xenophobia is by now so deeply ingrained into the attitudes of the young that it bodes ill for the future.

What can be done to change the hate-filled, quasi-totalitarian mindset of East Germans? Thierse mentions, of course, the need for a dramatic lowering of unemployment, but also a politics of optimism and, most emphatically, addressing the syndrome of violence and xenophobia head on. Politicians and the media[38] must speak out forcefully. The police and judiciary must intervene promptly and with determination. Local politicians, parents, teachers and businessmen must support the quiet resistance to prejudice and violence. Another pertinent comment is by Wilhelm Heitmeyer, a well-known youth sociologist and expert on the challenge of the violent skinheads, especially in the context of the debate of the year 2000 about suppressing the NPD. Heitmeyer warns against the stereotypes of this debate – which personalizes, pathologizes, or even biologizes the misbehaviour of the young. Like other thoughtful commentators, he also fears that outlawing the NPD might make its activists into attractive martyrs for other youths. He also sees the problems of street violence not only with the violent thugs but in terms of flaws of German society in general. The prevalence of domestic violence in Germany tends to lower the threshold for all violence and to encourage disrespect for all individuals. A fear of losing one's job and home is a very real and rational problem in German society with its high youth unemployment. Finally, Heitmeyer would like to see the problems of migration and multicultural coexistence publicly and positively addressed and debated rather than allowing public indifference to stifle initiative and encourage alienation.[39]

In spite of the accumulation of hate crimes in Germany in 2000, including a bomb attack on a Düsseldorf commuter train – which injured ten immigrants from the former Soviet Union – plans to outlaw the violent NPD are not universally considered an effective weapon against the radical right. 'If the NPD is banned today', opined Berlin's security chief Eckart Werthebach, 'a new organization will rise in its place tomorrow with the exact same people, and we'd have to run after them with a new banning order.' In the largest German state, North Rhine Westphalia, such a ban only scattered the neo-Nazis and made it harder to keep track of them. The German Basic Law (constitution) has a procedure for outlawing political parties, but it requires that they pose a clear and present danger to the constitutional order. Many German politicians, with the exception of the Greens, also fear that a ban would violate basic principles of free speech and association. Chancellor Schroeder seems to favour a ban but mostly in sensitive places, such as on the site of the future Holocaust memorial and at the Brandenburg Gate, both matters of local police authority.[40]

There are also debates between CDU and SPD, for example in Mecklenburg-Vorpommern, over proposals to permit right-wing youths to meet in municipally owned clubrooms under the supervision and influence of youth social workers.[41] Conservative critics argue that such examples of *akzeptierende Jugendarbeit* (youth work based on acceptance) might imply an acceptance of anti-democratic, Nazi thought. Youth psychologists and social workers, on the other hand, point out that the 'non-accepting attitudes' of the establishment are a major factor in pushing the very young into the alienated and xenophobic attitudes of right-wing youth. One has to break the vicious circle, not perpetuate it. The German problematique obviously has some very German features, and yet there can be little doubt that the political socialization of French, British and Scandinavian neo-fascists has much in common with it, and similar efforts at 'accepting youth work' have been suggested by the Norwegian social scientist Tore Bjorgo, among others.[42]

NOTES

1. For an analysis of relevant aspects of right-wing reaction to the great upheaval of the 1960s and 1970s, see for example Herbert Kitschelt, *The Radical Right in Western Europe: A Comparative Analysis* (Ann Arbor, MI: University of Michigan Press, 1995), pp. 57–8 and 253.
2. See Henry Carey, 'Postcommunist Right Radicalism in Romania', in *The Revival of Rightwing Extremism in the Nineties* (London: Frank Cass, 1997), pp. 149–77, esp. pp. 162–3, 165–8.
3. Haider took over the 30-year-old FPÖ in 1986. Ibid., pp. 1, 33, 52–3, 59. See also Ch. 8 of this volume.
4. Werner A. Perger, 'Der Skandal zur rechten Zeit', *Die Zeit*, 4 June 1998. The FPÖ originally came from the *deutschnational Lager* and German opinion has always been particularly provoked by manifestations of German nationalism in Austria. On the occasion of the 1998 German Athletic Festival (*Deutsches Turnerfest*) in Munich, for example, the local *Süddeutsche Zeitung* recalled an acrimonious dispute of 75 years earlier, in the crisis year of 1923, when the anti-Semitic Austrian *Deutscher Turnerbund* was dramatically disinvited by the city from attending a predecessor of the *Deutsches Turnerfest* in Munich, because the Nazis would have taken advantage of its presence to politicize the event. *Süddeutsche Zeitung*, 6 June 1998.
5. See also 'Wien überschätzt Azorenhoch', ibid., 10 May 2000.
6. Martin A. Lee has described the extensive network of Gadafy's contacts with international arms dealers, terrorists, Licio Gelli, the mastermind behind the Italian P-2 Masonic Lodge, and Gelli's Argentine connections in an article, 'Ties that bind Gadafi and Neo-fascists', *Los Angeles Times*, 13 August 2000.
7. Cited by *Searchlight*, December 1999. Hans-Georg Betz describes the FPÖ as a 'rightwing populist', rather than a neo-Nazi party in his book *Radical Rightwing Populism in Western Europe* (New York: St Martin's, 1994), pp. 12–13, 63, 108, 112–14, 124–6 and 160.
8. Quoted from Tony Judt, 'Tales from the Vienna Woods', *New York Review of Books*, pp. 8–9.
9. *Süddeutsche Zeitung*, 22 September 2000.
10. See Kevin Donegan in the *Los Angeles Times*, 4 February 2000. Even the *Rough Guide to Ireland*, a popular tourist guide 'with an attitude' has accused Ireland of being 'shamefully intolerant of minorities', although this is denied by the authorities.
11. *Le Monde*, 30 May 2000, p. 8. Socialist adherents rejected this anti-immigrant statement by a narrow 51 per cent to 43 per cent, and the young by 55 per cent to 41 per cent. Among blue-collar workers and right-wing adherents (UDF, RPR, DL), anti-immigrant sentiments command majorities of between 73 and 86 per cent.
12. See also the illuminating essays and reviews on the politics of race in *French Politics and Society*, Autumn 2000.
13. On the Vlaams Blok, see also Christopher Husbands, 'Belgium: Flemish Legions on the March', in Paul Hainsworth (ed.), *The Extreme Right in Europe and the USA* (London: Pinter, 1994), pp. 126–50.
14. See Peter Merkl, 'Rollerball or Neo-Nazi Violence?' in Merkl (ed.), *Political Violence and Terror* (Berkeley and Los Angeles, CA: University of California Press, 1986), pp. 229–33 and 'A New Lease of Life for the Radical Right?' in Merkl and Weinberg (eds), *Encounters with the Contemporary Radical Right* (Boulder, CO: Westview, 1993), pp. 208–12. Also Peter Merkl, 'Are the Old Nazis Coming Back?' in Merkl (ed.), *The Federal Republic of Germany at Forty-Five* (London: Macmillan, 1995), pp. 434–60, *passim*.
15. In 1984, after the British defeat in Paris, a million francs-worth of destruction marked the scene. In Brussels, one fatality and 200 arrests marred the game against the FC Anderlecht. A year later, a collapsing wall at Heysel Stadium killed 39, mostly Turin fans, and injured hundreds during the match between Liverpool and Juventus.

16. The same year, 133 Manchester hooligans were arrested after completely trashing their Istanbul hotel. See the history of hooliganism and its repression by Jon Garland, 'Policing Racism in Football', in Jon Garland and Michael Rowe, *Racism and British Football* (Basingstoke: Macmillan, 2001), Ch. 4, which also has a fine list of references on this subject. Another brief history appeared in 'La résurgence du mal anglais', in *Le Figaro*, 20 June 2000.

17. The *Observer* also remarked: 'It is English society that produces violence and xenophobia.' But as the Home Affairs Committee in the House of Commons also pointed out in a report, most British soccer stadiums are such nasty, overcrowded and underequipped places (e.g. lacking restrooms, restaurants, etc.) that we should not be surprised if the working-class fans sometimes 'behave like the animals' for which these stadiums seem designed. See Garland and Rowe, *Racism*, Ch. 4.

18. Germany has reinstituted temporary passport control for international matches in the hope of catching its own hooligans. After the *Observer* blamed the British boulevard press and its World War II chauvinism for the excesses between German and British hoolies, the *Sunday Mirror* wrote: 'The actions of a band of criminals who call themselves fans brought shame not glory, to England.' Quoted by the *Frankfurter Allgemeine Zeitung*, 19 June 2000.

19. *Guardian*, 24 June 2000. The European soccer association UEFA threatened to oust England from the Eurocup 2000 'if the terror did not end'. It also denied Turkey and England a 'Euro 2000 Fair Play' rating.

20. See Moran's 'Racism in Football: A Victim's Perspective', which refers also to David Meller's Football Task Force and its 1980s report, *Eliminating Racism from Football*. Racism has always been present in soccer, especially in local and domestic games, long before it invaded international matches.

21. East German hooligans are less inhibited in racist violence and share the display of flags and nationalist slogans with their neo-Nazi groups without however exhibiting any great desire to be recruited into their organizations. See Merkl, *The FRG at 45*, p. 460. Concerning Charleroi, see also *Der Spiegel*, 16 June 2000, on the preparations for violence.

22. *Economist*, 1 July 2000.

23. See Table 10 in Ch. 4 of Garland and Rowe, *Racism*, which details incidents between the late 1950s and 1995 and offers commentary.

24. The REP arose in the 1980s from older right-wing groups and CDU/CSU dissidents and, by 1989, were poised to become an important right-wing populist party when German unification took away one of their popular propaganda lines. Racked with internal factionalism and rivalry among several would-be *Führers*, they never quite recovered from this turn of events even though they engaged themselves strongly on the issue of immigrants and asylum-seekers.

25. On the escalation of anti-foreign violence, see Merkl, 'Are the Old Nazis Coming Back?', pp. 441–50. Also Michael Minkenberg, 'The Radical Right in Unified Germany: Dividing the Nation in the Name of the People', *Politik*, Summer 2001. On German immigration policies and problems, see esp. William M. Chandler, 'Immigration Politics and Citizenship in Germany', in Merkl, *The FRG at 45*, pp. 344–56.

26. Other left-wing violence typically involves nuclear energy plants and transports, and giant construction projects such as the extension of Frankfurt Airport, Startbahn West, and most recently globalization conferences.

27. BKA Report by Director Klink, presented at a conference at George C. Marshall European Centre for Security Studies, 21 September 2000.

28. Under the prevailing electoral law, the voter has two ballots, one for a candidate for the individual district and one for a state party. The latter determines the party's proportional share of seats in the state legislature.

29. The NPD and its youth organization, the Young Nationalists (JN), cultivate more of a dynamic, aggressive and revolutionary image, but it had only about 150 members in

the entire state. For details of the contest, see Rainer Erb, 'DVU und NPD im brandenburgischen Wahlkampf', *Deutschlandarchiv*, November/December 1999, pp. 947–52.

30. See Merkl, *The Making of a Stormtrooper* (Princeton, NJ: Princeton University Press, 1980), pp. 160–67.

31. Klaus-Dieter Fritsche, 'Politischer Extremismus in Deutschland – ein aktuelles Lagebild', George C. Marshall European Centre for Security Studies, 22 September 2000.

32. He also found more than twice as many active neo-Nazi skinheads in East Germany (3,000) than in West Germany (1,200) which has a population four times the size of East Germany. There are various other skinhead groups, even leftist and anti-racist ones (e.g. SHARPS: Skinheads Against Racism and Prejudice).

33. See Klaus Wasmund, 'Neo-Nazi Attitudes and Violent Behaviour Among German Youth', paper presented at 17th IPSA World Congress, 17–22 August 1997 in Seoul. Wasmund also discusses the 'uniforms' (bomber-jackets and Doc Marten boots with white shoelaces, flags and symbols, and the neo-Nazi rock music 'scene'. On this last-mentioned subject, see also *Der Spiegel*, 30 (1997).

34. Compare the general essays in *The Revival* ... for example on Italy, Germany and Romania.

35. 'Was alles normal ist', *Süddeutsche Zeitung*, 2 October 2000.

36. See the report on a pro-foreigner enlightenment campaign in a village school near Leipzig, 'Fremdenfeindlichkeit bleibt zu oft unwidersprochen', in *Kulturchronik*, 5 (2000), pp. 18–20.

37. Reprinted in *Kulturchronik*, 5 (2000), pp. 21–2.

38. Ibid., pp. 22–3. Thierse is particularly critical of the sensationalism and the focus on the violent few rather than on the quiet resistance of many to the anti-foreign excesses.

39. Quoted from the *Kulturchronik*, 6 (June 2000), pp. 21–3.

40. In the face of the mounting and often lethal attacks on such sensitive targets, the Ministers of the Interior of federation and states met in Düsseldorf and agreed on a tougher stance against right-wing extremism.

41. In the GDR, communist youth policy gave young people access to many such municipal youth clubs under the supervision of communist social youth workers. Upon unification, however, all such public services and facilities were closed down, a foolish measure on a par with past American conservative arguments against after-school basketball facilities for ghetto youth – on the grounds that they might 'coddle juvenile criminals'.

42. In his oral presentation at the Marshall Centre on 22–23 September 2000.

CHAPTER TWO

Ten Theories of the Extreme Right

Roger Eatwell

INTRODUCTION

DURING THE last 20 or so years, a variety of extreme right political parties have leapt to electoral prominence across Western Europe.[1] Consider the four most cited examples. The first major breakthrough came in France, when Jean-Marie Le Pen's FN won 10 per cent of the vote in the 1984 European Parliament elections. By 1995 Le Pen was supported by 15 per cent of French people in the first round of the French presidential elections. In Italy, the AN (the reborn neo-fascist MSI) won 15 per cent of the vote in the 1994 elections, and together with the LN briefly entered government with Silvio Berlusconi's conservative Forza Italia. In 2001 the same parties again formed an administration under Berlusconi. In Austria, the FPÖ won a record 27 per cent of the poll in 1999 and entered government early on in 2000, in coalition with the conservative ÖVP (although its controversial and media-genic leader, Jörg Haider, was forced to relinquish hopes of immediate national office in the face of a wave of international protest). In Belgium, by 2001 the VB enjoyed the allegiance of 33 per cent of voters in its Antwerp heartland, and more like 20 per cent in Flanders as a whole. However, the general European pattern of extremist voting is by no means one of ever-growing support – nor is the pattern of such support amenable to simple explanation.[2]

Even where it has been 'successful', the extremist electoral record has often been volatile. During 1998–99, the FN split badly and support dropped to under 10 per cent – before Le Pen rebounded in the 2002 presidential elections to enter the second ballot with 17 per cent of the vote. The FPÖ has lost votes since entering office – reflecting the dangers of 'anti-system' parties appearing to become part of the system. Both the AN and LN lost votes in the 2001 elections compared to their 1990s' peak, when they attracted around 15 per cent of the vote nationally and 30 per cent of the northern vote respectively. Extremist support has often risen and fallen rapidly especially at the local level (although it is important to note that there are also long-standing extreme right strongholds, such as FPÖ leader Jörg Haider's home state of Carinthia, where his party has polled over 40 per cent of the vote). The German DVU won 13 per cent of the vote in the 1998 Saxony-Anhalt regional elections, but slumped to a tenth of this level in the same area for the subsequent 1998 federal elections. Conversely, the British BNP won less than 4 per cent of the vote in the 1999 European Parliament elections in Oldham West, but won over 16 per cent in the 2001 general election (the common argument holds that fringe parties do better in 'second order' rather than major national elections). Support can also vary notably within similar areas of a country at the same time. The first local breakthrough of the FN came in Dreux during 1982–83, a town which was experiencing notable structural change. Yet Evreux, a relatively similar town just a few miles away, saw no such breakthrough. And in some countries, such as Ireland, Portugal and Spain, the extreme right hardly exists (although there is evidence that anti-immigrant sentiment is growing in some of these countries).[3]

The purpose of this chapter is not to expand on selected examples of these particular cases. Rather, the main focus is methodological and theoretical. This chapter seeks to set out better tools and hypotheses which could help answer a number of questions – although the more individualistic, complex nature of postmodern society means that such predictions would always need to be accompanied by considerable caveats.

In the opening two sections of this chapter, I develop a critique of the current main theoretical explanations of electoral support for the extreme right.[4] I identify five key 'demand' and five 'supply' side arguments. By 'demand', I mean arguments that focus primarily on socioeconomic developments, such as the impact of immigration, unemployment or rapid social change. By 'supply', I refer more to the messages which reach voters – which means studying factors such as the leadership and programmes of the insurgent and mainstream parties, or the media. Although many arguments overlap, separating them in this way has heuristic advantages – not least, by raising the issue of the primacy of agency or structure. In line with recent historical and social science fashion, approaches typically stress the primacy of demand factors over supply, of structure over agency.[5]

Unquestionably, Europe has experienced major socioeconomic changes in recent years, changes which have weakened the allegiance to (if not always voting for) mainstream parties. However, in the conclusion I argue that there is a need to develop a (double) three-dimensional model, which focuses on the attitudes of individuals (the *micro*-level), who are embedded in various groups and local (*meso*) and wider national and international (*macro*) contexts.[6] More specifically, this chapter concludes that a fertile avenue for further empirical work is the hypothesis that extreme right supporters tend to be characterized by a combination of three traits which are strongly influenced by supply-side factors as well as demand-side factors, namely: growing perceptions of 'extremist' *legitimacy* + rising personal *efficacy* + declining political *trust*.

DEMAND–SIDE THEORIES[7]

The single-issue thesis[8]

Initially, the most common demand-side approach to the revival of extreme right voting in Western Europe was the single-issue thesis.[9] This places considerable emphasis on the attractiveness of anti-immigrant politics – or issues which can be related to this, such as law and order, unemployment or welfare.[10]

The rise of the FN in France during the 1980s appears to offer an excellent verification of this thesis. The party made its electoral leap forward after adopting an increasingly strident anti-immigrant line. By the time of the 1995 presidential elections, 22 per cent of the French electorate considered immigration as a top political priority – and a remarkable 53 per cent of Le Pen's voters. Xenophobia was a particularly good indicator of the likelihood of FN voting.

The single-issue approach implies that extreme right parties will do especially well at times when there are major concerns about new immigration. Austria appears to provide a good example of such a linkage. Here the number of legal immigrants more than doubled between the late 1980s and 1993, and illegal immigration rose too as communism collapsed. By the late 1990s, over 9 per cent of Austria's population were immigrants (the second highest figure in the EU, after Luxembourg). The immigration issue was forcefully exploited by the FPÖ, which saw its vote surge during these years. Recently, Haider has continued to exploit the issue, arguing that the EU's eastward expansion polices would open Austria's borders to a flood of new immigrants, which he characterized as in effect declaring war on his country.

However, there are several problems with the single-issue thesis. The most fundamental problem stems from the fact that most extreme right parties do have broad programmes, covering more than race-related matters.[11] For example, when the FN began life in 1972 it was not primarily concerned with immigration. Even after picking up the issue forcefully, it has put forward a variety of well-publicized and relatively detailed policies on economic and social matters. At the local level, the FN occasionally did not concentrate on immigration as it tried to build support, preferring instead to cultivate sympathetic coteries and their ideological concerns (most typically, nostalgia for past forms of the right, such as Marshall Pétain's Vichy government).[12]

Moreover, whilst xenophobia was unquestionably important to the FN vote, a notable minority of its supporters were attracted by what they saw as its underlying authoritarian-conservative (even revolutionary-right) ideology.[13] Another important group of 'neither left nor right' ('*niniste*') supporters were motivated more by their general disillusionment with the left as the defender of their economic interests.[14] Turning to other cases, immigration did not play any significant role in the AN's breakthrough in Italy during 1992–94.[15] There is also little evidence that immigration was the major cause of voting for the LN at its peak in the 1990s. Indeed, LN support waned at the turn of the new millennium, precisely the time it adopted a more strident anti-immigrant stance (at the same time, the focus turned from immigrants coming from Southern Italy to the growing numbers entering Italy from outside the EU).[16]

A further problem for the single-issue thesis concerns chronology. Extreme right success does not necessarily follow new waves of immigration. The FN leapt forward during the early 1980s when immigration to France was relatively low. Similarly, the German REP made its first major breakthrough in the 1989 European and Berlin senate elections, when immigration was not a national public issue – although immigration had for some time been an issue in Berlin.

This last factor highlights yet another problem with the single-issue thesis: namely the meso-spatial relationship between immigration and extremist voting. The most common argument has been to claim that there is some form of 'halo' effect, that anti-immigrant voting is strongest in areas surrounding concentrations of immigrants – areas where there is a perceived threat of 'invasion' into housing and job markets.[17] However, there is no necessary connection, as can be seen from the fact that the extreme right in Britain has in general been weak in spite of significant concentrations of 'immigrants' in some urban areas. Extreme right parties can even be strong in areas where there are few immigrants.

In many ways, the immigration issue appears to be one of perception more than reality. For example, in Germany support for the extreme right tends to rise when immigrants in a particular area are perceived as causing some form of socioeconomic problem or receiving over-favourable treatment. Turning to the more macro-level, the revival of the Norwegian FRPn during the 1990s (a time when polls showed that Norwegians were becoming more tolerant towards immigration) was almost certainly related to the belief that immigrants were entitled to the generous welfare benefits accorded to Norwegians.

The protest thesis

During the 1990s and after, commentators have increasingly stressed protest or 'anti–politics' as the key factor explaining the rise of the extreme right.[18] This thesis typically holds that such parties lack any serious ideology and that their programme amounts to little more than a negative attack on the political establishment (even the immigration issue can be turned against elites by blaming past governments for laxity in this field). Extreme right 'supporters' are seen as vehicles for expressing discontent with the mainstream parties. As a result, there is little or no social structure to the extremist vote, which tends to be volatile.

Evidence for this thesis can be found in features such as the declining share of the vote going to most mainstream parties, and falling turnouts in most European countries (often dramatic falls, such as the record low 59 per cent in Britain in 2001). Attendance at political meetings has in general slumped, with voters now quenching their (distinctly limited) thirst for political information by imbibing television news (which in turn has gone down market in an attempt to maintain viewer interest). German-language states even have a specific word for being fed up to the teeth with party politicians: '*Politikverdrossenheit*'.

FPÖ voters at the time of the 1999 legislative elections rated immigration behind hostility to the political establishment (66 per cent mentioned the latter to pollsters, compared to 47 per cent who said they voted FPÖ because of immigration). FPÖ voters resented the mainstream parties' domination of Austrian life since World War II, particularly the clientelistic-corrupt 'party-card economy'. In France, dislike of the political establishment was second only to xenophobia in the traits which help identify the typical 1990s FN voter. For many, this was part of a wider loss of faith in parties as legitimate democratic vehicles. To avoid being tarred by the same brush, some groups, such as the FPÖ, have sought to call themselves a 'movement' rather than a party (a terminological sleight of hand which seems unlikely to inoculate them from the voters' ire should they achieve office).

There can be no denying that conventional 'politics' is held in increasing contempt by many, but this does not mean that the protest thesis is essentially correct. One crucial problem concerns the fact that it is possible both to protest and to make a rational choice in terms of voting. For instance, whilst polls clearly show that VB voters do not like mainstream parties or the Belgian state, many have chosen the party precisely because they are attracted to its policies.[19] In most countries, there is a choice of 'protest' parties, but it is the extreme right which recently has made the main electoral progress in Western Europe. Alternative extreme left and green parties, which in general tend to be 'pro-immigrant', have in some cases even lost votes – the main exception before the 2002 elections was the PDS in East Germany, whose ideology bears some resemblance to that of the extreme right. People tend to vote for parties with which they have some form of ideological affinity.[20] They also act rationally by voting for parties which they believe will have some form of policy impact (though this does not necessarily mean that such parties have to enter office). The last point is especially important, as it implies that small parties tend to stay small because they are perceived as powerless.[21] This has been especially true where a relatively large conservative party, such as the Dutch Conservative Party (VVD), German CDU/CSU or British Conservatives have at times played on anti-immigrant sentiments.

The protest theory also posits that the extreme right vote is socially unstructured and transient. Certainly such parties can exhibit 'flash' characteristics, where they suddenly rise and fall. However, in general the major contemporary West European extreme right parties have had relatively stable and socially structured electoral constituencies. During the 1980s, when the first major signs of extreme right revival became clear, parties such as the French FN had most typically recruited from centre-right supporters, or people who were normally non-voters. Sociologically, they tended to be strongest among males, middle-aged-to-older voters, and within the small business and artisan sectors of the economy. Aspects of this profile remained important in the 1990s; especially the male-oriented side (although there are exceptions, for instance the Italian LN). But during the 1990s the extreme right also came to pose a threat to centre-left parties. In the first ballot of the 1995 presidential elections, Le Pen attracted more working-class votes than any other candidate (30 per cent); by this time, the FN supporters were the most loyal in France. Similarly, by 1999 the FPÖ was attracting major working-class support in Austria (47 per cent). Nevertheless, it is important not to overstress extreme right working-class support. For example, the Italian AN typical voter has tended to be a lower-middle-class public functionary.

The social breakdown thesis

Some commentators have sought to relate the revival of the extreme right to anomie, which leads to feelings of insecurity and inefficacy.[22] More specifically, the thesis holds that traditional social structures, especially those based on class and religion, are breaking down. As a result, individuals lose a sense of belonging and are attracted to ethnic nationalism, which according to psychological research increases a sense of self-esteem and efficacy. For similar reasons, they may be attracted to family and other traditional values. Young people especially, who have never experienced a secure milieu, are most likely to fall victim to this syndrome.

Certainly extreme right groups tend to defend traditional values. The FPÖ, for example, developed in the late 1990s the idea of a *Kinderscheck*, a form of new child benefit designed to help keep women in the home (previously welfare programmes had not figured in FPÖ campaigns, other than through its stress on immigrant parasites). They also tend to be hostile to forms of sexual liberation, such as homosexuality. Extreme right groups also tend to be nationalist, although a notable minority stress ethnoregionalism as the primary source of identification (the homogenous, relatively limited geographic region is often portrayed as a 'natural' rather than bureaucratic barrier to immigration). As such, it is important not to overstate the extent to which the current extreme right discourse is nationalist and centralist: it can even celebrate a form of ethnic diversity, albeit within a more overarching unity (thus Padania, the LN's term of Northern Italy, as a separate but integral part of white, Christian Europe – and so on).

There are undoubtedly studies which have found a connection between a high level of urban social isolation, including low religious and trade union ties, and voting for parties such as the FN or the REP. In the Netherlands, a significant correlation has been found between ethnic Dutch nationalism, a preference for anti-immigrant parties and feelings of social isolation.[23] Work on anti-immigrant voting in a former 'red' working-class district in Belgium indicated that the typical supporter was rarely a member of any form of organization, even a club.[24] Conversely, in Germany practising Catholics whose views in many ways coincided with those of the REP tended not to vote for this party, but remained loyal to the CDU/CSU. Potential French FN supporters also tended not to switch voting if they were part of traditional, leftist working-class networks (although culturally such milieux could be notably racist).[25]

However, there are major problems with the social breakdown thesis. One crucial issue concerns the fact that no matter how isolation is measured, it is clear that many extreme right voters are not suffering from anomie. Certainly the rate of associational membership is not significantly different for French FN voters than for other parties. In Italy, whole (extended) families could go over to voting for the LN, with the young often acting as the socializing agent.[26] These examples points to two important perspectives. First, that the family is often a more powerful form of socialization (including reverse socialization) than the associational group. And secondly, that networks can be both a prophylactic and recruiting agent. Strong opinion leaders within networks can be an especially important form of influence (and help resolve the rational choice paradox of why people vote at all). There are major problems in hypothesizing that associational membership encourages a sense of belonging, and democratic traits, without considering the specific nature of groups. For example, *pieds noirs* (Algérie française) sub-cultures have been strongly related to voting for the FN in areas such as the south of France.

A variation on the social breakdown thesis holds that its impact has been particularly notable on the party system in countries such as Austria, Belgium and Switzerland. In these countries the classic consociational party system was founded on socially isolated groupings, in particular through the Church and working-class organizations. Although the resulting elite accommo-dation-clientelistic politics opened the way for populist attacks, the social structure made it difficult for parties to emerge which sought a horizontal, trans-class appeal. However, as these structures broke down, so opportunities opened for new parties – especially ones which celebrated the national (or regional) community. This process was helped by the old antagonisms between the various pillars at the mass social level, which made it difficult for voters to switch to another established party. Moreover, as sociopolitical structures within the pillars had tended to be deferential, their voters were open to the new authoritarian, leader-oriented appeals of the extreme right.

This argument undoubtedly contains some insights, but most countries in Europe have not had party systems based on pillared societies. Even within those that have, most voters have not turned to extreme right parties. Moreover, in the Netherlands – another of the classic consociational Euro-pean democracies – before 2002 there was relatively little extremist voting (possible explanations for the weakness of the extreme right in the Nether-lands include: a relatively open elite; the existence of left oppositional groups; a Calvinist culture which has limited corruption; and various forms of repression). The late Pim Fortuyn's sudden rise (his party won 17 per cent of the vote in the 2002 parliamentary elections) illustrates the potential for new party breakthrough. But whilst the breakdown of traditional partisanship may be a necessary condition for the rise of an insurgent party, it is by no means a sufficient condition.

The (reverse) post-material thesis

During the 1970s and 1980s many sociologists came to argue that the more wealthy Western societies were moving towards a 'post-material' society, characterized by features such as a diminishing concern with traditional class and economic interests; greater concern for lifestyle issues, such as feminism and environmentalism; a loss of faith in traditional parties and growing interest in more issue-based and protest politics; and a declining faith in national institutions. The rise of green movements seemed to demonstrate that these cultural changes were exerting an important political impact.

By the 1990s this argument was adapted to explain extreme right voting in Western Europe.[27] The new post-material agenda is seen as irrelevant for many voters. It may appeal to a section of the educated and young, but it has little appeal for many others – especially unskilled males. Such voters see the new post-material agenda as totally unconnected to their material concerns, which if anything have become greater against a background of globalization and growing job insecurity in many countries. Moreover, the post-material emphasis on sexual and other freedoms threatens traditional values both within the family and society. The thesis further holds that mainstream, especially left of centre, elites are typically blamed for social liberalization, which increases the alienation from conventional politics.

Certainly many extreme right parties have picked up aspects of the Anglo-American New Right agenda of the post-1970s, including both its traditionalism and its more economic agenda focusing on the need for greater efficiency through free markets (thus boosting growth and rewarding the hard-working). However, it is important to note that many extreme right parties – such as the VB and DVU, and to a lesser extent the French FN – have an anti-materialist philosophy. They overtly stress the primacy of politics over economic matters. More specifically, many have picked up aspects of the post-material rhetoric, such as a stress on political participation, even environmentalism. It is true that the latter aspect often has 'blood and soil' conservationist connotations rather than radical ecological ones. Extreme right environmentalism is also sometimes a surrogate for overt anti-immigrant politics – 'this land is *your* land'. Nevertheless, the activist aspect can be more genuine, and marks an important difference with traditional conservative (and Anglo-American New Right) politics.

It could be countered that the study of party programme and 'philosophy' tells us little or nothing about voting. The fact that the main support for most extreme right parties comes from less-skilled males seems to offer strong sociological credence to the reverse post-materialist thesis's emphasis on alienation among this group. The strong nationalism and xenophobia exhibited by many extreme right voters may also in part be a reaction against post-material internationalist values. However, whilst the reverse post-material thesis has a general plausibility at this level, it offers little by way of specific explanation.

The broad hypotheses of the thesis is that extreme right voting will be greatest where post-material values have developed most strongly and weakest where they are least developed. This may help to explain why the extreme right is so weak in Eastern Europe, but it has only a weak fit in Western Europe. Post-material values are generally seen as being strongest in countries such as (West) Germany, the Netherlands and the Scandinavian ones. But these are countries where in general the extreme right is weak electorally. Post-material values are lower in France, but it was here that the extreme right made its first major breakthrough during the last generation. Post-material values were even lower in Britain in the 1970s, but this did not stop the National Front (NF) making notable headway in some areas, such as the East End of London and Leicester where it could attract 20–30 per cent of the vote in these economically depressed, high immigrant areas.[28]

The last point highlights the fact that extreme right success is often very localized. What does the reverse post-material thesis tell us about why the BNP has been relatively successful in the 2001 general election in a handful of northern cities such as Oldham, but not in neighbouring Blackburn (though it won a 2002 local election seat here)? A comparative political science theory cannot be refuted by a single counter-example, but clearly the reverse post-material thesis is incapable of explaining variation within like socioeconomic cases.[29]

The economic interest thesis

In spite of the anti-materialist philosophical side of many extreme right parties, there has been a long tradition of trying to associate economic interests with extremist voting, typically arguing that such support comes from the losers in the competition over scarce resources and/or those who suffered from some form of relative deprivation. Predictably, this approach has been used to explain contemporary extreme right voting.[30]

Some extreme right parties undoubtedly play on economic interest as part of their appeal. For instance, in February 2000 Haider claimed that the FPÖ had replaced the social democrats as the true defenders of the working class. Whilst such rhetoric has to be understood within the context of his campaign to play down extremism, Haider was also pointing to the way in which his party's anti-EU and anti-immigrant policies promised job protection for many workers. The Italian LN also stressed economic issues during the 1990s, including the threat from parasitical Southern Italian and other 'immigrants', and the rapacious Italian state (which over-taxed and interfered in the Northern economy).

Specific studies of voting further seem to bear out the broad socioeconomic correlation. For example, in Germany the unemployed at the turn of the 1990s were especially likely to vote for the REP; so too were those who felt some form of relative deprivation. Fears about social exclusion and the future appear to have been especially strong among the young in many countries. In France, 47 per cent of unskilled young voters supported the FN in the 1997 legislative elections.[31] The FPÖ vote also tends to come from younger rather than older working-class voters.

The economic argument can be expanded by hypothesizing that extreme right voters are not simply likely to come from those already suffering disadvantage, but from those who fear economic change. Globalization poses a particular threat to two types of worker. First, there are those who work in industries vulnerable to foreign competition. Secondly, there are state-sector employees likely to be hit by the pressures to cut taxes and state expenditure, which have accompanied the general process of globalization (although most Western European countries have so far not significantly undertaken reform programmes in this area, not least because of the electoral dangers of such change). Thus the crucial socioeconomic cleavage is not a working-class versus middle-class one, but is more sectoral. Certainly, there is evidence in both Austria and Northern Italy that this type of structural change has affected voting (though it is important to note that public-sector worker support for the MSI/AN has more historic roots in fascist clientelistic politics). This helps to explain why relatively rich countries and regions may spawn extreme right support.

However, the exact linkages between socioeconomic interest and extreme right voting in Western Europe are far from clear. Most unemployed people, poor people, those suffering from relative deprivation, or holding fears about the future, do not vote for the extreme right (this is also true in Eastern Europe, where the economic situation is in general much worse). This includes people who see a significant threat from immigration/ethnic minorities. In Britain, for example, a study at the turn of the new millennium found that more than half of the working class agreed that immigrants took jobs away from people, and over a third agreed that equal opportunities for blacks had gone too far.[32] But extreme right voting remains unimportant outside a handful of localities. In France, economic issues are central for all the mainstream parties, but this is much less true for FN voters – who tend to be more concerned with Arabs, etc. Intriguingly, in Belgium the FN has, in general, done poorly in French-speaking Wallonia, which has suffered notable economic decline – yet the VB has been one of the most successful parties in the more affluent Flemish part of Belgium.

Nevertheless, picking up a point made earlier, there is some evidence that socioeconomic problems have a particular impact when immigrant groups, especially in a localized context, are seen as being in some ways treated more favourably, that 'they do more for them than us', to quote one study of the industrially depressed, and former 'red', area of Seraing (Liège) in Belgium.

The same point could be made about extreme right support in Britain in areas such as Oldham.[33] The issue is one of perception more than reality – which raises the crucial question of how people move beyond simple socioeconomic interest to understand the political world.

SUPPLY SIDE THEORIES

The political opportunity structure thesis

The political opportunity structure (POS) thesis has increasingly been adopted by commentators in recent years.[34] The approach focuses on two broad sets of political factors which are largely external to the insurgent party. First, it stresses the extent to which the actions and programmes of mainstream parties help or hinder insurgents. Secondly, there is the question of the degree of 'openness' of political institutions to insurgent parties.

The POS approach holds that extremist parties are likely to make a breakthrough when mainstream parties cluster around the centre, and fail to pick up issues which are of growing voter appeal. For example, the French FN increasingly exploited anti-immigrant sentiment at the turn of the 1980s when this was being ignored by the mainstream parties (the socialists were even promising more rights to immigrants).

More indirectly, the extreme right can be legitimized when political discourse becomes contaminated by its themes, especially ones relating to immigration.[35] For example, by the mid 1980s, key figures within the French centre-right, notably Jacques Chirac and Charles Pasqua, had clearly discerned the threat from the FN and modified their language accordingly. Even some socialists dabbled in watered-down forms of anti-immigrant politics. Moreover, at the local level, informal electoral arrangements emerged between the mainstream and 'extreme' right. At times this contamination of discourse can defuse the insurgent movement, as happened when the German CDU during 1991–92 picked up the issue of constitutional reform to limit the arrival of asylum-seekers (over 400,000 arrived in 1992 alone, a trend which helped to provoke extremist violence during 1991–92). But the technique can backfire too. During 1997 in Hamburg, the local Social Democrats adopted policies such as opposition to the Euro currency and stricter treatment of foreign criminals, but it was the DVU which was the main beneficiary locally. Although the connection is less clear-cut, British politicians taking an increasingly hard line on the growing number of asylum-seekers helped to legitimize the BNP in 2001–2 (and to inflame ethnic minority alienation, which helped fuel rioting during 2001).

The mainstream can also legitimize extremism directly. The rise of the Italian AN was helped by the way in which President Cossiga was clearly willing to accept that the 'post-fascists' could be made part of a new centre-right to replace the Christian Democrats (DC), who were drowning in a sea of corruption (the fact that the MSI, like the DC, were good anti-communists was an important credential). Cossiga called for hammer-blows to demolish the corrupt old Republic – a theme which the MSI picked up in its 1992 election campaign, when it produced a campaign badge showing a pickaxe and ran on the slogan 'every vote a hammer-blow'. The extensive support of the media magnate, Silvio Berlusconi – whose new Forza Italia party allied with the AN in the run up to the 1994 elections – added further legitimacy to the MSI/AN. This situation was very different to the one in Austria in early 2000, when the president was far more suspicious of the FPÖ's entry into government and virtually invited the EU to intervene (the ban was also influenced by the Belgian prime minister's and French president's desire to tag their own extreme right parties as beyond the pale).[36]

Institutional aspects of POS approaches often focus on electoral systems – typically claiming that proportional representation helps new parties. For instance (socialist) President Mitterrand altered the French National Assembly election system from single-member constituencies to regional lists for the 1986 elections in order to increase FN representation, and weaken the mainstream right. In Germany, the 5 per cent cut-off in many elections makes it more difficult for small parties to convince voters they will be successful and gain some form of bandwagon effect. Conversely, federal systems can offer extremists the chance to make a major breakthrough locally. Haider, for example, has been most successful in his home region of Carinthia. Another important institutional aspect concerns the power to ban, or brand parties. The German Office for the Protection of the Constitution (BVS) can effectively de-legitimize a party by officially labelling it 'extreme'. Although this does not mean a party will necessarily fail to attract support, this device almost certainly harmed the REP in the early 1990s (previously they had been labelled merely 'radical'). Tough court sentences on racist violence or harassment also send out powerful signals about what is socially acceptable.

The POS approach undoubtedly offers important insights. However, it has a variety of problems. In particular, it is possible to find countries where there has been 'space' for extremist parties, where there has been a proportional electoral system, etc., but where there has been minimal extremist voting. For instance, the Netherlands has a highly proportional electoral system with a low entry threshold, but has not seen a sustained, successful extreme right movement. And countries such as Portugal and Spain, which also have proportional representation systems, have seen no significant extreme right activity. The electoral argument can be shored up if the stress is placed on district magnitude (namely the number of seats per district: the greater the number, the more small parties tend to benefit). However, it is important to remember that the FN has done well in terms of votes (if not in terms of representation) in legislative elections based on a form of majority voting. In Sweden the leading parties, especially the Social Democrats, have taken a major role in anti-racist campaigns, but there has been no sustained, successful extreme right party, although there is space for such a party. Is the issue that this is de-legitimized space? Or are extreme right parties more successfully marginalized by mainstream parties picking up part of their rhetoric (a trend which has helped halt the rise of the greens)? The POS approaches seem to have little to say about this. Ultimately, they seem of more use for *ad hoc* national explanations rather than systematic international comparison.

The mediatization thesis

A further criticism of the POS approach is that even within its own 'high politics' terms, it tends to ignore what is now arguably the most important instrument in political communication – the media.[37] Certainly, there is a growing literature on the role of the media in promoting racism.[38] Studies have sought to prove that the media are riddled with positive stereotypes of the indigenous population and a negative presentation of the 'Other'. Among the specific issues which the media tend to focus on are illegal immigration, bogus asylum-seekers, overly favourable treatment of immigrants, crime (especially drugs and prostitution), and problematic cultural differences (especially the impossibility of assimilating Islamic immigrants).

However, whilst the media may at times pander to racial stereotyping, in general they are hostile to the extreme right. The reporting of violence against immigrants is often linked to the dangers of a revival of Nazism (a common tabloid moral panic). Whilst this may encourage copy-cat violence, its main effect has probably been to further de-legitimize the extreme right electorally. At times, the media attack the electoral extreme right directly. For example, in Britain the tabloid press picked up the 'National Front is a Nazi front' theme (begun by anti-fascist activists) during the late 1970s, when there were fears that the Front was about to make a major electoral breakthrough. More typically, the extreme right is largely starved of publicity. While Italian television was heavily under state influence, it rarely mentioned the MSI; and more recently, the media seem to have taken a decision to avoid giving the LN excessive publicity.

Nevertheless, there have been occasions when parts of the media have overtly supported the extreme right. The rise of the MSI/AN during 1993–94 coincided with remarkably favourable coverage from the Berlusconi media empire, which included the three most-watched private television channels. The FPÖ too, especially key statements on immigration by Haider, has received important support from the *Neue Kronen Zeitung* which, relative to potential readership, is the most widely read newspaper in the world (over 40 per cent of adults have read the paper in recent years).

The media have also indirectly helped the extreme right through their agenda-setting function. The issue is not simply one of their coverage of issues such as the threat from immigrants. The media, especially television, encourage a focus on personality, which helps leader-oriented parties. The growth of face-to-face debates and interview programmes makes it more difficult for journalists to act as gatekeepers. Declining state control and the growth of private media channels has also stressed entertainment values, which further encourages a concentration on lively personalities and the new. It has also encouraged more quizzing of mainstream politicians, especially about broken promises and corruption.

It is also important to consider local as well as national media. Sometimes the local media are more apolitical, prone to report events neutrally. For instance, in Oldham before the 2001 general election the local press reported the growing BNP activities, including their own press releases, with little or no editorial comment. The Oldham press also gave considerable coverage to three events in 2001 which fitted the BNP's agenda: a police report stating that racially motivated attacks on whites were more common than those by whites on non-whites; an apparently racially motivated serious attack on a 76-year-old war veteran; and a claim made by an Asian youth on BBC national radio that there were 'no go' areas for whites in Oldham. In spite of this, the BNP launched its own Oldham website which stated: 'This site cuts through the controlled media's paper curtain of politically correct censorship about what's going on in Oldham.'[39]

It seems easy to conclude that the media played a major part in the BNP's ensuing general election 'success'. However, it is important to note that there are major methodological problems involved in assessing media effects. Discourse analysis tends to adopt a Gramsciian approach which accords the media considerable power on the basis of alleged 'hegemonic' content without any empirical analysis of voters. It is true that apparent correlations can be found, as in Oldham. But it is not clear what role the media played compared to demand-side factors, or shrewd local BNP campaigning (including how to use the media). Nevertheless, noting methodological problems serves as a warning about sweeping claims concerning media power rather than as a refutation of more limited claims. Circumstantially, it seems clear that the media can play an important role in legitimizing (or de-legitimizing) issues and parties. A sudden increase in coverage of a fringe party also seems likely to create a sense that the party is on the move, creating a form of bandwagon.

The national traditions thesis

The national traditions thesis helps to illustrate another methodological problem – namely, the dangers of grand social science theory which is blind to specific national cultures. The thesis holds that extreme right parties are most likely to be successful when they can portray themselves as in some way a legitimate part of the national tradition.

One version of this thesis holds that parties which exhibit clear affinities with fascism (especially Nazism) find it difficult or impossible to legitimize themselves.[40] For example, the German DVU and NPD, whose propaganda shows a marked fascination with the Nazi era, have failed to gain sustained support in spite of evidence that in 1981, 12 per cent of West Germans had an extreme right view of the world and 37 per cent shared aspects of this worldview; in 1998, 12 per cent in the old *Länder* still held such views, and 17 per cent in the new *Länder*.[41] Several subsequent studies have shown that such views are even more common in the former East Germany. The problem is less serious in Italy, where historians during the last generation have been increasingly willing to normalize rather than demonize the fascist era. Certainly AN leader Gianfranco Fini was for a time in the 1990s Italy's most popular politician, in spite of his enigmatic references to the AN as 'post-fascist' and his defence of Mussolini as a great statesman.

In other countries the fascist legacy is also highly problematic. For instance, part of British national identity is linked to anti-fascist images (the 1940 Battle of Britain, etc.). This has posed a major problem for the British NF and BNP, whose main leader – John Tyndall – openly wore Nazi-style uniform before joining the NF. A study in the late 1970s found that 76 per cent of voters thought the NF had a Nazi side to it. In France, Le Pen was chosen to lead the FN, which included small fascist *groupuscules*, partly because he had no overt fascist past. Nevertheless, the claim that the FN was 'fascist' has undoubtedly limited its appeal in traditional left-wing areas where 'anti-fascism' has long been a rallying cry.

The national traditions thesis has also been applied to the issue of the extent to which extremist parties can create a legitimate discourse about immigration and conceptions of citizenship (sometimes referred to as the 'discursive opportunity structure').[42] This is important because psychological work has revealed that in the contemporary Western world 'prejudice' tends not to be expressed in unambiguous statements about racial hierarchies. People like their views to appear reasonable and acceptable to peers.[43]

Across Europe, there have historically been very different conceptions of who can become a member of the national community. Although practice is more complicated, three ideal types are typically delineated. The first is the French Jacobin conception, which holds that anyone willing to be assimilated into the culture could become French. The second is the German model where citizenship has traditionally been based on 'blood'. The third is the British model, which is multi-national/cultural – a reflection of the fact that Britain was historically made up of different nations and was the 'Mother' country to an empire. The British conception has made it difficult to construct a legitimate discourse of exclusion. On the other hand, the French FN has been able to point to Arab immigrants as unwilling to assimilate. Opinion polls at the time of the 1989 Creil incident, when Muslim girls were turned away from school because their traditional garb was seen as flouting secular rules, highlight the continued resonance of the Jacobin model. The German model also potentially underpins anti-immigrant politics (although in this case the Nazi legacy provides a powerful counter).

A comparison of British, French and German traditions highlights another point about democracy. The dominant British historic discourse has stressed parliamentary sovereignty and the role of intermediary organizations. The Jacobin tradition has celebrated the 'Republic one and indivisible', and has been hostile to parties and pressure groups. Clearly the latter tradition serves further to legitimize a discourse which demonizes mainstream parties, and backroom parliamentary deals. An element in the French political tradition also celebrates strong leadership, which also helps legitimize forms of extreme right politics. This last point also applies to Germany. Whilst the Nazi legacy provides a powerful counter, it is worth noting that the two longest-standing of Germany's postwar Chancellors, Konrad Adenauer and Helmut Kohl, have attracted a father-like, personalist following.

However, national traditions are clearly facilitating factors rather than direct causal ones. In particular, they need interpreting, recounting, by others – not least by an insurgent party capable of constructing a sophisticated general political discourse.

The programmatic thesis

Sometimes the programmatic thesis essentially argues that extreme right parties – contrary to the protest thesis – do have a serious ideology, but do not seek specifically to relate this to voting.[44] Two versions directly relate programme to support. The first holds that political campaigning is becoming increasingly issue-based – and extremist parties have often been successful at exploiting specific issues, especially when they form part of a broad party programmatic 'direction' which can be picked up by even the least politically sophisticated.[45]

The second holds that there is a particular 'winning formula', which involves combining authoritarian anti-immigrant politics with free market economics (an approach linked in its most sophisticated, although ultimately misleading, form with a sectoral demand-side analysis).[46]

There has been a growing tendency among academics to use the term 'populist' for many of the more successful contemporary parties, like the FPÖ. One reason for this is to highlight the way in which they pick up issues which concern the electorate, but which are largely ignored by the mainstream parties. The term 'populism' is also used to denote the way in which parties like the FN and FPÖ portray themselves as the true democrats and representative of the people. For instance, the 1993 FN programme devotes three chapters to different procedures which could increase the power of the people. Arguably, the most commonly suggested answer is an increased use of the referendum.[47] More generally, the epithet 'populist' is designed to underpin the claim that this family of parties is not truly 'extreme'.

Certainly some extremists, for instance the BNP, have recently concluded from the FPÖ's success that a relatively democratic-moderate approach attracts voters (although they are aware that this can cause problems with hard-core members). For this reason, the BNP has changed its core policy from the compulsory repatriation of 'immigrants' to one of voluntary repatriation. The BNP has also attempted recently to follow the French FN line of playing down the traditional racist language in favour of a 'new racism' which stresses cultural difference. Thus Arabs in France are not so much inferior as a people who have their own culture, which cannot be assimilated.[48] Exclusion can even be made 'democratic' by extremists who ask whether people in Dreux (Oldham, etc.) were ever asked if they wanted local schools which are entirely or primarily Muslim, and so on.

The FPÖ's economic policies also reveal a notable break with the interwar extreme right. Like all the successful contemporary extreme right parties, it is critical of highly statist economics. However, commentators who stress the free market side of these parties gloss over crucial points.[49] One concerns the fact that the state sector is too large in many Western European countries, and has often been 'colonized' by the mainstream parties. More fundamentally, it is important not to confuse market values with market mechanisms. For example, the AN's Verona theses of 1998 accept the necessity of more market capitalism so long as *homo œconomicus* does not supersede spiritual and political man. The Euroscepticism of many extreme right parties also in part reflects this suspicion of globalization and markets. Nevertheless, it is important to note that not all extreme right parties are Eurosceptic: the LN in particular has used a 'Europe of the regions' rhetoric to help legitimize its attack on the central state.

Some on the contemporary extreme right are more accurately characterized as supporters of 'Third Way' economics (even if the actual term is not always employed). Put another way, they seek to achieve a modern balance between private and public sector. Haider, for instance, has stated that 'We are neither right nor left, we're just in front.'[50] Many other parties, including the FN, LN and Norwegian FRPn, have at times all used some form of neither left nor right rhetoric. Whilst such rhetoric can have an electoral dimension (Third Way rhetoric potentially appeals across the political spectrum), such syncretism has been a classic feature of extreme right ideology. Especially since the New York terrorist attacks on 11 September 2001, Third Way rhetoric has also pointed to the twin dangers of Islamic fundamentalism and US global capitalism. In countries with significant Islamic populations, the extreme right has tended to see the Twin Towers attack as a godsend for its cause – although this has sometimes been tempered, for instance in the case of Le Pen, by pro-Arab and anti-Israeli and anti-US sentiments.

These arguments point to three broad conclusions about the relationship between support and programme. The first is that specific issues can attract support, especially if the issues are portrayed in a way which gives them some form of legitimacy. Such issue-based politics seems to be especially attractive to voters who are relatively unsophisticated. The second is that the most successful parties have tended to have a somewhat ambivalent economic programme, which allows them to attract both supporters of freer markets and others who still look to the state for protection (at the time of the 1997 legislative elections in France, such *ninistes* made up 25 per cent of the electorate, with the largest single group voting for the FN). More generally, except perhaps at times of major crisis, most voters are risk averse and prefer to seek change which seems limited rather than 'extreme'.

The charismatic leader thesis

There is a growing literature suggesting that party democracy is in decline and, especially for a de-aligned electorate, media-oriented leaders become crucial.[51] Some commentators hold that the emergence of 'charismatic' leaders, such as Jean-Marie Le Pen, is an important factor in the rise of the extreme right.[52] This charismatic impact is normally considered in terms of the leader's direct appeal to voters, but it can also be considered in terms of an ability to hold a party together (the external and internal dimensions of charisma).

An immediate problem concerns definition. The social science use of the term 'charisma' stems from Max Weber, who associated it with a leader characterized by a quasi-religious sense of great vision, and who attracted a body of unquestioning, affective supporters. Defined this way, there have been few – if any – major charismatic leaders in the last hundred years. (Hitler is perhaps a rare European example.)[53] This has led some commentators to use a weaker definition of charisma, or to use terms such as 'pseudo-charisma'. In this case, the emphasis moves towards a more diverse set of characteristics.

This still leaves open the question of what defines a (pseudo) charismatic leader. Usually a formal definition is not offered, but it is possible to set out some commonly ascribed attributes of contemporary charismatic leadership. These include: oratorical confidence and especially an ability to use the media; a sense of mission which tends to be inclusionary and/or about building identity; the use of narratives about the leader's life, often stressing sacrifice and struggle; the use of friend–enemy, Manichaean, categorizations; and the use of macho language and symbolism. However, a problem which afflicts this approach is one which afflicts all list-definitions. Namely, is it necessary for a leader to possess every trait in order to be deemed charismatic? Umberto Bossi, the leader of the LN, has often been termed 'charismatic', but his gangly appearance and unkempt dress do not conform to the classic image.

This points to the fact that the concept of charisma is about audience receptivity as well as leadership traits. Here the focus turns more to the demand side, to why leadership may appeal to voters. Various arguments relating to this have already been considered in passing. For instance, leadership is to some extent culture-specific. (Bossi's appeal may in part be a reaction to Mussolinian machismo.) The more authoritarian extreme right voter is clearly attracted to strong leadership (a feature of an important section of the FN vote). The decline of class- and religious-based parties also raises the issue about how voters receive political signals in a de-aligned world. Although rational choice theory tends to be hostile to vague concepts like 'charisma', it is possible to write leadership into utility-maximizing analysis by seeing it as a form of low-cost signalling. Voters are attracted to appealing leaders because they offer an easy way of understanding the political message. Leader-oriented parties are also appealing if this means that dissent, which could cause dissonance, is minimized. The extensive focus on Haider in parts of the Austrian media, and his control of the party before splits began to emerge during 2000–2, almost certainly played its part in the rise of the FPÖ. Charismatic appeal can further be related to arguments about rapid socio-economic change and/or economic crises. Such developments can produce a sense of powerlessness, which may lead to non-voting. The charismatic leader increases voter efficacy because they can create a sense that politics is not pointless. This is achieved both through the belief that the leader can change things, and by encouraging the belief that the leader is somehow part of the people, that he can be influenced by the people. This can be termed 'proxy control',[54] a term which illustrates the dangers of believing that voters attracted by charismatic leaders are necessarily seeking some form of authoritarian dictatorship.

This discussion highlights something which has been implicit in much of the preceding argument. This is that whilst there is a relatively large body of work which probes issues such as the age, class and sex basis of voting for the main extreme right parties, ultimately there are still major gaps in our knowledge. The charismatic thesis offers an excellent illustration of this point. In general, the existing empirical evidence counts against the thesis. For instance, more voters seem deterred by Le Pen, especially his gaffes on issues such as the Holocaust, than are attracted by him. Similar sentiments appear to apply to Bossi. But there are major problems operationalizing the charismatic thesis, and there has been a lack of original research design (such as focus groups) which might help further our knowledge of the cybernetic processes by which voters are attracted to the extreme right. It is also important not to ignore the internal charismatic dimension of leadership – namely the ability to hold often ideologically diverse parties together, with little or nothing to offer by way of spoils.

MOVING ON

The preceding arguments clearly underline the complexity of the task which faces anyone who seeks to theorize about the extreme right. It is particularly important to underline that there is no single extreme right supporter, corresponding to the 'authoritarian personality' or any other model. Indeed, there are notably different types of extreme right voters.

It should be clear from the foregoing analysis that no one factor can explain such a diverse pattern of extreme right voting. Demand factors are undoubtedly the necessary prior condition for extreme right success. But they are clearly not sufficient. A complex mix of supply factors are necessary to help launch a party. A key argument in the above analysis is that most of those who vote for the more successful extreme right parties are not random protesters, but voters who are choosing a party which is seen to approximate to their views. But the way in which voters perceive such parties is influenced by a variety of factors, such as mainstream parties' campaigning, the media and the activities of the extremist parties themselves.

Moreover, as well as considering demand and supply factors, contingency must also be added into the equation. For instance, the 'success' of the BNP in Oldham in the 2001 general election stemmed in part from chance factors which attracted notable media coverage.

Nonetheless, it is important not to lapse into a postmodernist mindset, where events have multiple and varied causes, lacking any discernible pattern. Comparative political science may not have the precision of the 'hard' sciences, but it should seek to develop methodologies which allow such complex issues to be studied and produce testable hypotheses. I therefore seek to make two main points by way of a forward-looking conclusion.

1. *The macro–meso–micro approach*: Current analyses place far too much emphasis on macro rather than meso and micro analysis. The meso-level is often ignored, not least because it requires detailed local and group level research. Moreover, such work would require repeating in different contexts, both national and international, in order to develop a 'grand theory'. Although some primary work has been done on individual extreme right voters, much micro-theory is deduced from mainly macro-level analysis since mass surveys are expensive (and sometimes fail to pick up extremist supporters, who prefer to hide such sentiments). More work needs to be done at the micro level, especially work which moves beyond the conventional socioeconomic categories, or age, sex, class, etc. We need to know more about 'extremist' beliefs. We need more work which relates macro-theory to micro-views/behaviour. We also need more evidence about what combination of political–psychological sentiments triggers extreme right voting.

2. *The legitimacy, efficacy and trust (LET) hypothesis*: Given the point about the diversity of extreme right support, there are clear dangers in constructing any new form of archetypal extremist voter. However, I want to argue on the basis of the above arguments that a notable increase in extreme right voting is likely to stem from a combination of three (partly related) percep-tions. These are

growing extremist *Legitimacy* + rising personal *Efficacy*
+ declining system *Trust*

It is impossible in a short chapter to develop fully this hypothesis. Nevertheless, some pointers can be given which briefly reiterate arguments which have already been noted above.

Legitimacy refers to the belief that a party is in some way socially acceptable, most typically by creating the impression that it is a legitimate part of the national tradition. Careful packaging of policies, for instance the 'new racism', can also help. This approach highlights the role of the party itself, especially its leaders and 'intellectuals', in constructing discourse. Legitimacy can also be accorded by mainstream politicians picking up 'extremist' themes and policies – even if these are adapted in a watered-down form (for instance, limiting immigration rather than totally banning it, let alone pursuing mass repatriation). Important opinion leaders, especially the media, can also play a part in setting an agenda which, whilst not necessarily endorsing extremist parties, can help their cause. Such legitimacy may be achieved at a relatively broad level, but it can emerge only within specific local political contexts (which may then give the party the boost it needs to expand in other areas).

Efficacy refers to an individual's belief that she/he can affect what happens politically (people with low efficacy tend not to vote). This raises two issues. First, what makes people feel more efficacious? And secondly, how do insurgent parties create the impression that they can become bigger/have an effect? Feelings of self-efficacy can rise for various reasons, including group membership and the impact of charismatic leadership. Small parties can gain credibility in various ways. Proportional representation can help (although, as has already been pointed out, there is no simple correlation between electoral system and extremist voting). Some form of agreement with mainstream parties can be crucial. Parties also need to be able to disseminate their message. In the past, this meant an effective organization. Today some form of access to the media is more important. Lack of division within the party also helps low-cost programmatic signalling (although discrete local differentiation can help, especially during take-off).

Trust refers to feelings about the ability of the economic and political system to deliver desired goods. The decline of class and religion has meant that specific issues have increasingly become important in determining voting. Economic ones tend to predominate in most voters' minds, although anti-immigrant politics reflect wider cultural concerns. Trust declines when governments fail to deliver on key issues: the World Values Survey seems to indicate that rapidly rising unemployment would have a particularly notable effect on trust. Trust also declines when politicians become involved in scandals – a trend which has attracted growing media attention in recent years. So far this decline in trust has mainly affected mainstream parties rather than the system itself. There have been no major economic crises in Western Europe in recent years which might de-legitimize capitalism (although social inequalities have grown in many countries). Moreover, democracy has become a near-universal shibboleth.

However, whilst democracy has become a near-universal concept, its exact connotations are being increasingly challenged. As long as the communist 'evil empire' existed, Western democracy could in an important sense define itself by the 'Other'. Following the collapse of the dictatorial Soviet empire, the spotlight has turned inward, towards democracy's basic principles and linked socioeconomic structures. What does democracy mean in a world increasingly characterized by 'globalization'? The reality seems to be one of growing multinational corporate power. What exactly does international 'multi-level governance' mean in terms of democracy? Such new institutions may seek to protect (liberal) democracy in terms of rights, but they offer little or no possibility for (direct) democratic participation. These arguments clearly point to the growing possibility of constructing a legitimate discourse which is critical of the system rather than just of mainstream parties. This in turn may affect voter attitudes. The proportion of authoritarians within the extremist constituency may well grow if democratic legitimacy declines. A serious economic downturn could have even more dramatic effects. In recent years it has been rational not to seek extreme solutions because 'crises' were of limited extent. Capitalism may have become increasingly inegalitarian, but it could still legitimize itself through 'big cake' arguments. Serious national or sectoral crises, brought about by growing globalization, could dramatically reduce trust in the system. So might the need to cut welfare and other benefits in the face of global economic pressures.

Such arguments are clearly highly speculative – and this chapter has not sought to predict the future. But they point to the dangers of assuming that the extreme right challenge can be tamed by mainstream parties, which are rapidly approaching their sell-by date. Indeed, the last paragraph points to the dangers of believing, like Francis Fukuyama, that history has ended and that liberal democracy truly has won.

NOTES

1. There is considerable controversy as to whether some of the parties discussed in this chapter are better termed 'radical right' or 'populist'. As this chapter is concerned with theory (support) rather than concepts (definition), it adopts the term 'extreme right', arguably the most common generic term, simply as a convenient shorthand. As has been noted in passing, there are undoubtedly important differences between the 'extreme right' parties – programmatic differences which play a part in some theories. For a distillation of the different definitions which have been given to the 'extreme right' and 'radical right' see C. Mudde, 'The War of the Words Defining the Extreme Right Party Family', *West European Politics*, 19.2 (1996). On the definition of 'populist' see P. Taggart, 'New Populist Parties in Western Europe', *West European Politics*, 18.1 (1995). See also M. Fennema, 'Some Conceptual Issues and Problems in the Comparison of Anti-Immigrant Parties in Western Europe', *Party Politics*, 3.4 (1997); and the excellent chapter by U. Backes, 'L'extrême Droite: les multiples facettes d'une catégorie d'analyse', in P. Perrineau (ed.), *Les Croisés de la société fermée. L'europe des extrêmes droites* (Paris: Editions de l'Aube, 2001).

2. Predictably, these developments have attracted an extensive academic literature. For notable recent surveys of the European scene in the last 20 years, see H.-G. Betz, *Radcal Right-Wing Populism in Western Europe* (Basingstoke: Macmillan, 1994); H.-G. Betz and S. Immerfall (eds), *The New Politics of the Right* (New York: St Martin's Press, 1998); L. Cheles, R. Ferguson and M.Vaughan (eds), *The Far Right in Western and Eastern Europe* (Harlow: Longman, 1995); P. Hainsworth (ed.), *The New Politics of the Right* (London: Pinter, 2000); H. Kitschelt (in association with M. McGann), *The Radical Right in Europe* (Ann Arbor, MI: University of Michigan Press, 1995); P. Merkl and L. Weinberg (eds), *The Revival of Right-Wing Extremism in the Nineties* (London: Frank Cass, 1997). Special issues of journals include 'Far Right in Europe: In or Out of the Cold?', *Parliamentary Affairs*, 53.3 (2000).

3. In Spain, a report published in 2000 by the government's Centre for Sociological Research found that 49 per cent of Spaniards were hostile to foreign cultures (Maghrebian influence was the main fear), a notable increase on the previous results.

4. There is some overlap between these theories and those which seek to explain extreme right violence, but violence is not a major concern of this chapter. Note, there has been some dispute about whether electoral success breeds extremist violence, or whether violence is more a substitute for electoral success. For the latter thesis, see R. Koopmans, 'Explaining the Rise of Racist and Extreme Right Violence in Western Europe: Grievances and Opportunities', *European Journal of Political Research*, 30.3 (1996).The thesis is difficult to analyse satisfactorily as there are major problems in terms of the collection of data on extremist violence.

5. See, for example, the empirical testing of four 'dominant' (demand) theories in M. Lubbers and P. Scheepers, 'Individual and Contextual Characteristics of the German Extreme Right-Wing Vote in the 1990s. A Test of Complementary Theories', *European Journal of Political Research*, 38.1 (2000).

6. On the importance of the macro–meso–micro approach, especially the neglected meso level, see R. Eatwell, 'The Dynamics of Ethnocentric Party Mobilisation' in R. Koopmans and P. Statham (eds), *Challenging Immigration and Ethnic Relations Politics* (Oxford: Oxford University Press, 2000). For more detail of this argument applied to the British and French cases, see R. Eatwell, 'The Dynamics of Right-Wing Electoral Breakthrough', *Patterns of Prejudice*, 32.3 (1998).

7. For the sake of brevity, this chapter does not seek to offer a full bibliographic survey of theories. Nor does it provide detailed referencing in relation to party programme, voting statistics, etc. The primary purpose of the notes is to list mainly English-language illustratory examples of each main theory and related points.

8. The various theories which follow are not always referred to in the same terms by commentators: for instance, the single-issue thesis is sometimes presented in terms of 'anti-immigrant' politics.

9. For example: D. Arter, 'Black Faces in the Blond Crowd: Populist Racialism in Scandinavia', *Parliamentary Affairs*, 45.3 (1992); C.T. Husbands, 'The Other Face of 1992: The Extreme Right Explosion in Western Europe', *Parliamentary Affairs*, 45.3 (1992).

10. J. Billiet and H. de Witte, 'Attitudinal Dispositions to Vote for a "New" Extreme Right Party: The Case of "Vlaams Blok"', *European Journal of Political Research*, 27.2 (1995).

11. C. Mudde, 'The Single-Issue Party Thesis: Extreme Right Parties and the Immigration Issue', *West European Politics*, 22.3 (1999).

12. On local differentiation see J.-P. Roy, *Le Front national en région centre, 1984–92* (Paris: L'Harmattan, 1993).

13. G. Ivaldi, 'Conservatism, Revolution and Protest: A Case Study in the Political Cultures of the French National Front's Members and Sympathies', *Electoral Studies*, 15.3 (1996).

14. N. Mayer, *Ces français qui votent FN* (Paris: Flammarion, 1999).

15. P. Ignazi, *Postfascisti?* (Bolgna: Il Mulino, 1994).

16. A. Bull and M. Gilbert, *The Lega Nord and the Northern Question in Italian Politics*

(Basingstoke: Palgrave, 2001).

17. For example, N. Mayer and P. Perrineau (eds), *Le Front national à découvert* (Paris: Presses de Sciences Po, 1989).

18. For example, P. Knigge, 'The Ecological Correlates of Right-wing Extremism in Western Europe', *European Journal of Political Research*, 34.2 (1998); H.-G. Betz, 'Conditions Favouring the Success (and Failure) of Radical Right-Wing Populist Parties in Contemporary Democracies', in Y. Mény and Y. Surel (eds), *Democracies and the Populist Challenge* (Basingstoke: Palgrave, 2002).

19. M. Swyngedouw, 'The Subjective, Cognitive and Affective Map of Extreme Right Votes: Using Open-ended Questions in Exit Polls', *Electoral Studies*, 20.2 (2001).

20. W. Van der Brug, M. Fennema and J. Tillie, 'Anti-Immigrant Parties in Europe: Ideological or Protest Vote?', *European Journal of Political Research*, 37.2 (2000).

21. M. Fennema and J. Tillie, 'A Rational Choice for the Extreme Right', *Acta Politica*, 33.3 (1998).

22. For example, W. Heitmeyer *et al.*, *Die Bielefelder Rechsextremismus-Studie* (Weinheim and Munich: Juventa, 1993); P. Perrineau, *Le Symptôme Le Pen. Radiographie des électeurs des FN* (Paris: Fayard, 1997).

23. M. Fennema and J. Tillie, 'Social Isolation: Theoretical Concept and Empirical Measurement', in M. Fennema *et al.* (eds), *In Search of Structure: Essays in Social Science Methodology* (Amsterdam: Het Spinhuis, 1998).

24. J. Faniel, 'Vote brun en banlieue rouge', *Les Cahiers du Cevipol*, 3 (2000), p. 19.

25. F. Haegel, 'Xenophobia on a Suburban Paris Housing Estate', *Patterns of Prejudice*, 34.1 (2000).

26. A. Bull, 'An End to Collective Identities? Political Culture and Voting Behaviour in Sesto San Giovani and Erba', *Modern Italy*, 1.2 (1996).

27. P. Ignazi, 'The Silent Counter-Revolution: Hypotheses on the Emergence of Extreme Right-Wing Parties in Europe', *European Journal of Political Research*, 26.3 (1992); M. Minkenberg, 'The New Right in Germany', ibid.; M. Minkenberg, 'The Renewal of the Radical Right: Between Modernity and Anti-Modernity', *Government and Opposition*, 35.2 (2000).

28. C.T. Husbands, *Racial Exclusionism and the City* (London: Allen & Unwin, 1983).

29. The meso-level is notably under-studied. For a notable exception see the study of the Vlaams Blok stronghold, Antwerp, by M. Swyngedouw, 'Anvers: une ville à la portée du Vlaams Blok?', in P. Delwit, J.M. de Waele and A. Rea (eds), *L'extrême Droite en France et Belgique* (Brussels: Editions Complexe, 1998).

30. For the classic version of this thesis see S.M. Lipset, *Political Man* (London: Heinemann, 1962). For a recent example see H. Kriesi, 'Movements of the Left. Movements of the Right: Putting the Mobilization of Two New Types of Social Movements into Political Context', in H. Kitschelt, P. Lange, G. Marks and J.D. Stephens (eds), *Continuity and Change in Contemporary Capitalism* (Cambridge: Cambridge University Press, 1999).

31. A. Muxel, *L'Expérience politique des jeunes* (Paris: Presses de Sciences Po, 2001), p. 44.

32. R. Jowell *et al.*, *British Social Attitudes* (London: Sage, 2000).

33. R. Eatwell, 'Out of the Ghetto: "Rights for Whites" and the New Extremist Moderation in Britain', in R. Eatwell and C. Mudde (eds), *Western Democracies and the New Extremist Challenge* (London: Routledge, 2003).

34. POS approaches were initially used as part of new social movement theory. See S. Tarrow, *Power in Movement* (Cambridge: Cambridge University Press, 1994). For the thesis specifically related to the extreme right see especially the introduction to Koopmans and Statham, *Challenging Immigration and Ethnic Relations Politics*.

35. M. Schain, 'The National Front in France and the Constitution of Political Legitimacy', *West European Politics*, 10.2 (1987).

36. M. Merlingen, C. Mudde and U. Sedelmeier, 'European Norms, Domestic Politics and the Sanctions against Austria', *Journal of Common Market Studies*, 39.1 (2001).

37. P. Statham, 'Berlusconi, the Media and the New Right in Italy', *Harvard International Journal of Press/Politics*, 1.1 (1996).

38. For instance, T.A. van Dijk, *Elite Discourse and Racism* (London: Sage, 1993), and R. Wodak, 'The Genesis of Racist Discourse in Austria since 1989', in C.R. Caldas-Coulthard and M. Coulthard (eds), *Texts and Practices: Readings in Critical Discourse Analysis* (London: Routledge, 1995).

39. A sentiment which has encouraged the extreme right generally to develop Internet resources. See R. Eatwell, 'Surfing the Great White Wave: The Internet, Extremism and the Problem of Control', *Patterns of Prejudice*, 30.1 (1996).

40. For instance, R. Karapin, 'Radical Right and Neo-fascist Political Parties in Western Europe', *Comparative Politics*, 30.2 (1998), esp. p. 216.

41. D. Loch. 'La Droite radicale en Allemagne: un cas particulier?', in Perrineau, *Les Croisées*, p. 305.

42. R. Koopmans and H. Kriesi, 'Citoyenneté, identité nationale et moblisation de l'extrême droite. Une comparaison entre la France, l'Allemagne, les Pays-Bas et la Suisse', in P. Birnbaum (ed.), *Sociologies des nationalismes* (Paris: PUF, 1997), pp. 316–17.

43. M. Billig. S. Condes, E. Edwards, M. Gare, D. Middleton and A. Radley, *Ideological Dilemmas* (London: Sage, 1988), and M. Billig, *Banal Nationalism* (London: Sage, 1995).

44. For instance, C. Mudde, *The Ideology of the Extreme Right* (Manchester: Manchester University Press, 2000).

45. See B. Maddens and I. Hjanl, 'Alternative Models of Issue Voting: The Case of the 1991 and 1995 elections in Belgium', *European Journal of Political Research*, 39.3 (2001).

46. See especially Kitschelt, *The Radical Right*.

47. For the argument that 'populist' parties raise legitimate problems about 'actually existing democracy', see M. Canovan, 'Trust the People! Populism and the Two Faces of Democracy', *Political Studies*, 47.1 (1999).

48. On the new extremist discourse, especially the impact of the French 'Nouvelle Droite', see P.-A. Taguieff, *Sur la nouvelle Droite* (Paris: Descartes & Vie, 1994).

49. For instance, H.-G. Betz, 'Haider and Revolution. Only Just Begun', *Contemporary Austrian Studies*, 9.1 (2002).

50. M. Sully, *The Haider Phenomenon* (Boulder, CO: East European Monographs, 1997), p. 35.

51. For example, B. Manin, *Principles of Representative Government* (Cambridge: Cambridge University Press, 1997).

52. For example, R. Barraclough, 'Umberto Bossi: Charisma, Personality and Leadership', in *Modern Italy*, 3.2 (1998); B. Klandemans and N. Mayer, 'Militer à l'extrême droite', in Perrineau, *Les Croisées*, esp. p. 156.

53. Compare the stress on Hitler's charisma in I. Kershaw, *Hitler. 1889–1936, Nemesis* (London: Penguin, 1998), with the rational choice explanation of W. Brustein, *The Logic of Evil. The Social Origins of the Nazi Party, 1925–1933* (New Haven, CT: Yale University Press, 1996).

54. D. Madsen and P.G. Snow, *The Charismatic Bond* (Cambridge, MA: Harvard University Press, 1991).

CHAPTER THREE

The Growing Threat of the Radical Right

Hans-Georg Betz

A MONG MAJOR political developments in established Western-style democracies, few have provoked as much interest and raised as much concern as the revival of different forms of right-wing radicalism and extremism in recent years. And for good reasons. In the past few years, new parties on the right have made advances at the polls, the scope and impact of which are unprecedented in the postwar period. The best-known case has been the Austrian FPÖ, which, under the leadership of Jörg Haider, within little more than a decade, managed to triple its popular support at the polls. Even more spectacular was the advance of the Norwegian FRPn, which within a span of only a few months saw its popularity in monthly surveys soar from 14 per cent in February to 34 per cent in September 2000, surpassing all other Norwegian parties. Even where these parties have done less spectacularly, the result was still often nothing short of a minor political earthquake. But the radical right has not only been increasingly successful in national and subnational elections. In a growing number of cases the new parties and movements of the right have also managed to gain positions of real power, on several levels. And this not only in Austria, where the FPÖ has shared power nationally, regionally and locally. Thus, in Italy, the LN as well as the AN were partners in the short-lived Berlusconi coalition government; at the same time both parties have held numerous executive positions in towns and cities as well as, on occasion, on the regional level. In France, in the late 1990s, the FN captured four city halls before splitting up into two competing movements. Finally in Norway, in 1999, the FRPn gained control of the mayoral office in the small town of Os. In most cases, the assumption of real power would not have been possible without the complicity of the established parties. As a result, the politically organized radical right has made considerable progress in moving 'from the margins to the mainstream' of political life.[1]

The electoral gains of new parties and movements on the right are merely the most visible aspect of a broader wave of right-wing activism and activities, ranging from racially motivated violence by skinheads and other juvenile delinquents; the growing virtual community of like-minded groups and individuals gathering around and linked up through various hate sites on the WorldWideWeb; to the peddling of 'historical revisionist' views and literature that trivialize or deny outright the Nazi crimes, especially the Holocaust.[2] Together with neo-fascist and neo-Nazi groups, *groupuscules*, and mini-parties (more often than not with overt transatlantic links) promoting various forms of national socialism and a hysterical ideology of White Resistance, they constitute a transnational right-wing radical underground loosely connected through the Internet, which serves as forum, means of communication and channel for the dissemination of ideas, as well as a unifying and identifying force.[3]

There can be no doubt that for the first time since the end of World War II the radical right has become once again a significant political factor in a growing number of established Western-style democracies. The response from the scholarly community has been rather quick. During the past few years, there has been a burgeoning literature painstakingly recording each and every development on the radical right, suggesting explanations for its rise and success, and warning of the consequences they might entail. Most of this literature has focused on individual parties, movements or groups in isolation. Attempts at comprehensive comparative research, either on a macro- or a micro-level, have been the exception rather than the norm.[4] As a result, there is still little agreement on certain fundamental questions. For instance: What do we mean by radical right? Which parties, movements, groups, ideologies and ideas belong to the radical right? What explains the current success of the radical right? What is its significance in and for contemporary politics?[5]

As Michael Minkenberg has recently suggested, any attempt to understand the contemporary radical right requires sensitivity to a few basic realities.[6] First, contemporary right-wing radicalism is a transnational phenomenon and can therefore only be fully understood from a comparative perspective; second, it is a modern phenomenon, which has to be understood in the context of contemporary socioeconomic and sociocultural trends and developments; and third, it is a complex and variegated phenomenon, which eschews simple taxonomy and typology. Among these points, the third one is of particular importance. It goes to the heart of a central problem in the study of the contemporary radical right: what can – and should – be included in this category. As the EU member-states' sanctions against Austria have amply demonstrated, how this question is answered can have very concrete and rather serious political consequences.

In the remainder of this chapter I propose a comparative analytical approach to contemporary right-wing radicalism designed to serve as a framework for further discussion. The analysis deals primarily with the question of categorization and definition. I suggest that despite the contemporary radical right's variegated nature, it is possible to advance theoretically and analytically meaningful propositions that go beyond mere description. A second, supplementary concern of the chapter is to situate the contemporary radical right in a larger sociocultural and political context. Here I argue that the contemporary radical right has benefited as much from the collapse of traditional ideologies characteristic of the 'postmodern condition', as it has from fundamental sociostructural changes affecting all advanced capitalist societies. The final part of the chapter draws some conclusions with respect to the contemporary radical right's position in capitalist democracies and its prospects for the future.

BEYOND FASCISM

There is a strong temptation to see the contemporary wave of right-wing radicalism as little more than a slightly updated version of fascism or at least neo-fascism.[7] As a recent note by the Secretary-General of the United Nations stated: 'Neo-fascism and neo-Nazism are gaining ground in many countries, especially in Europe. This is reflected by the electoral victories of extreme right parties advocating xenophobia, attacks on ethnic, national and religious minorities, and racial or ethnic purity in the countries where they are active.'[8] Although intuitively appealing, this interpretative approach is seriously flawed, not least because it ignores important recent advances in our understanding of fascism. These suggest that fascism should be primarily seen as a revolutionary form of radical nationalism aimed at the general mobilization of a nation's collective energies in the service of national rehabilitation, regeneration and revival.[9] From this perspective, fascism constitutes above all 'a response to national vulnerability and decay in an intensely competitive international environment that is perceived as intrinsically unfair' and to the established elite's perceived inability to advance a nation's power position.[10] This explains why, ideologically, fascism, like Marxism–Leninism, is 'collectivist in orientation', 'fundamentally anti-liberal' and deeply hostile to pluralism, which it considers a source of divisiveness that prevents the nation from realizing its potential.[11]

Undoubtedly, among the contemporary radical right there have been groups, such as Britain's Combat 18, and splinter parties that share fascism's hostility to liberalism, pluralism and democracy, and which are quite prepared to advocate the use of violence in their struggle against the established democratic order.[12] However, these groups constitute a relatively small minority on the fringes of the larger movement. The majority, including most electorally relevant parties, is neither revolutionary nor (overtly) anti-democratic. On the contrary, as Roger Griffin has pointedly put it, most have adopted a politics that 'enthusiastically embraces the liberal system' while, at the same time, making 'a conscious effort to abide by the democratic rules of the game and respect the rights of others to hold conflicting opinions and live out contrasting value-systems'.[13] What distinguishes the contemporary radical right from other movements is less their stance on democracy and the rule of law; rather it is their espousal of an explicitly radical nativist position reflected in an overtly 'ethnopluralist' notion of cultural protectionism, based on the notion that cultures and ethnicities are incompatible with each other and that cultural mixing should therefore be resisted.[14]

EXCLUSIONARY POPULISM

The result is a form of exclusionary populism, which has become the dominant – and arguably most successful – strand of contemporary right-wing radicalism. The core of its ideology – if the statements and programmatic positions of these groups deserve to be characterized as constituting an ideology at all – is a restrictive notion of citizenship, which holds that true democracy is based on a homogeneous community (what some on the radical right have referred to as 'organic democracy'), that only long-standing citizens are full members of civil society and that a society's benefits should only accrue to them.[15] As G.M. Tamás has pointed out, this type of radical nativism – or what Robert J. Antonio has called 'reactionary tribalism' – is a thoroughly modern phenomenon fully compatible with the ethos of advanced industrial capitalism since it is grounded in a '"homogeneous" world-view' that measures human beings in terms of 'productive usefulness'.[16] Unsurprisingly, among the most characteristic features of exclusionary populism has been a range of demands focusing on the expulsion of unemployed foreigners (based on the argument that an unemployed foreign worker is a contradiction in terms) and foreigners charged with having committed a crime; an immediate stop to all transfer payments to refugees and asylum-seekers; and the 'repatriation' of asylum-seekers whose application has been denied.

A second characteristic of the most successful radical right-wing parties and movements has been their espousal of populist tactics and rhetoric. Although the term has been widely accepted to describe the contemporary radical right, its meaning is not always very clear.[17] In journalistic and academic discourse alike, populism often comes across as nothing more than a pseudo-

democratic, manipulative, opportunistic if not demagogic strategy designed
to market politics to a thoroughly cynical electorate. The problem with this
usage of the term is that it seriously underestimates the appeal of the populist
challenge. A measured account of contemporary populism has recently been
advanced by Margaret Canovan who defines it as 'an appeal to "the people"
against both the established structure of power and the dominant ideas and
values of the society'.[18] From this perspective, populism derives its legitimacy
and popular appeal primarily from its anti-establishment posture, which in
turn is grounded in a promise 'to redress the balance of power' in society 'in
such a way that genuinely popular government might persevere'.[19] This means
that populism, at least programmatically, also always involves a claim for
genuinely popular participation and representation by means of a radical
reform of the established political institutions and the whole political process.

At the same time, contemporary political populism, especially in its
exclusionary form, relies heavily on the mobilization of popular *ressentiments*.
According to Max Scheler's classic definition, *ressentiment* is a 'psychic
mechanism' that is based on the experience of individual inferiority and/or
weakness.[20] It is the result of a strong feeling of powerlessness combined with
the inability to let go of that experience and resign oneself to one's objective
weakness, which in turn leads to a deep sense of having suffered an indignity
and injustice. One of its most important manifestations is 'a characteristic
inclination … to attend frequently or even predominantly to supposedly
negative qualities of other individuals who are "different" … in some
significant respect'.[21] The populist right has derived much of its appeal from
its ability to repackage and articulate popular *ressentiments* and direct them
against specific targets. Particularly in the initial phase of mobilization, right-
wing populist parties have tended to focus on country-specific problems that
promised to be sources of popular *ressentiment*. Some parties such as the
regionally based LN, VB and Canadian Reform Party played on latent
animosities between north and south (LN, VB) and west and east respectively
(Canadian Reform) or, as in the Australian case, on indignation over the
'special treatment' of indigenous people.[22]

Of particular importance in this context have been attempts to appeal to
latent popular *ressentiments* generated by the official interpretation of national
history. For example in Germany, the radical right's core demand focused
on the 'decriminalization' of German history as a first step toward the
'normalization' of the country. In a similar vein, Christoph Blocher, the leader
of the Zurich branch of the SVP, sought to exploit latent *ressentiments*
generated by the controversy that erupted in the late 1990s over Switzerland's
role during World War II. In strong words Blocher voiced sympathy and
understanding for the 'innumerable citizens' whose feelings 'for our native

land are being repeatedly offended', and especially for the 'elder among them' who 'are being hurt with respect to their lifelong efforts and achievements for this country'.[23] Declaring that 'We are not ashamed of our history' and vowing that 'The people of Switzerland cannot be blackmailed', he lashed out against Switzerland's critics at home ('young representatives of the left, a few theologians, numerous sociologists, professors, artists and journalists') and abroad. He singled out particularly the Jewish World Congress as 'the leader of the campaign against Switzerland of the past and the present', and other Jewish organizations, 'which are demanding money' while denying 'that they are interested in money'.[24] Blocher went so far as to compare the threats of these organizations to boycott Swiss goods to the Nazi-instigated boycott of 'Jewish business in Germany that initiated the atrocious extermination of the Jewish people'.[25] Blocher's populist strategy of resentment proved highly successful. In the most recent national election, the SVP emerged as the most popular political party in Switzerland.

In addition to country-specific *ressentiments*, virtually all right-wing populist parties have pursued a mobilization strategy that focuses particularly on the political and intellectual elite. As Margaret Canovan has maintained, this strategy aims not only to challenge the established power-holders; it also, and perhaps most importantly, seeks to debase their values. The ultimate goal is to rob them of their basis of political and moral legitimacy in order to replace the dominant values with the 'common sense of the people' as a new basis of legitimacy. Characteristically, all successful parties on the contemporary radical right have espoused a pronounced anti-elite rhetoric (as we have seen in the case of Christoph Blocher) in an attempt to undermine and discredit issues and projects generally identified with the cultural and political establishment, such as immigration, multiculturalism, affirmative action and 'political correctness' in general.

Radical right-wing parties have been most successful when they have managed to combine a strong appeal to anti-establishment *ressentiments* with an equally strong claim to democratic reform or renewal. The most prominent case in point is the FPÖ, which has consistently promoted itself as 'the driving force behind the political renewal of Austria', seeking to bring about an 'Austrian cultural revolution with democratic means' which would lead to the overthrow of 'the ruling class and the intellectual caste'.[26] Similar claims were made by the LN, the Scandinavian Progress Parties, and even by the FN. But perhaps the best example of the new populist politics of resentment came from Australia, home of Pauline Hanson's One Nation Party. Among other things, Hanson marketed her party as a 'chance for change. The chance to finally rid ourselves of the inequity that has grown from years of political correctness, where we have not been able to speak our mind, or express our views without being called names intended to make us look backward, intolerant or extremist.'

It was Hanson again who expressed most forcefully what has become a major trope in exclusionary populist rhetoric, namely the charge that 'the majority of Australians' faced the threat of becoming 'second-class citizens in their own country, under a government who panders to minority interests and denies the majority the right of decision'. With One Nation, Hanson claimed, Australians were finally given back their voice allowing them to decide 'if it is the elite of the media, of academia and those others who see themselves above ordinary Australians who dictate our future, or whether it will be the people themselves who decide our fate'.[27] With these words, Hanson skilfully combined the three major elements of contemporary right-wing populist mobilization: the appeal to widespread anti-establishment *ressentiments*; the claim to return power to the ordinary people; and the promotion of the right of citizens to be accorded priority treatment in their own country. The recent electoral record of right-wing populist parties suggests that these elements constitute a powerful formula for political success, particularly when articulated by a strong charismatic leader figure, who has a firm grip on the party's organizational structure.

FROM NEO–LIBERALISM TO *VÖLKISCH* SOCIALISM

While populist demands for 'true' democracy and the limitation of rights of citizenship have remained central to the radical right's mobilization efforts, neo-liberal economic demands (the second major element in what Herbert Kitschelt's has called the contemporary radical right's 'winning formula') have not.[28] The reason might be that for most parties, economic positions played a rather subordinate role. And even in those parties where they played a more substantial role (e.g., the FPÖ and the LN), demands for substantial tax cuts, privatization, more room for markets and greater individual initiative and responsibility (all of which figured prominently on most parties' agenda in the 1980s and early 1990s) were not so much policy goals in and for themselves as the means of weakening decisively the established parties, which were seen as deriving much of their position and power from their control of the state and its resources.[29] In any event, given their strong support for policies that promote national preference, it is much more plausible for these parties to espouse a programme of economic nationalism aimed at safeguarding the nation's 'capacity and autonomy to make independent decisions about its economy', thus guaranteeing its economic and political independence as well as safeguarding its cultural identity.[30]

Economic nationalism is particularly important for a second group of parties that are part of the contemporary radical right movement. Unlike the exclusionary populist right, these parties have largely remained marginal political actors on the fringes of their respective party systems. Among its more prominent representatives are the German NPD and (arguably) the German DVU, the Italian MSIFT and the BNP. What distinguishes them from other parties on the radical right is their espousal of an explicit national (or, perhaps more appropriately, *völkisch*) socialist agenda. Douglas Holmes has summarized their position as being 'based on a critique of the moral economy of multiculturalism, with a bisecting critique of the political economy of an impaired welfare state'.[31] The result is a politics of 'exclusionary welfarism', based on a mixture of claims to social justice and revived community, and regulated by 'a racialized delimitation of citizenship'.[32]

These tendencies have been especially pronounced in the programmatic evolution of the German NPD, which defines itself as an anti-capitalist national revolutionary force fighting for a new social order in Germany.[33] This represents a significant radicalization of the party's programmatic orientation, which came in response to its growing (if very limited) support in the 1990s, particularly in the eastern part of the country. As a result, the NPD abandoned its traditional national-conservative position and adopted a militant 'German socialist' stance in response to the challenge of globalization. The new position was reflected in slogans such as 'More social justice!' and 'Work! Our goal: full employment and social security!' At the same time, the leader of the party, Udo Voigt, deplored the fact that the 'outstanding achievements of the German social system are being more and more replaced by minimal standards' and that the 'intended elimination of millions of jobs and the creation of intolerable and permanent unemployment is driving large populations all around Europe into poverty and debt'.[34] But the most strident attack against globalized capitalism was advanced by the party's unofficial chief ideologue and former Red Army Fraktion (RAF) member, Horst Mahler, who in a speech to the party conference in 1999 denounced 'globalism as the highest stage of imperialism' which demanded the 'revival of the German nation'.[35]

Ironically, in a world where theoretical anti-capitalist positions have largely been abandoned, the national socialist wing of the contemporary radical right is one of the last political forces to pay tribute to core demands of the traditional socialist and communist left, which the latter have largely jettisoned. Today it is groups such as the Italian MSIFT, which proclaim that there can be 'no compromise with capitalism' while raising their voice against privatization, the 'savage market', globalization, mass unemployment and the gradual destruction of the social welfare state.[36] The alternative to the competitive market capitalist model advanced by these groups is founded on a comprehensive and (compared to the demands of exclusionary populist parties) radicalized notion of national preference, where jobs, housing and other social benefits are strictly reserved for the 'indigenous' population ('DVU: Deutsche zuerst!') and where the state is called upon to intervene in favour of indigenous companies to safeguard jobs. Like exclusionary populist parties, most of them pay at least lip-service to the constitutional order and democratic rules. However, the extent of their radicalism sets them apart as a distinct group, which borders on right-wing extremism.

THE BOND THAT BINDS: WHITE RESISTANCE

The call for national preference is part of a larger project, which in various ways and to varying degrees informs all aspects of contemporary radical right programmes and activities: White Resistance. For most of the postwar period, the hard core of the White Resistance movement was predominantly American. This is hardly surprising, given the United States' long history of racist nationalism and white supremacism.[37] Recently, however, its ideas have begun to exert considerable influence on a number of radical right-wing groups (such as militant skinhead organizations) and parties outside the United States, ranging from Scandinavia to Russia.[38] The central idea informing White Resistance is the notion that during the past couple of decades, the survival of the white race and particularly of Western culture and civilization has become fundamentally threatened. As the American White supremacist and former Ku Klux Klan leader David Duke has put it: 'Our race faces a world-wide genetic catastrophe. There is only one word that can adequately describe it: genocide. It is a relentless and systematic destruction of the European genotype.'[39] White Resistance groups blame the 'systematic and planned extermination of an entire national, racial, political, or ethnic group' on low birth-rates, abortion ('aborticide'), mass immigration from developing countries, affirmative action ('anti-white prejudice') and particularly intermarriage ('interracial genocide'), which are supposed 'to integrate whites out of existence or at least to a controllable level [sic]'.[40]

Groups and parties such as the BNP that subscribe to the basics of White Resistance charge the political establishment with promoting policies that systematically discriminate against whites while 'champion(ing) the racial interests of non-whites. They [the white race] must sacrifice their own future on the altar of "diversity" and cooperate in their own dispossession' and promote and even subsidize the displacement of their own people and culture by 'alien peoples and cultures. To put it in the simplest possible terms, white people are cheerfully to slaughter their own society, to commit racial and cultural suicide. To refuse to do so would be racism.'[41] But the BNP is not the only party to disseminate ideas that come from the transnational White Resistance movement. In the late 1990s – and particularly during the Kosovo crisis – even a relatively moderate right-wing populist party such as the LN adopted an increasingly noticeable White Resistance rhetoric.

At the time, the party claimed, among other things, that immigration represented a kind of 'demographic imperialism' designed to promote social alienation, weaken internal cohesion, and thus make Europe ready to be taken over by outside powers. For the LN, the main promoter of this 'mondialist' strategy was the United States which, in the party's view, aimed at constructing a 'totalitarian "global village" on the ruins of the peoples'. Given the circumstances, Europe was faced with a choice between a 'mondialist American multicultural society' and a 'European society based on its peoples'.[42] The LN's increasingly strident anti-Americanism also explains why immediately after the beginning of the NATO campaign against Yugoslavia the LN sided with Milosevic and the Serbs, 'a great people, which keeps its word, solid and serious' (Umberto Bossi in the Italian parliament) against the agents of a global and total liberal exchangism that sought to destroy the peoples and their traditional values and establish a new global order.[43]

In the context of White Resistance, the question of National Socialism (Nazism) and especially of the Holocaust plays a crucial role. White Resistance groups tend to have strong links to Holocaust negationist circles: groups and individuals who either insist that the planned extermination of vast numbers of human beings never happened at all (or, at any rate, not in gas chambers), or who deny that there ever was a concerted Nazi policy to annihilate the Jews and other groups that the Nazis considered *lebensunwert* (unworthy of life) – or, at the least, that if it occurred it happened unbeknownst to Hitler himself.[44] At first sight, it is not entirely obvious why anybody would spend time and energy to try and refute the crimes of a regime, which after all was instrumental not only in causing the death of millions of Europeans but in fatally weakening Europe's position in the world. This seeming paradox can only be explained if one subscribes to the notion that Nazism was above all an exemplary case of White Resistance. From this perspective, as the Swiss Holocaust negationist Jürgen Graf has charged, the 'Holocaust story' represents a threat because it is 'a major weapon in the growing campaign to discredit Western culture and to break down European racial–cultural consciousness. It is used to subvert national sovereignty, and [to] promote massive Third World immigration into North America and Western Europe.'[45]

Graf's intervention confirms that what distinguishes the radical right from other contemporary social and political movements is above all their pronounced nativism. This is not to say that all, or even a majority, of these groups subscribe to the explicitly raci(ali)st position of White Resistance ideology. Rather, the majority on the radical right espouses a 'post-racist' position of ethnopluralism, which aims at the protection and preservation of 'one's own' society, culture and way of life rather than the disparagement, subjugation and extinction of other cultures.[46] Radical right-wing nativism thus stands above all for a cultural nativism, which increasingly concerns itself with the (allegedly endangered) future of European identity and particularly of the Western value system.

In Western Europe, right-wing cultural nativism has especially focused on the challenge posed by the growing number of Muslim residents, who are increasingly seen as the main threat to Western culture.[47] As Jörg Haider stated in the early 1990s: 'The social order of Islam is opposed to our Western values. Human rights and democracy are as incompatible with the Muslim religious doctrine as is the equality of women. In Islam, the individual and his free will count for nothing, faith and religious struggle – *jihad*, the holy war – for everything.'[48] Other parties have echoed these charges, going so far as to claim that Islam is seeking to inundate Europe with Muslim immigrants in an effort to destroy Western civilization and thus attain world domination.[49] Thus at the time of the NATO intervention in Kosovo, Umberto Bossi argued that the conflict in Kosovo was fundamentally between Christian Serbs and 'the Albanian immigrants – I underline immigrants, for future memory – who are Muslims'. The connotation was clearly that the Muslim Albanians had pushed the Serbs out of the land which was 'the root of [Serbian] political and historical existence', a fate which might befall Europe as a whole if it did not defend itself against being invaded and inundated by streams of immigrants from Muslim countries. In this conflict, the LN clearly stood on the side of Serbian nationalism, which it considered an expression of the kind of 'patriotism' which represented 'the ultimate obstacle to the advance of the global American and Muslim empires'.[50]

Since the end of the Kosovo conflict, the mood in Italy and other Western European countries has hardly changed. On the contrary. The mobilization against the threat from 'fundamentalist Islam' to European culture and identity has become a central unifying theme in the debate about (and attacks against) multiculturalism. This reaches far beyond *völkisch* socialist and exclusionary populist circles, as demonstrated by the recent debate in Italy (which involved among others Giovanni Sartori) about the future of immigration from Muslim countries.[51] Again, it was the LN which was at the forefront of the struggle against the 'Damocles sword' hanging over Europe, warning in the pages of the party's official newspaper of the 'subversive character of Islamic proselytism', which 'is in reality an even more dangerous threat to our fundamental values and for our democracies than the *jihad* which expresses itself with bombs'.[52] No doubt, by raising the 'Islamic problem' and transforming it into a question of cultural resistance, the radical right has put itself into a favourable position to take advantage of the emerging identity politics in Western Europe.[53]

FILLING THE VOID

It is hardly a coincidence that the recent upsurge of right-wing radicalism in advanced capitalist democracies has occurred at a time of enormous turmoil and profound change affecting virtually all aspects of individuals' lives. In this situation, radical right-wing parties and movements propose themselves as alternatives to the traditional forces, filling a void created by the erosion and collapse of the established structures. In recent years, these developments have been primarily associated with globalization and 'postmodernization'.[54]

Undoubtedly, globalization has played a significant role in the radical right's ability to rally voters to its cause, although the links are not always entirely clear. On a more general level it has been suggested that the connection lies in 'the economic and social climate characterized by fear and despair engendered by the combined effects of globalization, identity crises and social exclusion' which has been exploited by the radical right.[55] In a similar vein, Roger Griffin has argued that in 'a situation where the very stability and globalization of liberal capitalism nourishes local fears of the erosion of cultural identity', it is 'ethnocentric and hence traditionally ethnocratic' passions 'which are the order of the day for those who feel threatened by the pace of change'.[56] Although suggestive, these interpretations remain both too sweeping and too vague to lead to firm conclusions.

Analytically, considerably more fruitful are observations that link the political success of right-wing radical parties and movements to theoretically expected or empirically observable consequences of globalization. Thus Vincent Cable has suggested that what 'is variously described as a "new nationalism", the "politics of cultural identity", the "politics of the soil", "positive nationalism", or the "new mercantilism" reflects, each in a different way, a reaction to the loss of authority of nation-states and an attempt to reassert it or to assert other forms of identity.'[57] This explanation suggests that there is a link between the transformation of the role and position of the state in advanced capitalist countries, which occurred in response to new competitive challenges, and the growing appeal of right-wing populist parties. As various analysts have argued, globalization (and here especially the dramatic increase in capital mobility) has induced a shift from the traditional corporatist

Keynesian welfare state toward a 'Schumpeterian workfare state with a managerial bias', or what Philip Cerny has called a 'competition state'.[58] Although there is little evidence that this process has led to a significant retrenchment of the welfare state, it is clear that it has significantly limited the state's range of options in economic and monetary policies. The result might very well be an increase in popular disenchantment with politicians and politics in general, favouring populist parties as protest vehicles.[59]

A second link is suggested by those who focus on the consequences of globalization on labour markets in advanced industrial societies. From this perspective, the intensified integration of global markets, and particularly the competitive pressures from developing countries with large pools of human labour, entail above all a decrease in demand for unskilled and semi-skilled labour in advanced industrial countries. At the same time, increased inter-national competition in product and capital markets has led to greater elasticity of labour demand. In Dani Rodrik's words, globalization means that 'the services of large segments of the working population can be more easily substituted by the services of other people across national boundaries'. As a result, these groups are likely to lose bargaining power, resulting, among other things, in slower wage growth, higher risk of redundancy and, above all, rising social inequality.[60] At the same time, there is a growing threat of capital flight, as companies are tempted to relocate their production facilities to low-wage and low-cost countries which promised higher returns on capital. These developments, it has been suggested, have contributed to the appeal of right-wing populist parties and, in the process, have raised 'the specter of a resurgent populist and xenophobic isolationism built on the support of losers from globalization'.[61] Unfortunately, the notion that the radical right is primarily a protest by 'modernization losers' finds little empirical support.[62] In the first place, radical right-wing parties have done particularly well in countries or regions that belong to the most affluent countries (such as Austria, Norway, Denmark and Switzerland) and regions (such as northeastern Italy and the Flemish region of Belgium) in Western Europe, where unemployment has generally been significantly below the OECD average, and where social welfare systems are among the most generous in the world and thus well-positioned to compensate potential losers of globalization. Moreover, although right-wing radical parties have attracted a disproportionate share of blue-collar voters, only a minority of these voters belongs to the group of poorly educated and unskilled workers most likely to be victimized by global change. This suggests that the link between globalization and the rise of right-wing radicalism is more complex than has generally been assumed.[63] Clearly, more research is needed to gain a better understanding of the relationship between globalization and party politics.[64]

A second major secular development linked to the rise of the radical right has been the process of postmodernization.[65] In its most abstract sense, postmodernization refers to the exhaustion of the Enlightenment project and the collapse of the legitimizing metanarratives of modernity that were grounded in this project. The ensuing 'condition of postmodernity' is characterized by a 'culture which has lost any sense of being part of a "grand narrative", and whose characteristic products are therefore marked by playfulness and inconsequentiality'.[66] Ironically, the degeneration of all 'mobilizing myths' of modernity might have been the very process, which, at least in the West, has robbed fascism of its revolutionary claim and thus of its distinct ideological and political identity.[67] At the same time, the emergence of a new cultural and sociostructural context characterized by uncertainty and fluid boundaries (the latter is also a main characteristic of globalization) might well have given rise to popular longings for security and predictability. If societal change exceeds 'the adaptive capacity of the established political parties', and these are therefore not capable of meeting these longings, some voters are likely to look elsewhere.[68] In support of this hypothesis one might cite the observation that the yearning for a strong man who leads the way and fixes everything seems to be particularly prevalent among supporters of right-wing radical parties.[69]

A second aspect of postmodernization that appears to be linked to contemporary right-wing radicalism regards the strains engendered by the gradual transformation of gender roles, reflected in the at least partial collapse of the traditional 'patterns of masculine role behavior, namely, the good-provider role'.[70] As Judith Newton has pointed out for the United States, the destabilization of the traditional male role has been caused by both economic and cultural developments giving rise to what variously has been described as a male crisis:

> The globalization of capitalism, economic restructuring, corporate downsizing, falling wages, the entry of married women into the labor market, the restructuring of domestic life by the dual incomes which middle-class families now require, foundational challenges to the gender order by organized feminisms and gay liberation in the United States and abroad, and the critique of white, middle-class, heterosexual masculinity by identity movements on every front – all have contributed either to the erosion of primary breadwinning as the foundation of dominant masculinities in the United States or the production of a related delegitimation of patriarchy on a global scale.[71]

One of the most striking aspects of the contemporary radical right is the fact that it finds considerably more support among men than women.[72] This has even been the case with parties headed by women, such as the Danish People's Party (Pia Kjærsgaard) and the Australian One Nation Party (Pauline Hanson). In fact, during the past ten years, the core supporters of radical right-wing parties have come from a relatively circumscribed social group – young white male blue-collar voters, a group which is presumably most affected by many of the developments Newton has listed.[73] Right-wing radical leaders, in turn, have made statements designed to appeal to the insecurities and *ressentiments* of white male voters. For example, Pauline Hanson referred to white Anglo–Saxon males as 'the most downtrodden person[s]' in Australia. With these words, Hanson appealed 'not only to those men feeling directly threatened by multiculturalism and feminism, but also to all these men threatened by changes in the rural and industrial sphere that have led to the disappearance of many traditional male jobs'.[74]

Again, it is far from clear to what degree the process of postmodernization has contributed to the rise and success of radical right-wing parties and movements. However, I would maintain that there are significant links which need to be explored if we want fully to understand the nature and cultural and political significance of the contemporary radical right.

THE THREAT FROM THE RIGHT

The contemporary radical right defines itself primarily as a social movement for the protection of national identity in a world which it sees as fundamentally hostile to Western values and culture. Its response is strikingly simple: 'The own people first', as the Belgian VB has put it. This is the war cry that represents the core of a new type of populist nativism, which is shared by virtually all relevant groups on the contemporary radical right, from exclusionary populists to White Resistance groups. What distinguishes the various groups is primarily their objective (e.g., assimilation of non-European foreigners versus their 'repatriation' and ethnic homogeneity) and the means proposed and accepted to reach their goal (restrictive legislation versus violence). Contemporary populist nativism goes beyond traditional nationalism as far as its extended goal is to safeguard the survival of a distinctly European culture. It is therefore principally compatible with projects of transnational integration such as the EU as long as it is limited to ethnically and culturally similar communities.

Much of the discourse of radical right-wing parties represents nothing more than a radicalized version of mainstream positions promoted and defended by the established political parties. Especially with respect to the question of immigration, the examples are myriad, ranging from Charles

Pasqua's public announcement when he was French Interior Minister under Balladur that the government's goal was 'zero immigration'; to slogans such as 'children instead of Indians' used by the German CDU in a recent state election.[75] What distinguishes the radical right is that it minces no words, whereas mainstream parties are more cautious. It is hardly surprising if radical right-wing parties are treated as political pariahs that need to be marginalized for, by exposing the hypocrisy of official practices, they tend to embarrass the political establishment.

Undoubtedly, in the current situation of profound change, uncertainty and instability the contemporary radical right represents a growing political and cultural threat. The threat is not that the radical right might undermine the democratic rules of the game. Rather, it stems from the fact that the radical right promotes values that are fundamentally opposed to the values that form the basis of postwar liberal democracies in Western Europe and elsewhere. The danger is that the growing appeal of radical right-wing policies and ideas will lead to a further erosion of openness, solidarity and historical sensitivity, while encouraging prejudice, intolerance, self-righteousness and blatant egoism. Unfortunately, there are few reasons to believe that the advanced capitalist societies are currently in a position and ready to adopt a decisive and militant stance in defence of liberal democracy.

NOTES

1. P. Hainsworth (ed.), *The Politics of the Extreme Right: From the Margins to the Mainstream* (London: Pinter, 2000).
2. H.-G. Betz, 'Contemporary Right-Wing Radicalism in Europe', *Contemporary European History*, 8.2 (1999), pp. 299–316.
3. See J. Kaplan and L. Weinberg, *The Emergence of a Euro-American Radical Right* (New Brunswick, NJ: Rutgers University Press, 1998); M. Ebata, 'The Internationalization of the Extreme Right', pp. 220–49 in A. Braun and S. Scheinberg (eds), *The Extreme Right: Freedom and Security at Risk* (Boulder, CO: Westview Press, 1997).
4. Exceptions are H. Kitschelt, *The Radical Right in Western Europe* (Ann Arbor, MI: University of Michigan Press, 1995); M. Minkenberg, *Die neue radikale Rechte im Vergleich* (Opladen: Westdeutscher Verlag, 1998); and, to a certain degree, C. Mudde, *The Ideology of the Extreme Right* (New York: Manchester University Press, 2000).
5. C. Mudde, 'The War of Words Defining the Extreme Right Family', *West European Politics*, 19.2 (1996), pp. 225–48.
6. M. Minkenberg, 'The Renewal of the Radical Right: Between Modernity and Anti-Modernity', *Government and Opposition*, 35, 2 (2000), pp. 170–71.
7. L. Cheles, R. Ferguson, M. Vaughan (eds), *Neo-Fascism in Europe* (Harlow: Longman, 1991); W. Laqueur, *Fascism: Past, Present, Future* (New York: Oxford University Press, 1996); M.A. Lee, *The Beast Reawakens: Fascism's Resurgence from Hitler's Spymasters to Today's Neo-Nazi Groups and Right-Wing Extremists* (London: Routledge, 1999). For a dissenting position see D. Prowe, 'Fascism, Neo-Fascism, New Radical Right', in R. Griffin (ed.), *International Fascism* (London: Arnold, 1998), pp. 305–24.
8. 'Measures to Combat Contemporary Forms of Racism, Racial Discrimination,

Xenophobia and Related Intolerance: Note by the Secretary-General', United Nations General Assembly, 53rd session, A/53/269, 17 August 1998, *http://www.unhchr.ch/ Huridocda/Huridoca.nsf/0811fcbd0b9f6bd58025667300306dea/dd1f86.*

9. This summary is derived from ideas advanced by R. Griffin, '"Fascism":An Ex-paradigm. Reflections on the Taxonomy of Contemporary "Authoritarian Movements"', *http://www.brookes.ac.uk/schools/humanities/Roger/2457/ex%20paradigm.htm*; A.J. Gregor, 'Fascism at the End of the Twentieth Century', *Society*, 34.5 (1997), pp. 56–63; Gregor, *The Faces of Janus* (New Haven, CT: Yale University Press, 2000).

10. Gregor, 'Fascism at the End of the Twentieth Century', p. 63.

11. Gregor, *The Faces of Janus*, p. 166.

12. See G. Gable, 'Britain's Nazi Underground', in L. Cheles, R. Ferguson and M. Vaughan (eds), *The Far Right in Western and Eastern Europe*, 2nd edn (Harlow: Longman, 1995), pp. 258–71.

13. R. Griffin, '*Interregnum* or Endgame? Radical Right Thought in the "Post-Fascist" Era', *Journal of Political Ideologies*, 5, 2 (2000), p. 173; 'Afterword: Last Rights?' in S.P. Ramet (ed.), *The Radical Right in Central and Eastern Europe since 1989* (University Park, PA: Pennsylvania University Press, 1999), p. 298.

14. Minkenberg, 'The Renewal of the Radical Right', p. 180.

15. Interview with C. Bouchet, *http://www.nationalbolshevik.com/nrf/nrfinterview2. html*; see also A. de Benoist, 'Democracy Revisited', *Telos*, 95 (1993), pp. 65–75; Griffin, '*Interregnum* or Endgame', p. 173; R. Eatwell, 'The Rebirth of the "Extreme Right" in Western Europe', *Parliamentary Affairs*, 53 (2000), p. 413.

16. G.M. Tamás, 'On Post-Fascism: How Citizenship Is Becoming an Exclusive Privilege', *Boston Review* (Summer 2000), *http://bostonreview.mit.edu/BR25.3/tamas.html*; R.J. Antonio, 'After Postmodernism: Reactionary Tribalism', *American Journal of Sociology*, 106.2 (2000), pp. 55–64.

17. Exceptions are P. Taggart, *Populism* (Buckingham: Open University Press, 2000) and Y. Mény and Y. Surel, *Par le peuple, pour le peuple* (Paris, Fayard, 2000).

18. M. Canovan, 'Trust the People! Populism and the Two Faces of Democracy', *Political Studies*, 67 (1999), p. 3.

19. A.J. Basevich, 'The Impact of the New Populism', *Orbis*, 40.1 (1996), p. 34.

20. M. Scheler, *On Feeling, Knowing and Valuing* (Chicago, IL: University of Chicago Press, 1992); R. Bittner, 'Ressentiment', in R. Schacht (ed.), *Nietzsche, Genealogy, Morality* (Berkeley, CA: University of California Press, 1994), p. 128; the classic account of *ressentiment* is M. Scheler, *Ressentiment* (New York: Schocken, 1972).

21. P. Poellner, *Nietzsche and Metaphysics* (Oxford: Clarendon Press, 1995), p. 253.

22. See R. Biorcio, *La Padania promessa* (Milan: Il Saggiatore, 1997), Ch. 6; T. Harrison, *Of Passionate Intensity* (Toronto: University of Toronto Press, 1995), Ch. 2; I.E. Deutchman, 'Pauline Hanson and the Rise and Fall of the Radical Right in Australia', *Patterns of Prejudice*, vol. 34.1 (2000), pp. 49–62. Belgian accounts of the rise of the VB generally tend to ignore or downplay the importance of the party's anti-Walloon platform, despite the fact that in the party's official position statement, independence for Flanders with Brussels as the capital of the new state comes before the question of immigration. See VB, 'A Party Unlike Any Other Party', *http://www.vlaams-blok.be/engelsfrans/engels/ frameset.htm.*

23. C. Blocher, 'Switzerland and the Second World War: A Clarification' (Zurich, 1997), *http://www.cins.ch/second.htm.*

24. C. Blocher, 'Switzerland and the Eizenstat Report' (Berne, 1997), *http://www.cins. ch/eiz.htm.*

25. Blocher, 'Switzerland and the Second World War'.

26. *The Nationalrat Election in Austria: Information on October 9, 1994* (Vienna: The Federal Press Service, 1994), p. 19; J. Haider, *Die Freiheit, die ich meine* (Frankfurt: Ullstein, 1993), p. 201.

27. Pauline Hanson's One Nation Launch Speech, 11 April 1997, *http://www.gwb.com.au/ onenation/speech.html*.

28. The first element is an authoritarian and particularist stance on political and cultural issues. See Kitschelt, *The Radical Right in Western Europe*, pp. vii–viii; on the non-significance of neo-liberalism see also C. Mudde, 'The Single-Issue Party Thesis: Extreme Right Parties and the Immigration Issue', *West European Politics*, 22.3 (1999), pp. 188–9.

29. In some cases (e.g., the FN) there was also considerable admiration for Ronald Reagan and especially Margaret Thatcher.

30. See A. Caplin, 'Economic Nationalism in the 1990s', *Australian Quarterly*, 69.2 (1997), p. 12.

31. D.R. Holmes, *Integral Europe: Fast-Capitalism, Multiculturalism, Neofascism* (Princeton, NJ: Princeton University Press, 2000), p. 114.

32. Ibid., p. 122.

33. U. Voigt, 'Bewegung muss Partei ergreifen', *Deutsche Stimme* (June 2000), *http:// www.ds.-verlag.de/zeitung/Ds6_20/mk002.html*.

34. See A. Pfahl-Traughber, 'The NPD setzt heute auf die Schlacht um die Strasse', *Die Welt* (30 August 2000); interview with Udo Voigt of the Nationaldemokratische Partei Deutschlands (NPD), *http://ds.dial.pipex.com/finalconflict/a19-1.html*.

35. 'Der Globalismus als höchstes Stadium des Imperialismus erzwingt die Auferstehung der deutschen Nation', *http://horst-mahler.de/texte/globalismus.html*.

36. See *http://www.msifiammatric.it/manif08.jpg*; similar rhetoric was advanced by the DVU during the election campaign for the regional election in Saxony-Anhalt in 1998, where the party focused almost exclusively on social issues. In the election, the DVU gained 12.9 per cent of the vote. See DVU, 'DVU-Wahlprogramm Sachsen-Anhalt 1998', *http://www.dvu.net*.

37. On the two major figures in American Nazism, see W.H. Schmaltz, *Hate: George Lincoln Rockwell and the American Nazi Party* (Washington, DC: Brassey's, 1999) and K. Koogan, *Dreamer of the Day: Francis Parker Yokey and the Postwar Fascist International* (Brooklyn, NY: Autonomedia, 1999). For a broad overview of the postwar history of right-wing movements in the United States, see S. Diamond, *Roads to Dominion* (New York: Guilford Press, 1995).

38. See B.A. Dobratz and S.L. Shanks-Meile, *'White Power, White Pride!' The White Separatist Movement in the United States* (New York: Twayne, 1997); J. Kaplan and L. Weinberg, *The Emergence of a Euro-American Radical Right* (New Brunswick, NJ: Rutgers University Press, 1998), Ch. 6.

39. D. Duke, 'Is Russia the Key to White Survival?', D. Duke *http://www.duke.org/dukereport/ 10-00.html*.

40. P. Hall, 'Inter-racial Genocide', *The Jubilee Newspaper* (July/August 1997), *http:// www.jubilee-newspaper.com/see_it_96.htm*.

41. British National Party, 'What is Racism?', *http://www.bnp.to/what.htm*.

42. 'Anche tu!', Lega Nord leaflet, 1999; *Enti Locali Padani Federali, Padania, identità e società multirazziali* (December 1998), *http://www.leganord.org/frames/politica.htm*, p. 14.

43. *Resoconto stenografico dell'Assemblea*, Seduta n. 513 (26 March 1999).

44. See M. Shermer and A. Grobman, *Denying History: Who Says the Holocaust Never Happened and Why Do They Say It?* (Berkeley, CA: University of California Press, 2000).

45. 'Spirited Twelfth IHR Conference Brings Together Leading Revisionist Scholars and Activists', *Journal for Historical Review*, 14.6 (1994), p. 2.

46. The term 'post-racist' is borrowed from A. Polito, 'Il Trionfo della signora Pia piccola Haider di Danimarca', *La Repubblica* (30 September 2000).

47. As early as 1991, the VB's mobilization against the Muslim immigrant population was a major factor accounting for the party's electoral success. See J.B. Billiet, 'Church Involvement, Ethnocentrism, and Voting for a Radical Right-Wing Party: Diverging Behavioral Outcomes of Equal Attitudinal Dispositions', *Sociology of Religion*, 56.3 (1995), p. 306.

48. Haider, *Die Freiheit, die ich meine*, p. 93.
49. See H.-G. Betz, *Radical Right-Wing Populism in Western Europe* (New York: St Martin's Press, 1994), p. 135.
50. *Resoconto stenografico dell'Assemblea; Enti Locali Padani Federali*, p. 14.
51. The debate was set in motion by the archbishop of Bologna, Cardinal Biffi, who suggested in a pastoral letter that Italy should favour Catholic immigrants over Muslims warning that 'either Europe will become Christian again or Islam will win'. Needless to say, Biffi's position found wholehearted support in the Lega Nord. See M. Menghetti, 'La Provocazione Biffi: immigrati sì, ma cattolici', *Il Messaggero* (14 September 2000); see also M. Smargiassi, 'Biffi: niente moschee in Italia', *La Repubblica* (1 October 2000). In a series of articles in major Italian newspapers and magazines, G. Sartori supported Biffi's position and questioned both whether Italy needed immigrants at all and whether Muslims would agree to integrate themselves into Italian society or whether they would create separate communities, which would become a fundamental threat to democracy. See 'Gli Islamici e noi italiani', *Corriere della sera* (26 October 2000); 'Gli Immigrati? Necessari, anzi no', *Il Sole 24 Ore* (21 July 2000).
52. A. del Valle, 'Una Spada di Damocle incombe sull'Europa. La Jihad e le minacce islamiche', *La Padania*, 23 July 1999; for an analysis of LN's war against Islam, see R. Guolo, 'I nuovi Crociati: la Lega e l'Islam', *Il Mulino*, 49.5 (2000), pp. 890–901; E. Mauro, 'Il Paese post-razzista di Bossi e Berlusconi', *La Repubblica* (30 March 2000); I. Diamanti, 'Allarme senza solide basi. La Chiesa e la Lega anti-Islam', *Il Sole 24 Ore* (5 November 2000).
53. On identity politics in Germany see, for example, R. Cohen, 'Is Germany on the Road to Diversity? The Parties Clash', *New York Times* (4 December 2000), p. A14.
54. D. Held, A. McGrew, D. Goldblatt and J. Perratton, *Global Transformations* (Stanford, CA: Stanford University Press, 1999); S. Crook, J. Pakulski and M. Waters, *Postmodernization: Change in Advanced Society* (London: Sage: 1992).
55. 'Measures to Combat Contemporary Forms of Racism, Racial Discrimination, Xenophobia and Related Intolerance.'
56. Griffin, 'Afterword: Last Rights?', p. 312.
57. V. Cable, 'The Diminishing Nation-State: A Study in the Loss of Economic Power', *Daedalus*, 124 (Spring 1995), p. 23.
58. B. Jessop, 'Post-Fordism and the State', *http://www.geo.ut.ee/inimtool/referaadid/krap/referaat_palhus.htm*; P. Cerny, 'Paradoxes of the Competition State', *Government and Opposition*, 32.2 (1997), pp. 251–74.
59. This might have accounted, at least in part, for the gains of the FN in the mid 1980s, after Mitterrand's famous 'U-turn', and also for the recent gains of the Norwegian FRPn, after Carl Hagen started to appeal to popular misgivings about the government's tight fiscal policy despite a growing budget surplus. See I. Thorbjörnsrud, 'Norwegens Ölboom beflügelt Rechtspopulisten', *Salzburger Nachrichten* (19 September 2000); R. Wolff, 'Reich und rechts', *Die Tageszeitung* (23 October 2000).
60. D. Rodrik, *Has Globalization Gone Too Far?* (Washington, DC: Institute for International Economics, 1997), Ch. 2, p. 4; see also A. Sapir, 'Who is Afraid of Globalization? The Challenge of Domestic Adjustment in Europe and America', *http://www.ksg.harvard.edu/cbg/trade/sapir.htm*.
61. G. Garrett, 'A Virtuous Global Circle', *Boston Review* (December/January 1997/98), *http://bostonreview.mit.edu/BR22.6/garrett.html*. A similar interpretation is advanced in Rodrik, *Has Globalization Gone Too Far?*, p. 69.
62. For an elaboration of the thesis see H. Kriesi, 'Movements of the Left, Movements of the Right: Putting the Mobilization of Two New Types of Social Movements into Political Context', in H. Kitschelt, P. Lange, G. Marks and J.S. Stephens (eds), *Continuity and Change in Contemporary Capitalism* (Cambridge: Cambridge University Press, 1999), pp. 402–3; for a critique see Minkenberg, 'The Renewal of the Radical Right', pp. 181–2.
63. See H. Beirich and D. Woods, 'Globalisation, Workers and the Northern League', *West*

European Politics, 23.1 (2000), pp. 130–43.

64. For a comprehensive approach to this question see D. Swank and H.-G. Betz, 'Globalization, the Welfare State, and Right-Wing Populism in Western Europe', unpublished paper, Department of Political Science, Marquette University, 2000.

65. For a thorough discussion of postmodernism and the radical right see Antonio, 'After Postmodernism'.

66. R. Skidelsky, 'What's Left of Marx?', *The New York Review of Books* (16 November 2000), p. 24.

67. Griffin describes the result as the 'structural impotence of the radical right today'. Griffin, '*Interregnum* or Endgame?', p. 172.

68. J.W.P. Veugelers, 'A Challenge for Political Sociology: The Rise of Far-Right Parties in Contemporary Western Europe', *Current Sociology*, 47.4 (1999), p. 82.

69. In 1995, 85 per cent of Le Pen supporters agreed with the statement that what France needed was a true leader who took command and fixed things. N. Mayer, 'Rechtsextremismus in Frankreich: Die Wähler des Front National', in J.W. Falter, H.-G. Raschke and J.R. Winkler (eds), *Rechtsextremismus: Ergebnisse und Perspektiven der Forschung, PVS*, Sonderheft 27/1996 (Opladen: Westdeutscher Verlag, 1996), p. 394.

70. R.F. Levant, 'The Masculinity Crisis', *The Journal of Men's Studies*, 5.3 (1997), p. 222.

71. J. Newton, 'White Guys', *Feminist Studies*, 24.3 (1998), p. 576.

72. This holds even true for multivariate analyses, which control for other factors such as education, income and values. See, for example, M.M.L. Crepaz and H.-G. Betz, 'Postindustrial Cleavages and Electoral Change in an Advanced Capitalist Democracy: The Austrian Case', in G. Bischof, A. Pelinka and D. Stiefel (eds), *The Marshall Plan in Austria*, Contemporary Austrian Studies, Vol. 8 (New Brunswick, NJ: Transaction Publishers, 2000), p. 520.

73. For an exploration of this question with regard to the FN see N. Mayer, *Ces Français qui votent FN* (Paris: Flammarion, 1999), Ch. 6.

74. A. Curtoys and C. Johnson, 'Articulating the Future and the Past: Gender, Race, and Globalisation in One Nation Discourse', *Hecate*, 24.2 (1998), p. 105.

75. The slogan was coined during a recent debate on whether Germany should seek to attract foreign hi-tech specialists to Germany to meet a growing need for highly trained personnel in the information technology sector. The CDU's answer was that instead of importing more foreigners, the government should see to it that German children get more and better computer training. A similar debate was also initiated in Austria, where the FPÖ advanced the argument that instead of importing more foreigners, Austrians should have more children. See M. Völker, 'Der Ausländerreflex der FPÖ', *Der Standard* (11 October 2000).

Part 2
Comparing Public Opinion Indicators

Racism and the Political Right:
European Perspectives

Charles Westin

INTRODUCTION

R ACISM HAS once more become a truly serious problem in Europe. It manifests itself in discrimination and social exclusion in the labour market, in segregation in the housing market, in unequal opportunities in the educational system, in marked differences in general health and well-being between migrant categories and majority populations, and in differential access to power and influence. Social stratification along these crucial variables is increasingly becoming determined by 'perceived race', culture, ethnicity and religion. Racism manifests itself in a new build-up of anti-Semitism, in popular demands to curb immigration and to repatriate migrants, and in the rise of National Front parties and it manifests itself in persecution of migrants and minorities, in threats and hostilities aimed at these people and in acts of political terrorism that include assault, arson and even murder. These developments in the member-states of the EU were accompanied in the 1990s by persecution and exclusion policies aimed at the Roma people in several central and Eastern European states.

Who would have thought some ten years ago that Nazis would march again? Who could have anticipated that several thousand well-educated young people in affluent Western countries would defend and believe in Nazi ideas again? Who could ever have imagined that the well-documented and detailed facts of the Holocaust would actually be questioned and even denied while some surviving victims are still alive and can witness to what took place in the death-camps?

Much work has been done on analysing conditions of attitude change and developments of public opinion. Comparatively little work has been done on analysing public opinion differences between countries or states, mainly because of economic and methodological obstacles to such research. This article takes a closer look at two Eurobarometer surveys of attitudes commissioned by the European Monitoring Centre on Racism and Xenophobia (EUMC). Interesting differences between the 15 member-states of the EU can be related to differential experiences of immigration, integration policies and anti-racist vigilance. Opinions affect policy-making, there is no doubt about that, but policies, and in particular the ideas pursued by parties on the far right, also mould figures of thought that have much more profound effects than momentary changes of opinion.

THE 1997 EUROBAROMETER SURVEY

The EUMC was established as an independent body by the EU in 1997. Its task is to combat racism, xenophobia and anti-Semitism in Europe. That same year a Eurobarometer opinion poll was carried out, gauging the European opinion on racism and xenophobia. Eurobarometer surveys had previously been employed in studies of the majority population's attitudes to immigrants and 'out-groups' in 1988 and 1993. The 1997 survey was carried out in all 15 member-states in March and April that year.[1]

The results show that almost 33 per cent of those interviewed describe themselves as 'quite racist' or 'very racist'. At first sight this measure of 'racism' by means of 'self-declaration' appears to be a neat way out of sticky methodological and partly ethical problems. On closer inspection, however, some unsolved questions concerning the reliability and validity of the instrument present themselves. Obviously the term 'racist' carries varying connotations in different European countries. In countries where racism has been regarded as a serious problem for a long time, the term means something else than in countries where racism has hardly been on the agenda. 'Race' and racism have been debated for 50 years in the UK, but the issue is a relatively new one in Greece. There is a social desirability bias associated with this measure that we have no means of assessing or controlling.

Nevertheless, it was established that self-declared racism was prevalent among those sympathizing with the political right, those over fifty-five, the less-educated, those holding negative views of the EU and, indirectly at least, among rural dwellers. People sympathizing with the political left, those younger than fifty-five, with higher education, people appreciating the EU and urban dwellers were less prone to declare themselves as racists. This is consistent with patterns that have been established in independent attitude surveys carried out in various individual countries.

Surprisingly, however, a large majority of the respondents expressed their support for the fundamental democratic rights and freedoms. Nine out of ten regarded 'equality before the law' and the 'right to education' as fundamental values that always need to be respected. Eight out of ten were in favour of the right to protection against discrimination, the right to one's language and culture, religious freedom and freedom of speech. The strong support for these classic democratic rights hardly seems logically or psychologically compatible with the unexpectedly large number of self-declared racists. As many as 75 per cent of the respondents thought positively of multiculturalism (some must be self-declared 'racists'), and some 60 per cent agreed that minorities enrich social life. However, a significant share of the respondents also believe that minorities must give up their cultures in order to become accepted.

If these findings correctly represent opinions (in 1997), and if methodological biases can be ruled out or are negligible, two (complementary) explanations present themselves. One is that public opinion is polarized, as illustrated by the case of Denmark with high values for both integration and assimilation attitudes. The second and more challenging explanation is that racism and xenophobia are interwoven in intricate ways into the very fabric of European culture. Jews in Europe have always been aware that supporters of liberal ideology could be anti-Semites at the same time. In the 1940s, Gunnar Myrdal showed that the American democratic creed prevailed alongside racist ideology, which denied African Americans political rights. This implies that the struggle against racism, anti-Semitism and xenophobia has to concern itself with something much more comprehensive than merely combating extremist expressions, opinions and organizations. The value systems, the belief systems, the histories and the institutions of mainstream society have to be critically scrutinized.

The most serious criticism of the methodology employed in the 1997 Eurobarometer survey is that only self-declaration was used as an indicator of racist and xenophobic attitudes. These are highly complex objects of thought that normally require an assembly of indicators to be determined adequately. Secondly, in view of the considerable differences between member-states with regard to immigration experiences, numbers and kinds of migrants, and immigration and integration policies, it is questionable whether an overall European opinion should be presented or rather divided up according to member-states.

A hypothetical division of the EU member-states into three groups seems to fit the 1997 data reasonably well. It came out most clearly (see Table 4.1) in the responses to the following two statements.

> For each of the following opinions, please state whether you tend to agree or tend to disagree:

1. In order to be fully accepted members of society, people belonging to these minority groups must give up such parts of their religion or culture which may be in conflict with the law.

2. In order to be fully accepted members of society, people belonging to these minority groups must give up their own cultures.

TABLE 4.1
OPTIONS FOR INTEGRATION OR ASSIMILATION

	Agrees with integration	*Agrees with assimilation*	*Disagrees with both*
Sweden	**65**	23	12
The Netherlands	**56**	26	18
Denmark	**55**	**37**	8
Finland	**54**	19	27
UK	**45**	26	29
Luxembourg	*43*	21	37
Germany	*40*	26	34
France	*44*	**32**	24
Belgium	31	**44**	25
Austria	25	**35**	*40*
Greece	24	**34**	*42*
Portugal	29	27	*44*
Ireland	27	16	*57*
Spain	16	17	*67*
Italy	21	10	*69*

Note: Figures in **bold** represent the five highest percentages for each option respectively (read ↓). Figures in *italics* represent the highest value for each state respectively (read →).

Statement 1 is taken as an indicator of being in favour of integration, statement 2 as an indicator of being in favour of assimilation. These operationalizations may obviously be criticized on similar grounds as the measure used to determine racist attitudes. One would want a battery of questions to assess respondents' preferences for assimilation or integration.

First, five countries high on 'integration' form a north European cluster:

Sweden, the Netherlands, Denmark, Finland and the UK. A second cluster of countries, mainly an EU-core, consists of Belgium, Austria and France, that all have high values for assimilation. (I have included Germany and Luxembourg in this intermediate group.) The third, basically south European, cluster consists of the five countries with the highest values on disagreement: Italy, Spain, Ireland, Portugal and Greece.

The Nordic states, the Netherlands and the UK, high on integration, have adopted integration policies and multicultural policies to handle the issue of incorporating migrant minorities into the polity. Types of immigration differ from postcolonial in the Netherlands and UK; labour migration from European peripheries into Denmark and Sweden; to virtually no immigration at all in the case of Finland. Another common element is that these are all Protestant (Lutheran, Calvinist and Anglican) countries with liberal democratic constitutions. Finland is a newcomer in the family of immigration countries but has adopted the Scandinavian approach. The Netherlands and the UK followed different paths but arrived at far-reaching policies of multiculturalism. Note that Denmark too places a high value on the assimilation option, which reflects a situation in which public opinion is polarized.

The countries in the intermediate group all have histories of guest-worker migration, and they all belong to the Franco-German bloc. Four are EU core states. Three have significant right-wing protest parties that have played an important role in influencing anti-immigrant opinions at home: VB in Belgium, FN in France and the FPÖ in Austria. Four of the countries are predominantly Catholic. Germany is divided between a Catholic south and a Protestant north. The French model of incorporating migrants through the citizenship model is of course very different to the German approach of not incorporating migrants at all. Although France and Germany actually have higher values for integration, it still seems reasonable to place these countries in this intermediate category.

The third cluster represents countries mainly situated in southern Europe with recent experiences of immigration. What they have in common is that they all until quite recently were major sending countries: Italy, Spain, Portugal, Greece and Ireland. Four are Catholic countries, Greece alone is Orthodox. These countries have not yet developed policies on immigration and incorporation. Hence, the question of whether migrants should assimilate or integrate in the receiving society was not an issue for public opinion in 1997.

This grouping of countries has proved to be helpful in organizing the information in the 1997 as well as in the 2000 Eurobarometer. Let us then have a look at the distribution of self-declared 'racism'.

Right-Wing Extremism

TABLE 4.2
SELF-DECLARED 'RACISM' IN THE 1997 EUROBAROMETER SURVEY
ACROSS EU MEMBER-STATES

	Most racism			→ *Least racism*	
Country	*Very racist* (4)	*Quite racist* (3)	*A little racist* (2)	*Not at all racist* (1)	*Means*
Sweden	2	16	40	42	1.78
The Netherlands	5	26	46	24	2.14
Denmark	12	31	40	17	2.02
Finland	10	25	43	22	2.23
UK	8	24	34	35	2.07
Luxembourg	2	12	33	54	*1.64*
Germany	8	26	34	32	2.10
France	16	32	27	25	**2.39**
Belgium	22	33	27	19	**2.60**
Austria	14	28	32	26	**2.30**
Greece	6	21	31	43	1.92
Portugal	3	14	25	58	*1.62*
Ireland	4	20	32	45	1.85
Spain	4	16	31	49	*1.75*
Italy	9	21	35	35	2.04

Note: Figures in percentages. The highest three mean figures are in bold; the lowest three mean figures are in italic.

Table 4.2 clearly shows that self-declared racism is highest in Belgium, France and Austria, with high values also for Finland, the Netherlands and Germany. With the exception of Luxembourg, racism almost seems endemic in the EU core countries. It is particularly striking that the three countries with the highest values are countries where right-wing populist parties have had significant electoral successes. These parties have obviously exploited a popular discontent among the general public, but they have also been instrumental in channelling this discontent into anti-immigrant expressions, on the verge of voicing racist standpoints. These parties have played an important role, then, in moulding, articulating, reinforcing and legitimizing a racist or semi-racist public opinion. Self-declared racism is also relatively frequent in the five northern countries. The lowest rates of self-declared racism are found in the southern countries.

An important variable in this context is people's trust in institutions and political establishments. A scale was constructed based on the following seven items:

1. The people who run the country are more concerned with themselves than the good of the country!
2. Corruption among politicians is increasing!
3. The way government and public bodies work is getting worse!
4. I have little control over what is happening in the world around me!
5. Public services look less and less after the interests of people like me!
6. The rich get richer and the poor get poorer!
7. There is nothing one can do to change things in our society!

TABLE 4.3
TRUST IN PUBLIC INSTITUTIONS AND POLITICAL ESTABLISHMENTS

Country	Lowest trust ⟶			Highest trust
	Negative (3)	*Critical* (2)	*Positive* (1)	*Means*
Sweden	16	47	37	1.79
The Netherlands	18	29	52	1.64
Denmark	13	26	61	1.52
Finland	36	33	31	2.05
UK	48	35	18	2.32
Luxembourg	15	35	50	1.65
Germany	54	29	18	**2.38**
France	41	37	22	2.19
Belgium	63	30	7	**2.56**
Austria	34	34	33	2.03
Greece	59	26	16	**2.45**
Portugal	37	36	27	2.10
Ireland	47	31	22	2.25
Spain	39	30	31	2.08
Italy	40	37	23	2.17

Note: Figures in percentages. The highest three mean figures are in bold.

As Table 4.3 shows, distrust in public institutions and political establishment is highest in Belgium, Greece and Germany. It is also quite noticeable in the UK, Ireland and France. Distrust is overall high in the core and southern clusters, but less so in the northern cluster of countries. At the time the survey was carried out, a number of scandals in connection with public institutions and government were uncovered in Belgium. Not the least was the exposure of a paedophilia ring responsible for the murder of several Belgian children held in captivity. This shook the nation and led to a political crisis. If political distrust in public institutions and government establishments may be an explanatory factor of racism in the core states, and conversely, if trust in institutions and government may account for the somewhat lower rate of racism in the northern states, this explanation obviously does not hold true in southern Europe with a high degree of distrust in the political establish-ment but a low degree of self-declared racism.

Two additional questions point to some other dimensions of attitude moulding that need to be considered in the overall picture. The first of these concerns the degree to which majority populations are aware of possible discrimination in the labour market directed against migrants and minorities. The second question concerns the extent to which people feel that their country can accept (more) minority groups. The distribution of responses to these two questions is given in Table 4.4.

We see a consistent response pattern in the core cluster. A significant share of the respondents is not aware of discrimination on the labour market that hits minority groups (Austria, Germany and Belgium). Luxembourg and Ireland are also low on this question, but in all likelihood for different reasons. Ireland has only a small migrant population, whereas Luxembourg has a large migrant population (but this is professional to a large extent and thus pre-sumably not the victims of discrimination). The same core countries are also high on the feeling that the country cannot accept more minority groups without serious consequences to the country. On the whole, the northern countries take an intermediate position in both these questions, whereas southern Europe is well aware of discrimination in the labour market, but does not think that continued immigration would cause problems for the country. The exception is Greece. The 1997 Eurobarometer produced some results of concern in view of the increasing racism in Europe. It also provided a hypothetical model of country grouping according to which some consistency of response patterns has been seen.

TABLE 4.4
AWARENESS OF DISCRIMINATION IN THE LABOUR MARKET AND
ACCEPTANCE OF (MORE) MINORITY GROUPS

	Least positive —————————————————→ *Most positive*	
Country	*People from minority groups are being discriminated against in the job market!*	*Our country has reached its limits; if there were to be more people belonging to these minority groups we would have problems!*
Sweden	89	60
The Netherlands	74	60
Denmark	85	64
Finland	73	27
UK	66	66
Luxembourg	**40**	61
Germany	54	**79**
France	72	69
Belgium	56	**82**
Austria	**39**	70
Greece	90	**85**
Portugal	86	60
Ireland	**51**	42
Spain	87	29
Italy	79	62

Note: Figures in percentages agreeing with statement. Least positive: the three lowest mean figures are in bold. Most positive: the three highest mean figures are in bold.

IMMIGRATION AND INCORPORATION POLICIES

What policies are likely to have affected or moulded public opinion? There is no simple answer to this question since the member-states have different histories of state-formation, minority policies and immigration histories. In this section I will take a closer look at immigration and incorporation policies in member-states where such policies have been formulated.

EU core states

When Jörg Haider's FPÖ won the 1999 Austrian elections and formed a government together with the Conservative Party, the EU reacted strongly and initiated sanctions against Austria. Within Austria itself, however, business carried on as usual. The boycott may have been unsuccessful, but the action did call attention to the presence of racism and xenophobia that Haider had so successfully managed to exploit. Austria's central position in Europe implied that it was a major gateway for refugees from communist Europe. It also recruited guest workers in the 1960s. A second wave of immigration started in the mid 1980s. Like Germany, Austria never considered itself to be a country of immigration. As some 16 per cent of its population is foreign-born, this stance is surprising. Mainstream political actors have largely neglected issues of racism.[2] Strong anti-Semitic sentiments were prevalent in Austria in the early parts of the twentieth century, influencing Hitler in his youth. Austria's dubious role during 1938–45 as, on the one hand, victim of Nazi aggression or, on the other hand, active perpetrator hit the country in the 1980s when the international community questioned Kurt Waldheim's presidency because of his collaboration with Nazi forces during World War II. In defence of a precarious national identity (Austrians regard themselves as more German than the Germans, according to a popular stereotype), there is restricted space for incorporating immigrants into the polity.

Belgium, one of Europe's oldest industrial nations, has a history of immigration since the early twentieth century. In the interwar years and after World War II migrant labour was imported from Italy, Spain and Greece to work in the mining and steel industries. These workers could be laid off when the economy went into recession and re-employed when manpower was needed. Although many migrants had been 30 years in Belgium they were not regarded as residents. Magnette[3] argues that the political system hesitated to develop ways of incorporating migrants into the polity (through naturalization or by extending the franchise) because of the intricate balance of power between the two nations within the state. There is a complex asymmetry in that national identity in Flanders is Flemish, whereas it is Belgian in Wallonia and Brussels. Although steps have been taken to promote integration of migrants residing in the country, measures in the field of immigration are characterized by toughness and restriction. The VB has played an essential role in moulding anti-immigrant opinions in Flanders. Multiculturalism is thus an inconceivable outcome of the contradictory Belgian policies.[4]

France has a longer history of immigration than other European states. It stretches back in time to the early nineteenth century. This early immigration to France was predominantly European. Since World War II, immigrants have come from Portugal and Italy, but also increasingly from former colonies and overseas 'Départements'. French incorporation policies thus trace their roots back to this need for manpower on the one hand, but also to the specifically French republican ideal on the other, stressing the equality of all citizens. In theory all residents of the French state are regarded as citizens. Incorporation is thus explicitly based on the acquisition of citizenship. Once newcomers become citizens they are entitled to the full social and political rights associated with this citizenship. It is up to the individual migrant to adapt and adjust himself to the ways of French society. The requirement to learn French is not a manifestation of ethnic or national chauvinism but an affirmation that French is a world language and the only recognized national language. Assimilation is the expected and unavoidable outcome of this policy.[5]

Germany was a major sending country in the nineteenth century and has thus a more concentrated history of immigration than France. Despite the fact that Germany has received more immigrants than the United States over the past 50 years, paradoxically it has not until quite recently seen itself as a country of immigration. Consequently it has not recognized people of migrant origin as a permanent part of its population. The redrawn German borders after World War II, and the division into the Federal Republic of Germany (FRG) and a Soviet puppet state, the German Democratic Republic (GDR), gave rise to massive population shifts from the East to the West. According to a right laid down in the constitution of the FRG, anyone who can present evidence of German ancestry is entitled to German citizenship. After the fall of the communist regimes in Europe, great numbers of *Aussiedler* made use of this provision. The rights of the *Aussiedler* are a striking contrast to the situation of the second- and third-generation descendants of guest workers, still expected to 'return home'. No targeted integration policies have been enforced pertaining to the guest workers and their descendants since these groups were never intended to settle permanently in Germany. Social exclusion is a logical outcome of this approach. A certain degree of integration has, nevertheless, taken place through the economic system and participation in the labour market.

Luxembourg, the smallest state of the EU both in terms of territory and population, has a foreign-born population of 35 per cent, which is the highest figure in the EU. Population policies have had to consider how to maintain a national identity, given the country's exposed position between France, Germany and Belgium and its large migrant population. The country has introduced legislation to ensure social and political rights to foreigners, while at the same time stressing the importance of the contribution aliens are expected to make to Luxembourgish society. The migrant population of Luxembourg consists to a larger extent than elsewhere in the EU of well-educated professionals. Even so, the authorities stress the restriction of immigration flows. Luxembourg has adopted an integration policy, but with certain reservations.

The northern cluster

For many years migration to Britain was dominated by post-colonial visible migrants who were British subjects. The Commonwealth Immigration Act of 1968, however, put an end to this spontaneous immigration. At the time this Act was implemented kinship networks were already well established between sending regions and migrant communities in the UK. People find ways of entering and settling in the UK legally. Families reunify. Marriages take place. Today a majority of the of the African-Caribbean, Pakistani, Bangladeshi and people of Indian origin are born in the UK as the second or third generation of the original migrants. Although British social, economic and political conditions have had their impact on minority cultures, certain distinctive values, traditions and belief systems have withstood pressures of cultural assimilation. The UK has no integration policy directly comparable with the Dutch or Swedish initiatives. On the other hand, the fight against racism and discrimination has a much longer history and stronger position than in any of the other countries of the EU. The challenge today is how to maintain ethnic diversity, how to support minority groups and how to voice ethnic and cultural interests.[6]

The Netherlands has a long tradition of immigration and of providing refuge for persecuted (religious) minorities. The country has strong libertarian traditions and is known for its toleration of life-styles on the margins of society. These traditions are partly an outcome of its geopolitical position between three major European powers but also of its history as a seafaring nation. Morality is an individual matter, not a concern of others – an attitude which reflects the founding liberal values of the Dutch nation. Assimilation of newcomers was never an explicit requirement.[7] Even quite far back in time, provisions were made to safeguard the autonomy of religious and cultural minorities. As one of the first states in Europe, the Netherlands adopted a multicultural policy. The aim to establish a multicultural society is producing a widespread acceptance of diversity, despite some infrequent backlashes of racist violence. The logical consequence of the Dutch policies is integration, and indications are that the Netherlands is managing to accomplish this objective.[8]

Migration to Sweden divides into two distinct phases: labour migration before 1972, and thereafter, refugee migration with family reunification. Sweden adopted an ambitious 'immigrant' policy in 1975 to promote equality and support for ethnic minorities. Because of its central focus on equality, integration and the fight against racism, it is sometimes seen as a multicultural policy. The mechanism of the welfare state serves as the driving force towards integration – a model that was developed several decades earlier to transform traditional class-structured society to a modern egalitarian state. The educational system is a cornerstone of the model. Another basic instrument is participation in the polity. This was achieved by extending the franchise to those foreign citizens who are permanent residents in local and county elections. A complementary strategy is to encourage naturalization and, as from 2001, to accept dual citizenship. The official policy in Sweden is to promote integration. But there is a hidden agenda. 'Ethnic diversity is all very well but things should be done according to the Swedish model!' These conflicting goals have furthered a situation of segregation rather than integration.[9]

TABLE 4.5
THE NORDIC STATES AND INTERNATIONAL MEMBERSHIPS

	Member of EU	*Member of EMU*	*Member of NATO*
Denmark	Yes	No	Yes
Finland	Yes	Yes	No
Sweden	Yes	No	No
Iceland	No	No	Yes
Norway	No	No	Yes

Although the Nordic countries differ in their orientation to international cooperation (see Table 4.5), they have a social welfare policy based on similar ideas. As integration policies are regarded as part of the welfare system, there are many similar components of the Nordic countries' policies directed to migrant minorities despite differences in migration histories. Denmark's history of modern immigration resembles Sweden's in many respects, although it is smaller in both absolute and relative terms. The Danish incorporation policies resemble the Swedish strategies. An important difference between the two countries is the presence of several protest parties representing up to 25 per cent of the Danish electorate. The most important of this is Fremskridtspartiet (the Progress Party). This party was founded in the early 1970s and its main target was criticism of the public sector and the taxation policies. However, it has gradually moved towards xenophobic positions with regard to immigration and is in favour of repatriation policies. The party has been instrumental in giving xenophobic forces in Denmark a voice. As a result public opinion is polarized on issues of immigration.

Finland has a short history of immigration. Up until the 1980s it was still an important sending country, having supplied Swedish industry with hundreds of thousands of workers in the 1960s and 1970s. Finland has also had a very restrictive refugee policy, for which it was criticized by the other

Nordic countries. The Finnish approach was largely determined by consideration of the country's particular relation to the Soviet Union during the Cold War period. Defectors from the Soviet Union were sent back if apprehended by the Finnish authorities. Secondly, close to 10 per cent of the population are Karelians or their descendants who were relocated to western Finland when Karelian territory was seceded to the Soviet Union in 1945. In addition to the heavy war damages that Finland had to pay the Soviet Union, this resettlement was a heavy strain on the economy. After the Cold War, Finland opened its borders to immigration of refugees. Small numbers of Vietnamese and Somalis have sought refuge in Finland. The country has adopted the Nordic welfare model of incorporation and has liberal views on minority rights. Finland has two official languages (Finnish and Swedish). Minority policies are largely determined in accordance with the framework developed to manage language rights.

The southern cluster

Italy, historically one of Europe's major sending countries, is now an important recipient of migrants. Large-scale immigration is a recent phenomenon, and within the space of little more than a decade the number of migrants in Italy has skyrocketed. There has been little time to develop well-conceived policies on integration. A major concern is the large number of undocumented migrants. The regularization of the undocumented migrants, in effect amnesty, has top priority today.[10] An awareness of the impact of immigration is growing at various levels, but nothing concrete has come out of it yet, since Italy is still struggling to come to grips with problems of political corruption, its fascist past and organized crime in the South. The lack of clear policies is creating a situation of confusion and panic. Griffin points to the fact that Europe's oldest radical right electoral party, the MSI, did not follow the example of Le Pen's FN when the occasion arose.[11] Instead its offspring, the AN, gave immigration issues a low profile, focusing its attention on regional differences, which are historically important issues in Italy.

Spain and Portugal have also become major countries of immigration in recent years, with migrants from North Africa and Latin America. In Portugal's case migrants also come from southern and western Africa via networks with former colonies (Angola, Mozambique, Guinea Bissau and Cape Verde). Neither country has developed policies to incorporate migrants into the polity. Racism does not appear to be as great a problem on the Iberian Peninsula as it is in France or Belgium. Both Spain and Portugal were freed from fascist dictatorships in the mid 1970s. Although fascist factions are still around, the radical right lost whatever political credibility it may have had during the period of transition to democracy. Membership of the EU has been immensely important in stabilizing democratic rule and modernizing these two countries that had been under the rule of Franco and Salazar for almost 40 years.

Immigration to Greece is possibly even more recent than it is to Spain and Portugal. One source of this immigration is the so-called Pontic Greek Diaspora, that is to say descendants of Greek settlers along the Black Sea coasts and in the Caucasus. The country is also a target for migrants from the Middle East and Albania. Little has been done to address questions of incorporation and integration of migrants. Greece stands out compared to the other Mediterranean countries. Distrust in public institutions and government establishment is widespread. After World War II, Greece suffered an agonizing civil war, and several military dictatorships (most recently in 1967–74). There is constant tension in its relationship with Turkey and Albania, and recently also with Macedonia. Greek immigration and minority policies must be placed in this context of a still ongoing process of Greek nation-state formation.

Ireland formed as an independent state after the struggle for independence (1919–21) from the UK. Ireland has a long history of supplying English industry with cheap labour. The United States and Australia were other main destinations of Irish emigration. Ireland has benefited from membership of the EU. Its economy has improved significantly and the country is now attracting international capital and professionals from the EU. Ireland has accepted refugees and asylum-seekers in recent years. More importantly, there is a significant return migration from the UK and the United States. Ireland has a long history of discrimination directed at travelling people.[12] Anti-racist policies are being developed, partly modelled on British experiences.

This incomplete survey of immigration histories and incorporation policies (or lack of them) clearly demonstrates the range of differences and disparities between the 15 member-states of the EU. In order to combat racism and xenophobia there is a need to define some common ground. One such starting point is Article 13 of the Amsterdam Treaty.

THE 2000 SURVEY

The most recent Eurobarometer survey on racism and xenophobia was carried out between 5 April and 23 May 2000. It was analysed and reported by the Institute for Social Research and Analysis (SORA), and published by the EUMC in March 2001.[13] The survey was carried out in all 15 member-states of the EU with an average sample size of slightly more than 1,000 respondents. More than 16,000 persons were interviewed. Some items from the 1997 Eurobarometer were used again. The data are treated as if they reflect current political debate in the member-states at the time the survey was conducted, that is to say, after the Amsterdam Treaty (including Article 13) was signed.

Methodological obstacles

A general methodological problem was that response rates were low with, however, considerable variations between the countries. Refusal rates varied from 75 per cent in the Netherlands (which is a methodological catastrophe) to 16 per cent in Austria (acceptable) and 19 per cent in France (barely acceptable). In nine of the 15 member-states, refusal rates were well over 40 per cent (totally unacceptable) and in five other, well over 50 per cent.[14] It is quite clear that this overall high refusal rate has seriously undermined the sample's representative quality. The problem is of course that non-response may be systematically related to the questions that the survey is dealing with. It cannot be ruled out that people refuse to participate because they sympathize with racist views, which would mean that the prevalence of racist and xenophobic views will be underrepresented in the sample. One can get around the problem to a certain extent by weighting, but when we are dealing with refusal rates of 60 and 70 per cent in some cases, even this does not suffice to repair the sample. In addition to the general problem of non-response there were missing values. The proportion of missing values varied between the participating countries. Furthermore, as with all comparative studies of this nature, questions could be interpreted differently in varying cultural contexts, despite meticulous efforts to translate the questions as correctly as possible.

From a social science point of view the problem is that market research has overexploited the general public. People's growing unwillingness to participate in surveys reflects negatively on studies undertaken for purposes of academic and policy research. High refusal rates in representative surveys have become a major problem to monitoring agencies. Obviously it must be hard to refrain from analysing the Eurobarometer data, in this case concerning a topic of great importance and a study that required considerable investment of time and money to carry out. The EUMC in Vienna was not willing to sacrifice the study because of its methodological deficiencies. The data were analysed as if there were no major methodological drawbacks. The EUMC has published the analysis reported by SORA giving it full visibility on the Internet (*www.eumc.eu.int*).

Since the EUMC not only has the remit *to describe* public opinion but also to take appropriate action *to change* it (to paraphrase Karl Marx) by affecting those who mould opinion, decision-makers and politicians, the report cannot be dismissed out of hand. It does certainly present an image of the situation in the EU. Policy-makers will act on this picture of the situation irrespective of whether or not it corresponds in all its details to the actual situation. It is the published (and official) image of public opinion (based on an expert study and analysis) that carries weight, influences policies, programmes and political decisions, not the unarticulated public opinion as such.

We should bear in mind that refusal rates are most likely to have affected the general image by underrating racist and xenophobic attitudes in countries with the highest refusal rates: the Netherlands, Denmark, Finland, Greece and Ireland in the first place, but probably also affecting the results in Sweden, Italy, Belgium and the UK quite significantly. The first three of these have come out with relatively low levels of expressed xenophobia.

The overall picture

During the 1997–2000 period, attitudes in the EU member-states towards migrants and minority groups changed in certain unexpected and partly contradictory ways. In the overall picture it appears that a large number of Europeans approve of policies aimed to improve relations between majorities and minorities, while at the same time a majority of the respondents expressed their concern that minorities were threatening social peace and welfare. Most Europeans are optimistic about multiculturalism and most reject repatriation programmes; however, a significant number of the respondents also voice the opinion that the presence of minorities is personally disturbing to them. At first sight these results present a contradictory impression. On second analysis, it is obviously non-committal to state that one accepts policies aimed to improve relations between majorities and minorities, whereas it takes more of personal nerve or audacity to state that one is disturbed by the presence of minorities. Some items, then, are more prone to social desirability effects than others.

Again it appears that European opinion is divided, to the extent of being polarized. Are there significant differences between states, or are the main divisions of opinion within the individual states? Or are we facing combined effects? Various statistical tools of analysis were employed by SORA (factor analysis, regression analysis and cluster analysis) in order to extract more detail in response patterns. The most important independent variables that were found to correlate closely with attitudes to minorities (the dependent variables) were education, family relationship to members of minority groups, employment status and political views (party preferences). These variables point to four social identity domains of central relevance: knowledge; emotional security; recognition (qualification and sense of worth); and power and influence. Age differences were also found. Younger people express more tolerant views than the elderly, and higher education is associated with positive attitudes to minority groups. But, surprisingly, having a parent or grandparent belonging to a minority group is not associated with positive attitudes. Experiences of unemployment as well as voting for parties on the right tend to be linked with negative views on minority groups. There are however significant differences between the member-states of the EU in these respects.

We need to question the notion of explanation in the type of statistical modelling employed in the analysis of data. In some cases voting behaviour may 'explain' the presence of xenophobic attitudes. By voting for a right-

TABLE 4.6
DISTRIBUTION OF TOLERANT/INTOLERANT ATTITUDES IN EUROPE

| Country | *Lowest tolerance* | | | → *Highest tolerance* | |
	Intolerant (4)	*Ambivalent* (3)	*Passively tolerant* (2)	*Actively tolerant* (1)	*Means*
Sweden	9	15	43	33	2.00
The Netherlands	11	25	34	31	2.18
Denmark	20	17	31	33	2.26
Finland	8	21	39	32	2.05
UK	15	27	36	22	2.35
Luxembourg	8	32	33	28	2.22
Germany	18	29	29	24	**2.41**
France	19	26	31	25	**2.41**
Belgium	25	28	26	22	**2.58**
Austria	12	30	37	20	2.31
Greece	27	43	22	7	**2.88**
Portugal	9	34	44	13	2.39
Ireland	13	21	50	15	2.30
Spain	4	18	61	16	2.08
Italy	11	21	54	15	2.30
EU-average	*14*	*25*	*39*	*21*	

Note: Figures given in percentages. Owing to the rounding off of decimals, the percentages for individual
        countries (and the EU-average) do not in all cases add up to 100 but to 99 or 101. The four highest
        mean values are in bold.

wing, xenophobic or national front type of party one is making a commitment
to the ideas and rhetoric upheld by that party. However, it is equally likely
that people's xenophobic attitudes 'explain' their voting behaviour. That is to
say, people who cherish xenophobic beliefs themselves are attracted to vote
for parties that reflect these values and belief systems. There are interactive
effects that would require panel data to analyse in more detail.

We need to be aware that a great many so-called background variables in
our analysis are actually outcomes of people's strivings, decisions and aims,
and affected by obstacles, enabling conditions and instruments that they may
employ in seeking to achieve their goals. Their intentions and values are
essential components of their attitude systems. Thus, not only do background
variables 'explain' attitudes. Attitudes also 'explain' some important background variables such as voting behaviour, education, occupation, self-
employment and (to a certain degree) place of residence, among others.

Attitude dimensions

Factor analyses identified the following attitude dimensions:[15]

1. Fearing social conflicts and loss of economic status
2. Believing in improvements of social coexistence
3. Advocating restrictive acceptance of minorities
4. Feeling threatened by other ways of life
5. Recognizing cultural enrichment by minority groups
6. Approving of repatriation of immigrants
7. Endorsing the promotion of cultural assimilation.

Six of these dimensions (2–7) were used to classify respondents into four
categories: actively tolerant (21 per cent), passively tolerant (39 per cent),
ambivalent (25 per cent) and intolerant (14 per cent). There are country
differences, as shown in Table 4.6

In terms of the proposed country grouping we find that new countries
of immigration, the southern cluster, are spread over the table. The core group
of countries tend to collect towards the intolerant end of the scale whereas
the northern cluster of states tends to converge towards the tolerant end of
the scale. But it needs to be borne in mind (again) that opinions are divided.
In Denmark there is (still) both a large actively tolerant opinion as well as
quite a significant intolerant opinion. Denmark is low on the intermediate
positions of being ambivalent and passively tolerant. Whatever the principal

TABLE 4.7

PERCENTAGE OF THE RESPONDENTS THAT AGREE WITH STATEMENTS
CONCERNING: (1) ANTI-DISCRIMINATION; (2) DIVERSITY-MANAGEMENT;
(3) EQUAL OPPORTUNITIES; (4) PARTICIPATION

Statements:

(1) 'Outlaw discrimination against minority groups!'

(2) 'Encourage the creation of organizations that bring people from different races, religions and cultures together!'

(3) 'Promote equal opportunities in all areas of social life!'

(4) 'Encourage the participation of people from minority groups in the political life of the country!'

	Least agreement			→ *Most agreement*
	Anti-discrimination (1)	*Diversity-management* (2)	*Equal opportunities* (3)	*Participation* (4)
Sweden	40	34	37	39
The Netherlands	37	29	51	26
Denmark	33	35	34	40
Finland	26	38	43	26
UK	31	28	39	25
Luxembourg	41	36	44	29
Germany	34	29	35	25
France	31	28	42	19
Belgium	29	31	38	21
Austria	**27**	**26**	35	20
Greece	34	**18**	**31**	**13**
Portugal	31	**22**	36	**11**
Ireland	**24**	29	**31**	16
Spain	**27**	27	39	16
Italy	33	34	**31**	**15**

Note: Figures given in percentages.

factors are that bring about tolerant attitudes in the northern welfare states (egalitarianism, long-standing democratic rule, multicultural policies in the domain of ethnic relations, liberal and social democratic traditions), something in the working of these factors generates the presence of a comparatively large actively tolerant opinion. Sweden and Finland come out as the most tolerant societies, and yet the most vicious neo-Nazi terrorism outside Germany is found in the Nordic states. The very fact that Sweden has a liberal constitution with regard to the freedom of the press, the freedom of assembly, the freedom of organization, etc. has been exploited by international Nazi organizations that encounter greater problems of establishing in countries where they are the object of much closer police monitoring. This is a typical liberal democratic dilemma.

TABLE 4.8
ACCEPTANCE OF MIGRANTS FROM DIFFERENT REGIONS AND FOR
DIFFERENT REASONS

	Lowest acceptance ⸻⸻⸻⸻⸻⸻⸻➤ *Highest acceptance*				
	Muslim countries	*Eastern Europe*	*Countries in conflict*	*Asylum-seekers*	*EU*
Sweden	2.15	2.28	2.33	2.26	2.46
The Netherlands	1.85	1.89	2.17	2.27	2.07
Denmark	2.11	2.22	2.33	2.28	2.53
Finland	2.02	2.12	2.13	2.08	2.37
UK	1.77	1.79	**1.75**	**1.69**	**1.89**
Luxembourg	1.75	1.83	2.01	2.01	2.26
Germany	**1.64**	1.79	1.93	1.95	**1.98**
France	1.85	1.96	2.12	2.02	2.22
Belgium	**1.74**	**1.77**	1.93	1.83	2.17
Austria	**1.69**	**1.69**	1.93	1.91	**1.82**
Greece	1.86	1.92	**1.77**	1.91	2.27
Portugal	**1.74**	1.83	**1.91**	1.87	2.17
Ireland	1.78	1.82	1.98	1.83	2.09
Spain	2.11	2.16	2.29	2.26	2.41
Italy	2.10	2.12	2.21	2.10	2.41

Note: Means on scale 1 (low acceptance) to 4 (high acceptance).

Several questions in the survey focus on issues pertaining to multicultural policies. In Table 4.7 attitudes to four of these issues are presented. John Rex[16] is one of several writers on multicultural societies who stresses that normative multiculturalism must promote and support policies of anti-discrimination, diversity management, equal opportunities and participation. It is therefore hardly surprising that we find respondents in EU countries that have adopted multicultural policies (the northern cluster) present greater sympathy with the importance of anti-discrimination, equal opportunities, etc. than respondents in the southern cluster of countries that have not (yet) adopted any such policies. But we must also take note of the fact that less than half of the respondents (with one exception) even in the most tolerant cases wholeheartedly support anti-discrimination, diversity management, equal opportunities and participation.

Some individual country response patterns deviate from the general trend. Equal opportunities are important in France and the UK – countries that on several other indicators come out as harbouring rather xenophobic public opinions. Diversity management has its highest value in Finland, a country that has two founding nations, two official languages and the means to deal with diversity in a highly practical manner. Interestingly, we find that Belgium too is among the better countries in attitudes to diversity management. The highest values for acceptance of participation are in the Nordic countries that have done most to incorporate migrants through the political system. Questions of participation in the polity have been dealt with theoretically by Hammar, Bauböck and Kymlicka.[17] Anti-discrimination is only supported by an average of 33 per cent of the respondents, although there are some variations between the countries. This is somewhat disheartening in view of the radical stand that the EU has made in the Amsterdam Treaty, Article 13, concerning the struggle against all forms of discrimination. These dimensions of multiculturalism have not been political issues in the southern cluster of states because immigration is a recent phenomenon, as already stated several times before. Nor have they been political issues in the guest-worker states belonging to the EU core because migrant labour was regarded as a temporary solution to the need for manpower.

Table 4.8 shows the mean values for acceptance of migrants of different categories. The core states, including the UK and Portugal, are on the whole least willing to accept migrants from Muslim countries, from Eastern Europe, countries in conflict, asylum-seekers or even from the EU. France departs from the trend by having a more positive acceptance of migrants from Eastern Europe and also of asylum-seekers. A low percentage of respondents from the southern cluster of states agreed with the various aspects of multicultural policies, but there was an indication of higher acceptance of immigrants than is the case with the EU core states. Public opinion in Spain and Italy, together with the Nordic countries, is most positively inclined to accept immigrants. What the large core countries, France and Germany, as well as the UK, have in common is that they have been the preferred countries of destination for the past 50 years. It is easy to get the impression that the large volume of immigration to these countries over a long period of time has brought about domestic opinions in Germany and the UK that seem rather indifferent to asylum-seekers' need for protection.

Explaining altitudinal differences in countries

How does one explain changes in public opinions? And how do we explain differences between countries? These two questions require different but interrelated answers. The first pertains to processes over time, the second to distributions of various (explanatory) factors in geopolitical/geocultural space. In both cases background variables serve as essential explanatory factors, but in different ways. In this section I can only sketch some possible approaches to the analysis of country differences in opinions. Let us, then, return to the independent background variables in the EUMC/SORA report.

No significant gender differences were established. It is of course always essential to take gender into account, but it does not help us in our present quest. In this case, age, on the other hand, is clearly correlated with the attitude dimensions. Older respondents hold significantly more negative views of migrants than younger respondents. Age, or to be more precise date of birth, is an essential variable when analysing changes in public opinion because of the time dimension it involves (the generational issue). In this case, however, age is hardly likely to explain attitudinal differences in countries as there are no distinctive demographic disparities between the countries with regard to age distribution. Differences between the EU member-states in demographic age composition are insignificant, particularly in comparison to the vast demographic differences between Europe and developing countries.

Education, as mentioned previously, was found not only to correlate with the attitude variables, but also with age. To a certain extent, then, the age effect may be colinear with education. Younger generations have on the whole spent more years in school than their parents. This is a result of the restructuring of the labour market and economy away from mass employment in low-skilled industrial jobs to a post-industrial economy requiring a well-educated, skilled workforce. Analysed as a sociological variable, education clearly serves several functions. Its most obvious task is to convey knowledge to students and scholars who want, or need, to learn basic skills, specific skills or acquire a general knowledge of the world or some facets of it. It is often assumed that knowledge promotes rational views of the world, society and human existence in which there is little place for ideas such as racism. However, it is also apparent that a secondary objective of the educational system is to grade students and hence to sort them according to their aptitude for higher education, an undertaking with far-reaching social and sociological consequences as higher education usually is a prerequisite for career opportunities and upward social mobility. The educational system (appearing in the analysis as the sociological variable 'education') serves, thus, directly or indirectly, to reproduce social structure.

School curricula probably do influence attitudes to migrants and minorities by promoting an understanding of their situation, but the main explanation of the correlation between higher education and positive attitudes to migrants is more likely to be the role that the educational system plays for social mobility and thus ultimately for career opportunities, self-confidence, life satisfaction and being in control of one's life circumstances. As far as country differences are concerned, educational systems differ markedly in Europe. In the Nordic countries comprehensive school systems are essential instruments for social transformation, whereas in Latin countries (France in particular) school systems appear to be more focused on traditional academic learning and elite scholarship. What the consequences of different school systems are for attitude formation *vis-à-vis* minorities and migrants have not been analysed systematically, but may well be a project worth pursuing.

An unexpected finding was that respondents defining themselves as (distantly) related to or descendants of members of a minority group tend to hold more negative attitudes towards minority groups in general than those who define their ancestry in terms solely of the majority population. This finding relates to deeper existential dimensions of identity. There are country differences here that could be analysed systematically. First, one would want to distinguish between respondents of migrant origin on the one hand and respondents belonging to ethnolinguistic and/or ethno-territorial minorities on the other. Finland, Belgium and Spain are multi-national states with constitutions that recognize the existence of more than one national group with founding rights in the state. Denmark, Austria, Germany, Ireland and Portugal, on the other hand, are examples of states that come reasonably close to the nation-state ideal, quite independent of the fact that several of them have large migrant populations. The remaining states have one dominant national group, in most cases large migrant popula-tions, and also some numerically small but still culturally distinct ethno-territorial or ethnolinguistic groups. An example of an analytical grid is given in Table 4.9. This could prove to be useful in pursuing an analysis of this finding.

A variable of great importance in all explanations of racism and xenophobia is employment status. It is linked to several identity factors (social recognition, locus of control, sense of worth, etc.). Sociologists sympathizing with the left

TABLE 4.9
COUNTRY DIFFERENCES

	Multinational states	*Majority dominated states with ethnoterritorial minorities*	*Close to the nation-state ideal*
Northern cluster	Finland (Finns, Swedes)	Sweden (*Saami*) The Netherlands (*Frisians*) UK (*Celts*)	Denmark
EU core countries	Belgium (Walloons, Flemings)	France (*Bretons, etc.*) Luxembourg (*Germans*)	Austria, Germany
Southern cluster	Spain (Castilians, Catalans, etc.)	Greece (*Turks, Albanians*) Italy (*Sardinians, etc.*)	Ireland, Portugal

have sought to explain why working-class respondents have assumed positions more negative to migrants than middle-class respondents. One such thinker is the Norwegian sociologist Ottar Brox[18] who launched a theory some 30 years ago that stated that low-skilled workers facing possible redundancy in times of economic recession were those who were most susceptible to adopting not only negative views of migrants but even more blatantly fascist ideals. He termed his theory structural fascism. Others have presented similar interpretations.[19] Theoretically much points in support of this theory. People whose social status is low and who are on the lowest rungs of the employment ladder compete with migrant labour for the same jobs in a labour market where these types of jobs are becoming increasingly scarce. Low-skilled native workers experience migrant labour as a threat to their positions and are therefore inclined to adopt negative views of migrants.

However, results from a series of four comparable attitude surveys undertaken in Sweden over the 24-year period 1969–93 do not directly support Brox's theory. Public opinion on migration changed during the period, but the fluctuations did not follow the economic cycle as predicted by Brox. The problem was that his theory did not take into account roles played by various other contributing or enabling factors in shaping people's views. The most important of these factors is the presence of movements, parties or factions that legitimize and articulate the ideas of unjust competition and the privileged right of native residents over those of migrants. Obviously right-wing extremist parties do just that. The European situation is of great interest to analyse in this perspective. Levels of employment and unemployment vary considerably among the EU member-states, as does the presence of right-wing extremist parties. These differences and their links to public opinion need to be explored systematically.

Country differences with respect to opinions on immigration and migrant presence are probably most adequately explained in terms of the political context. This context varies significantly with regard to party structure, voting behaviour, policies on migration and minority issues, etc. The 2000 data clearly show that sympathies with the political right are more closely related to xenophobic attitudes than sympathies with the political left and centre. This comes out clearly on all seven attitude dimensions. In the analysis presented by SORA 'voting behaviour' is said to 'explain' xenophobic attitudes. There is, in other words, a strong positive correlation between voting for parties on the far right and xenophobic attitudes. 'Moving', as it were, towards the left along the political scale is accompanied by a 'decrease' in these attitudes. This relation is evident in several countries, but is seen most clearly in Austria, Belgium, Denmark and France. These are all countries in which right-wing protest parties and National Front-type parties have achieved considerable electoral success. No such party plays a significant role in Finland, Netherlands, Sweden or the UK. The protest parties in Austria, Belgium, Denmark and France are EU-critical, which is consistent with their nationalistic views. In Sweden, the EU-critical niche was already occupied by parties on the left (the Left Party and the Greens), with no or very little expression of xenophobic ideas. So in this particular case, right-wing protest parties cannot monopolize the EU-critical platform, which may explain why they have only a marginal position in Swedish politics.

CONCLUSION

It would not be out of place to qualify the relationship between extremist positions and public opinion. Obviously there is not one monolithic public opinion, but rather a spectrum of different views. Some opinions are more frequently expressed than others, even though they may not be representative of the most commonly held views. It is normally those views that are voiced by moulders of opinion that become reinforced by repeated exposure in the media that come to be regarded as 'public opinion'.

Public opinion, then, represents a wide spectrum of viewpoints, some of which are totally opposed to each other. Nevertheless, it does make sense to speak about certain tendencies of opinion, 'gravitational centres', which shift from time to time, partly as a result of direct opinion moulding, partly as a result of people's accommodation to the changing conditions and realities of everyday life. The media play a significant role in the formation of public opinion, more, it seems, as reinforcers of existing movements of opinion than as independent moulders. It goes without saying that changes of opinion are influenced by what goes on beyond the gravitational centre. If public opinion on any specific issue may be conceived of in terms of a continuum of view-points, then any change of opinion implies a (slight) shift of centre towards either of the extremes.

Political movements operating at the extremes may not expect to achieve mass support. Nevertheless, the political mobilization of extremist groups is of importance in affecting public opinion in terms of shifting its gravitational centre. Beliefs, representations, values, figures of speech, derogatory jokes and stereotypes work themselves in towards the centre; way beyond the circle of committed activists. Words that used not to be acceptable ways of expression, may, if they are catchy, suddenly spread and eventually also become accepted.

When protest parties such as the VB or FN receive a considerable share of the vote, the gravitational centre of public opinion is shifted significantly to the right. The danger is that other competing parties may opportunistically adapt their proposed policies to a somewhat milder, but basically similar, position in the hope of winning back votes. It is easy to recommend parties not to follow that course of action. They should stay firm in their egalitarian, anti-racist and democratic views and serve as political buffers against racist and anti-democratic tendencies.

Ruud Koopmans[20] launched the proposition that xenophobic and racist violence seems to be less frequent in countries in which far-right parties have made electoral gains or are embedded within the political system, and vice versa. Wolfgang Kühnel[21] found support for this hypothesis. Austria, Belgium, Denmark, France and Italy are countries in which parties to the far right have made significant electoral gains. Germany, Sweden and the UK on the other hand are countries where extremist groups have resorted to racist violence. Spain could possibly be included in this latter category through the terrorist actions of ETA. Table 4.10 presents a grid for comparative analysis of far-right factions in the EU member-states.

Racism and xenophobia is a European problem and must be combated on a European level. The measures to combat discrimination taken by the EU in the Amsterdam Treaty represent an important step forward. The 15 member-states all have some constitutional provisions to prevent racism and discrimination. However, they differ considerably. Some states have specific non-discrimination clauses in their constitutions. In other cases constitutions may be less specific, referring to the issue in more general terms of human rights. All EU member-states have introduced laws to combat racist violence. Several have enacted specific legislation to outlaw racial discrimination in certain fields of employment. It is fair to say that these legal provisions express

TABLE 4.10

PROTEST PARTIES AND EXTREMIST ORGANIZATIONS IN THE EU

	Large right-wing protest parties	*Small extremist, neo-Nazi splinter groups*	
Northern cluster	Denmark	Finland, the Netherlands	Sweden, UK
EU core countries	Austria, Belgium, France	Luxembourg	Germany
Southern cluster	Italy	Greece, Ireland, Portugal	Spain

a will to combat racism and to counteract discrimination on grounds of race and ethnicity. However, there is still a lot of ground to be covered in order to eradicate the most malevolent forms of racism in Europe. The most challenging task is to critically scrutinize the value foundations, nationalistic rhetoric and institutional forms that enable racist and xenophobic organizations to thrive.

NOTES

1. See Eurobarometer Opinion Poll no. 47.1: *Racism and Xenophobia in Europe* (Luxembourg, 1997).
2. See K. Wachter, 'State Construction, Minorities, Immigration and the Racist Consensus in Austria', in C. Westin (ed.), *Racism, Xenophobia and the Academic Response: European Perspectives* (Stockholm: CEIFO Publications, 2001).
3. P. Magnette, 'Racism and the Belgian State', in Westin, *Racism, Xenophobia and the Academic Response*.
4. See B. Cambré, H. de Witte and J. Billiet, 'The Attitude towards Foreigners in Belgium', in Westin, *Racism, Xenophobia and the Academic Response*.
5. See J. Doomernik, *The Effectiveness of Integration Policies towards Immigrants and their Descendants in France, Germany and the Netherlands* (Geneva: ILO, 1998).
6. See Commission on the Future of Multi-Ethnic Britain, *The Future of Multi-Ethnic Britain* (London: Runnymead Trust and Profile Books, 2000).
7. See J. Doomernik and M. Fennema, 'Past and Current Racism and Policy Responses in the Netherlands', in Westin, *Racism, Xenophobia and the Academic Response*.
8. See F. Bovenkirk, M. J. I. Gras and D. Ramsoedh, *Discrimination against Migrant Workers and Ethnic Minorities in Access to Employment in the Netherlands* (Geneva: ILO, 1994).
9. See C. Westin, *The Effectiveness of Settlement and Integration Policies for Immigrants to Sweden* (Geneva: ILO, 2000).
10. See U. Melchionda, 'The Immigration Urgency in Italy: Its Social Representation', in C. Westin (ed.), *Racism, Ideology and Political Organization* (Stockholm: CEIFO Publications, 1998).
11. See R. Griffin, 'Ce n'est pas Le Pen: The MSI's Estrangement from Overt Xenophobia',

in Westin, *Racism, Ideology and Political Organization.*

12. See M.Tannam, S. Smith and S. Flood, *Anti-Racism:An Irish Perspective* (Dublin: Harmony, 1998).
13. See E.Thalhammer, Z.Vlasta, E. Enzenhofer et al., Attitudes towards Minority Groups in the European Union: A Special Analysis of the Eurobarometer 2000 Survey, 2001, www.eumc.eu.int
14. See SORA (E. Thalhammer, Z.Vlasta, E. Enzenhofer *et al.*), *Attitudes towards Minority Groups in the European Union:Technical Report*, 2001, www.eumc.eu.int
15. I am not using the same terminology as SORA for these dimensions.
16. John Rex, 'The Concept of a Multicultural Society', in John Rex and Guibesnau Montserrat (eds), *The Ethnicity Reader: Nationalism, Multiculturalism and Migration* (Oxford: Polity Press, 1997).
17. T. Hammar, *Democracy and the Nation State* (Aldershot: Gowers, 1990); R. Bauböck, *Transitional Citizenship: Membership and Rights in International Migration* (Aldershot:Edward Elgar, 1994); and W. Kymlicka, *Multicultural Citizenship:A Liberal Theory of Minority Rights* (Oxford: Clarendon Press, 1995).
18. O. Brox, *Strukturfascismen och andra essäer* (Stockholm: Prisma, 1972).
19. See J. Solomos and J.Wrench (eds), *Racism and Migration in Western Europe* (Oxford: Berg, 1993).
20. R. Koopmans, *A Burning Question: Explaining the Rise of Racist and Extreme Right Violence in Western Europe*, The Public and Social Movements, Discussion Papers FS III 95–101 (Berlin: Science Centre, 1995).
21. W. Kühnel, 'Right-Wing Extremism, Migration and the German Political System', in Westin, *Racism, Ideology and Political Organization.*

CHAPTER FIVE

Explaining National Variations in Support for Far Right Political Parties in Western Europe, 1990–2000

Allen Wilcox, Leonard Weinberg, William Eubank

FOR MORE than a decade now, academics, clerics, journalists, along with public officials from countries belonging to the EU, have voiced alarm about the revival of right-wing extremism in the seemingly stable democracies of Western Europe.[1] The alarm has been set-off by two broad trends. First, in various EU countries there have been serious episodes of violent attacks on Third World immigrants, 'guest workers', members of the Roma community and other racial and religious minority populations.[2] In Sweden, Germany and elsewhere these assaults have often been carried out by members of right-wing youth gangs displaying Nazi era parapher-nalia and chanting slogans, 'Foreigners Out!' reminiscent of the Hitler dictatorship.

The second trend, or suspected trend, to have aroused serious concern involves growing voter support for political parties of the radical or extreme right. The electoral successes achieved by the French FN, Austria's FPÖ, the Italian LN and NA formations and, at least at the regional level, the VB in Belgium caught many analysts by surprise.[3] Prior to the 1980s, far-right parties in Western Europe occasionally enjoyed short bursts of popularity, such as the movement led by France's Pierre Poujade during the 1950s. But there was no period of high electoral support for these parties sustained over the years, and certainly not on a Europe-wide basis.[4] But alarmed observers noted that beginning in the 1980s and continuing at a seemingly accelerating pace in the 1990s, there has been growing voter support for these parties to a point where a long-term trend has become discernible. Furthermore, recent EU-wide public opinion surveys have reported high percentages of Euro-peans possessing racist and xenophobic attitudes, at levels much higher than those achieved at the polls by the radical right parties. The implication was that these parties' electoral bases were potentially far bigger than their current vote totals would suggest. Aside from this hypothetical possibility, there were in fact two instances during the last decade in which far-right parties entered government coalitions and shared in the exercise of power. In Italy both the 'post-fascist' NA headed by Gianfranco Fini and the xenophobic LN movement of Umberto Bossi participated in the short-lived right-wing government of Silvio Berlusconi in 1994. And, as a result of the 2001 Italian parliamentary elections, Berlusconi and his far-right allies have returned to power. In Austria, the FPÖ of the charismatic Jörg Haider has become a fully-fledged participant in his country's ruling coalition. In both the Italian and Austrian cases leaders of various EU countries expressed concern about these developments, and in the latter case sanctions were applied, at least briefly.

Analysts of far-right politics, including ones whose work have been included in this volume, were quick to point out that the more electorally successful parties belonging to this genre were substantially different from their fascist predecessors (or in a few cases contemporary rivals).[5] To quote Betz:

> Distancing themselves both from the backward-looking, reactionary politics of the traditional extremist (i.e., neo-fascist and neo-Nazi) Right as well as its proclivity for violence, these parties are posing the most significant challenge to the established structure and politics of West European democracy today … Generally, the majority of radical right-wing populist parties are radical in their rejection of the established socio-cultural and socio-political system and their advocacy of individual achievement, a free market, and a drastic reduction in the role of the state without, however, openly questioning the legitimacy of democracy in general. They are right-wing first in their rejection of individual and social equality and of political projects that seek to achieve it; second, in their opposition to the social integration of marginalized groups; and third in their appeal to xenophobia, if not overt racism and anti-Semitism. They are populist in their unscrupulous use and instrumentalization of diffuse public sentiments of anxiety and disenchantment and their appeal to the common man and his allegedly superior common sense …[6]

In short, the new or recently remodelled (from such old neo-fascist organizations as the Italian MSI) right-wing 'populist' parties which Betz defines in this way are adapted to the social and economic conditions prevailing in the advanced industrialized societies of Western Europe.[7] And particularly when they come to be led by such cagey or charismatic figures as Jörg Haider, they represent serious contestants for political power.

THEORIES

The purpose of the present enquiry is to explain the sources of electoral volatility among far-right parties in Western Europe in the last decade of the twentieth century. What were the prevailing economic, social and political conditions in the countries where far-right voting rose and fell most widely between 1990 and 2000? However, before introducing the collection of variables we have employed in order to answer this question, it seems essential that we comment on the magnitude of the far-right parties' growth in voter support in these years. How formidable a challenge do these parties pose?

TABLE 5.1
FAR-RIGHT VOTING IN WESTERN EUROPE: 1990–2000

Country	*Source of data★*		*c.1990 vote: far right (%)*	*Latest vote c.2000: far right (%)*	*Far-right vote change 1990–2000 (%)*
	1990 elections	*2000 elections*			
1 Austria	1990	1999	16.6	26.9	10.3
2 Belgium	1991	1999	7.7	11.4	3.7
3 Denmark	1990	1998	6.4	9.8	3.4
4 Finland	1991	1999	3.1	4.2	1.1
5 France	1988, 1993 (average)	1997	11.2	15.0	3.8
6 Germany	1990	1998	2.4	3.0	0.6
7 Ireland	1989, 1992 (average)	1997	0.0	0.0	0.0
8 Italy	1992	2001	14.1	26.7	12.6
9 The Netherlands	1989	1998	0.9	0.6	−0.3
10 Norway	1989	1997	13.1	15.3	2.2
11 Spain	1989	2000	0.0	0.0	0.0
12 Sweden	1991	1998	6.7	0.0	−6.7
13 Switzerland	1991	1999	9.4	3.0	−6.4
14 UK	1992	1997	0.0	0.0	0.0
Mean			6.54	8.28	1.74
Standard deviation			5.79	9.60	5.22

★ Elections were compared as close as possible to 1990 and 2000 – allowing for the different years in which elections were held in the 14 countries.

If we examine the national election results recorded in Table 5.1 the overall impression is that there was a very limited Europe-wide growth in voter support for far-right parties during the 1990s. Despite the extensive commentary mentioned at the beginning of this essay, the average (mean) national increase in support for these parties over the decade was 1.7 per cent, a positive figure to be sure, but one which should hardly be a cause for alarm. In other words, in c.1990 a little over 6.5 per cent of voters on average in the various West European democracies chose to support far-right parties, while by 2000 the figure had grown to slightly over 8 per cent. Nor do the data suggest a Europe-wide trend. The far right certainly expanded its electorate in Austria and Italy and grew modestly in Belgium, France, Denmark and Norway, but it declined somewhat or remained a negligible force elsewhere. Illustratively, the magnitude of the standard deviation in national levels of far-right voting, a measure of dispersion, increased markedly over the decade. For historical reasons Germany always remains a subject of intense scrutiny when it comes to right-wing extremism. Accordingly, during the 1990s, a period during which the entire electorate of the economically depressed, socially dislocated and formerly communist East Germany was incorporated in the Federal Republic, support for far-right parties grew by the end of the decade to a still modest 3 per cent of the electorate.[8] In general, it seems that support for far-right parties expanded measurably in the 1980s, but in more recent years it has tended towards slower growth, again with a handful of exceptions. We should view these findings against a background in which analysts have repeatedly stressed growing voter volatility and the electorate's disenchantment with the longstanding ruling parties in their respective countries.[9] As a consequence, we think that understanding the sources of variability in far-right voting may be of more theoretical interest than explaining the overall magnitude of its support in the electorate.

To return to our central concern: what then explains the variation in the level of far-right voting during the 1990s in the 14 Western European countries included in our analysis? Three well-known interpretations come to mind. They are by no means mutually incompatible but they do emphasize different aspects of the situation. Further, their proponents developed these interpretations as attempts to explain the overall level of voter support for far-right parties in the West European democracies, not their rise in some countries and their decline in others. As a consequence, these views should prove helpful but we should not expect them to represent a perfect fit between their goals and our objectives in this effort.

In their well-known formulation, the German political scientists Erwin Scheuch and Hans-Dieter Klingemann stress that right-wing radicalism represents a 'normal pathology' in all rapidly changing industrial societies.[10] There are elements in the population of such societies that are unable to cope with the economic changes and concomitant cultural and social dislocations. These 'losers' in the modernization or post-modernization process react with rigidity, closed-mindedness, elevated levels of xenophobia and by blaming minority groups for their plight. Such individuals constitute the base of electoral support for radical right parties in Europe and elsewhere.

If Sheuch and Klingemann place the emphasis on the explanatory power of social structure, Herbert Kitschelt's interpretation (our second hypothesis) on the other hand pays particular attention to party politics and the role of political leadership. Far-right parties do well at the polls, he reasons, when major parties of the conventional left and right move towards the centre or, better still, join each other in sharing power in a coalition government. Under these circumstances far-right parties are able to exploit popular dissatisfaction with the country's political establishment, and the accompanying system of spoils, to fill an electoral space vacated by the party/parties of the conventional right. The brief rise of the German NPD during the period of the 'Grand Coalition' between the CDU and Social Democrats (1966–69) offers an example of the kind of arrangements Kitschelt has in mind. The long-standing coalition between Austria's Christian Social and Social Democrats would be a better one. Another factor is the role of the political entrepreneur. For a far-right party to become electorally meaningful it needs a leader capable of recognizing and then exploiting the opportunities with which he or she is presented. The truculent Umberto Bossi, leader of Italy's LN, and France's Jean-Marie Le Pen use of street language (often including profanity) to communicate with large numbers of angry voters for whom the abstract rhetoric of conventional party politicians seems at once boring and inaccessible.

The third interpretation calls our attention to the role of values or a clash of values as an important basis of support for radical right parties. Much of this discussion was initiated by Piero Ignazi's argument about the resurgence of the far right representing a 'silent counter-revolution' in Western European politics. This view, in turn, was a response to Ronald Inglehart's well-known study of the rise of post-materialist values among younger, better-educated voters.[11] Inglehart maintained that support for green and left-libertarian parties was an expression of the values of this prosperous and environmentally conscious segment of the electorate. For Ignazi, the rise of new right-wing populist parties, such as Switzerland's anti-environmental Automobilist Party, represented a backlash against the essentially 'new left' or post-materialist values Inglehart identified. Parenthetically, if the contemporary far-right parties represent a backlash against post-materialism, we might expect the electoral performances of green and left-libertarian parties and right-wing populist parties to vary together: the higher the level of voter support for one, the higher for the other.

The case for the potential importance of values in promoting growth in support for far-right parties over the course of the 1990s is strengthened when we consider overall changes in the behaviour of Western European electorates. As Russell Dalton and other analysts note, with the achievement of higher levels of education and expanded exposure to the mass media,

European voters have become substantially more sophisticated than was the case earlier in the last century.[12] As one of the consequences of this develop-ment, the relationship between voters' background social characteristics, e.g., social class, income, religious affiliation, regional origins, and their voting preferences have become attenuated. Nowadays, voters in the Western Euro-pean democracies are more likely to vote on the basis of short-term attitudes and long-term value preferences. If this is the case, we would expect that the growth in support for far-right parties (for which we seek an explanation here) would be strongly associated with voters' subjective assessments of their environment.

The way in which we have sought to adapt the three alternative hypotheses described above for our purposes and explain national variations in voter support for far-right parties over the 1990s is as follows. First, we assembled and aggregated data at the national level for 14 West European countries.[13] Thus we are constructing our explanation based upon the national characteristics of the countries involved rather than the attributes, distinctive or otherwise, of far-right voters. In what type of national settings have far-right parties gained and lost the most support over the 1990s?

METHODOLOGY

In order to pursue our investigation we assembled data from a number of sources and then aggregated them, when necessary, at the national level. Two of our principal sources were the *World Value Survey*[14] and the *Political Data Handbook*.[15] Since our focus is on psychological variables, the coverage provided by the *World Value Survey* determined our sample – namely, Austria, Belgium, Denmark, Finland, France, Germany, Ireland, Italy, the Netherlands, Norway, Portugal, Spain, Sweden, Switzerland and the UK. We classified political parties in these 14 Western European democracies primarily upon the reputational rating scheme devised by Inglehart and Huber.[16] That is, experts from the respective nations rated all the parties in each system on a ten-point scale anchored by the labels 'left' and 'right'. Based upon the earlier work by Castles and Mair,[17] other expert sources, and our own knowledge, we then used the average ratings to sort the parties into far left, left, centre, right, and far-right categories. For this chapter, our focus will be exclusively on the far-right category (see Appendix 5.1).

A few more detailed observations about the variables included in the study are necessary. (A complete list is available from the authors.) Questions were selected from the *World Value Survey* on the basis of their plausible relationship to one or more 'theories' of ideological voting, particularly those mentioned previously. If we erred, we erred on the side of exclusivity. To compensate somewhat for the large number of relevant questions, we reduced them (when possible) to a smaller number of variables. Specifically, we used factor analysis and reliability analysis on sets of items with common format and content. When these techniques pointed to similar dimensionality and reliability across all 14 nations, we combined items into scales. We then constructed aggregate measures for both scales and single-item questions by calculating means and standard deviations (for some items, percentages were more appropriate). The calculations of standard deviations in addition to means is not a common practice. When discussing the process of aggregation, it occurred to us that, in addition to knowing and comparing the average values of variables across nations, it might also be useful to compare differences in variation across nations. Put another way, knowledge about the comparative homogeneity or heterogeneity of values and other psychological variables might prove equally informative. This proved to be the case.

Our source for many of the non-psychological variables was the second edition of the *Political Data Handbook*. Again we chose variables that were plausibly theoretically relevant and, when possible, values of those variables corresponding to the *World Value Survey 1990–1991* time-frame. Included were measures of population, social structure, employment, the economy, public finance, government structures and political communications. Most of these need no explication (a complete list is available from the authors). Two composite indexes might be noted. 'The Index of Social Progress consists of 44 welfare-relevant social indicators distributed among eleven sub-indices as follows: education, health, women's status, defense effort, economics, demography, geography, political stability, political participation, cultural diversity, and welfare effort.'[18] The Human Development Index 'is a composite measure of human development containing indicators representing three equally weighted dimensions … longevity (life expectancy at birth), knowledge (adult literacy and mean years of schooling), and income (purchasing power parity dollars per capita).'[19]

In addition to the *Handbook*, variables were extracted from a variety of other sources. Foreign resident population variables were taken from Fassman and Munz, 'Patterns and Trends of International Migration in Western Europe'.[20] Measures of decommodification and conservative, liberal and socialist welfare regimes came from the *Three Worlds of Welfare Capitalism* by Esping-Andersen.[21] The degree of corporatism was extracted from Lehmbruch's chapter in Goldthorpe's *Order and Conflict in Contemporary Capitalism*.[22] Income maintenance types and the feminist welfare classification were based on information in Hill's *Social Policy: A Comparative Analysis*.[23] Asylum-seeker

data was derived from an OECD migration publication.[24] The dispropor-
tionality indexes, effective number of political and parliamentary parties, and
frequency of parliamentary and manufactured majorities all came from
Lijphart's *Electoral Systems and Party Systems*.[25] Specific indicators of constitutional structure and a summed index of constitutional openness were taken
from Huber, *et al.*, 'Social Democracy, Christian Democracy, Constitutional
Structure, and the Welfare State'.[26] The two types of democratic regime dimensions and the number of issue dimensions came from Lijphart's *Democracies:
Patterns of Majoritarian and Consensus Government in Twenty-One Countries*.[27]

Expert estimates on a variety of policy issues and on a series of party-
system parameters (both means and standard deviations for the latter) were
taken from Laver and Hunt, *Policy and Party Competition*.[28] A number of
measures of electoral systems came from *Party System Change: Approaches and
Interpretations*, by Mair.[29] *Comparing Democracies: Elections and Voting in Global
Perspective* by LeDuc, *et al.* supplied measures of cleavage voting and issue
correlates of left/right attitudes and party preference.[30] An extensive set of
additional political variables was obtained from Lane and Ersson, *Politics and
Society in Western Europe*.[31] Measures of conflict among parties and left/
right change were drawn from Knutsen's 'Expert Judgements of the Left–
Right Location of Political Parties: A Comparative Longitudinal Study'.[32]
The remaining political and cultural variables were drawn from a variety of
sources.[33]

In the analysis that follows, we have relied on simple bivariate correlation
analysis. The small number of cases (14) makes the use of multivariate analysis
(that is, factor analysis and regression analysis) questionable at best. Although
these techniques and similar ones may be explored at a later date, for now it
seems wiser to rely on a more straightforward bivariate approach.

FINDINGS

Our findings provide some support for each of the three interpretations of
far-right voting we described at the beginning of this chapter, but not in
ways expected by their advocates. That is, we find that comparatively high
variations in far-right voting are positively associated with particular sets of
social values, certain national political conditions and a few measures of
national economic performance, but not exactly in ways we would have
anticipated given the hypotheses. This outcome is probably the inevitable
result of employing the nation as the fundamental unit of analysis rather than
the attributes of far-right voters themselves and of our focus on electoral
volatility rather than magnitude of support.

Having said this, high levels of change in far-right voting during the 1990s tended to occur in countries whose citizens expressed a distinct set of values and where there also existed significant levels of disagreement among some citizens with the views expressed by other citizens. So far as the latter is concerned, in addition to reporting the magnitude of the relationship between various social values and the variability of far-right voting when they meet conventional criteria of statistical significance, we have also (see above) recorded the standard deviations for these same linkages.

TABLE 5.2
RELATIONS BETWEEN VALUE MEANS AND FAR-RIGHT VOTING

Relationships between values and far-right voting

Far-right voting is higher in countries where:

People are more likely to believe that they have little freedom of choice and control over the way their lives turn out. (V95-mean)★ (−0.629)

People are more likely to be dissatisfied with their lives as a whole. (V96-mean) (−0.636)

People are more likely to say they are religious. (V151-mean) (−0.557)

People are not as likely to trust their own countrymen. (V341-mean) (0.545)

People are more likely to believe that 'Wealth can grow so there's enough for everyone' rather than 'People can only accumulate wealth at the expense of others'. (V256-mean) (0.668)

People were less likely to like to have as neighbours people of a different race, religion, or nationality. (V70,V74,V76,V77,V81,V82-mean) (−0.597)

People were less likely to agree that scarce jobs should be shared with disadvantaged groups such as women, the elderly, immigrants and the handicapped. (V.128 to V131-mean) (−0.675)

People are more likely to believe that if their countrymen live in need, it is because of laziness and a lack of willpower. (V97–V98) (0.614)

People are more likely to believe that owners should run their businesses or appoint managers rather than government or employees having a role. (V126) (0.547)

★Variable numbers refer to the *World Value Survey*.

It remains to be seen whether or not the societies in which the far right has risen the furthest over the last decade are experiencing a 'silent counter-revolution', but it does seem clear that, in the aggregate, they are relatively pessimistic, conservative ones (see Table 5.2). (Some observers might even say they are mean-spirited.) In countries where the far right's fortunes at the polls have shown the greatest variability, people tend both to believe that they have little control over the way their lives turn out (−0.629) and, at the same time, to express dissatisfaction with the direction their lives have taken

(–0.636). Feeling dissatisfied with themselves and relatively powerless to alter course, these citizens are inclined to be mistrustful of others in society (0.545) and to assign blame and wish to inflict punishment on others (0.614). They are inclined to blame others for their life situations while judging themselves blameless because they believe events determining their own lives are beyond their control. They are more likely to report being religious (–0.577) while simultaneously concluding that, if their fellow citizens are needy, it is the result of their own laziness and lack of will power (0.614) and that scarce jobs should not be shared with such disadvantaged groups as the elderly, immigrants and the handicapped (–0.675). And, it should hardly come as a surprise when we report that European societies in which the far right did well during the 1990s were ones where citizens tended to prefer not to have people of different racial, religious or national backgrounds as neighbours (–0.597).

Further, these are not national settings in which a consensus exists over the above value preferences. Variation in popular support for the far-right parties is highest where significant levels of dissent and disagreement exists over some of these same values. In particular (see Table 5.3), the far right is most volatile where the public exhibits strong disagreement over the desirability of living close to individuals of different racial or religious backgrounds (0.557), the fundamental questions of personal life satisfaction (0.614) and the ability to control the way their lives turn out (0.591).

TABLE 5.3

RELATIONSHIPS BETWEEN STANDARD DEVIATIONS OF VALUES AND
FAR-RIGHT VOTING

Far-right voting is higher in countries where:

There is greater variation among people in how much freedom of choice and control they believe they have over their lives. (V95–st. dev.) (0.591)*

There is greater variation among people in how satisfied they are with their lives as a whole. (V96–st. dev.) (0.614)

There is greater variation among people in how many children they believe constitutes an ideal family. (V213–st. dev.) (–0.555)

There is greater variation in respondents' estimated household income. (V363 – st. dev.) (–0.649)

There is greater variation in the extent to which people would like to have as neighbours people of a different race, religion, or nationality. (V70,V74,V76,V77,V81,V82–st. dev.) (0.577)

*Variable numbers refer to the *World Value Survey*.

The overall pattern then is of national volatility in voter support for radical right parties appearing in relatively unfriendly, punitive settings, but ones where significant members of the public disagree with one another over at least two important values: self-control and life satisfaction.

In some respects this characterization fits the countries' economic circumstances as well (see Table 5.4). We find that wide variation in the electoral performances of radical right parties during the 1990s occurred in countries that experienced higher levels of working days lost as the result of strikes and other industrial disputes (0.538). The context is also one in which citizens express strong opposition both to government ownership of business enterprises and to employees' playing a role in their management (co-determination) (0.547) (see Table 5.2). Respondents also reported greater variation in their estimated household incomes (−0.649) (see Table 5.3). Further, by Western European standards the welfare state measures in place are relatively less generous and display wider differences in benefits based upon occupational status than is true for countries where radical right voting is not as volatile (0.731). On the other side of the ledger, defence expenditure as a percentage of GDP is also significantly lower than in countries with more stability in far-right voting (−0.551). The same may be said in regard to general government debt (−0.636). The wider the variation in far-right voting, the lower is the debt as a percentage of GDP. These are clearly countries, in the aggregate, where the spirit of post Cold War economic enterprise prevails and which display wider than average differences in their citizens' economic status.

TABLE 5.4

RELATIONSHIPS BETWEEN ECONOMIC VARIABLES AND FAR-RIGHT VOTING

Far-right voting is higher in countries where:

Working days lost through industrial disputes are higher. (0.538)

Central government defence expenditures as percentage of GDP are lower. (−0.551)

General government deficit as percentage of GDP is lower. (−0.636)

Conservative welfare regime is in place (as measured by 'the degree to which social insurance is differentiated and segmented into distinct occupational- and status-based programmes' with 'large variations between the bottom and top in terms of benefits' and with privileges accorded civil servants relatively high.[a] (0.731)

Income maintenance type.[b] (−0.584)

Notes
a See Esping-Andersen, *The Three Worlds of Welfare Capitalism*, p. 69.
b A scheme similar to that of Esping-Andersen. See Hill, *Social Policy*, pp. 43–4.

When we examine the political correlates linked to wide variations in voter support for far-right parties, we are left with the impression that we are dealing with a syndrome or a single coherent and underlying factor (see Table 5.5). This is the case because the political characteristics of these countries fit so well with the social values their citizens express and with their economic attributes.

TABLE 5.5
RELATIONSHIPS BETWEEN POLITICAL VARIABLES AND FAR-RIGHT VOTING

Far-right voting is higher in countries where:

Average elected government duration is lower. (−0.619)

Salience to party leaders of taxes vs spending as an issue is lower (expert rating). (−0.556)

Salience to party leaders of religion as an issue is higher (expert rating). (0.560)

Cabinet portfolios valued more as rewards of office rather than as means to affect public policy. (0.649)

Cabinet members more likely to make public their disagreement with decisions. (0.652)

More variation in estimates of policy autonomy of cabinet members. (0.553)

More variation in estimates of frequency of cabinet assignment changes. (0.638)

Electoral participation is higher. (0.554)

Government durability (proportion of maximum time governments stay in power) is lower. (−0.577)

Voters in the countries in question were not apathetic during the 1990s. In fact, electoral participation was significantly higher than in states with less variation in far-right voting (0.554). Evidently, dissatisfaction with their lives and mistrust of their fellow citizens were not values that inhibited voters from casting their ballots. If electoral turnout was high, the durability of governments the voters selected was low (−0.619). Compared to states with more stable levels of support for far-right parties, we are dealing with countries where cabinet governments did not last long (as measured by the proportion of the maximum time governments were permitted to hold office before the next election cycle) (−0.577). Their relative brevity may in part have been the result of cabinet members not being reticent in criticizing one another (0.652). In the countries with wider variation in support for the far-right, members of the cabinet were thus more likely to attack one another in public and cabinet shuffles were relatively common (0.638). This, despite the fact that cabinet portfolios in these governments were more likely to be valued in personal terms as a tangible reward than as a means for influencing public policies (0.649).[34]

Austria, Belgium, France and Italy were the countries that most strongly embodied the collection of social values, economic conditions and political characteristics we have just described. (Denmark, Sweden and Switzerland were the least likely to display these traits – see Appendix 5.2.). In all four countries, far-right voting increased during the 1990s. And, perhaps unsurprisingly, recent survey evidence suggests that Austria, Belgium, France and Italy cluster together in other ways as well. Among other things, their citizens (except for France) tend to have less than average confidence in their public institutions. In addition, corruption in the public sphere is viewed by experts as being greater than the average for advanced industrial democracies.[35]

CONCLUSIONS

Our investigation has departed in two ways from most empirical studies of contemporary far-right party politics in Western Europe. First, instead of focusing on the magnitude of the far-right vote, we chose instead to pay attention to its variability over time. Our dependent variable, really a measure of the degree of volatility in far-right voting, reveals declines in some countries along with increases in others during the 1990s. (This was a time when many political scientists stressed the erosion of traditional voting patterns, the collapse or transformation of old social cleavages and the disappearance of such old political parties as the Italian Christian Democrats.)

Second, while many studies of far-right voting patterns aim at identifying the specific attributes of the new right-wing populist electorate, who votes for the new radical right and why, our strategy has been to consider the general conditions prevailing in the countries in which these parties participated in national elections during the last decade of the twentieth century. In other words, we have tackled the problem of the West European far-right from a somewhat different angle than many observers. Our findings inevitably reflect these differences in approach.

These findings suggest that the far-right vote has shown the greatest increase, at least in recent years, in socially and economically conservative nations whose highly individualized citizens express low levels of trust in others, and dissatisfaction with the direction their lives have taken. They are also prepared to express 'moral indignation' at the failings of others but not themselves and do not wish to have as neighbours people of different backgrounds.

In addition, the countries where these qualities are most prevalent – Austria, Belgium, France and Italy – appear to be highly contentious societies. There is widespread disagreement over important social values as well as in the economic and political realms. Strikes and other labour stoppages are common phenomena, while governments come and go at a substantially faster than normal pace. Moreover, the narrowly self-interested members of the various governments seem to have considerable difficulty in getting along with one another: witness the frequency with which they criticize each other in public forums. All these traits leave us with the impression of a not so silent counter-revolution against growing social pluralism and institutional weaknesses. They also add up to a less than flattering portrait of the societies involved.

APPENDIX 5.1
FAR-RIGHT PARTIES c. 1990 AND 2000★

	1990	*2000*
Austria	Freedom Party	Freedom Party The Independents
Belgium	Vlaams Blok Front National	Vlaams Blok Front National
Denmark	Progress Party	Progress Party Danish People's Party
Finland	Christian League	Christian League
France	Front National	Front National (diverse right wingers)
Germany	Republikaner New Democratic Party	Republikaner New Democratic Party German People's Union
Ireland		
Italy	National Alliance Lega Nord	National Alliance Lega Nord Social Movement Three Colour Flames
The Netherlands	Centre Democrats	Centre Democrats
Norway	Progress Party	Progress Party
Spain		
Sweden	New Democrats	
Switzerland	Swiss Motorists' League Swiss Democrats Federal Democratic Union	Swiss Democrats Federal Democratic Union
UK	British National Party	British National Party

★Only those parties are included which received a high enough percentage of the vote (usually 1 per cent) to be recognized as possibly significant. In most cases they were the only parties receiving votes.

APPENDIX 5.2
NUMBER OF TIMES EACH NATION REGISTERS AMONG THE TOP THREE
NATIONS IN THE FAR-RIGHT DIRECTION ACROSS THE 28 VARIABLES AND
AMONG THE TOP THREE IN THE NON-FAR-RIGHT DIRECTION

	Far Right	*Non-Far Right*	*Difference*
Austria	15	1	14
Belgium	12	0	12
Denmark	1	10	−9
Finland	4	8	−4
France	12	2	10
Germany	4	3	1
Ireland	4	6	−2
Italy	25	0	25
The Netherlands	3	3	0
Norway	2	8	−6
Spain	4	5	−1
Sweden	0	17	−17
Switzerland	1	13	−12
UK	2	6	−4

NOTES

1. For a recent example see N. Fraser, *The Voice of Modern Hatred* (Woodstock, NY: Overlook Press, 2001).
2. See, for example, T. Bjorgo and R. Witte (eds), *Racist Violence in Europe* (New York: St Martin's Press, 1993).
3. See, for example, P. Ignazi, 'The Silent Counter-Revolution', *European Journal of Political Research*, 22 (1992), pp.101–21.
4. For a discussion, see R. Eatwell, 'The Rebirth of the "Extreme Right" in Western Europe', *Parliamentary Affairs*, 53.3 (July 2000), pp. 407–25.
5. The most obvious examples are H.-G. Betz, *Radical Right-Wing Populism in Western Europe* (New York: St Martin's Press, 1994); H. Kitschelt, *The Radical Right in Western Europe* (Ann Arbor, MI: University of Michigan Press, 1995); and P. Ignazi, *L'Estrema destra in Europa* (Bologna: Il Mulino, 1994).
6. Betz, *Radical Right-Wing Populism*, pp.3–4.
7. Greece and Portugal, less economically developed members of the EU, have no competitive far-right parties. See, for example, T. Davis, 'The Iberian Peninsula and Greece', in H.-G. Betz and S. Immerfall (eds), *The New Politics of the Right* (New York: St Martin's Press, 1998), pp. 157–72.
8. On the limits of voter support for the far right in Germany, see *The Appeal of the Far*

Right (Washington, DC: European Branch, Office of Research, US Department of State, 2000), p. 5.

9. See, for example, R. Putnam, S. Pharr and R. Dalton, 'What's Troubling the Trilateral Democracies?', in S. Pharr and R. Putnam (eds), *Disaffected Democracies* (Princeton, NJ: Princeton University Press, 2000), pp. 3–27.

10. E. Scheuch and H.-D. Klingemann, 'Theorie des Rechtsradikalismus in westlichen Industrieesellschaften', *Hamburger Jahrbuch für Wirtschafts-und Gesellschaftspolitik*, 12 (1967), pp. 11–29. For an earlier expression of these ideas applied to the American case, see D. Bell, 'The Dispossessed', in D. Bell (ed.), *The Radical Right* (Garden City, NY: Doubleday, 1963), pp. 1–38.

11. See, for example, R. Inglehart, *The Silent Revolution* (Princeton, NJ: Princeton University Press, 1977), pp. 262–90.

12. See, for example, R. Dalton, *Citizen Politics in Western Democracies* (Chatham, NJ: Chatham House, 1988), pp. 200–2.

13. Austria, Belgium, Denmark, Finland, France, Germany, Ireland, Italy, Netherlands, Norway, Spain, Sweden, Switzerland and the UK. Portugal was not included because the law prohibits the participation of far-right parties in its national election contests.

14. World Values Study Group, World Values Survey, 1981–84 and 1990–93. 2nd ICPSR version (Ann Arbor, MI: Institute for Social Research [producer], 1999. Ann Arbor, MI: Inter-university Consortium for Political and Social Research [distributor], 1999).

15. J.-E. Lane, D. McKay and K. Newton, *Political Data Handbook: OECD Countries*, 2nd edn (New York: Oxford University Press, 1997).

16. J. Huber and R. Inglehart, 'Expert Interpretations of Party Space and Party Locations in 42 Societies', *Party Politics*, 1.1 (1995), pp. 73–111.

17. F. Castles and P. Mair, 'Left–Right Political Scales: Some Expert Judgements', *European Journal of Political Research*, 12 (1984), pp. 73–88.

18. Lane *et al.*, *Political Data Handbook*, p. 32.

19. Ibid., p. 33.

20. H. Fassman and R. Munz, 'Patterns and Trends of International Migration in Western Europe', in H. Fassman and R. Munz (eds), *European Migration in the Late Twentieth Century* (Laxenburg, Austria: International Institute for Applied Systems Analysis, 1994).

21. G. Esping-Andersen, *The Three Worlds of Welfare Capitalism* (Princeton, NJ: Princeton University Press, 1990), pp. 52, 74.

22. G. Lehmbruch, 'Concentration and the Structure of Corporatist Networks', in J.H. Goldthorpe (ed.), *Order and Conflict in Contemporary Capitalism* (Oxford: Clarendon Press, 1984), p. 66.

23. M. Hill, *Social Policy: A Comparative Analysis* (London: Prentice-Hall, 1996), pp. 44–5.

24. OECD, *Trends in International Migration Annual Report 1994* (Washington, DC: OECD Center), p. 195.

25. A. Lijphart, *Electoral Systems and Party Systems: A Study of Twenty-Seven Democracies 1945–1990* (New York: Oxford University Press, 1994), pp. 160–2.

26. E. Huber, C. Ragin and J.D. Stephens, 'Social Democracy, Christian Democracy, Constitutional Structure, and the Welfare State', *American Journal of Sociology*, 99.3 (1993), pp. 7111–49.

27. A. Lijphart, *Democracies: Patterns of Majoritarian and Consensus Government in Twenty-One Countries* (New Haven, CT: Yale University Press, 1984), p. 216.

28. M. Laver and W.B. Hunt, *Policy and Party Competition* (New York: Routledge, 1992).

29. P. Mair, *Party System Change: Approaches and Interpretations* (New York: Oxford University Press, 1997).

30. L. LeDuc, R. Niemi and P. Norris, *Comparing Democracies: Elections and Voting in Global Perspective* (Thousand Oaks, CA: Sage, 1991).

31. J.-E. Lane and S.O. Ersson, *Politics and Society in Western Europe* (Thousand Oaks, CA: Sage, 1994).

32. O. Knutsen, 'Expert Judgements for the Left–Right Location of Political Parties: A Comparative Longitudinal Study', *West European Politics*, 21.2 (April 1998), pp. 63–91.

33. Z.F. Arat, *Democracy and Human Rights in Developing Countries* (Boulder, CO: Lynn Riemer, 1991); D.Altman and A. Perez-Linan, 'Beyond Polyarchy: Measuring the Quality of Democracy', paper, annual meeting of the Midwest Political Science Association, April 1998; and M. Caldwell, 'Constitutional Structure and the Shaping of Welfare States', paper, annual meeting of the American Political Science Association, 1997.

34. See, for example, E. Browne and J. Dreijmanis (eds), *Government Coalitions in Western Democracies* (New York: Longman, 1982), pp.352–3.

35. See, especially, R. Dalton, 'Political Support in Advanced Industrial Democracies', in P. Norris (ed.), *Critical Citizens* (New York: Oxford University Press, 1999), p. 68; and D. della Porta, 'Social Capital, Beliefs in Government, and Political Corruption', in Pharr and Putnam (eds), *Disaffected Democracies*, p. 207.

CHAPTER SIX

The Development of the Extreme Right at the End of the Century*

Piero Ignazi

INTRODUCTION

IN THE last two decades of the twentieth century the extreme right re-emerged as a relevant phenomenon all over Europe. Before the 1980s only one party had gained continuous parliamentary representation since the first postwar elections – the Italian MSI – while two more parties, the Scandin-avian Progress Parties – the Danish FRPd and the Norwegian FRPn (formerly the Anders Lange Party) – had surfaced in the 1970s. One more entry may be represented by the National Action and the Republican Swiss parties, both located at the extreme right of the system.

In the other European countries, until the 1980s, the extreme right had shortlived and irrelevant manifestations. In Germany, after the spread of right-wing extremism in the first federal election – estimated at 10.1 per cent of the votes[1] – a 'second wave' of right-wing extremism emerged in the late 1960s when the NPD suddenly rose and entered most of the *Land* parlia-ments while failing to cross the 5 per cent hurdle at the 1969 Bundestag elections; mainly because of that, it disappeared immediately afterwards. In Austria the somewhat nostalgic VdU of the 1950s had progressively left room to more liberal-conservative components leading to the FPÖ and so depriving the Austrian extreme right of a solid representation. Norbert Burger's Austrian NDP was a very minor and unappealing substitute. In France, the Poujadist movement of 1956–58 has been frequently associated with the extreme right but it was of a different kind and lasted only two years. Otherwise, right extremism was dispersed in various tiny chapels. Finland experienced repeated attempts at a proto-fascist re-emergence, but

---

*Part of this paper revises the last two paragraphs of Chapter 12 in my recent book, *West European Extreme Right Parties* (Oxford: Oxford University Press, 1993).

no overt nostalgic party won parliamentary representation. In Britain, a factionalized and quarrelsome extreme right never escaped its absolute marginality. In Belgium and the Netherlands, there were only minor *groupuscules* and in Ireland and Sweden there were none. The late-comers into the democratic systems – the Mediterranean countries – had never shown any likelihood of recasting the old fascist-like forces: there were only isolated flare-ups without any impact on the party system in the late 1970s and afterwards.

Until the 1980s the extreme right had gained parliamentary representation only in four European countries; before the 1970s only the Italian MSI could boast parliamentary and local representatives. In the 1980s the extreme right made its breakthrough in six more countries: France above all, which gave the real impetus to this political family with the FN's resounding and stable performances over 10 per cent; Belgium and the Netherlands (the latter less than the former); Switzerland whose right extremism proliferated into various parties; Austria with the right extremist turn of Haider's FPÖ; and

TABLE 6.1
ELECTORAL TREND OF THE EXTREME RIGHT PARTIES BY COUNTRY
(1980–99)

	1980–89	*1990–99*	*1980–99*	*Difference* *1980–99/1990–99*
Austria	7.36	21.79	17.10	+14.61
Belgium	2.76	9.73	6.40	+6.97
Denmark	6.57	7.53	6.98	+0.96
France	6.53	13.60	9.36	+7.07
Germany	0.33	2.53	1.43	+2.20
Italy★	6.53	11.50	9.46	+5.15
The Netherlands	0.80	1.80	1.18	+1.00
Norway	7.06	10.80	8.56	+2.74
Sweden	–	2.70	2.70	+2.70
Switzerland	5.05	8.36	7.04	+3.31
Mean	4.28★★	9.05	7.02	+4.77

★Calculated excluding the LN. Where the LN was included the 1990–99 mean would have been 20.90 (+13.55) and the 1980–99 mean 15.08.
★★Calculated over the ten countries. Excluding Sweden the mean would be 4.75.
Source: Official sources.

Germany with the coming of the 'third wave' which became a constant nuisance for the political system after the 1989 European election, even if it never entered the Bundestag. The map is completed by the ephemeral success of the Greek ENEP, KP and then EPEN in the early 1980s in the European elections; by the isolated emergence of the Portuguese PDC/MIRN; and by election of Blas Pinar, the Fuerza nueva leader, to the 1979 Spanish Cortes. Taking into consideration also these latter marginal performances, only Britain, Ireland, Finland and Sweden had been immune to the extreme right resurgence in the 1980s: this was the decade of the extreme right spreading across Europe, the so-called browning of Europe.[2]

The 1990s, notwithstanding some retrenchments — the newly democratized Mediterranean countries have finally rid themselves of any sizeable right-extremist presence — the evolution of the former Italian bastion of the extreme right (the Italian MSI becoming a post-fascist party the AN) signalled the consolidation of this political family. In the 1990–99 decade, the mean percentage of the extreme right parties reached 10.9 per cent of votes compared to 4.7 per cent in the 1980s.

In sum, the extreme right parties have rearranged and reaffirmed themselves in the last 20 years (see Table 6.1). We may ask how different are they from the pre-1980s extreme right parties and what are the conditions which favoured their arrival and their persistence?

THE IMPACT OF POST-INDUSTRIALISM AND THE RECASTING OF THE EXTREME RIGHT

As I have already argued,[3] the 1980s represented a watershed in the history of right extremism because the revitalization of that political family implied *a change in its nature*. The ideological source of the postwar extreme right and, above all, of its major interpreter, the Italian MSI, depended on the old fascist theory and practice: fascism was the ultimate and unanimous reference. Since the arrival of the Scandinavian Progress parties — they were almost irrelevant in the European setting given the 'peripheral' nature of these countries and the peculiarity of the parties — and of the French FN, a new kind of ideological profile, or rather, of political discourse, has emerged. These parties denied any lineage from old fascism and the fascist regimes of the 1930s whereas, still in 1990, the MSI party leader, in his address to the National Congress, proclaimed 'the eternal and unchangeable values of fascism'.[4] They presented a new discourse which discarded positions such as the overthrow of the democratic setting, the primacy of the state, the authoritarian-corporatist socioeconomic architecture and the express adoption of violent means in politics. Nevertheless, notwithstanding these changes, their discourse maintained an anti-system profile as they displayed:

> those attitudes and behavior patterns that challenge in particular the *Rechtsstaat* [state of law] and its fundamental values and principles in favour of an organic view of society, an ethnically or racially-based concept of the nation, and an authoritarian view of politics and political leadership, often coupled with an anti-liberal and anti-communist bias.[5]

Anti-egalitarianism, anti-pluralism and anti-parliamentarism, albeit veiled or reframed, still represent the ideological core of the newly formed extreme right parties.

Following this approach, the extreme right family is made up of two ideal-types of party: the 'traditional' one, associated with the fascist tradition, and the 'post-industrial' one which denies any overt reference to fascism, display-ing instead a set of anti-liberal/anti-democratic beliefs, values and attitudes, all nurtured by the novel issues and needs of post-industrial society. The first type is fading away. The recent and incipient distancing of the AN from its fascist inspiration, plus the disappearance of the other neo-fascist parties, especially in the Mediterranean countries, leaves only the German NPD and the BNP to represent this tendency (with the DVU and VB on the margin of this type). The second type, on the other hand, comprises the vast majority of the present extreme right parties in Western Europe. This is not the only way to classify the internal variation of the extreme right parties. Various categorizations have recently been presented. They offer a valuable under-standing of the present nuances and streams within this political family. In this chapter, however, we will limit ourselves to emphasizing the divide between an old setting, where neo-fascist nostalgia dominated, and a new one where such nostalgia has been discarded and new ideas and perspectives have taken its place.[6]

The emergence of the latter type is related to the development of post-industrial society. The decline of the industrial economic sector and the relative weakening of the class conflict have left more and more room for 'value-based' conflicts. While for almost two decades, from the mid 1960s to the mid–late 1980s, this change has seemed to foster post-material leftward value systems, it has, *at the same time but underneath*, favoured a diverging political–ideological outcome.

More generally, the societal atomization and individualization that are consequences of the process of post-industrialization have provoked a two-fold and opposite reaction: on one side, an emphasis on individual *self-affirmation* – which, in turn, follow two different paths, the libertarian post-material line and the neo-conservative exaltation of individual economic entrepreneurship – and, on the other side, an emphasis on (individual and collective) *self-defence*. In the former case, the atomization process is counterbalanced by the mobilization of individual resources. In the latter case, the same process produced a demand for the recovery of 'organic solidarity', for the recasting of collective identities, for more integration. In fact, to take one example, where the crisis of conventional moral standards was greeted as a liberation event by the left-ward offspring of post-industrialism, the same issue was lamented as a negative occurrence by its right-wing counterpart.[7] The collapse of the social bonds produced by class and religious de-alignment – plus the decline in national identity via both the supranational institutions' growing role and globalization – coupled a vitalistic and self-directed reaction by the most affluent and educated part of the society, with the diffusion of a state of uncertainty and displacement within the less articulated strata.

The displacement and alienation consequent upon the development of post-industrial society, while denounced in the intellectual domain, were long discarded by the political discourse. Only when neo-conservatism arose did some of these questions get enough audience. Until then, they had remained 'silent' because of a lack of interpreters – contrary to what had happened on the left where new social movements and left-libertarian parties achieved the representation of the post-material constituencies.

The demand for physical security from crime and violence, for an (ethnically) homogeneous and harmonious community, and for strong, reassuring leadership and institutions (even at the cost of reducing the 'excessive' individual rights) reflects the need for being taken care of, being part of an aggregate, and being provided with an identity.[8] As these needs have fermented in Western countries for a while, that is since post-1968, without finding a political interpreter to represent them; they have propelled a sort of 'silent counter-revolution' in attitudes. The value set was changing on the right-wing side too, and the rapid diffusion of the neo-conservative mood was the first sign of such change. However, the surfacing of these sentiments of alienation and displacement could not be fully interpreted by the neo-conservatives; even the neo-conservative agenda did not, and could not, offer a fully satisfactory answer to the demands arising from the 'displaced and alienated' electoral constituency. Over and above the interplay between political supply and demand, the conservatives could not push the new issues brought to the political fore too far because of intrinsic political/ideological barriers. Only more radical parties could fully voice sentiments that reflected the demands of identity (hence nationalism), of homogeneity (hence xenophobia), of order, hierarchy and strong leadership (authoritarianism). And finally, only non-established parties could assault the democratic representative system by undermining its legitimacy because of failings, unaccountability, corruption, mismanagement, selfishness, etc.[9] As Kitschelt has argued:

> [the] new radical right stands for strong authoritarian-paternalist procedures and rejects participatory debate, pluralism based on equal worth of citizens' voices, tolerance for disagreements in the decision-making process and compromise between conflicting interests. In economics ... they advocate the spontaneous allocation of resources through market institutions but reject redistributive schemas. The state should be strong and authoritarian but small ...[10]

In short, the process which led post-industrial society has deepened the critical status of that section of the population (mainly self-employed and manual workers) who had suffered from the process itself. In particular, the loss of social bonds and the feeling of distance and isolation (*vis-à-vis* institutions and representative mechanisms) heightened sentiments of displacement and alienation and, potentially, of resentment.[11] These sentiments were transferred politically into the issues of tough law and order, national identity and pride, traditional moral standards, and state enforcement, all of which reflect the need for recasting a symbolic belonging, in other words, self-defence. These strains – rather than articulated demands – were unrepresented until the traditional cleavages had lost (part of) their salience in favour of a 'new axis of conflict' and until a new ideological discourse (neo-conservatism) had surfaced to voice them. This underground change in value priority, which has been labelled a 'silent counter-revolution', found its effective and authentic interpreters only when new political entrepreneurs in tune with these non-material rightward demands emerged by exploiting a favourable structure of opportunity.

Actually, the existence of an adequate political partisan offer in the extreme right domain was necessary too to meet the above mentioned demands.[12] Needed in particular was the pre-existence or rapid creation of an organizational structure to provide the potential electoral constituency with a strong sense of belonging; a clear-cut set of themes to identify the party and distinguish it from all the other parties; an appealing, charismatic and uncontested leadership which could prevent or control internal factionalism and catch media attention; and the strategic flexibility to exploit whatever favourable circumstances might arise. All the successful parties of the extreme right have displayed these characteristics. The strong and appealing leadership together with the highest adaptability to strategic needs have been the keys to success stories such as Jean-Marie Le Pen's FN, Jörg Haider's FPÖ,

Umberto Bossi's LN, Filip Dewinter's VB, Pia Kjaersgaard's FRPd, and Hagen's FRPn.

Finally, a recent empirical validation of this hypothesis asserts that:

> the new right is more responsive to contemporary politics than to the past. [The data confirms] the hypothesis of a silent counter-revolution and not of a resurgence of the older nostalgic fascist tradition. The electoral performances of left-libertarian and contemporary right-wing extremist parties have a lot more to do with one another ... Contemporary right-wing extremism and left-libertarianism go together and both appear to be the outgrowth of the current post-industrial circumstances in Western Europe.[13]

FACTORS OF DEVELOPMENT AND ENDURANCE

Many factors contribute to explaining the rise of extreme right parties. The electoral system (PR without hurdles versus plurality and/or majority) and especially the type (local and 'second order') and sequence of contested elections (the 'second order' elections before the most important ones) played a crucial role in the appearance and consolidation of the extreme right parties. Jackman and Volpert's empirical analysis found that a low electoral threshold, in a multiparty system, positively affects the extreme right parties' performance.[14]

The changing relationship between voters and parties brought about the breakthrough of new parties. The electoral and partisan indicators of de-alignment – higher volatility,[15] lower party identification[16] and party recruitment[17] – highlight the growing availability of voters for new political offers. A similar trend has been affecting party identification and party recruitment. The data shows that the rising curve of the 1980s[18] turned towards a steep decline in the 1990s. The number of party members has dropped everywhere in the established democracies[19] and the same goes for the level and intensity of party identification.[20]

Furthermore, the process of radicalization and polarization, together with the politicization of new, salient and misconceived issues, fostered the rise of extreme right parties. This occurred in particular in France, Germany, the Netherlands, Belgium, Sweden, Austria and, with some caveats, also in Denmark and Norway. Where radicalization and/or polarization decreased and no issue of the new right agenda was successfully politicized, as in Italy, Spain, Portugal, Greece[21] and Britain, the 'old' extreme right parties declined to the point of disappearing or were forced to change to survive, as in the Italian case.

One more factor seems at work in this framework. A factor which, to our understanding, is at the heart of the process of extreme right endurance: the 'crisis of legitimacy' of Western societies. The rationale for the linkage between decline of confidence in the system and performance of the extreme right is the following: the extreme right parties' peculiarity is not limited to their exclusionist, nationalist, or xenophobic agenda. It is also their opposition to the legitimizing bases of the liberal-democratic systems: individual freedom and representation through collective agencies (political parties), pluralism and managed conflict among individuals and groups, and human equality are under attack. The holistic and monistic political culture of the extreme right is antagonistic to the system. Well beyond their official and programmatic declarations, which cannot overtly stipulate any anti-democratic proposals, the extreme right parties – with the partial exception of the Scandinavian Progress Parties – nonetheless display an anti-system pattern. The German REP's adaptation to the prescriptions of the BVS in order to avoid a legal ban is a case in point. Thus, if the extreme right parties are 'anti-system' in this sense, their development might be linked to a crisis of confidence in the democratic system itself: whenever confidence declines, more opportunities are set up for these parties.

The thesis of a crisis of legitimacy has circulated since the mid 1970s, when the Frankfurt School's criticism of capitalist and consumerist society and the pending fiscal crisis of the state merged together, putting on trial the essence and the workings of the democratic system. A series of researches attempted to provide empirical ground for that common wisdom. Actually, democracy *per se*, as an ideal political system, proved to be accepted by the overall majority (around 95 per cent) across Western Europe.[22] On the other hand, however, satisfaction with the *workings of democracy* drew quite a lower percentage (57 per cent) with high fluctuation across time and countries.[23] The ratings of particular political institutions presented a rather worse picture:'less than half of the public in each nation expresses confidence in the national legislature, rating it eighth in the list of ten institutions'.[24] In short, while democracy as an ideal system (by contrast to authoritarianism or dictatorship) receives almost unanimous support, the evaluation of the political institutions and of system performance is more critical.

This overall positive picture darkens further when attention is focused upon the people located on the right-end side of the political continuum: in every country (Denmark differs in a couple of cases) *those located at the extreme right are less supportive of democracy*. Moreover, the supporters and/or voters for the extreme right parties are by far the most alienated *vis-à-vis* the democratic institutions and their workings. While the mass public has not shifted towards anti-system and antidemocratic attitudes, the politically alienated people are *concentrated on the right pole and in the extreme right parties.* Empirical evidence has been provided for Germany,[25] Austria[26] and the Scandinavian countries.[27] It has also been confirmed for Belgium,[28] the Netherlands,[29] France[30] and for Italy.[31]

Given the over-representation of extreme right voters among those dissatisfied with the system, the relationship between decline in the overall citizens' confidence in the system and extreme right success could be demonstrated. The case of France illustrates the working of such a relationship quite well: the confidence in the system and in the institutions (plus the more general life-satisfaction) was at the lowest point in 1984, precisely when the FN broke into the system.[32] In Germany, system support declined before 1989, setting the conditions for the success of the REP, and then German unification provided a sentiment of euphoria which depressed the REP. Its fortunes recovered when confidence went down again in 1992. The same applies for Norway where confidence sharply declined in 1985–89,[33] and in Austria after 1989,[34] in Denmark in 1970, in Belgium throughout the 1990s, in the Netherlands and in Italy in the early 1990s (Eurobarometer).

A comparative and more formalized assessment of this relationship is provided by Pia Knigge's test of the intention to vote for extreme right parties in Belgium, France, Italy, Denmark, Germany and the Netherlands and the public's dissatisfaction with the political regime in the ten years from 1984 to 1993.[35] This empirical analysis supports the political dissatisfaction thesis.[36] This consideration is further validated by a 12-country analysis which assesses that political dissatisfaction increases the likelihood of voting for the extreme right parties.[37] The centrality of this relationship has been more and more frequently recognized. Nonna Mayer, for example, has argued that 'the FN vote cannot be reduced to a racist or xenophobic vote, as it comes from a complex combination of motivations where the criticism of the parties and the political system has the same weight as the demand for a national preference'.[38]

If we go beyond the assessment of the working of democracy, which proved not so negative, and enquire about the attitudes regarding the 'linkage agents' of the democratic system – political parties and politicians – the picture becomes quite gloomy. On one hand, the 'increasing public skepticism of political elite appears to be a common development in many advanced industrial democracies'.[39] This anti-establishment mood[40] is reinforced by a diffuse 'anti-party sentiment':[41] 'There is a wide gap of confidence between the elites of the established parties and their electorate'.[42] This loss of trust affects, to varying degrees, the whole of Europe (with the exception of the British Isles). In Germany, new words have been coined to express this sentiment, *Parteiverdrossenheit* (disaffection with party) and *Politikverdrossenheit* (alienation from politics).[43] In Belgium, the Netherlands and Austria the consociational role of parties has come under attack. In France the loss of confidence dates back to the early 1980s[44] and the trend has been inverted only very recently.[45] In Italy the absence of confidence in parties and politicians (and politics in general) represents an enduring element of national political culture (see the seminal Almond and Verba[46] and more recently Morlino and Tarchi[47]). In Scandinavia, finally, the emergence of the extreme right parties (1973 in Denmark and Norway, 1991 in Sweden) has also been related to 'the fact that the electorate in Denmark, Norway and Sweden was influenced by feelings of distrust towards politicians'.[48]

This creeping and widespread sentiment needed political entrepreneurs in order to be represented. Once more, as in the case of the new right agenda, the extreme right parties were, and are, the best-qualified for expressing the anti-party sentiment. Extreme right parties are anti-party because in their genetic code one finds the ideal of 'harmonious unity' and the *horror vacui* of divisions: the national, local or ethnic *community* must be preserved against any sort of division. Pluralism is extraneous to the extreme right political culture: unity, strength, harmony, nation, state, *ethnos*, *Volk* are the recurrent references. The individual never attains his own specificity: individual self-affirmation pertains to liberalism and therefore is totally alien to the political culture of extreme right parties. Extreme right parties seek a national or subnational collective identity. They cannot conceive of a community where people are not 'similar' one to another, because differences would entail division. And as division is the essence of liberal-democracy, their search for unity and identity leads them to conflict with the principles of the democratic system. This search does not come from 'fascist' inspiration. It is the byproduct of a (widely shared) worldview that society must be a harmonious community. What else should the rationale for xenophobic messages be? With very minor exceptions no one supports biological racism any longer. The answer lies in the adherence to a monistic worldview, to anti-pluralism. And what are the natural targets of anti-pluralism? Political parties at the political level and foreigners at the social level.

The distrust in politicians and parties (both established parties and the party *per se*) in fact permeates the extreme right political discourse. Parties and politicians are the target of the populist messages of the extreme right. The French FN leader, Jean-Marie Le Pen, used to address the four established French parties as the 'gang of four' emphasizing the extraneousness of the FN to that 'club'. The same goes for all the other leaders of the extreme parties, from Haider to Dewinter, from Bossi to Karlsson, from Glistrup and Kjaersgaard to Lange and Hagen, from Ferret to Schoenhuber, from Frey to

Janmaat. Only the MSI rather deviates on this point.[49] The attitudes of the FN voters are in tune with such feelings: 58 per cent, against a national mean of 36 per cent, think that the politicians do not care for people like the average voter on the street.[50] The FPÖ voters pointed out that the most important motive for voting for Haider's party was precisely the extraneousness of that party to the other parties' scandals and privileges. The Glistrup party 'tried to undermine the legitimacy of the regime of the old parties'[51] by voicing anti-political feelings as long as its Norwegian sister-party did. In Belgium and the Netherlands, anti-party statements flowed from the party pro-grammes of the VB and of the CD and CP/CP '86.[52] All this sketchy evidence supports the relationship between the diffusion of an anti-party sentiment and the growth of the extreme right parties.

PROLETARIZATION AND RADICALIZATION, OR APPEASEMENT AND EMBOURGEOISEMENT?

The 1980s represented a watershed in the history of the postwar extreme right. In that decade the political landscape of the right-wing pole changed. The French FN emerged from a 'decade of darkness and sarcasm', as Le Pen declared after the 1984 European elections, and became a prominent party in the French political system. In a few years, newly born parties such as the Belgian FN and the German REP, or pre-existing ones such as the Belgian VB, the Dutch CD and, above all, the Austrian FPÖ, followed the French example. With national variations, all represented hostility to their repre-sentative liberal–democratic institutions, both because of their malfunction-ing *and* their intrinsic features: therefore, the extreme right parties played upon the advocacy of traditional *and* reframed right extremist issues centred on ethnocentrism, authoritarianism and moral traditionalism, distrust towards the establishment, the traditional parties, the politicians, and more generally, party politics itself.

The rise of extreme right parties was linked to their capacity for mobil-izing resources (citizens unsupportive of the system, alienated from politics, attentive to non-politicized issues such as immigration, law and order enforcement, morality and national identity) by political entrepreneurs who exploited a favourable structure of opportunity at the political level (system polarization and radicalization) and at the cultural level (the rise of a neo-conservative movement in the intellectual elite with its impact on mass beliefs).

At the end of the century, with the exception of Ireland, Britain, Sweden (plus the questionable case of Finland) and the Mediterranean countries, the extreme right parties took hold. Strongholds of the extreme right have moved north. The transformation of the MSI/AN into something different but predictably away from this political family has reduced the significance of the Italian example, although there is still a question mark pending over the LN). On the other hand, Spain, Portugal and Greece are still missing in the new extreme right landscape. With the recent crisis of the French extreme right, moreover, even this remaining Mediterranean country is losing its signal role. Austria's FPÖ now leads the group, followed by the Norwegian FRPn, the VB, the new Danish DFP, the surviving FN (and its minor splinter party, Bruno Megret's MNR), the FNb, the Swiss SD, FDP and Tessin League, and the German – electorally weak but militant – REP, DVU and NPD. After its recent electoral fiasco, the Dutch CD is going to dissolve, the BNP manages to survive in absolute marginality as before, and the Swedish NyD has followed the typical flash party fate. In the last 20 years postwar neo-fascism has almost disappeared. With the exception of the BNP and the NPD (plus the questionable cases of DVU and VB), by now no other party could be defined as a truly neo-fascist party.

The diverging development of new 'post-industrial' parties and traditional, neo-fascist parties is, in a way, related to their different historical origin: the former are the offspring of the present post-industrial society, and they reflect demands and needs that are different from those which nurtured the neo-fascist parties. The post-industrial extreme right parties are the byproduct of dissatisfaction with government policies on issues such as immigration and crime and, at a more profound level, of their uneasiness in a plural, conflicting, multicultural and globalizing society, while they dream of a monist, well-knit and identity-providing (idealized) society.

In the most recent years, we can discern a two-fold development. On one side, some parties (the Norwegian FRPn, the Italian AN and, partly, the newly born French MNR) have gone along a path of 'moderation' and the search of an agreement with the conservative right. The same path seems followed less convincingly, for mere tactical reasons, by the FPÖ and the LN because of their entry into their respective governments. On the other hand, the majority of the extreme right parties have fostered a spiral of 'radicalization' leading to sharper confrontations with the 'system' and to offering themselves as the only and ultimate alternative 'for the sake of the country'. This diverging strategy has rewarded both groups and it is difficult to assess which option will prevail.

However, both the accommodating and the confrontational parties share (with the major exception of the AN) the same transformation in the sociodemographic profile of their supporters. The larger parties of the 1990s – FN, FPÖ, VB, LN, Progress parties and their offspring – plus the German,

Dutch and British ones have all become 'workers' parties'. In some cases, the quota of blue-collar and low-income people is even larger than in the socialist parties. The massive presence of working-class people in the extreme right electorate is the most novel aspect compared to the 1980s. Except for the German REP, party supporters are predominantly male and young.

This sociodemographic profile reinforces the impression that the extreme right parties are no longer the collectors of the protest votes of those moderate sectors (employees, professionals, middle-aged), radicalized by dissatisfaction with the mainstream conservative parties and willing to 'send them a signal'. Instead, the present extreme-right voters represent a specific constituency mobilized by feelings of alienation towards the political system and dissatisfaction towards the socioeconomic dynamics of postmodernization and globalization, which they do not control and feel excluded from. This constituency is mainly composed of the weakest strata of the 'risk society'. Their feeling of powerlessness and marginality finds an echo in the populist anti-establishment and anti-system appeals, fostered by the extreme right parties.

The political–electoral development of this political family has thrived during the last years of the twentieth century. Its persistence and further development is basically related to the overall deepening of the 'crisis of confidence' in the political institutions, including parties, politicians and politics *tout court*.[53] The mistrust towards political institutions and their performance produces that sentiment of alienation and detachment which leads either to the rejection of politics (abstentionism is the most direct manifestation) or to radical anti-system options of which the support for the extreme right is one of the outcomes. The latter is so attractive nowadays because it permits the highest expression of extraneousness to the system and offers a world apart from the political mainstream. Even more appealing is the perspective of a new integration in an ethnoreligious homogeneous and holistic community – at national or subnational levels – tied up with strong and hierarchical social relationships within the boundaries of a *völkisch* community.

The post-industrial development of the Western societies and its most recent supranational tendencies, both economically and politically, have displaced a growing constituency of people whose lack of confidence in the face of such a development has directed them to embrace an anti-liberal (authoritarian), anti-pluralist (monistic), and anti-egalitarian (xenophobic) worldview: precisely that offered by the extreme right parties. Whether these parties will cease to emphasize their rejection of the political and economic systems (as in the case of the Norwegian FRPn, the Italian AN and the newly born French MNR) or not, is the question for this new century.

NOTES

1. See R. Stoess, *Politics Against Democracy* (New York/Oxford: Berg, 1991); and P.H. Merkl [1988:AQ]

2. See C.Ysmal, 'The Browning of Europe: Extreme Right Parties in the 1989 European Election', paper delivered at the ASAP meeting, San Francisco, CA, 1989.

3. See P. Ignazi, 'The Silent Counter-Revolution: Hypotheses on the Emergence of Extreme Right-Wing Parties', *European Journal of Political Research*, 22 (1992), pp. 3–34; Ignazi, 'New Challenges: Post-Materialism and the Extreme Right', in M. Rhodes, P. Heywood and V. Wright (eds), *Developments in West European Politics* (London: Macmillan, 1997), pp. 300–19; Ignazi, 'The Extreme Right in Europe: A Survey', in P. Merkl and L. Weinberg (eds), *The Revival of Right-Wing Extremism in the Nineties* (London: Frank Cass, 1997), pp. 47–64.

4. See Ignazi, *Il Polo Escluso: Profilo del Movimento Sociale Italiano*, 2nd edn (Bologna, Il Mulino, 1998).

5. M. Minkenberg, *Die Neue Radikale Rechte im Vergleich: USA, Frankreich, Deutschland* (Opladen/Weisbaden: Westdeutscher Verlag, 1998).

6. See P. Perrineau, *Le Symptôme Le Pen* (Paris: Fayard, 1997), pp. 343–9; N. Mayer, *Le Français qui votent Le Pen* (Paris: Flammarion, 1999), pp. 18–19; J. Billet and H. de Witte, 'Attitudinal Dispositions to Vote for a "New" Extreme Right-Wing Party: The Case of "Vlaams Blok"', *European Journal of Political Research*, 27 (1995), pp. 181–202; H.-G. Betz, 'The New Politics of Resentment: Radical Right-Wing Populist Parties in Western Europe', *Comparative Politics*, 25 (1993), pp. 413–27; M. Swyngedouw, 'Les nouveaux clivages dans la politique belgo-flamande', *Revue française de science politique*, 45 (1995), pp. 775–90; and H. Kitschelt (with A.J. McGann), *The Radical Right in Western Europe: A Comparative Analysis* (Ann Arbor, MI: University of Michigan Press), p. 43.

7. See Ignazi, 'The Silent Revolution'; Betz, 'The New Politics of Resentment'; M. Minkenberg, 'The New Right in Germany: The Transformation of Conservatism and the Extreme Right', *European Journal of Political Research*, 22 (1992), pp. 53–68; Minkenberg, *Die Neue Radikale Rechte im Vergleich*; and Kitschelt, *The Radical Right in Western Europe*; Minkenberg, 'Context and Consequence: The Impact of the New Radical Right on the Political Process in France and Germany', *German Politics and Society*, 16 (1998), pp. 1–23.

8. See Z. Bauman, *Globalization: The Human Consequences* (New York: Columbia University Press, 1998).

9. See Ignazi, 'The Silent Counter-Revolution'; and Minkenberg, *Die Neue Radikale Rechte im Vergleich*.

10. Kitschelt, *The Radical Right in Western Europe*, p. 20.

11. See Betz, 'The Politics of Resentment'; and Betz, *Radical Right-Wing Populism in Western Europe* (New York: St Martin's Press, 1994).

12. See Kitschelt, *The Radical Right in Western Europe*; J. Veugelers, 'A Challenge for Political Sociology: The Rise of Far-Right Parties in Contemporary Western Europe', *Current Sociology*, 47, 4 (1999), pp. 78–105; and Veugelers, 'Social Cleavage and the Revival of Far-Right Parties: The Case of France's National Front', *Acta Sociologica*, 40 (1997), pp. 31–49.

13. L.B. Weinberg, L.E. Eubank and A.R. Wilcox, 'A Brief Analysis of the Extreme Right in Western Europe', Department of Political Science, University of Reno, Nevada (mimeo), p. 8.

14. R. Jackman and K. Volpert, 'Conditions Favouring Parties of the Extreme Right in Western Europe', *British Journal of Political Science*, 26 (1996), pp. 501–21; esp. 515–16.

15. See P. Mair, 'In the Aggregate: Mass Political Behaviour in Western Europe', in H. Keman (ed.), *Comparative Democratic Politics* (London: Sage, 2002), pp. 122–40.

16. R. Dalton, *Citizen Politics* (Chatham: Chatham House, 1996); and P. Norris (ed.), *Critical*

Citizens (Oxford: Oxford University Press, 1999).

17. See P. Mair and I. van Biezen, 'Party Membership in Twenty European Democracies, 1980–2000', *Party Politics*, 7 (2001), pp. 5–21.

18. See R. Katz and P. Mair (eds), *How Parties Organize* (London: Sage, 1994); and P. Mair, *Party System Change: Approaches and Interpretations* (Oxford: The Clarendon Press, 1997).

19. See Mair and van Biezen, 'Party Membership'.

20. See Dalton, *Citizen Politics*; and Norris, *Critical Citizens*.

21. See L. Morlino and R. Montero, 'Legitimacy and Democracy in Southern Europe', in R. Gunther, N.P. Diamandouros and H.-J. Puhle (eds), *The Politics of Democratic Consolidation: Southern Europe in Comparative Perspective* (Baltimore, MD/London: Johns Hopkins University Press, 1995), pp. 231–60.

22. See D. Fuchs, G. Guidorossi and P. Svensson, 'Support for the Democratic System', in H.-D. Klingemann and D. Fuchs (eds), *Citizens and the State* (Oxford: Oxford University Press), pp. 325–53; esp. p. 349.

23. Ibid., p. 341.

24. See Dalton, *Citizen Politics*, p. 269.

25. See D. Fuchs, 'Trends in Political Support', in D. Berg-Schlosser and R. Rytlewski (eds), *Political Culture in Germany* (London: Macmillan, 1993), pp. 262–3; Minkenberg, *Die Neue Radikale Rechte im Vergleich*; R. Stœss and O. Niedermayer, *Rechtsextremismus, politische Unzufriedenheit und das Wählerpotential rechtsextremer Parteien in der Bundesrepublik im Frühsommer 1998*, Arbeitspapiere des Otto-Stammer-Zentrums No. 1 (Berlin: Berlin Free University, 1998); Stœss, 'Rechtsextremismus und Wahlen 1998', in J. Meckenburg (ed.), *Braune Gefahr: DVU, NPD, REP, Geschichte und Zukunft* (Berlin: Elefanten Press, 1999), pp. 146–76; and H.-G. Jaschke, 'Die Rechtsextremen Partein nach der Bundestagswahl 1998: Stehen sie sich selbst im Wege?', in O. Niedermayer (ed.), *Die Parteien nach der Bundestagswahl 1998* (Leverkusen: Leske-Budrich, 1999), pp. 141–57.

26. See K.R. Luther, 'Austria: From Moderate to Polarized Pluralism', in D. Broughton and M. Donovan (eds), *Changing Party Systems in Western Europe* (London: Pinter, 1999), pp. 118–42; and M. Riedlsperger, 'The Freedom Party of Austria: From Protest to Radical Right Populism in Betz', in H.-G. Immerfall and S. Immerfall (eds), *The New Politics of the Right* (New York: St Martin's Press, 1998), pp. 27–43.

27. See H.-J. Nielsen, 'The Uncivic Cultures: Attitudes towards the Political System in Denmark and the Vote for the Progress Party, 1973–1975', *Scandinavian Political Studies*, 2 (1976), pp. 47–155, esp. pp. 149ff.; J.G. Andersen and T. Bjørklund, 'Radical Right-Wing Populism in Scandinavia: From Tax Revolt to Neo-Liberalism and Xenophobia' (forthcoming); and M.P.J. Gooskens, 'How Extreme are the Extreme Right Parties in Scandinavia?' MA thesis, University of Leiden, 1993.

28. See M. Swyngedouw, M. Beerten and J. Kampen, 'De vernaderingen in de samenstilling van de kiezerskorpsen 1995–1999', *ISPO Bulletin*, 35 (1999).

29. See J. Tillie and M. Fennema, 'A Rational Choice for the Extreme Right', *Acta Politica*, 33 (1998), pp. 223–49, esp. p. 239.

30. See P. Brechon and B. Cautres, 'La cuisante défaite de la droite moderé', in P. Perrineau and C. Ysmal (eds), *Le vote surprise* (Paris: Presses de Sciences Po, 1998), pp. 225–51.

31. See P. Ignazi, *Il potere dei partiti: La politica in Italia dagli anni Sessanta ad oggi* (Bari: Laterza, 2002).

32. See Mayer, *Ces française qui votent Le Pen*, p. 213.

33. See H.A. Miller and O. Listhaug, 'Ideology and Political Alienation', *Scandinavian Political Studies*, 16 (1993), pp. 167–92.

34. See Luther, 'Austria: From Moderate to Polarized Pluralism'.

35. See P. Knigge, 'The Ecological Correlates of Right-Wing Extremism in Western Europe', *European Journal of Political Science*, 34 (1998), pp. 249–79.

36. Ibid., p. 271.

37. See R. Gibson and T. Swenson, 'The Politicization of Anti-Immigrant Attitudes in

Western Europe: Examining the Mobilization of Prejudice among the Supporters of Extreme Right-Wing Parties in EU Member States, 1988 and 1994'. Paper presented at the 95th Annual Meeting of the American Political Science Association, Boston, MA, 1999.

38. See Mayer, *Ces française qui votent Le Pen*, p. 149.
39. See Dalton, *Citizen Politics*, p. 269.
40. See A. Schleder, 'Anti-Political-Establishment Parties', *Party Politics*, 2 (1996), pp. 291–312; and Y. Meny and Y. Surel, *Par le peuple, pour le peuple* (Paris: Fayard, 2000).
41. See T. Poguntke and S. Scarrow (eds), 'The Politics of Anti-Party Sentiment', *European Journal of Political Research*, Special Issue no. 29 (1996).
42. See K. Deschouwer, 'Political Parties and Democracy: A Mutual Murder', *European Journal of Political Research*, 30 (1996), pp. 263–78, esp. p. 276.
43. See S. Scarrow, 'Politicians against Parties: Anti-Party Arguments as Weapons for Change in Germany', *European Journal for Political Research*, 29 (1996), pp. 297–317, esp, pp. 309ff.
44. See Mayer, *Ces française qui votent Le Pen*; and R. Cayrol, *Le grand Malentendu: Les Française et la politique* (Paris: Seuil, 1994).
45. See P. Ignazi and P. Perrineau, 'L'extrême droite en Europe: marginalité du néo-fascisme et dynamique de l'extrême droite post-industrielle', in G. Grunberg, P. Perrineau and C. Ysmal (eds), *Le Vote de Quinze: Les élections européennes du 13 juin 1999* (Paris: Presses de Sciences, 2000), pp. 223–42.
46. G. Almond and S. Verba, *The Civic Culture* (Boston, MA: Little, Brown and Co., 1963).
47. L. Morlino and M. Tarchi, 'The Dissatisfied Society: The Roots of Political Change in Italy', *European Journal of Political Research*, 30 (1996), pp. 41–63.
48. See Goosken, 'How Extreme are the Extreme Right Parties in Scandinavia?', p. 17; and Andersen and Bjørklund, 'Radical Right-Wing Populism in Scandinavia'.
49. See Ignazi, *Il Polo Escluso*.
50. See Perrineau, *Le Symptôme Le Pen*, pp. 116–18.
51. See L. Bille, 'Denmark: The Oscillating Party System', *West European Politics*, 12 (1989), pp. 42–58, esp. 49.
52. See Swyngedouw, 'Les nouveau clivages'; C. Mudde, 'The War of Words: Defining the Extreme Right Party Family', *West European Politics*, 19 (1996), pp. 225–48; Mudde, 'The Extreme Right Party Family', PhD thesis, Leiden University, 1998; and R.B.J. de Witte, 'De onbegrepen Verkiezingsuitslag voor extreem-rechts', *Acta Politica*, 16 (1991), pp. 449–70.
53. See Norris, *Critical Citizens*; also M. Dogan, 'Déficit de la confiance dans les démocraties avancées', paper presented at the sixth national conference of the Association Française de Science Politique, Rennes, 28 September–1 October 1999.

Part 3
Changing National Contexts

The Front National in Context: French and European Dimensions

Michael Minkenberg and Martin Schain

INTRODUCTION

IN THIS chapter we look at the French FN from a comparative perspective. Although the emergence of this party of the radical right must be understood in the context of the dynamics of the French party system, its development should also be understood in comparative context in two different ways.

First, cross-nationally, these parties have developed in Western European societies at a time of transition into what has been termed 'post-industrial society'. Voter attachments to both left and right have been undermined by a restructuring of the labour force and by severe challenges to traditional forms of national identity. The restructuring of the labour force has not only meant the decline of smokestack industry in favour of the service sector, but also a growing cleavage between workers involved in the emerging global economy and those who work in the public sector and more nationally oriented business and industry. Europeanization and globalization have shifted the influence and power of associational interest groups, and have challenged traditional political loyalties.

Second, these same trends have challenged traditional forms of national identity in every European country. The accelerated process of European integration has embedded French identity in an emerging EU that is both political and economic. Problems of democratic deficit in France have been accentuated by the even more severe problems of democratic deficit on the European level. However, these same problems of democratic responsibility have been noted in every European country. Moreover, the growing globalization of European economies has encouraged a political rhetoric that appears to narrow political alternatives sharply, and question the ability of national governments to develop and maintain their own social agendas.

These similar socioeconomic and sociocultural trends, however, have been processed differently through the political system of each country. This presents us with a crucial comparative question: how and why the radical right has emerged and developed in different ways in different countries. In the following sections, we look first at the common context from which the radical right has emerged. We then look at how these common factors have been processed in the French political and party system: the electoral emergence of the radical right; the forms it has taken and not taken; the dynamic impact on the party system, agenda formation and public policy.

A CONCEPT OF THE NEW RADICAL RIGHT

In this chapter the new radical right is conceptualized here as a radical reaction to fundamental social and cultural changes in postwar Western societies.[1] In addition, the radical right, in general, is understood first as a collective actor (that is, a political party and/or a social movement), with a specific ideological core or collective identity, and as a complex network of right-wing political entrepreneurs, ideologues and various political groups.

For a workable definition of right-wing radicalism in comparative perspective, it seems preferable to avoid the shopping-list quality of most definitions and tie it to theoretical concepts of social change which underlie most analyses of the radical right. Here, modernization theories are useful since they provide some conceptually grounded criteria for such analyses. A promising starting point is Dieter Rucht's concept of modernization, which he broadly understands as a growing autonomy of the individual (status mobility and role flexibility) and an ongoing functional differentiation of the society (segmentation and growing autonomy of societal subsystems).[2] In this context, right-wing radicalism can be defined as the radical effort to *undo* such social change. The counter-concept to social differentiation is the nationally defined community; the counter-concept to individualization is the return to traditional roles and status of the individual in such a community. It is this overemphasis on, or radicalization of, images of social homogeneity which characterizes radical right-wing thinking.

Ideology

At the core of right-wing radicalism is thus a political ideology, the key element of which is a myth of a homogenous nation, a romantic and populist ultra-nationalism which is directed against the concept of liberal and pluralistic democracy and its underlying principles of individualism and universalism. The nationalistic myth is characterized by the effort to construct an idea of nation and national belonging by radicalizing ethnic, religious, cultural and political criteria of inclusion/exclusion and to condense the idea of nation into an image of extreme collective homogeneity.

An explanatory approach of the success of right-wing radicalism, which dwells on these aspects of nationalism and modernization theory, and which follows earlier work by Theodore W. Adorno and Seymour M. Lipset, is provided by German sociologists Erwin Scheuch and Hans-Dieter Klingemann.[3] Their model is based on the assumption that the potential for radical right-wing movements exists in all industrial societies and should be understood as a 'normal pathological' condition. In all fast-growing modernizing countries there are people who cannot cope with economic and cultural dislocation, and who react to the pressures of readjustment with rigidity and closed-mindedness. These reactions can be mobilized by right-wing movements or parties offering political philosophies that promise an elimination of pressures and a simpler, better society. These philosophies do not contain just any utopia but a romanticized version of the nation before the first large wave of modernization. The core of the problem consists of a specifically a-synchronous dealing with the past, especially a dissent about the evaluation of modernity in the respective societies.

Structures

Starting from the concept of party (or movement) 'families',[4] it is important to ask the questions: 'What are the conditions under which the radical right manifests itself in the form of a movement rather than a party?', and 'To what extent do other organizational forms of the radical right support or constrain the particular organization's mobilization efforts?'[5]

The field of right-wing collective actors is structured in terms of ideological variations and organization types (see Table 7.1). The ideological types are derived from the respective concept of nation and the exclusionary criteria applied. Thus, authoritarian-fascist, classical racist (including colonialist), xenophobic or ethnocentric, and religious-fundamentalist versions can be distinguished. All four variants have in common a strong quest for internal homogeneity of the nation and populist, anti-establishment political style but the latter two share the characteristic of a culturally defined rejection of differences which informs the 'ethnocratic' ideology especially of the new radical right.[6] The organizational variants are distinguished by their approach to institutional political power and public resonance. Parties and electoral campaign organizations participate in elections and try to win public office. These are the most visible and politically relevant right-wing radical organizations. In Western Europe, 19 radical right-wing political parties were established between 1965 and 1995, with half of them gaining an average of at least 4 per cent in national or European elections in the 1980s and 1990s.[7]

But the focus on political parties alone obscures other organizational variants of the radical right which are significant on their own, or in terms of their interaction with the party spectrum. Among the non-party types, we distinguish two. Social movement organizations also try to mobilize public support, but do not run for office; rather they identify with a larger social movement (a network of networks with a distinct collective identity) and offer interpretative frames for particular problems.[8] Smaller groups and sociocultural milieux, on the other hand, operate relatively independently from either parties and larger social movements and do not exhibit formal organizational structures, but can also be characterized as networks with links to other organizations and a collective identity which is more extreme than that of the parties or movement organizations (including higher levels of militant protest or violence). They represent a 'micro-mobilization potential' for the radical right,[9] and in terms of their strength, they seem to be in an inverse relationship with political parties. Where radical right-wing parties are strong, independent subcultural milieux tend to be underdeveloped (for example France, Italy, Austria); where those parties are weak or fragmented, they tend to evolve more (UK, Germany, Sweden).

In light of the notion that the mobilization of the radical right occurs often in times of accelerated social and cultural change, or functional differentiation,[10] the new radical right is understood as a result of a general modernization shift which occurred in most Western democracies in the wake of '1968', and specific mobilization shifts in the context of each country's opportunity structures. The latter are most important in influencing whether the new radical right appears predominantly as a social movement type or a political party type.[11] The transition of Western industrial societies into a phase of advanced industrial capitalism, or 'post-industrialism', brought about fundamental and challenging changes. New political dynamics opened opportunities for new parties on the left and right, along a new value-based cleavage, and this cleavage created a mobilization potential for the 'normal pathological' right wing.[12]

Thus, the new radical right is not simply the extension of conservatism towards the extreme right but the product of a restructuring of the political spectrum and a regrouping of the party system. Sociologically, it represents the right-wing pole of a new conflict axis which cuts across the established lines of partisan conflict and societal cleavages, while ideologically it performs a bridging function between an established (neo)conservatism and an explicitly anti-democratic, latently violent right-wing extremism.[13]

THE RADICAL RIGHT SCENE IN FRANCE : THE PARTY AS HEGEMON

The following remarks contain a brief overview of the respective radical right 'landscape', i.e. groups and organizations as collective actors, in France (see Table 7.1).

TABLE 7.1

DOMINANT ACTORS IN THE FRENCH RADICAL RIGHT-WING FAMILY
(POST-1965)

	Party/campaign organization	*Social movement organization*	*Subcultural milieu*
Fascist right		FANE	FNE
Racist right	Tixiér–Vignancourt		GUD skinheads
Ethnocentrist/xenophobic right	FN	(Nouvelle Droite)	GUD skinheads
Religious-fundamentalist right		F: CCS	

Abbreviations: CCS: Comités Chrétienté-Solidarité (Christianity-Solidarity Committees); FANE: Fédération Action Nationalle-Européenne (Federation of National European Action); FN: Front National; FNE: Faisceaux nationalistes européens (European National Fascists); GUD: Groupe Union Defense (Union Defence Group)

Unlike Germany, Britain or the United States, the French case demonstrates strong centripetal tendencies towards a clustering of various groups and organizations around the FN.[14] Movement organizations such as FANE and the skinhead milieux are underdeveloped in comparison to Germany.[15] Before the split in early 1999, the FN had about 70,000 members and achieved a normal share of about 15 per cent of the vote in national elections by the late 1990s. By 1997, it was the second largest party of the right, and had established itself as the hegemon in the radical right-wing sector. But as French research shows, the FN had also increasingly adopted characteristics of a mass party organization by systematically constructing subcultures and subsocieties,[16] i.e. its own 'movement society'.

The FN was created in 1972 by leaders of the Ordre nouveau, a nationalist movement that was itself founded three years earlier to overcome the fragmentation on the far right. Under the leadership of Jean-Marie Le Pen, who combined the political experience of anti-Gaullism; poujadism and Tixiérism – he was the campaign manager of the far-right presidential candidate Tixiér-Vignancour in 1965 – with his military experience in Algeria, the FN tried to attract anti-republicans, authoritarians, conservative Catholics, imperialists and racists.[17] In none of the elections prior to 1983 did the FN attract more than 1 per cent of the national vote, and the party reached its electoral low-point in 1981 when Le Pen was not able to find the necessary 500 'sponsors' for his presidential candidacy. Clearly, prior to 1981 Le Pen was unable to mobilize a significant portion of the electorate, although the themes and issues that he developed through the FN were generally the same as those he used after 1981. The FN rose from obscurity to prominence after its breakthrough in the 1983 local elections in a Paris suburb and the 1984 European elections. Since then, and until the split into the FN and the Mégretist MNR in early 1999, the FN consolidated its national vote share at a stable level of 15 per cent.

Part of the reason for the rapid electoral success of the FN – next to the personal charisma of its leader – was an ambiguous platform and a flexible strategy at a time of growing dissatisfaction of segments of the French public with the established parties and an increasing sense of crisis (see above). Although the party has different factions or *familles*, the authority of Jean-Marie Le Pen as its leader was undisputed until 1998, and the party's image was streamlined into homogeneity.[18] Thus Le Pen's and the party's platform were almost indistinguishable. Immigration became the FN's major campaign theme by the late 1970s, but the party's ideology was more complex than that, and defied the notion of a single-issue movement.[19]

The FN ideology

Echoing the diagnosis of the intellectual New Right, Le Pen interpreted the signs of an economic crisis as an indicator of a crisis of the French nation and culture. The FN reasserted a notion of French national identity that comprises both revolutionary-republican traditions and the entire '4,000 years' of French history. It attacked all notions of egalitarianism (including the idea of human equality as preached in the Bible and in the literature of the Enlightenment),[20] and blamed the left and immigrants as the major reasons for social and economic problems in France. At the same time, the FN promoted the values of individual freedom, private property and law and order. Le Pen finally rejected internationalist policies, and after 1992 became the most ardent critic of the process and policies of European integration. He was the only major politician in France to oppose the US-led war against Saddam Hussein in 1991.[21]

Although there has been a certain consistency of themes presented by the FN, there have also been significant changes of position over the years. The initial FN programmes after 1972 reflected the party's origins among the groups of the extreme right of Vichy and Algérie française: order, moral values and Catholicism. The economic programme called for a 'third way' between capitalism and communism, a withdrawal of the state from the economy and a defence of small business. There was little mention of limitations on immigration in public rhetoric, although racist rhetoric about North African immigrants as a 'wild minority' was more frequent in internal propaganda. On the other hand, the FN supported a European confederation that would include Britain.[22]

As the party achieved electoral success in the 1980s it both modified and expanded its issue presentation. Its economic programme became increasingly modelled after the Reagan/Thatcher model of market liberalism and anti-statism, combined with the core issues of immigration and law and order.[23] Thus, by the time of the presidential and legislative elections of 1988, in addition to the core issues, the programme of the FN was clearly market-liberal and more or less pro-European, with frequent allusions to the New Right in both the United States and Britain. Indeed, within the party, the programme was often seen as 'pro-American' – a position that distanced the FN from many of the hardline neo-fascist militants who had joined the party in the early years before the electoral breakthrough.

> To reassert the formula of M. Reagan, '… I want the state off my back and out of my pocket …' Today the alliance with the United States remains necessary for France and will remain so for Europe as long as [Europe] remains a military dwarf confronting a Soviet giant. This requires that Atlantic solidarity to prevail wherever possible against the menace of Soviet imperialism and Muslim extremism.[24]

This orientation changed in the 1990s. Two events were particularly significant: the Gulf War of 1990 and the Maastricht Referendum of 1992. During each of these events, the FN took positions that served to reverse its issue orientation of the 1980s in key areas. Responding to pro-Iraq sympathies among those in the fundamentalist wing of the FN, but surprising many others, Le Pen strongly condemned United Nations intervention in the Gulf War, and French participation in that intervention in particular. Indeed, he went so far to as to visit Baghdad, and was received by Saddam Hussein as part of a delegation of right-wing parties from Europe.[25]

FN literature would later interpret this initiative as part of a larger effort by the party to oppose the United States and its influence on the global economy. By 1996, this broad expression of anti-Americanism had become a centrepiece of FN doctrine that was elaborated by Le Pen in a special issue of the party revue, *Identité*:

> It is by considering this construction of the New World Order that our change in attitude about the policies of the United States must be understood. When the Cold War was at its worst, and the Red Army was threatening, NATO had its *raison d'être*. The American presence contributed to contain Soviet expansionism, and to assure our liberty. Now, things have changed. NATO is being reconverted into the mailed fist of the New World Order. Far from being 'Europeanized' … it

imposes on the nations of Europe an Americanization of their diplomatic and military concepts ... In truth, the problem for today ... [must be seen] in terms of cleavage between the pruning shears of the New World Order and defenders of identities, that is defenders of nations ... This is the sense of my rallying-cry: 'Nationalists of all countries unite!' ... The White House has become the Trojan Horse of globalization ...[26]

Thus, by the time of the 1997 National Assembly elections, the FN had moved strongly to oppose the United States as a symbol of the larger issues of globalization.

This passionate anti-Americanism was combined with an opposition to key aspects of the Maastricht Agreement. Together with the Communists, the FN was the only important French political party to take a united stand against approval of the agreement. The leadership of all other major parties was divided on the referendum, and the electorates, particularly those of the Gaullist RPR and the moderate right Union pour la démocratie française (UDF), were deeply divided.[27] In the years after the referendum, the FN did not advocate the dismantling of the EU, but continued to advocate a Gaullist '*Europe des patries*' and 'a renegotiation of the European treaties and denunciation of the Schengen and Maastricht accords'.[28] The link with the anti-American orientation is established by Blot, when he argues that current institutions of the EU are a tool of Americanization.[29] This position was supported by Bruno Mégret, who would lead the break with Le Pen in December 1998, in stark terms in his manifesto for the 1997 legislative elections:

> The Europe of Brussels and of Maastricht is a machine to crush the nations and the peoples [of Europe]; it manufactures unemployment, taxation, bureaucracy and recession. Power is in the hands of a handful of anonymous and irresponsible high civil servants who impose a uniformity of legislation, a leveling by the lowest common denominator of our social systems, the opening of our frontiers to low-priced imports and to immigration from the whole world, the insertion into a new world economic and political order entirely dominated by the United States.[30]

Thus, whether for strategic-electoral reasons (to attract a larger working-class electorate), or for ideological reasons (to cement its coalition of militants within the organization), by 1997 the FN had established itself as a pole of opposition both to the American version of the global economic system with its objective of tariff reduction and free trade, and to the development of a united Europe with open internal borders. Instead, the party developed a programmatic compromise that linked racist rhetoric to anti-statist pro-capitalism, protectionism and anti-Americanism. Together with the Communists, the FN arguably became the most ardent defender of the idea that Europeanization and globalization undermined the safety network of the French welfare state.[31]

The leaders of the FN made it repeatedly clear that within France, their main political enemy was the Partie socialiste (PS) under François Mitterrand, although they generally lash out against the 'gang of four' – PS, PCF (Parti Communiste Française), RPR and UDF – for selling out French interests.[32] Le Pen continuously sought to distinguish himself from the political establishment by a more radical political discourse. On the other hand, the condemnation of the 'gang of four' did not prevent Le Pen from seeking respectability for his party through partial collaboration with the parties on the right, mostly at the local level, and a more moderate appearance in parliament.

The ideology and behaviour of the party raise the question of its orientation towards democracy and the French political system, and invite historical comparisons. Its origins in the Ordre nouveau, Le Pen's statement about the Holocaust as a small historical 'detail', his racism and disguised anti-Semitism, and some similarities between Hitler and Le Pen in style and appeal has lead some analysts to see fascist elements in the FN, and to see the party as a threat to French democracy.[33] However, these elements are outweighed by the differences not only in content but also in context. FN is neither revisionist nor revanchist (regarding Algeria, or the entire European order), nor does it propose a centrally directed economy or sociobiological elitism (thus setting it apart even from the more radical views of the Groupement de recherche et d'études pour la civilisation européenne (GRECE)). From Poujadism, the FN has inherited the populist style but not its opposition to economic modernization, and it is clearly more structured, hierarchically organized and has a broader platform.

The FN stands for authoritarian presidentialism, but not for the elimination of parliament and the democratic rules of the game, and it does not question the legitimacy of the Fifth Republic. If anti-system party means a party that '… abides by a belief system that does not share the values of the political order within which it operates'[34] the FN is not anti-system as far as the *political* aspect of the values are concerned. Values such as equality and tolerance are not essential ingredients of the current political order in France, but, as (controversial) components of the French political tradition, they have been part of the French belief system and key elements of what it means to be on the left.

The FN electorate

The electoral fortunes of the FN reflect a trend towards consolidation of voter support. The electoral emergence of the FN in 1983–84 has been well documented and analysed: from the sudden breakthrough in the European elections in 1984 with over 11 per cent of the vote (2.2 million), to the 14.4 per cent of the vote that Jean-Marie Le Pen attracted in the first round of the presidential elections in 1988 (4.4 million votes), to the record 15.1 per cent (4.6 million votes) vote for Le Pen in the first round of the presidential elections in 1995, and the record 15 per cent of the vote in the 1997 legislative elections.[35] The overwhelming majority of FN voters in 1984 'converted' from the established parties of the right; until 1999, the growth in the FN electorate can be attributed to its ability to attract a large percentage of new voters (and former abstainers), while holding on to its former voters better than any other party in France. In the European elections of 1999, in the aftermath of the split, FN (Le Pen) received 6 per cent with the MNR (Mégret) scoring 3.5 per cent.

The early successes from 1984 to 1986 depended to a large part on protest voting, fuelled by anti-party and anti-immigration sentiments, and characterized by a relatively low level of inter-election voting consistency. But after 1986, levels of consistency grew rapidly (to 91 per cent for FN voters loyal from 1993–97), and an increasingly even spread of FN support emerged across regions, classes and partisan background. This distinguishes FN support from the Poujadist movement of the 1950s, which drew its support mainly from disgruntled shopkeepers and farmers and the breakdown of the petty bourgeoisie. In fact, the FN attracts voters from middle-class and (disproportionately from) working-class backgrounds. Indeed, its proportion of the working-class vote in the 1990s has been as high or higher than the working-class vote for any party of the left. It has attracted former voters of the political right, as well as voters who support many of the issues of the political left.[36]

Overall, the most distinctive characteristic of the typical FN voter is not his or her sociodemographic profile but rather a strong concern with 'Frenchness', nationalism and immigration along with materialist-value orientations and high levels of insecurity, pessimism and authoritarianism. Electoral analyses of FN voter support show that traditional cleavage structures in French society (class, religion, region) play little role in the vote for Le Pen, but that value dimensions and issue concerns, in combination with constituency-level measures such as crime, immigration and unemployment, are decisive.[37] Thus, ideology has become a driving force behind the vote for Le Pen, and the FN is anything but a protest movement. Rather, despite its recent split, it is well rooted in the French electorate as the party of a new radical right and survived even the return from proportional representation to the single-member constituency system of elections in 1988 and the lack of parliamentary representation.

THE FRONT NATIONAL AND ITS SUCCESS: THE PECULIAR ROLE OF IMMIGRATION

Although it is generally presumed that there is a link between immigration and support for the extreme right, this link is by no means clear or obvious in the expanding volumes of research that have thus far appeared. Indeed, there has been a tendency for research to focus on factors other than immigration to explain variations in support for extreme right parties. The problem is that it is difficult to establish a spatial/ecological link between concentrations of immigrants and voting for the extreme right cross-nationally. The proportion of immigrants in the population is neither closely related to the existence of an important party of the extreme right nor to the level of electoral support for an extreme right party.

Immigrant concentrations

The lack of cross-national variation, however, does not rule out the importance of this relationship within countries. It is unlikely that the FN could have achieved an electoral breakthrough in the 1980s without these issues gaining political priority. In this sense, the FN was successful in converting a longstanding concern (that, as we will see, changed remarkably little over a long period of time) into a political issue. Mobilization around issues of immigration was important at the stage of electoral breakthrough, because voters who gave priority to this issue were willing to break their allegiances with parties with which they had formerly identified. Once the FN had achieved a significant electoral breakthrough, the areas in which it was successful became bases for further expansion because the impact of success expanded the impact of the immigration issues on voters in other areas and on voters of other political parties. The question of the relationship between immigration and the development of the French FN has been the subject of considerable debate. The spatial/ecological linkage between FN support and immigrant presence has never been convincingly established, primarily because FN has, over time, attracted a high proportion of the vote even in areas in which there are low concentrations of immigrants. Kitschelt, for example, finds little evidence to support a relationship between levels of immigration and the emergence of the far right at the national level. He skilfully summarizes a large group of studies that find only a weak relationship between the presence of immigrants and FN support in France, a relationship that grows weaker as we move from region to department to commune, and according to some studies, grows weaker over time.[38]

Nevertheless, Pierre Martin demonstrates first that, between 1984 and 1997, the difference in FN support in those departments with the largest concentration of North Africans and those with the smallest concentration was consistent over time: those with the largest concentrations consistently attracted about twice the level of support. He also shows, however, that the level of FN support *grew* most over time where the proportion of immigrants was *smallest*. (See Table 7.2.) It is also clear from Martin's data that the variation in support among various kinds of elections has been greatest where the proportion of immigrants is smallest, and least where it is largest.

TABLE 7.2
SUPPORT FOR THE FRONT NATIONAL BY PERCENTAGE OF NORTH
AFRICANS AND TURKS IN *DÉPARTEMENTS*

	Highest percentage (32 départements)	Medium percentage (32 départements)	Smallest percentage (32 départements)
FN 1986 (legislative)	13.7	9.1	5.9
FN 1997 (legislative)	18.4	15.3	9.7
Percentage change	+34.3	+68.1	+64.4

Source: Pierre Martin, *Comprendre les évolutions électorales* (Paris: Presses de Sciences Po, 2000), p. 276.

This implies two possible conclusions. The first is that the presence of immigrants was most important in the early years of the establishment an electoral breakthrough of the FN. As the party became better established nationally, it was able to make significant gains even in areas in which the concentration of immigrant populations was small or non-existent, building on a smaller base of support.

The second is that the reason why the relationship between immigrant concentration and the FN vote breaks down as we move from larger to small areas is that 'French [voters] most hostile to immigrants choose to live where housing is not too expensive and where there are few immigrants: urban working-class neighborhoods close to immigrant neighborhoods, or rural areas on the periphery of urban areas.'[39]

Moreover, although there does not appear to be any correlation between the *level* of immigrant presence and the FN vote at the commune level, this does not mean that there is no relationship at all. There does seem to be some threshold effect. If we look at Table 7.3, we can see that there was an 'advantage' for the FN in 1996 where there is a concentration of immigrant population, but this advantage tends to level off when the proportion of

TABLE 7.3
PARTY SUPPORT AND THE PRESENCE OF IMMIGRANTS AT THE
COMMUNE LEVEL IN 1996

Percentage of immigrants in commune	*None*	*1–4%*	*5–10%*	*10+%*
PC	4.7	2.7	6.5	6.3
PS/MG	23.6	29.9	24.9	29.2
UDF	9.4	8.0	4.4	4.3
RPR	15.6	10.7	10.9	11.0
FN	*5.5*	*5.9*	*8.5*	*8.3*
No ID	27.3	31.6	30.4	31.1
Total	100%	100%	100%	100%

Source: CSA survey 9662093, November 1996, RS10/RS12, ETR.

immigrants rises above 5 per cent.[40] While electoral support for the party tends to rise with the presence of immigrants, it appears to rise at a relatively low threshold, rather than in a linear fashion.[41]

The link between immigrant concentrations at the commune level is similar to what Nonna Mayer wrote about this relationship at the département level in the legislative elections of 1997, which in turn confirms the earlier analysis of Pierre Martin reported in Table 7.2 above:

> Our study of 1997 shows that the tendency to vote FN in the last legislative elections varies with relation to the local importance of the immigrant population, whatever the age, sex, social milieu, religious practice or level of education of the respondents. It is always stronger among voters linked to the working class milieu, but even among those who have no link to this milieu, the scores for Le Pen's party almost triple when we move from zones where there are few foreigners to those where there are many of them (6 per cent to 16 per cent) ... even among the better educated respondents, the rate of the declared vote for the FN increase directly with the presence of foreigners (8 per cent ... to 12 per cent ...).[42]

Although there is no way of demonstrating a direct shift from the established right to the FN at the commune level, the presence of immigrants appears to be related to the support among right-wing voters in favour of the FN (see Table 7.3). In the 32 départements with the highest levels of immigrants analysed by Martin, the proportion of votes for the French right increased marginally more than in the 32 départments with the lowest levels of immigrants. In both groups of départments, the right showed sharp gains in 1984 over 1981 – gains that have endured. However, these gains appear to be attributable to increased voting for FN in both cases (see Table 7.2): the vote for RPR/UDF actually declined by 9.6 per cent in zones of highest immigration and in zones of lowest immigration. As a result, the established right was supported by 35.5 per cent of the electorate in the former zones, compared with 40.5 per cent in the latter zones in 1997.[43] These electoral results at the départment level are generally supported by the survey results in Table 7.3: support for the established right (RPR/UDF) tends to be far higher in communes where there is no immigrant population, and then falls sharply even where there is a small proportion of immigrants.

The implication is that the presence of immigrants worked to the benefit of the FN after 1983, and to the detriment of the parties of the established right, in départments in which immigrants were most concentrated. However, many of the départments (and localities) in which there are high concentrations of immigrants are also areas in which the left has been historically dominant, and where municipalities of the left had politicized the question of immigration long before it had become an issue at the national level.[44]

Jeanette Money carries this analysis one step further in her recent book on the political geography of immigration control. She presents new evidence that as early as 1971 the right-wing national majority began to take immigration control and the 'problem' of immigrants much more seriously at the constituency level, as part of a strategy to defend their majority against the resurgent left. She demonstrates that there was a high proportion of swing constituencies in départments with high concentrations of immigrants (where the left was strong), and that the majority targeted anti-immigrant appeals to those constituencies.[45] These appeals were widespread during the legislative election campaign in 1973, and were even more widespread during the presidential election campaign in 1974. Therefore, although immigration was certainly not an important national issue in either of these campaigns, it was of far greater importance at the local level.

Thus, local government leaders, most of them from the left, and most of those from the PCF, were instrumental in challenging government policy on immigration, and forcing increased attention from both the right and the left.[46] In the process, they most likely set the groundwork for the FN breakthrough in specific areas and constituencies. In areas where the established parties of the right were not successful in stimulating transfers of votes from the left, the FN was far more successful in luring transfers from the established right and attracting new voters from the potential working-class constituency of the left.

Attitudes

The link between *attitudes* towards immigration and support for the FN is more decisive in a number of ways for helping us to understand both the initial success of the FN and its subsequent ability to mobilize additional voters. The process of constructing a stable electorate appears to have been built first – in the early years – on voter response to the core issues of the party: immigration and law and order (*sécurité*). After the initial breakthrough, the very success of the party appears to have had the impact of changing political priorities not only for those who have voted for the FN, but also for voters who have supported other parties as well, thus changing the terms of political conflict to those most favourable to the FN.

This process is indicated by the priority that voters have given to various issues from election to election. In 1984, what most clearly differentiated the voters for the FN from those of the more established right (as well as other parties) was the priority that they gave to the issue of immigration. Of the sub-sample who claimed to have voted FN in the European elections that year, 26 per cent cited 'immigrants' as their primary concern and 30 per cent cited 'law and order', compared with 6 per cent and 15 per cent for the entire sample (see Table 7.4). By 1986, as the FN electorate began to solidify, the priorities of party voters also solidified, with 50 per cent giving priority to law and order and 60 per cent to immigration (several responses were possible).

By many measures, attitudes towards immigrants had grown more favourable during the height of Third World immigration during the decade between the mid-1960s and the formal suspension of immigration in 1974. Thus between 1951 and 1971 the sentiment for giving native French priority over immigrants in housing and employment (if there should be a 'crisis of unemployment') diminished from 85 per cent to 55 per cent for the first, and from 84 per cent to 60 per cent for the second; in addition, agreement with the sentiment that foreigners do good for the country rose from 50 per cent to 68 per cent.[47] Then, after the flow of immigrants had diminished, but had not been halted in the late 1970s, some negative attitudes began to increase, but others, including priority for native French for employment, continued to diminish. Thus there is no convincing evidence that the electoral movement towards the FN emerged from a general *growing* sense of 'crisis' about immigration. Rather, it was the specific sense of crisis, and the priority of immigration issues among the potential electorate of the FN that was mobilized by the party.

THE FRONT NATIONAL AND ITS ENVIRONMENT: INTERACTION AND
IMPACT

In order to assess the FN's interaction with other political actors and its
impact on various levels, we must take into account both structural and
dynamic aspects of mobilization and involvement. Social movement research
offers the concept of 'opportunity structures' to summarize the mobilization
context in terms of perceived costs and benefits of collective political action,[48]
but a process model must consider the interaction of the radical right with
other political actors in a dynamic perspective.

The new radical right such as the FN represents a shift in political
placement, and a change in the discourse on nationhood towards the right
along the New Politics cleavage. The impact of this change is interactive; it
does not occur in a linear fashion but can be observed on various levels and
to varying degrees.[49] For example, the typical reaction of other political party
actors can range between demarcation and confrontation on the one hand,
and co-option and incorporation on the other.

The levels of interaction begin with control over the arena of right-wing
collective action; then the development of issue priorities among voters for
other parties, as well as those who transfer their support to the FN. We then
look at patterns of coalition formation with other parties; the impact on the
policy agenda of government and opposition; and finally the impact of governance at the local level. In general, compared with more conventional political
parties that have achieved an electoral breakthrough in European multi-party
systems, radical right parties have been relatively unsuccessful in developing
coalitions for governing. On the other hand, they have been relatively more
successful in gaining influence over the political agenda and policy formation.

Collective action

The rise of the FN has had a direct impact on the activities of extreme right
movements in France. This arena of extra-parliamentary and non-partisan
collective action includes two related but diametrically opposed dimensions
that must be considered: first, radical right-wing and xenophobic or racist
protest and violence; and second, the effects of movement-type counter-
mobilization and anti-fascist protest and violence. As we indicated above, the
French spectrum of the radical right is dominated by the FN; no significant
splinter groups or rival organizations have emerged (except of course for the
split in the FN itself in 1999). The rise of the FN has helped the party to
absorb a variety of small groups and to integrate parts of the radical right
subculture.

In international comparison, the size of the French skinhead scene is rather small.[50] There are currently about a thousand right-wing skinheads, somewhat fewer than the 1,500 estimated during the mid-1980s.[51] Frequent reports about the links between the FN and the militant right-wing subculture, repeatedly denied by FN leaders, indicate that dual membership in the Front national de jeunesse (FNJ), the FN's youth organization) and a violent student organization, the Groupe union défense (GUD, or Union Group Defence), is common; moreover, there has been a growing politicization and radicalization among skinheads and the FNJ.[52]

Thus, despite the rather high level of ethnocentrism in the French public, racist or extremist protest activities on the right are limited in scope. The numbers of racist or right-wing activities (such as threats or actions against people or property) are generally less frequent in France than in Germany, although different methods of tracking such incidents make direct comparisons difficult. The limited militancy among the French extreme right does not correspond with the comparatively high propensity for protest and direct action in France.[53]

This development has been accompanied by a substantial countermobilization which has attracted only little academic attention.[54] Moreover, between 1983 and 1995 the share of those in France who considered FN leader Jean-Marie Le Pen a danger to democracy has steadily increased from 38 per cent to 68 per cent, while the number of those who did not consider him dangerous has not decreased but stayed at a level of 25 per cent since 1987.[55] In sum, at the level of public opinion trends, the rise of the FN and its ongoing entrenchment in the French electorate has resulted in a growing polarization in the French public along the New Politics axis. This growing polarization reflects some tension in the French concept of nationhood between the political and the cultural dimension. Since the number of immigrants in France, particularly those of non-European origin, has tended to be rather stable during that period compared to the decades prior to the 1980s,[56] these changing attitudes are not a reaction to actual demographic changes but rather reflect the politicization of immigration.

Since the local elections in Dreux in 1983, some 200 anti-Le Pen rallies have taken place in France. Overall, during the course of 12 years, several hundred thousand people have been mobilized in a variety of protest activities, thus contributing to the emergence of a distinct anti-FN, anti-racist subculture across the spectrum of the entire left. Led by organizations such as Sections Carrément Anti-Le Pen, or Sections Definitely Against Le Pen (SCALP) and L'Appel des 250 (Appeal of the 250) with their newspaper *Ras l'Front* (Fed Up with the Front), this movement (which consists of a vast array of networks and several thousand members)[57] is directed primarily against the FN, but at times also targets the ethnocentrist policies of the Gaullists, the police and even projects of socialists.

Impact on issue priorities

It is striking how the issue priorities of the FN and its voters appear to have influenced the priorities of those voting for other political parties, as well as those new voters who began voting FN. Relatively few voters aside from those that supported the FN considered either immigration or law and order to be a strong priority at the time that FN achieved its electoral breakthrough. By 1988, however, the importance of these issues ranked with such issues as social inequality, and were far higher than concerns about the environment, corruption and the construction of Europe; only concern with unemployment ranked higher.[58] (See Table 7.4.)

TABLE 7.4
THE MOTIVATIONS OF VOTERS: 1984–97

Per cent	Law and order				Immigrants				Unemployment				Social inequality			
	84	88	93	97	84	88	93	97	84	88	93	97	84	88	93	97
PC	9	19	29	28	2	12	16	15	37	59	77	85	33	50	52	46
PS	8	21	24	29	3	13	19	15	27	43	71	83	24	43	40	47
Rt	17	38	37	43	3	19	33	22	20	41	67	72	7	18	23	21
FN	*30*	*55*	*57*	*66*	*26*	*59*	*72*	*72*	*17*	*41*	*64*	*75*	*10*	*18*	*26*	*25*
TT	15	31	34	35	6	22	31	22	24	45	68	75	16	31	32	35

Note: Figures refer to percentage of party voters voting for these reasons. Since several responses were possible, the total across may be more than 100 per cent. For 1988, the results are for supporters of presidential candidates nominated by the parties indicated.

Sources: Exit Poll, SOFRES/TF1, 17 June 1984, *Le Nouvel Observateur*, 22 June 1984; and SOFRES, *État de l'opinion, Clés pour 1987* (Paris: Seuil, 1987), p. 111; P. Perrineau, 'Les Etapes d'une implantation électorale (1972–1988)', in N. Mayer and P. Perrineau (eds), *Le Front National à découvert* (Paris: Presses de la FNSP, 1988), p. 62; P. Perrineau, 'Le Front National la force solitaire', in P. Habert, P. Perrineau and C. Ysmal (eds), *Le Vote sanction* (Paris: Presses de la FNSP/Dept. d'Etudes politiques du Figaro, 1993), p. 155, CSA, 'Les Elections législatives du 25 mai, 1997', *Sondage Sortie des Urnes pour France 3, France Inter, France Info et Le Parisien*, p. 5.

We can look at the relationship between the rise of the FN and its impact on other parties in a somewhat different way. In 1993 fewer than half of the voters who identified themselves ideologically as 'centrist' said that they had voted for a candidate of the established right – RPR/UDF – (most of the others had voted for the left), compared with 63 per cent in 1986; on the other hand, 63 per cent of those who identified as 'extreme right' voted for the established right in 1993, compared with 55 per cent in 1986 (then a smaller group). By 1993, 'We find ourselves ... in the presence of a political

TABLE 7.5
PUBLIC OPINION ON IMMIGRATION: 1966–91

	1966	1971	1973	1974	1977	1984	1987	1988	1990	1991
'Too many immigrants in France'	57	52		49		58		71	68	
'Send unemployed immigrant workers home'			70			46				40
'Limit family unification'		15		11	61	68	55		50	39
'If there was a crisis of unemployment, fire immigrant workers first'		60		65						45

Note: Figures in percentages.
Average of three surveys in 1990.
Source: Surveys reported in Y. Gastaut, *L'immigration et l'opinion en France sous la Ve République* (Paris: Editions du Seuil, 2000), pp. 306, 321, 329, 449.

radicalization of the moderate right electorate [that is, those who vote for the moderate right], probably linked to the increase of its audience among working-class categories.'[59]

Schain has argued elsewhere that the emergence of the FN in electoral politics in the early 1980s at first reflected the preceding weakening of the party system, as well as conflict about the political agenda on integration and incorporation among political actors involved in the policy-making process across the political spectrum. Later, the ability of the party to build an electoral following, and its increasingly important role in the political debate, appears to have had an impact on the priorities of all voters.[60]

However, in the 1990s the growth dynamics that we have analysed above gradually levelled off. The percentage of FN voters (indeed, all voters) who gave priority to issues of immigration and law and order stabilized. In addition, opposition to immigrants and immigration in public opinion appears to have diminished somewhat (see Table 7.5). In general, the presence of immigrant communities seemed to be less important as a dynamic for FN electoral *growth* than it was for electoral breakthrough. In 1997 the FN attracted only 28 per cent of its supporters from towns in which the immigrant population is more than 10 per cent; almost 10 per cent of its supporters lived in towns in which there were no immigrants at all. Thus, although the breakthrough sources of FN support seemed to have stabilized, the party continued to attract large numbers of new voters.

We have some evidence that immigration issues were less important for

TABLE 7.6
COMPARING FRONT NATIONAL LOYALISTS WITH NEW FN VOTERS
IN 1997

Questions dealing with race and immigration	*New voters vs. loyalist*	*Agree* %	*Do not agree* %
'Some races are better endowed than others'	Loyal	40.7	57.4
	New	30	66.7
'There are too many immigrants in France'	Loyal	98.2	1.9
	New	91.7	8.3
'North Africans who live in France will one day be French like everyone else'	Loyal	31.5	66.7
	New	35	61.6
'Now, we no longer feel as much at home as before'	Loyal	79.7	18.5
	New	75	25

Source: CEVIPOF/SOFRES survey of voters, 26 May 1997.

new voters than for those who transferred to the party earlier on. If we look at the data in Tables 7.6 and 7.7, we can see that there are some important differences between those new voters who voted for the party for the first time in 1997, and those who voted FN in the previous legislative election (1988) and the last presidential election in 1995 (loyalists). All of these voters are far more prone to see the world in racist terms than are supporters of other political parties, but the new voters are considerably less oriented in that direction, and are somewhat more optimistic about bridging the gap between native citizens and immigrants of North African origin.

However, by the 1990s, there was growing evidence of the role of the party itself in stabilizing the link with immigration issues. The core electorate in 1997 had become far less concentrated in the largest cities and towns, less masculine and even less Catholic than it had been before. Between 1988 and 1997 the loyal electorate (in both cases about 27 per cent of the total FN electorate, and therefore larger in number in 1997 than in 1988) of the FN changed in important ways, but mostly in terms of its broader distribution around the country. Therefore, it is striking that a larger and more broadly entrenched core group appears to have become *more* ethnocentric, with stronger identification with the FN and greater interest in politics. By 1997, the issue orientations of the new loyalists were even more solidly supportive of the core issues of the FN than they had been a decade before.

Therefore, in the process of integration, new voters seem to incorporate the core anti–immigrant, racist and authoritarian values of the party rather

TABLE 7.7
LOYAL FRONT NATIONAL VOTERS IN 1997 COMPARED WITH 1988

	1988	*1997*
Social/demographic:		
Men	67	59.3
Age 45+	55	53.7
Cities 200,000+	54	37.0
Practicing Catholic	18	5.6
Attitudes and values:		
Authoritarian★	82	79.6
Ethnocentrism★	61	89
Political Attitudes:		
Interest in Politics★	41	63
FN party ID	74	81.5

Note: Figures refer to percentage of loyal voters in each category.
Source: CEVIPOF/SOFRES survey of voters, 26 May 1997, and N. Mayer and P. Perrineau, 'Pourquoi
votent-ils pour le Front National?', *Pouvoirs*, 55 (1990), p. 177.
★The indices used for 1997 are somewhat different from those used by Mayer and Perrineau in 1988,
since the questions used were not the same in the two surveys (1997 index for authoritarianism average
attitudes on the death penalty, with those on discipline in schools; index for ethnocentrism averages
attitudes on 'no longer feeling at home in France' with 'too many immigrants').

than to dilute these values. The party itself appeared to have become an effective mechanism not only for mobilizing a growing electorate, but also for *encadrement*. At the same time, the new voters of the 1990s, many of whom came from outside the core areas of FN support and identified less with the party itself, were closer to the core values of the FN than their counterparts of 1988. The priority of these issues may have levelled off, but they continued to be important for developing and maintaining ideological links among party loyalists.

Coalition formation

Until their 1983 breakthrough, there was hardly any interaction between the FN and the established parties. The consensus on immigration was undermined by the very different manner in which the established parties handled the FN at the electoral level. The dynamic of alliance formation, however, and the reciprocal relationship between the FN and its political environment (evident in the shifting control response of the established parties from seeing the FN first as irrelevant, then as representing an opportunity), contributed to the FN's political breakthrough and the subsequent readjustments of the other parties' positions. The right's decision in the Dreux municipal election of 1983 to utilize the FN against the left was a major step.

In the FN's consolidation phase between 1984 and 1988, the following pattern of strategic interaction emerged. National leaders of the Gaullist RPR and the moderate right UDF vehemently opposed alliances with the FN but avoided stigmatizing the party and its voters. At the local and regional level, this allowed tolerance of further alliances in the elections of 1986 and 1988.[61] After 1988, the party leadership of the RPR decided on a strict demarcation from the FN and a strategy of containment. From then on, the FN's growing local electoral successes – especially its victories in Toulon, Marignane, Orange in 1995 and, later, Vitrolles – were generally the result of the party's own efforts in electoral isolation and the voters' response, not of the established party elites' strategic response.[62] However, because of the FN's expanding electoral strength throughout the country in the 1990s, isolation and containment became difficult to enforce.

In the local elections of 1995, the FN presented a record 25,000 candidates, and about 2,000 municipal councillors were elected (1,100 in larger towns with a population of 20,000 or more). Its capacity to present this vast army of candidates was a good indication of the political distance that the FN had travelled in the previous decade, and the success at the municipal level provided a building bloc for future candidacies. The 275 regional councillors elected in 1998 (concentrated in the Ile de France, Provence-Alpes-Côtes-D'Azur and the Rhône-Alpes) was only a 15 per cent increase over the number elected in 1992, but vastly increased the political leverage of the party.

Since 1983, the ability of the party to win seats at the sub-national level, where there is some dose of proportionality, increased with its ability to field candidates; and its ability to field candidates increased with success in political and social elections. In 1986, FN lists were presented in each of the 22 regions in France. With almost 10 per cent of the vote, the party elected 137 (out of 1,682) regional councillors; not a lot, but enough to exert some strategic influence over coalition formation in 12 of the 22 regions. In six regions their votes were needed to elect a council president from the established right. In Languedoc-Roussillon the Gaullist president reached a formal accord on a 'Programme of Action' with the FN; in five other regions the FN was able to negotiate positions in the regional government, and in five additional regions it gained some lesser positions.[63] Six years later, the FN increased its regional representation to 239, with representation in every region. In 14 of the 22 regions the right depended for its majority on the councillors of the FN, who carefully demonstrated their ability to arbitrate in the election of regional presidents and the selection of regional executives.[64]

In the regional elections in March 1998, with 15.3 per cent of the vote, the party gained little more than 1 per cent of the vote over its score in 1992. The real success, however, was that it had now become a major player in coalition formation at the regional level. The FN now had more regional councillors (275) than the UDF (262), and almost as many as the RPR (285). Under the guidance of Bruno Mégret, the party offered to support RPR or UDF candidates for the regional presidency who accepted a minimal programme of the FN which would *not* include *priorité nationale*.[65] In five of the 22 regions, the FN was successful in negotiating governing coalitions through which it has gained not only influence over the political agenda, but considerable patronage as well.[66] This was accomplished in the face of a direct prohibition by the national leadership of both the RPR and the UDF, and in the face of two major speeches by the President of the Republic opposing such alliances.[67] It was clear that both established right parties were under severe pressure from their local units, for whom the stakes in terms of position and patronage were significant.[68] Thus, the political compromises at the regional level became a direct challenge to the stability of the established right. One indication of this challenge was the statement in June 1998 of Edouard Balladur, the former RPR prime minister, who broke with his party by openly supporting a national debate on *préférence nationale* for social services – a key FN policy position – and refusing to exclude the FN as an opposition partner.[69]

Policy agenda formation

The story of immigration politics after 1983 is less about the struggle over policy orientation than about the struggle by political parties on both the right and the left to undermine the ability of the FN to sustain the initiative in portraying and defining these issues. The RPR/UDF have been deeply divided in their competition with the FN for voters who are frightened by the problems of a multiethnic society, between those who advocate co-operating with the FN and accepting their issues in more moderate terms, and others who are tempted to try to destroy their rival on the right through isolation and rejection of their portrayal of the issues altogether.

The problem first became acute after the 1986 legislative elections, when, as a result of proportional representation, the FN gained significant representation in the National Assembly. During the two years of parliamentary existence in the National Assembly from 1986 until 1988, the FN's legislative initiatives were successfully blocked by the other parties. Efforts to challenge the Chirac government in question time were tempered by Le Pen's desire for respect. Thus, the FN group adjusted quickly to the parliamentary routine and tried to acquire an image of a serious and hard-working body.[70] With 6 per cent of the deputies they produced a total of 9,152 or 13.4 per cent of the legislative amendments. But in the entire two-year span of the FN's presence in the National Assembly, only one legislative bill which emanated from them was debated and adopted, and it concerned a rather marginal issue: the official recognition of the French-speaking group in the international Association of parliamentarians.[71]

Each time the right felt it had succeeded in outmanœuvring the FN (the legislative elections of 1988, the municipal elections of 1989, and the immigration legislation of 1993), it was reminded nevertheless that the challenge would not disappear (the by-election victories of the FN in Marseilles and Dreux in December 1989; the legislative elections of 1993; the presidential and municipal elections of 1995; the legislative elections of 1997; and the regional elections of 1998). More and more, the electorally weak parties of the right needed the 10–15 per cent of the electorate that voted FN.

As for the Socialists, throughout 1993 they struggled to defuse the rhetoric of the FN with a variety of approaches: by policy initiatives (strengthening border controls whilst trying to develop a policy of integration) when they controlled the government; by agreeing with the established right when they were electorally threatened by the opposition, as did Socialist Prime Minister Laurent Fabius while debating with Chirac in 1985 that 'the Front National poses some real questions'; and, more generally, by alternating between the pluralist rhetoric of a 'right to difference' approach to immigrants and an individualistic 'right to indifference' approach.[72] Despite the confusion, the dynamics of party competition resulted in redefinition of the issue of immigration in national politics, from a labour market problem, to an integration/incorporation problem, to a problem that touches on national identity, to problems of education, housing, law and order, and to problems of citizenship requirements.

In a number of respects the reactions of the Jospin government to the electoral success of the FN after 1997 were an impressive result of the FN's ability to influence priorities of the national political agenda. Because of pressures from its own constituency and the weight of the FN, the government could not avoid dealing with the issues. In one of its first moves, the government announced that it would appoint a commission to study the broad question of immigration legislation, and that it would then quickly decide on what action to take with regard to new legislation on immigration and nationalization.

Within a month of its appointment, the commission issued its report, and recommended that the government try a bold new approach to the immigration issue: to accept with modifications the changes in immigration and naturalization legislation that had been made by the right since 1993, and to develop an explicit centrist approach that would tend toward consensus and to isolate the FN.[73] In the short term, this centrist approach was largely rejected by the opposition, and created emotional divisions within the Left as well. Nevertheless, in the debate on the immigration and naturalization proposals by the Minister of the Interior, considerations of how these bills would relate to the strength of the party were frequently explicit, and never far below the surface.[74]

Local power

Of course the impact of the FN has been felt most where the party had acquired political power by conquering the mayor's offices in Toulon, Marignane, Orange (all 1995) and, later, in Vitrolles (1997). In all these cases, they coordinated their agenda and emphasized the issue of law and order, in particular an increase of the local police force even while budgets were cut, and social and cultural activities such as the cleansing of libraries and the application of the *préférence nationale* to the allocation of social benefits. As Schain concluded, 'What most characterizes these first attempts to govern at the local level appears to be an attempt to create a symbolic and substantive image of FN government. However, beyond this, is a project to develop an institutional framework that will be a springboard to further success.'[75]

The fiscal policies were intended to underline the substance of FN government: while public funding of social, economic and cultural services came to a halt, taxes were increased – contrary to the FN's campaign promises. In practice this meant, for example, that between August 1997 and the beginning of 1999, when an administrative court intervened, the mayor of Vitrolles had refused to sign the contracts of 31 civil servants who had already been hired by the municipality. But most importantly, the cultural life in the cities governed by the FN underwent a severe transformation. Many cultural projects (theatre groups, music festivals, cinemas, clubs and coffee shops) had to abandon their activities for lack of funding or withdrawal of their licence, binational marriages were blocked, and anti-FN activities were suppressed at the expense of civil liberties.[76] Not only did this change the political climate in those municipalities, it also produced national repercussions, because other mayors or regional prefects who were not members of the FN made overtures to the party or emulated some of its policies. Despite the split in the party in 1999, only Toulon was lost to the radical right in the municipal elections of 2001.

CONCLUSIONS

In many ways, the development of the French FN has been unique and exceptional. The party emerged in the mid-1980s at a moment when opposition to the governing Socialists and Communists was growing, and when support for the established parties of the right was weak. The FN attracted voters who related strongly to the anti-immigrant and law and order issues espoused by the party. The rapid electoral success of the party coincided with its strong mobilization capacity that undermined non-party groups that focused on collective action. The political success of the FN increasingly politicized the electorate around the party in several ways.

First, the party electorate, while growing in size, developed into an increasingly loyal *and* ideological bloc of voters. In this, the French case diverges from other Western European cases such as Germany and Austria. Second, the immigration issues were successfully politicized by the FN *before* other established parties of the right used this issue in the electoral field. (In the UK and West Germany the major parties of the right utilized the issue in order to marginalize an early challenge by the radical right and to challenge the political left.) Third, the structure of the political right was much more fragmented than in most Western European countries, and provided the FN with the political space needed for its breakthrough and consolidation.

However, while there were certainly system-specific aspects of the establishment of the radical right in France, its development also raises comparative issues for the rest of Europe. First, the socioeconomic environment is common to most EU countries. This is, among other things, reflected in the growing proportion of working-class voters among the electorate of the radical right, most notably in Austria, Belgium and Germany. Second, the very fact that there is a radical right phenomenon in most 'post-industrial societies' is relevant to the foregoing argument that right-wing radicalism is a 'normal pathological condition', rather than an exceptional anomaly, in fast-changing modern societies. The form of that phenomenon is determined by the specific structures and dynamics of the political system in each country. Where right-wing radical parties are strong, the movement-type radical right is weak, but where the parties are weak or fragmented, radical right-wing movements and subculture, and often levels of right-wing violence, are stronger. Thus, the fight against right-wing radicalism is not over when such parties are successfully marginalized or banned.

Finally, our work suggests that radical right parties are strongly resisted in coalition formation, at least until their support proves to be indispensable. On the other hand, their impact on agenda formation and policy development is important, even when they are outside governing coalitions.

NOTES

1. See H.-G. Betz, *Radical Right-wing Populism in Western Europe* (New York: St Martin's Press, 1994); M. Minkenberg, 'The New Right in France and Germany. Nouvelle Droite, Neue Rechte, and the New Right Radical Parties', in P. Merkl and L. Weinberg (eds), *The Revival of Right-Wing Extremism in the Nineties* (London: F. Cass, 1997), pp. 65–90; M. Minkenberg, *Die neue radikale Rechte im Vergleich. USA, Frankreich, Deutschland* (Opladen/Wiesbaden: Westdeutscher Verlag, 1998).
2. See D. Rucht, *Modernisierung und neue soziale Bewegungen* (Frankfurt/New York, 1994).
3. E. Scheuch and H. D. Klingemann, 'Theorie des Rechtsradikalismus in westlichen Industriegesellschaften', *Hamburger Jahrbuch für Wirtschafts- und Gesellschaftspolitik*, 12 (1967), pp. 11–29.
4. K. von Beyme, *Parteien in westlichen Demokratien* (Munich: Piper 1984); Rucht, *Modernisierung*.
5. Minkenberg, *Die neue radikale Rechte im Vergleich*, Ch. 8.
6. Ibid., Chs 1, 7.
7. H. Kitschelt (with A. McGann), *The Radical Right in Western Europe* (Ann Arbor, MI: University of Michigan Press, 1995), p. 52
8. S. Tarrow, *Power in Movement* (Cambridge: Cambridge University Press, 1994), pp. 135ff.; Rucht, *Modernisierung*, p. 177.
9. W. Bergmann, 'Ein Versuch, die extreme Rechte als soziale Bewegung zu beschreiben', in: W. Bergmann and R. Erb (eds), *Neonazismus und rechte Subkultur* (Berlin: Metropol, 1994), pp. 183–207.
10. Rucht, *Modernisierung*, pp. 122–6.
11. Minkenberg, *Die neue radikale Rechte im Vergleich*, Ch. 1.
12. R. Inglehart, *Culture Shift* (Princeton, NJ: Princeton University Press, 1990); R. Dalton, *Citizen Politics* (Chatham, NJ: Chatham House, 1996).
13. See M. Minkenberg, *The New Right in Comparative Perspective: The USA and Germany* (Ithaca, NY: 1993); Kitschelt, *The Radical Right*.
14. The recent break-up of the FN into the old party under Le Pen's leadership and the new FN–MNR which is headed by Le Pen's rival and former number two in the party, Bruno Mégret, cut the party apparatus into two halves. But as the 1999 European elections show, this is a division at the level of party elites, delegates and activists, rather than that of the voters: both groups scored 9 per cent, but two-thirds of the vote went to the FN who thus re-entered the Strasbourg parliament.
15. According to a recent estimate of the French ministry of the interior, there are about 1,000 skinheads in France who account for as much as 80 per cent of registered right-wing violence (unpublished bulletin of DCRG, 22 June 2000). Data from Germany are discussed in detail below.
16. G. Birenbaum, *Le Front national en politique* (Paris: Balland, 1992).
17. See J.-Y. Camus, 'Origine et formation du Front national, 1972–1981', in P. Perrineau and N. Mayer (eds), *Le Front national à Découvert* (Paris: Presses de la Fondation Nationale des Sciences Politiques, 1989), pp. 17–19; W. Safran, 'The Front National in France: From Lunatic Fringe to Limited Respectability', in P.H. Merkl and L. Weinberg (eds), *Encounters with the Contemporary Radical Right* (Boulder, CO: Westview Press, 1993), p.20.
18. See Birenbaum, *Le Front National*, Ch. 1.
19. See S. Mitra, 'The National Front in France: A Single-issue Movement?', in *West European Politics*, 11, 2 (April 1988), pp. 47–64.
20. See Safran, 'The Front National in France', p. 21.
21. See P.-A. Taguieff, 'Un programme "révolutionnaire"?', in N. Mayer and P. Perrineau (eds), *Le Front National à Découvert*, pp. 195–227; H. Lagrange and P. Perrineau, 'Le syndrome lepeniste', in Mayer and Perrineau (eds), *Le Front National à Découvert*, pp. 228–47; P. Hainsworth, 'The Extreme Right in Post-war France: The Emergence and

Success of the Front National', in Hainsworth (ed.), *The Extreme Right in Europe and the USA*, pp. 48–53.

22. See H.G. Simmons, *The French National Front: The Extremist Challenge to Democracy* (Boulder, CO: Westview Press, 1996), pp.63–4.
23. See Kitschelt, *The Radical Right*, pp. 94–5.
24. FN, *Passeport pour la victoire* (Paris: 1988), pp.56–7. This is the programme for the 1988 elections.
25. See Simmons' excellent analysis of this episode in, *The French National Front*, pp. 100–2.
26. *Identité*, 23 (July–August–September, 1996), p. 3.
27. See A. Appleton, 'The Maastricht Referendum and the Party System', in Keeler and Schain (eds), *Chirac's Challenge* (New York: St Martin's Press, 1996).
28. *A Program for Governing*, on the National Front party web-page: *http://www.front-nat.fr*
29. Blot, 'La vassalisation du monde', p. 12.
30. B. Mégret, *Le grand Changement: et si on essayait le Front national?* (1997), pp. 53–64.
31. See M.A. Schain, 'Immigration, the National Front and Changes in the French Party System'; prepared for presentation at the Annual Meetings of the American Political Science Association, 3–6 September 1998, pp. 14–17.
32. See Birenbaum, *Le Front National*, pp. 79–96
33. See H.G. Simmons, *The French National Front*.
34. G. Sartori, *Parties and Party Systems: A Framework for Analysis* (Cambridge: Cambridge University Press, 1976), p.133.
35. See, M.A. Schain, 'The National Front in France and the Construction of Political Legitimacy', *West European Politics*, 10, 2 (April 1987); and the excellent collection by Mayer and Perrineau, *Le Front National*.
36. See P. Perrneau, *Le Symptôme Le Pen. Radiographie des électeurs du Front national* (Paris: Fayard, 1997); N. Mayer, *Ces Français qui votent FN* (Paris: Flammarion, 1999).
37. See M. Lewis-Beck and G.E Mitchell, 'French Electoral Theory: The National Front Test', in *Electoral Studies*, 12, 2 (June 1993), pp. 112–27. See also Minkenberg, *Die neue radikale Rechte*, Ch. 8, and N. Mayer and P. Perrineau, 'Why do they vote for Le Pen?', in P. Ignazi and C. Ysmal (eds), *Extreme Right-wing Parties in Europe: European Journal of Political Research*, Special Issue, 22, 1 (July 1992), pp. 129, 131; M. Schain, 'The National Front and the French Party System', *French Politics and Society* (Winter, 1999); Hainsworth, 'The Extreme Right in Post-war France', in Hainsworth (ed.), *The Extreme Right in Europe and the USA*, pp. 46ff.
38. Kitschelt, *The Radical Right*, pp. 103–5.
39. P. Martin, *Le Vote Le Pen: L'électorat du Front national* (Paris: Fondation Saint-Simon, 1996), pp. 20–1.
40. My thanks to Roland Cayrol, the director of CSA and Pascal Perrineau, the director of CEVIPOF, for permitting me to use the two data sets cited in the tables below. Of course, they have no responsibility for my interpretations of this data.
41. This analysis generally agrees with that of P. Martin in *Le Vote Le Pen*, pp. 20–3.
42. Mayer, *Ces Français*, p. 258.
43. See P. Martin, *Comprendre les évolutions électorales: La théorie des réalignements revisitée* (Paris: Presses de Sciences Po, 2000), pp. 270–81.
44. See M. Schain, 'Immigrants and Politics in France', in J.S. Ambler (ed.), *The French Socialist Experiment* (Philadelphia, PA: Institute for the Study of Human Issues, 1985), p. 187.
45. J. Money, *Fences and Neighbors: The Political Geography of Immigration Control* (Ithaca, NY/ London: Cornell University Press, 1999), pp. 135–47.
46. Ibid., p.156.
47. See A. Girard, 'Attitudes des français a l'égard de l'immigration étrangère', *Population* (November/December, 1974). The one measure that did not diminish was the sentiment that 'there are too many immigrants in France.'
48. See Tarrow, *Power in Movement*.

49. See Minkenberg, *Die neue radikale Rechte*, Ch. 9.
50. There is hardly any literature on the skinhead scene in France. One of the few French publications on skinheads contains little information about the French but a lot about the German scene; see A. Peralva, 'La violence skinhead', in P. Perrineau (ed.), *L'engagement politique. Déclin ou mutation?* (Paris: Presses de la Fondation nationale des sciences politiques, 1994), pp. 141–56. Recently, an unpublished memo from the French Ministry of Interior put the estimated number of French skinheads at some 1,000; DCRG, 'Brèves considérations sur la violence de l'extrême droite en France', presented at conference, 'Zwischen Prävention und Reaktion: zum Umgang mit Rechtsradikalismus und rechter Gewalt in Frankreich und Deutschland', Europa-Universität Viadrina Frankfurt (Oder), 29 June–1 July 2000.
51. See CRIDA (Centre de Recherche d'Information et de Documentation Antiraciste), *Rapport 1996. Panorama des actes racistes et de l'extrémisme de droite en Europe* (Paris: 1996), p. 42.
52. See J. Marcus, *The National Front and French Politics. The Resistible Rise of Jean-Marie Le Pen* (London: Macmillan, 1995), p. 192; Commission nationale consultative des Droits de l'Homme, *1996. La lutte contre le racisme* (Paris: La Documentation française, 1996), p. 41; CRIDA, *Rapport 1996*, p. 40.
53. Rucht, *Modernisierung*, pp. 161–84.
54. See N. Mayer, *Les collectifs anti-Front national*, cahiers du CEVIPOF, No. 13 (Paris: Centre d'étude de la vie politique française, 1995).
55. See N. Mayer, 'The National Front Vote and Right-wing Extremism', in F. Weil (ed.), *Extremism, Protest, Social Movements, and Democracy*, Vol. 3 of the Yearbook *Research on Democracy and Society* (Greenwich, CT/London: JAI Press, 1996), p. 215.
56. J.F. Hollifield, 'Immigration and Republicanism in France: The Hidden Consensus', in W. Cornelius, P.L. Martin and J.F. Hollifield (eds), *Controlling Immigration. A Global Perspective* (Stanford, CA: Stanford University Press, 1994), p. 151.
57. Ibid., p. 212.
58. See P. Perrineau, 'Le Front national, la force solitaire', in P. Habert, P. Perrineau and C. Ysmal (eds), *Le Vote sanction* (Paris: Presses de la FNSP/Dept d'Etudes Politiques du Figaro, 1993), p. 155.
59. J. Chiche and E. Dupoirier, 'Les Voies contrastées de la reconquête électorale. L'électorat de la droite modérée en 1993', ibid., p. 133.
60. See M.A. Schain, 'The Immigration Debate and the National Front', in Keeler and Schain, *Chirac's Challenge*, pp. 169–99.
61. See P. Perrineau, 'Le Front national', in M. Winock (ed.), *Histoire de l'extrême droite en France* (Paris: Seuil, 1993), pp. 275–7; Marcus, *The National Front*, pp. 136–43.
62. See J.-M. Donegani and M. Sadoun, 'Le jeu des institutions', in J.-F. Sirinelli (ed.), *Histoire des droites en France*, Vol. 1. *Politique* (Paris: Gallimard, 1992), p. 458.
63. See Birenbaum, *Le Front national*, pp. 79–80.
64. See C. Patrait, 'Pouvoirs régionaux en chantier', in P. Habert, P. Perrineau and C. Ysmal (eds), *La vote éclatée* (Paris; Presses de la FNSP/Dept. d'Etudes Politiques du Figaro, 1992), p. 311.
65. See *Libération*, 20 March 1998, p. 8, for a summary of the statement of the Political Bureau of the Front National.
66. After the smoke cleared, these were: Bourgogne, Bretagne, Languedoc-Roussillon, Picardie and Rhône-Alpes. To this list we should probably add Franche-Comté, where a UDF president was elected on 3 April 1998, with the FN and the left abstaining. However, after the Conseil d'État invalidated the election of Charles Millon in the Rhône-Alpes in December 1998, he was ousted by right–left majority in a new election in January. See *Le Monde*, 8 January 1999.
67. See the summaries of the speeches by Jacques Chirac in *Le Monde*, 21 March 1998, p. 6, and 25 March 1998, p. 6.

68. See *Le Monde*, 19 March p. 12 and 24 March, p. 1.

69. *Le Monde*, 17 June 1998, p. 5.

70. C. Maisonneuve, Le Front national à l'Assemblé Nationale, dissertation, Paris, IEP: 1991, p. 37.

71. See Maisonneuve, ibid., p. 39.

72. *Le Monde*, 11 February and 7 December 1989; See J. Vichniac, 'French Socialists and *Droit à la différence*', *French Politics and Society*, 9, 1 (Winter, 1991), pp. 40–57.

73. The basis for this approach is contained in the report by P. Weil, *Mission d'étude des législations de la nationalité et de l'immigration* (Paris: La Documentation Française, 1997); see pp. 47–8. Also see the commentary in *Le Monde*, 31 July 1997, p. 6.

74. See the discussion of this in *Le Monde*, 30 November 1997, p. 6.

75. See Schain, 'The National Front and the Politicization of Immigration in France: Implications for the Extreme Right in Western Europe', prepared for *Conference on Citizenship, Immigration and Xenophobia in Europe: Comparative Perspectives*, Wissenschafts-zentrum Berlin (WZB), 13–15 November, 1997.

76. See, for example, the dossier 'Le Front national, c'est ça', *Le Monde*, 21 March 1998, and *www.mrap.asso.fr.fiche5.htm* of 10 August 2000. At a recent conference on the far right in France and Germany in Frankfurt (Oder) on 29/30 June 2000, anti-FN activists from Toulon reported of a variety of measures by the local government to suppress any anti-FN activity which resulted in a recourse to modes of behavior modeled after the Résistance of World War II.

CHAPTER EIGHT

The FPÖ: From Populist Protest to Incumbency

Kurt Richard Luther

SINCE THE mid 1990s there has been a considerable advance of certain radical right-wing movements 'from the margins to the mainstream'. This has been nowhere more pronounced than in Austria, where on 4 February 2000, Jörg Haider's FPÖ succeeded in its ambition to enter national government. The prelude to the formation of the coalition between the FPÖ and the ÖVP caused enormous domestic and international controversy.[1] Moreover, the swearing in of the FPÖ ministers triggered the threatened diplomatic 'measures' (i.e. sanctions) of 14 of the EU governments and their associates.[2]

The inclusion in this volume of a chapter[3] on the recent development of right-wing radicalism in Austria thus requires little justification. There is a plethora of Austrian sociocultural and political phenomena to which the label right-wing radical (or right-wing extremist) can be – and has been – applied.[4] But the most important contemporary manifestation of Austrian right-wing radicalism is the FPÖ and our aim is to address two previously largely neglected dimensions: the internal dynamics of Europe's most successful right-wing radical party and the possible impact of its entry into government upon core dimensions of the party itself.

Political parties play a central role in modern liberal democratic theory, constituting an indispensable link between the sovereign people and the politicians to whom the exercise of the affairs of the state is temporarily entrusted via the electoral process. In sum, political parties can be regarded as perhaps the most important structures by means of which it is possible to bridge the inherent tension within all modern democracies between the authorizing *demos* on the one hand and the authorized politicians on the other (the principal–agent relationship).

Empirical political science has concerned itself above all with five key dimensions of political parties. First, political parties are vote-seeking organizations, which participate in public elections, where they present candidates and conduct campaigns. Second, there are the ideological values that are usually most firmly rooted amongst party functionaries ('mid-level elites') and ordinary party members and are reflected in the selection and marketing of policy preferences. Third, political parties (and above all their elites) are office-seeking. Fourth, research on political parties has of late stressed how political parties structure and organize themselves in order to exercise their mobilization and linkage function *vis-à-vis* society, but also to recruit political elites, or potential holders of public office. As has been argued since the time of Robert Michels,[5] a corollary of this organizational dimension is that political parties are inevitably very much concerned with self-maintenance, which requires them to secure adequate resources (e.g. financial, political and personal) and to mitigate intra-party tensions. Finally, political scientists have focused upon the constant external competition between political parties that comprises the relevant party system.

If one examines the history of the FPÖ with reference to these five empirical dimensions one can divide the development of the party between its foundation in 1956 and the general election of 4 October 1999 into four broad periods.[6] These are its period as a *ghetto party*, which lasted until the mid 1960s; the *normalization* period until the mid 1970s; the period of acceptance, which began in the late 1970s and lasted until September 1986; and, finally, the period of *populist protest* that was triggered by Jörg Haider's assumption of the party leadership on 15 September 1986. With its hotly contested entry into Austria's federal government on 4 February 2000, the FPÖ entered a new period, which one might perhaps designate as that of *governmental responsibility*.[7]

All political parties undertaking the shift from opposition to governmental responsibility are confronted with significant challenges and it was only to be expected that this transition would be particularly demanding for the FPÖ. For one, there is the impact of the external democratic delegitimation of the FPÖ embodied in the sanctions of the EU-14 (member-states of the EU). Closely related to this is what Anton Pelinka refers to as the 'singularity' (*Besonderheit*) of the FPÖ, which according to him is located less in the structure and issues of the party than in its rootedness in Austria's National Socialist past.[8] Third, the party's entry into government came immediately after a period of populist protest *par excellence*, which had lasted from 1986 to 1999. During this period, which coincides with Jörg Haider's leadership, the FPÖ had succeeded in advancing from a position in which its very survival was in question, to one where it had become Austria's second strongest electoral force. The vehemence of the political confrontations of these years resulted in relations between FPÖ politicians and other political actors becoming in part very strained, which could in turn undermine the capacity of the current party leadership to find partners willing to support its political objectives. Fourth, the new period in which the FPÖ finds itself will necessarily require a fundamental rethinking and restructuring of its position in Austria's electoral market, of its policy preferences, of its internal organization and recruitment, as well as of its relations to Austria's other political parties. In short, the FPÖ's entry into national government may well constitute the peak of its very steep upward development since 1986, but its transition from populist protest to governmental responsibility necessarily implies profound strategic challenges for the party with respect to each of the core dimensions of political parties outlined above.

This chapter will restrict itself above all to a consideration of the FPÖ's role in Austria's electoral market, as well to the party's internal organization and elite recruitment. We will first seek to establish how and with which strategic orientation the party operated in respect of both aspects in the period(s) prior to its entry into government. Thereafter, we will identify the most important challenges and strategic dilemmas facing the FPÖ as a consequence of its entry into Austria's federal government. As this chapter was finalized less than two years since this radical change in the party's political circumstances, it is as yet too early to be sure about the extent to which the structures and behaviours which the party employed prior to February 2000 will prove appropriate for the period of governmental responsibility. There has also been only a relatively short period of time to observe any possible changes in the party's electoral and organizational profile. Accordingly, this chapter's assessment of the strategic and organizational challenges facing the FPÖ is thus necessarily provisional.

THE FPÖ IN AUSTRIA'S ELECTORAL MARKET

Figure 8.1 illustrates the development of the FPÖ's share of the vote at general elections held between 1956 and 1999. Electorally, the *ghetto period* was characterized by decline, whilst the *normalization period* was above all a time of stabilization of the party's share of the vote, albeit at a relatively low level.[9] Under the liberal leadership of Norbert Steger, the party's period of *acceptance* peaked in the first ever FPÖ participation in national government. In terms of its position in the electoral market, however, the party was located at the edge of the political abyss. Its 1983 general election result constituted an historic low (4.98 per cent), and in public opinion surveys conducted during 1985 and 1986, it appears that only 2–3 per cent of Austrian voters supported the party. It was largely as a consequence of the intra–party dissatisfaction generated by this existential crisis that Jörg Haider was able to

FIGURE 8.1
PARTY SHARES OF THE VOTE AT AUSTRIAN GENERAL ELECTIONS:
1945–99

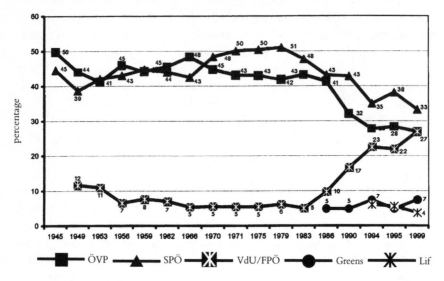

take over the leadership in a hotly contested internal election. This initiated a strategic reorientation of the FPÖ, which henceforth became a party of *populist protest*.[10] This reorientation was electorally extremely successful. At the general election of 1986, held merely a few weeks after Haider became leader, the party immediately doubled the share of the vote it had received in 1983. By the general election of 15 October 1999, the party's share of the national vote had grown to some 27 per cent, five times more than its 1983 share.

If one examines the results of the general election exit polls regularly conducted by Fessl+Gfk, it is clear that the increase of some 17 points in the FPÖ's electoral share between 1986 and 1999 was distributed very unevenly between the different segments of the electorate.[11] (The changes are indicated in Table 8.1.) The FPÖ's electoral growth was lowest amongst white-collar voters (+9) and farmers (+5). By contrast, the party's electoral support grew most among men (+20), but above all among blue-collar voters (+37). Haider's party was also disproportionately successful in mobilizing the support of young voters (mainly male but also female); in 1999, the FPÖ's share of the under-29-year-olds was 35 per cent. In 1986, it had been merely 12 per cent.[12] One of the most distinctive results of this ongoing reorientation of Austria's electorate is the fact that between 1979 and 1999 the party was able to increase its share of the blue-collar vote from 4 to 47 per cent, making the FPÖ the strongest party in this segment of the electorate.[13]

These changes in FPÖ support within the various segments of Austria's electoral market have had a less marked impact upon the sociostructural profile of the FPÖ electorate itself.[14] When compared with the electorates of Austria's other parliamentary parties, that of the FPÖ is still dispropor-tionately male (1986: 61 per cent; 1999: 62 per cent), and has unusually high levels of voters with vocational education (1986: 56 per cent; 1989: 55 per

TABLE 8.1
FREIHEITLICHE PARTEI ÖSTERREICHS VOTE WITHIN
SELECTED SOCIAL GROUPS (1986 AND 1999)

	1986	*1999*	*Change*
Overall	10	27	+17
Men	12	32	+20
employed	13	33	+20
unemployed	11	34	+23
pensioners		28	
Women	7	21	+14
employed	7	22	+15
unemployed	8	22	+14
pensioners	5	19	+14
Age			
18–29	12	35	+23
30–44	11	29	+18
45–59	6	21	+15
60–69	8	21	+13
70+	9	25	+16
Occupation			
self-employed/professionals	15	33	+18
farmers	5	10	+5
civil servants/public service	9	20	+11
white-collar	13	22	+9
blue-collar skilled	11	48	+37
blue-collar un/semi-skilled	8	45	+37
housewives	8	25	+17
pensioners	7	24	+17
in adult education	9	23	+14

Source: Fessel+Gfk exit polls.

cent). It shares with the Austrian SPÖ the distinction of having the lowest proportion of voters qualified for university study and/or with a degree (30 per cent). In respect of occupational structure, the FPÖ electorate is distinct by virtue of still having the lowest proportion of civil servants.[15] In other respects, however, there have indeed been changes in the profile of the FPÖ electorate. In 1986 white-collar workers constituted 27 per cent and blue-collar workers only 22 per cent of the party's vote. By 1999, white-collar workers (27 per cent) had just pipped blue-collar voters (26 per cent) into first place as the largest occupational group within the FPÖ's electorate. Compared to Austria's other parties, the FPÖ's electorate now has the highest proportion of workers and shares with that of the ÖVP the distinction of having the lowest proportion of salaried voters.[16] Young voters (i.e. those under 29 years of age) and those between 30 and 44 years old are over-represented in the FPÖ's electorate. The former group is only more strongly represented within the electorate of the Greens (38 per cent as opposed to 27 per cent in the FPÖ) and the latter group only in the electorate of the Greens and Liberal Forum (FPÖ 34 per cent; Greens and Liberal Forum each 38 per cent). However, if one examines the change between 1986 and 1999 in the age profile of the FPÖ electorate, one sees that the 18–29 year-olds' share of the FPÖ electorate has fallen by four percentage points, whilst that of the 30–44 year-olds has increased by two points (and that of the 45–59 year-olds by some seven points). It is too early to draw firm conclusions from these data, but it does appear that we are possibly witnessing a certain ageing of the FPÖ electorate, possibly as a result of a cohort effect.

The scale of the FPÖ's electoral success during its period of populist protest is not only unique in the history of the Second Austrian Republic but has indeed barely been equalled in any other Western European country during this period. The FPÖ's success has, of course, been facilitated by a range of different factors. Examples of external factors militating in its favour include global socioeconomic and cultural changes, the geopolitical up-heavals in Europe and the further weakening of Austria's political *Lager*. These developments have created uncertainty amongst the electorate and weakened its traditional party attachments. Second, elements of the opportunity structure have been important. Examples include Austria's proportional electoral system, the existence of the *Länder* as a second level of political power and the constitutionally required proportional composition of most *Land* governments, but also (subjective) political and economic failures of the political elite.[17]

Electoral success is, of course, never merely a product of external factors, but instead usually requires the identification and implementation of appropriate political strategies. During the period of populist protest, the dominant principle of the FPÖ's political strategy was vote maximization. Haider summarized this strategic maxim in the phrase '*attackieren statt arrangieren*' (attack not accommodation).[18] One of the most important and consciously chosen targets of this strategy were the overlapping electoral segments comprising those voters who were politically frustrated and those usually characterized as (potential) 'modernization losers'. In order to win over these voters, the FPÖ opted for an aggressive campaigning style and employed political rhetoric that was often unbridled. Its core electoral issues included political corruption, over-foreignization (*Überfremdung*), (immigrant) criminality, the alleged arrogance of the EU and a celebration of the sup-posedly exemplary values of the 'little man'.[19] The fact that during this period the FPÖ had no political responsibility whatsoever for national politics and was dismissed by its competitors as qualitatively unsuitable for government (not least precisely because of the unrestrained nature of its campaigning style), only made it all the easier for the party constantly to engage in irresponsible electoral outbidding of the then governing parties.[20] Moreover, when compared to the SPÖ and ÖVP, the FPÖ had a markedly small party organization and very few auxiliary organizations. Paradoxically, this worked to its advantage, since it allowed greater flexibility (or opportunism) in terms of the policy preferences it used to mobilize voters. As has already been demonstrated above, the predominantly negative and literally 'irresponsible' campaigning which the FPÖ undertook during its period of populist protest was highly successful electorally.

In the first three *Landtag* (provincial parliamentary) elections held since 4 February 2000, the party experienced a marked downturn in its hitherto constantly improving electoral fortunes. At the Styrian elections of 15 October 2000 the FPÖ slumped from 17.2 per cent (1995) to 12.4 per cent of the vote. A more modest decline at the Burgenland elections of 3 December 2000 (12.6 per cent vs. 14.6 per cent in 1996) nonetheless cost the party its only seat in the *Land* government. To date, the most significant loss the FPÖ has experienced since entering government has been at the Viennese provincial elections of March 2001. In 1996 the party had won 27.9 per cent of the vote, but was now supported by only 20.3 per cent of Vienna's electorate. The significance of this result lies not only in the magni-tude of the party's electoral decline, but also in the fact that Vienna comprises approximately one-fifth of Austria's population.

The reasons for these electoral reversals are closely related to the fundamental change that has taken place in the FPÖ's position in the electoral market. With its entry into national government, the FPÖ has surrendered the electoral advantage of 'irresponsibility' it had enjoyed. The party's claim to represent the 'small man' against 'the bigwigs' has understandably lost credibility. As in 1983, when Steger led the party into government with the SPÖ, the FPÖ has again immediately lost the support of many of those politically disgruntled voters whose vote for the party was motivated above all by the desire to express political protest. It is possible that we may soon witness a similar development amongst modernization losers, whom the party had assiduously courted in recent years.

The importance of the FPÖ's electoral losses should not, however, be exaggerated. First, we have to date, seen 'only' *Landtag* elections, which are of course second-order elections and often strongly influenced by *Land*-specific factors. Second, the party's loss of votes has been far less extensive than many external observers had predicted and numerous party insiders had feared.[21] A possible reason for this are the 'sanctions', which from the EU-14's perspective may well have been somewhat counterproductive. For, notwithstanding the considerable domestic political polarization caused by the formation of the government, the sanctions militated in favour of a growth in Austrian patriotism/nationalism and may thus well have resulted in a degree of solidarity with the governing parties. They also put the main opposition party in a very difficult position. For one, the SPÖ was clearly loath to criticize the EU-14's decision to implement sanctions in response to the participation in Austria's government of a party that the SPÖ had itself for many years claimed to be beyond the political pale. On the other hand, the SPÖ did not wish to further expose itself to the charge (frequently levied in particular by the governing FPÖ) that by failing to speak out strongly against the sanctions it was being disloyal to Austria (*Staatsvernaderer*). More-over, given the predominance of the sanctions issue during the first six months or so of the government's life, the opposition was unable to focus public attention upon those aspects of the government's policy in respect of which the SPÖ felt the ÖVP and FPÖ were most vulnerable to attack. (Examples include increased taxation and cuts in welfare benefits.) Whether or not the lifting of sanctions will result in a normalization of political competition and thus a worsening of the position of above all the FPÖ in Austria's electoral market can as yet not confidently be predicted.

On the other hand, there is as yet no convincing evidence to suggest that the electoral shifts since the FPÖ entered government constitute a real threat to the continued existence of the coalition, let alone to the survival of the FPÖ (as between 1983 and 1986). Finally, it is important to note that lead-ing FPÖ figures have for years been aware of the likely consequence for the party's electoral fortunes if its strategy of vote maximization were ever to enable it to enter government. As early as spring 1988, for example, Haider told this author that the party must resist the temptation of entering govern-ment until it had achieved a share of the vote such that the inevitable electoral losses that would follow such a move would not place the party in the kind of existential crisis it had experienced under Steger's leadership. He was also of the opinion that by entering government on the basis of a massively increased electoral following, the party would be much more likely to be in a position to influence the substance of government policy in a manner that would help minimize the loss of electoral support and might indeed even enable the party to mitigate those losses by increasing its support among other segments of the electorate.

The FPÖ's decision to enter government did not indicate a rejection of the goal of vote maximization, which many members of the party leadership had in any event always seen as a means to the end of government participation. Instead, it should be regarded as a prioritization of (remaining in) government. This priority will presumably dominate the party's strategic thinking for the next few years. The relative strength of Austria's parliamentary parties and the markedly poor relations between the FPÖ on the one hand and the SPÖ and the Greens on the other, mean that if the FPÖ is to realize its goal of remaining in government, it will for the foreseeable future have to do so in a 'black–blue' coalition, i.e. in cooperation with the ÖVP.

The FPÖ needs to formulate a revised electoral strategy if it is successfully to counter its expected loss of votes. The electoral strategy which the party employed with such success during its period of populist protest is likely to be much less suited for a governing party. The party has to make important strategic decisions in respect of at least three dimensions of its relationship to Austria's electoral market. First, it is likely that the very negative campaigning issues the party has consistently utilized since 1986 will no longer be as electorally profitable. The party will thus have to identify new core issues. The party leadership has already decided to make much of the FPÖ's alleged governmental competence. However, it is not yet clear how – if at all – the voters can be convinced that a party which during the years 1986 to 2000 constituted the embodiment of populist protest has now become a competent party of government. During the first year or so of its governmental term, given the party's lack of experience in government, FPÖ ministers have committed a number of political blunders, and ministerial turnover has been high. Another important test of the party's credibility as a government party will be whether it is able, in its new capacity, to remain aloof from the practices of political patronage (*Proporz*) which it did much to delegitimize and label as corrupt. Whether or not the FPÖ is successful in this endeavour will of course in large measure be determined by the party's behaviour and that of its ministerial team, as well as the extent to which the FPÖ is able to convince the electorate to attribute the government's more beneficial policy outputs to itself.[22]

The second strategic challenge for the FPÖ is closely related to the issue of its public image and has to do with how it proposes to change its hitherto very aggressive style of voter mobilization. It is no longer appropriate for the FPÖ to conduct itself in the electoral market in the manner it did during its period of populist protest. In the first place, the main target of the aggressive rhetoric of this period was above all the incumbent political class. In view of the fundamentally changed political role of the FPÖ, such an approach is likely to be regarded by the electorate as somewhat unconvincing; it could not of course be applied to the FPÖ ministers themselves and would be viewed by the party's coalition partner as unacceptable. In addition, retaining this unrestrained mobilization style would in all likelihood bring renewed difficulties for Austria's external relations, especially since the formal lifting of the sanctions has most certainly not resulted in the end of Austria's 'ostracism' or its full international 'rehabilitation'. Since the aggressive political style of the period of populist protest is closely associated with Haider himself, however, it is likely to be very difficult for the party to change the tone of the manner in which it operates in the public arena. For there is no doubt that, despite the fact that he resigned the party leadership in favour of Susanne Riess-Passer on 1 May 2000 and is himself now allegedly merely an 'ordinary member', Haider remains not only a member of the government coalition committee but also plays a key role in the making of most of the FPÖ's strategic decisions.

A third strategic decision in respect of the party's electoral role – and one that is also unresolved – concerns the identity of those segments of the electorate which the FPÖ should prioritize. At least two questions are important here. The first relates to the priority that should in future be given to attracting blue-collar voters. Some influential members of the party believe that the FPÖ must maintain – and seek to make increasingly credible – its claim to represent the interests of the working classes. It would, these persons believe, seriously undermine the political credibility of the party if it were now to abandon the interests of the 'small man', whose vote the party has in recent years assiduously sought. Accordingly, they argue that this defence of working-class interests should not only be underscored verbally but also by ensuring that the party is seen to be acting within the governing coalition in support of workers' interests, in particular via targeted changes in the areas of fiscal and social policy.[23] Other key figures within the FPÖ consider this strategy to be mistaken. In their opinion, it would serve no useful purpose for the party to target its electoral strategy at a segment of the population that is declining overall, is disproportionately composed of modernization losers and has hitherto been decidedly clientelistic in its orientation. This second group maintains that this blue-collar segment is also being targeted by the SPÖ and that the proposed measures exceed what is economically viable and would in turn thus undermine the party's strategy of seeking to create for itself the image of governmental competence. This group has been referred to as the economic wing of the FPÖ and its alternative strategy is for the party to place much more emphasis on mobilizing white and self-employed voters.[24] The intra-party conflict between these opposing strategies is still underway. However this conflict is eventually resolved, there is a second strategic question the FPÖ needs to address: namely, which additional electoral segments the party ought to target. In purely numerical terms, a promising target would of course be women, who have to date been disproportionately underrepresented in the party's electorate (see above). The party has been aware of this for years and has made deliberate efforts to appeal to women voters. Its first tactic was to recruit women to leading positions on the party's electoral list, but this tactic was not very successful.[25] Since the mid-1990s, the party adopted an additional tactic, namely, to supplement the 'hard' themes with which it was associated (e.g. anti-immigration, corruption and crime) with 'softer' themes such as increasing child allowances – the 'cheque for children' (*Kinderscheck*) – which the party's electoral strategists believe would appeal more to women. There is little evidence to date that this has indeed been the case.

In short, the party's entry into government has forced it to review the themes, tone, style and targets of its behaviour in Austria's electoral market. The actual extent of the electoral losses that will be suffered by the FPÖ – which has for so long and so vehemently pursued a strategy of populist protest – will of course depend to a considerable extent upon whether the party is able to develop a new electoral strategy which is more appropriate to its changed political role in Austria's party system. A further determinant of the political future of the party relates to the extent to which it is able to ensure that such a revised strategy is accepted by all the important groups within the party and successfully implemented through their wholehearted application.

INTERNAL ORGANIZATION AND ELITE RECRUITMENT

Political parties are very complex organizations, within which there is a constant struggle between competing personalities, groups and goals. Katz and Mair have suggested that it is useful to conceive of the internal life of political parties as comprising three 'faces', which reflect differing interests. These are (1) the 'party on the ground', the most important elements of which include the party membership and the party organization, usually based upon the principle of territoriality; (2) the 'party in public office', which relates above all to those office-holders organized in parliamentary parties, but also encompasses members of the political executive; and, (3) the 'party central office' and the key national party bodies that are closely associated with it (e.g. the party executive and the party directorate).[26] Katz and Mair of course accept that this heuristically motivated simplification is of necessity unable to capture the whole complexity of internal party life and that the three 'faces' in reality overlap. This caveat is potentially even more important in respect of Austria, a country in which there is an above average frequency of role accumulation. The following discussion of the FPÖ's internal tensions, and the resulting strategic challenges for the party is structured according to Katz and Mair's framework.

The party on the ground

Extent of membership Figure 8.2 depicts the development of the FPÖ's total membership during the four periods of the party's history. The *ghetto period* was one during which the party's organization was built up and which is thus predictably characterized by an increasing membership. In the second half of the *normalization period* the membership stagnation of the 1960s was replaced by a visible upwards trend of some 35 per cent during this period. The modest decline in the party's membership of the *period of acceptance* was followed by another rise during the period of *populist protest*; by 1999 it had increased by a further 40 per cent.

FIGURE 8.2
FREIHEITLICHE PARTEI ÖSTERREICHS PARTY MEMBERSHIP: 1956–2000

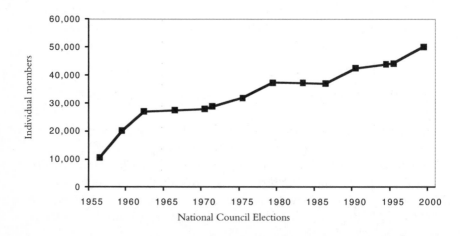

The relationship between the party's political behaviour on the one hand and its electoral results and membership development on the other is hinted at in Figure 8.3.[27] The strategy of normalization halted the electoral decline the party had experienced during its ghetto period; it stabilized the FPÖ's share of the electorate and helped the party recruit new members. On the other hand, the period of acceptance, during which the party entered government for the first time, resulted not only in a very worrying decline in its share of the electoral market, but also led to the first and to date only decline in its membership figure. To be sure, that decline was limited, but it is likely to have given the present leadership considerable cause for concern about the potential development of its membership base since it re-entered government in February 2000. During the period of populist protest, the party's membership rose from 37,000 to over 51,000, which constitutes an average annual increase of approximately 1,135 persons (see also Table 8.2).

The fact that the party's increased membership during this most recent period was accompanied by an even more dramatic increase in its electoral success meant that the party's membership density – as measured in terms of M/V – declined significantly (see Figure 8.3).[28] Some observers of the FPÖ have interpreted this as a failure of the party and/or as a development that would be worrying for the FPÖ from the perspective of normative

FIGURE 8.3

FREIHEITLICHE PARTEI ÖSTERREICHS VOTE AND MEMBERSHIP DENSITY
DURING ITS FOUR PERIODS OF DEVELOPMENT: 1956–2000

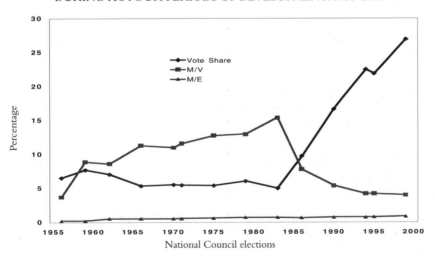

Key: M/V = FPÖ-members/FPÖ voters
M/E = FPÖ-members/Austrian electorate

democratic theory. There are at least four reasons why such an interpretation is inappropriate. Firstly, the first criticism appears to be predicated upon the erroneous assumption that the party had during this period set itself the goal of achieving a membership increase commensurate with its electoral growth. There were of course attempts made during this period to recruit new members, but voter maximization was *the* strategic priority of the party. The FPÖ never pursued the goal of developing in the direction of a membership-based mass party, as is indicated by the leadership's plans (which in the event were never fully implemented) to transform the party into a 'citizens' movement' that would have had much looser links with individuals.[29] Second, if one examines the development of the FPÖ's membership in relation to the total electorate (M/E), it is clear that – contrary to the expectations of many analysts – the FPÖ has indeed increased its organizational density during the period of populist protest. At the same time, the membership figures of both ÖVP and SPÖ declined markedly.[30] Thirdly, the ideal typical mass party is only one of the many existing party types. The ÖVP and SPÖ still embody features of this type much more than do the political parties of most other countries. However, many other organizational forms of political parties are compatible with normative democratic theory. As long ago as in the work of Michels,[31] empirical political science demonstrated that the internal processes of the mass party should not be regarded as a realization of democratic ideals. After all, the function of democratic legitimization of political parties should be seen as deriving less from their organizational penetration of society than from interparty competition in the electoral market.

Membership composition For most of the 45 years of the FPÖ's existence, the constituent provincial party organizations with the highest absolute levels of membership were those of Upper Austria, Carinthia, Styria and Salzburg (in that order). In 1986, together, they still comprised over three-quarters of the party's total membership. By October 2000 their combined share had dropped to 'only' 58 per cent (see Table 8.2). During the period of populist protest the party's total membership rose, but the development within each individual provincial party group varied considerably. In absolute terms, membership figures changed from +4,742 and −2,072, i.e. between +196 per cent and −28 per cent (see Table 8.1), though it is worth noting that the decline in absolute membership levels was to a significant extent a product of an exercise in weeding out from the lists of party members those persons who were members merely on paper. The four provincial party units where the membership levels increased most dramatically were those whose organizational density had traditionally been rather low and where the party's potential for mobilizing additional members was as a consequence greatest. The best examples are the Lower Austrian and Viennese party groups, the membership of which increased by 4,742 (+196 per cent) and 3,483 (+194 per cent) respectively. By contrast, Carinthia suffered a decline of some 2,072 members (−28 per cent).

These developments had at least three interesting consequences for intra-party relations. First, there was a change in the *Land* groups' relative strength in terms of party membership levels. Upper Austria remained first (24.4 per cent), but the second place is now held by Styria, albeit on the basis of a smaller share of the total party membership (down from 18.2 to 13.4 per cent). The second strongest *Land* group had been that of Carinthia, which in 1986 boasted some 20.4 per cent of the FPÖ's total membership. By 2000 it had a share of only 10.6 per cent. The greatest relative gain has been on the part of the *Land* groups of Tyrol (5.4 to 9.5 per cent), Vienna (5 to 10.3 per cent), but above all on the part of the Lower Austrian party (6.6 to 14.0 per cent). Second, the disparity in the relative size of the *Land* groups has declined further. Since the relative size of the *Land* groups' memberships determines the number of delegates the *Land* group is entitled to at the

TABLE 8.2

DEVELOPMENT OF THE FREIHEITLICHE PARTEI ÖSTERREICHS
MEMBERSHIP: 1986–2000

Land *group*	*Members*		*Change: 1986–2000*		*Share of Members (%)*		*Change of share (%)*	*Women %*
	1986	2000	abs.	%	1986	2000	1986–2000	2000
Burgenland	603	1,567	+964	+160	1.6	3.1	+1.5	20.0
Carinthia	7,488	5,416	−2,072	−28	20.4	10.6	−9.8	20.9
Lower Austria	2,423	7,165	+4,742	+196	6.6	14.0	+7.4	25.7
Upper Austria	9,124	12,497	+3,373	+40	24.9	24.4	−0.5	26.7
Salzburg	4,287	4,830	−543	+13	11.7	9.4	−2.3	27.3
Styria	6,679	6,870	+191	+3	18.2	13.4	−4.8	27.0
Tyrol	1,973	4,871	+2,898	+147	5.4	9.5	+4.1	26.2
Vorarlberg	2,310	2,801	+491	+21	6.3	5.5	−0.8	24.1
Vienna	1,796	5,279	+3,483	+194	5.0	10.3	+5.3	33.9
Austria (total)	36,683	51,296	+14,613	+40	100.0	100.0	–	26.4

Source: Federal Party Central Office and author's own calculations.

Bundesparteitag (Federal Party Congress), this shift in membership levels has also resulted in an adjustment to the relative intra-party strength of the various *Land* organizations.

Unfortunately, there are only very few data available regarding the social structure of the FPÖ's membership and there are no useful longitudinal data at all. If one examines the material that is available (the latest of which date from October 2000), there are nonetheless a few points one can make.[32] First, it is clear that the overwhelming majority of FPÖ party members are male. Accordingly, the proportion of women in the FPÖ's total membership was in October 2000 a mere 26 per cent and in Burgenland and Carinthia merely 20 and 21 per cent, respectively (see Table 8.2). Women are most strongly represented in the urban party organization of Vienna, but even here, they comprise a mere 34 per cent of the members. Looking at the development of the age structure of the membership since 1986, it is clear that Haider's assumption of the party leadership resulted in a rejuvenation of the party. This occurred above all in those *Land* groups where the party's membership levels increased most. For example, in 1992 the age cohort of those under thirty comprised some 27 per cent in Burgenland and 22 per cent in Tyrol. In 1994 this age cohort made up 13 per cent of the FPÖ's total membership, but has since declined somewhat and in October 2000 was a mere 11 per cent. During the same period the proportion of those over 60 has remained constant at about a quarter (1995: 25 per cent; 2000: 24 per cent). One possible interpretation of these data is that the phase of strong membership recruitment amongst young Austrians is now over. There is, unfortunately, only an incomplete set of data regarding the occupational structure of the FPÖ's membership, but if one compares what we know on the basis of those data about the occupational profile of the party's membership in 1992 with what most people believe the situation to have been between the 1960s and early 1980s (albeit on the basis of no hard data), there do appear to have been some significant changes. In the former period it was assumed that the party's membership was made up above all by civil servants, self-employed and professionals. In October 2000, however, blue-collar workers comprised approximately one-sixth of FPÖ members; self-employed and farmers each made up 11 per cent and students less than 2 per cent. It is worth noting that the occupational structure of the party's membership bears little relation to that of its electorate, in which blue-collar workers are extremely strongly represented (see above).

The size and composition of the FPÖ's membership may well be significant for the party's strategy. On the one hand, maintaining a large membership can be costly for a party. It requires the investment of a considerable amount of financial, organizational and other resources. It may also be costly for the party's leadership by virtue of the fact that it can result in an undesirable narrowing of the latter's room for political manœuvre, especially in respect of the party's selection of policy preferences. On the other hand, it may offer the party and/or its leadership considerable advantages. For one, a large membership is of considerable symbolic value, not least since it enables the party to make a credible claim to represent a large proportion of the citizenry. Second, a densely organized party is simply more visible in society, which in turn militates in favour of the party's mobilizational and legitimizational capacity. The membership can also be of considerable material advantage for the party (leadership). Despite the fact that political communication is nowadays conducted above all via electronic media, political parties still rely upon members when it comes to electoral campaigning. The more members a party has, the greater is the resource of unpaid labour at the party's disposal. In addition, notwithstanding the fact that membership contributions are a much less significant source of political parties' overall revenue than used to be the case,[33] membership dues still constitute an important source of party income. When calculating the costs and benefits of a large membership base for a political party and its leadership, however, the most important consideration may well be the extent to which the membership provides a key reservoir for elite recruitment. It is extremely important for the maintenance and external political success of any political party – and especially for one like the FPÖ that is a fledgling governmental party – that it has at its disposal a significantly large reservoir from which it can recruit party functionaries and office-holders.

The party in public office

The electoral successes which the FPÖ experienced during the period of populist protest resulted in a massive increase in the number of public offices to which it was entitled. Thus between 1981 and 1999, for example, the party experienced a fourfold increase in the number of elected offices it held. At the communal level, the number of FPÖ councillors grew from 1,766 to 4,876; FPÖ deputy mayors rose from 46 to 127, and the party's 27 mayors in 1981 had by 1999 become 36. At the *Land* (provincial) level, the number of FPÖ *Landtagsabgeordnete* (provincial parliamentarians) grew from 25 to 101, whilst the number of *Landesräte* (members of the provincial government) increased from 4 to 12. Nationally, the FPÖ's caucus in the popularly elected lower chamber (*Nationalrat*) grew from 11 to 52, whilst its caucus in the indirectly elected territorial chamber (*Bundesrat*) now comprises 15, but in 1981 the party had no members at all. Between 1989 and 1991, and again since 1999, the party's leader, Jörg Haider, held the governorship (*Landes-*

hauptmann) of Carinthia. If one were also to include all the positions which the FPÖ holds in the various new-corporatist organizations such as the Chamber of Labour and the Chamber of Commerce, the total number of FPÖ office-holders would be approximately 8,000. This has had important internal consequences for the party: it has posed new challenges both to the party and its leadership and has to some extent also required strategic reorientation.

First, there has been a shift of power away from the party on the ground towards the party in public office. This has resulted in part from existing provisions in the party's statute, according to which holders of public office are ex officio full members of the most important party committees. Also important have been strategic decisions made by the FPÖ leadership in the mid 1990s when it was decided that the intra-party weight of the parliament-ary caucus should be increased, in particular as regards the development and determination of policies and goals.

Second, it became increasingly difficult for the party to find people willing to stand on its electoral list and to hold public office in its name. The immediate, but poorly considered response by the party at all levels was to bring on board virtually anyone willing to stand for election. However, this soon changed the quantitative problem of political recruitment into an at times highly embarrassing qualitative problem. Many of these new candidates all too soon turned out to be people whose background, political opinions, or public behaviour were such that the FPÖ often felt obliged to distance itself from them, or even to remove them from office. The party introduced a series of measures that were designed not only to address this problem of unsuitable candidates but also to effect a general strengthening of the leader-ship. For example, all potential FPÖ candidates for public office now have to undergo a screening process, and decisions regarding the ordering of candidates on party electoral lists have been considerably centralized.

Third, there has been an increased tendency for the party leadership to place at or near the top of its electoral lists (especially at general elections) high-profile public figures who are selected above all because they represent certain key issues which the party wishes to emphasize in that specific campaign, or because they are felt by the leadership to be likely to attract a specific segment of the electorate which the party is targeting. Those *Quereinsteiger* – i.e. non-party personalities 'parachuted in' – have typically been used to highlight issues such as the fight against political corruption, or against crime. The system has also led to a prominent role for female *Quereinsteiger* whose visibility would, the party leadership hoped, help address its electoral deficit amongst female voters.[34] Such practices created not inconsiderable internal party dissatisfaction. The latter was to be found above all amongst longstanding party functionaries, who had little sympathy for a strategy which involved giving secure positions on party electoral lists to newcomers who – unlike them – had not made any significant contribution to the party's success. This dissatisfaction was also located amongst those 'believers'[35] who feared that the entry of these 'outsiders' would result in a highly undesirable de-ideologization of the party.

The party central office

In reality, Katz and Mair's three 'faces' of political parties obviously overlap and thus some aspects of the recent development of the FPÖ central office have already been alluded to. Therefore, this section will confine itself to summarizing these developments and the strategic challenges they present. First, the material resources of the FPÖ have increased considerably since 1986, above all because the party's electoral successes have resulted in the FPÖ being entitled to a much larger share of Austria's very generous level of public funding. This has permitted the party to strengthen and increase the staffing resources of its central office. Second, between 1986 and 1999 there has been an marked improvement in the technical resources of its central office. For example, the party has at last been able to establish a central index of all members, something which its leadership had been seeking for some 30 years to establish. The central office has also been equipped with the latest electronic communication equipment, by virtue of which there has been a considerable speeding up of internal and external communication, as well as a marked improvement in the flow of intra-party information. Also worth mentioning in this context is the fact that the central party office has in recent years increasingly sought the support of professional political experts, who have been employed above all in the training of party function-aries, but also in respect of the planning and conduct of election campaigns. As these people are often employed on a short-term or contract-specific basis, they do not constitute an intra-party factor that might wish (let alone be able) to form an oppositional group. On the contrary, their dependence upon the party leadership strengthens the position of the latter *vis-à-vis* the party on the ground. Bearing in mind these changes in above all the party central office and its relationship to the party on the ground, one is tempted to conclude that during its period of populist protest the FPÖ has moved a considerable way towards Panebianco's organizational ideal-type of the 'electoral-professional party'.[36]

Third, since February 2000 there has been a certain disorientation within the party central office. This was in part a consequence of the challenges posed by the physical and psychological changes resulting from the FPÖ's transition from an oppositional party to a party of government. It was, however, also related to the fact that, notwithstanding the above-mentioned increases since 1986 in the central office's staffing levels, the party apparatus remains relatively small. In the spring of 2000 many of those staff members and functionaries deemed most competent were either required to work in support of the party's governmental team, or were indeed physically relocated from their positions in the central office to work in the cabinets of the FPÖ's federal ministers. As a consequence, the efficiency and political competence of the central office has been undermined. From the perspective of the party's new strategy of governmental responsibility, the functional reorientation and relocation of these former central office staff appears eminently logical. Bearing in mind party-internal considerations, however, this development might be considered to constitute a plundering of the personnel resources of the central office, which in turn places the party in a position where it urgently needs to replace these people who were disproportionately well informed about the internal processes of the party. An even more important strategic issue for the party relates to the extent to which the central office will be able to rise to the challenges presented by the party's entry into government. That this transition may prove extremely difficult for the FPÖ's modest apparatus was demon-strated during the short period of government participation which the party experienced between 1983 and 1987 under the leadership of Norbert Steger. It is clear that during this first period of FPÖ government participation, the central office was unable to cope with the simultaneous demands of supporting the FPÖ's government team and ensuring the party's smooth internal operation. It proved incapable, on the one hand, of conveying to the party on the ground and to the general public the alleged successes of the FPÖ ministers,[37] and, on the other, of maintaining the internal workings of the FPÖ in a manner consistent with the goals of the party leadership. One of the most significant consequences of the overload which the party central office experienced between 1983 and 1987 was the fact that the leadership lost control of the party. Haider mobilized the party on the ground against the leadership and was himself elected leader in September 1986.

A fourth important strategic consideration, and one closely related to the previous point, is the extent to which the party leadership will succeed in maintaining the degree of consensus necessary to ensure the party is able to function externally as an effective political actor. Observers of the FPÖ during its period of populist protest often commented that its internal decision-making processes were highly centralized, or even authoritarian. Though there is some substance to such assertions, they have often been exaggerated. Moreover, the FPÖ has since its foundation always been charac-terized by strong internal conflicts, which derive from personal, territorial and ideological tensions, but are of course also the product of considerations predicated upon the pursuit of power politics.[38] During the period of populist protest the FPÖ leadership was able to manage these conflicts, even if this at times required the implementation of exceptionally tough measures – an example of which was the temporary removal from office of all party functionaries in the Salzburg *Land* party group. A key factor explaining the leadership success is to be found in the fact that its strategy of vote maximization led to continuous electoral successes and thus to an increase in material resources such as money, public office and other posts. These were available to the party leadership in the form of selective benefits by means of which the leadership was able to placate potential intra-party critics.[39] If the period of governmental responsibility were to result in the predicted reversal of the party's electoral fortunes, the leadership is likely to have at its disposal fewer such selective incentives and this may in turn lead to a revitalization of the FPÖ's traditionally very strong intra-party conflicts.

In assuming governmental responsibility on 4 February 2000, the FPÖ has prioritized government over vote maximization. This implies that the hitherto very close relationship between the party leadership (i.e. Haider) and the party on the ground will come under increasing pressure. For if Panebianco is correct, the party on the ground is likely to have a disproportionately high concentration of 'believers', i.e. of party members whose motivation is predominantly ideological.[40] Alternatively, it is to be expected that the party leadership – amongst whom there is a disproportionately high percentage of persons in public office – will comprise above all 'careerists' whose political priorities are the achievement, maintenance and exercise of political power. The hard political decisions and compromises that are an inevitable feature of government responsibility will most probably be unwelcome to the party on the ground and to the FPÖ's provincial functionaries. Given that the selective incentives available to the leadership to ensure the compliance of the party on the ground may well decline, increased intra-party conflict seems to be very likely.

Moreover, there will probably be a reactivation of the longstanding territorial conflict within the party, albeit a result of a logic that reverses that which applied during the FPÖ's period of populist protest. During the latter period, the FPÖ was able to achieve at least one governmental seat in every single *Land* government, and in Carinthia it even won the governorship. At the federal level, however, the party was unencumbered by governmental responsibility and pursued its strategy of vote maximization by means of a populist style that utilized unbridled political rhetoric. That rhetoric proved electorally successful, but did cause political discomfort to some *Land* party groups. This was particularly the case with the Vorarlberg group. Unlike that of most Austrian *Länder*, Vorarlberg's constitution does not require all parties that receive more than a given percentage of the popular vote at *Landtag* elections automatically to be represented in the provincial government. On the one hand, this was an advantage for the local FPÖ, inasmuch as it meant that they were members of a genuine – as opposed to an obligatory – government coalition. On the other hand, whilst most of the FPÖ's other provincial ministers could not easily be removed from office, the FPÖ's membership of the Vorarlberg government was not guaranteed and could be terminated by its dominant coalition partner (the ÖVP). The all too frequent occasions on which the party leader made what might euphemistically be termed a verbal *'faux pas'*[41] thus placed the Vorarlberg *Land* group in a very difficult position.

The position is now reversed. The federal party carries governmental responsibility, whilst in all *Länder* other than Vorarlberg the party is at best a member of an obligatory coalition, but has elsewhere lost its governmental seat either as a result of electoral decline (e.g. Burgenland), or because the constitutional rules have been changed to eject them from *Land* government (e.g. Salzburg and Tyrol). The FPÖ thus faces a situation that might well be analogous to that of 1983–86, when the federal party was blamed by the more ideologically motivated 'believers' of the provincial 'party on the ground' for the failings of an unpopular government.

In sum, it can be said that the FPÖ's assumption of governmental responsibility implies numerous strategic challenges in respect of organization and elite recruitment. Moreover, these apply to all three 'faces' of the party. It is to be expected that intra-party tensions will rise, whilst the resources available to the leadership in its attempts to overcome these tensions will decline. It is too early to say whether the leadership will be able to square these circles. However, it is very likely that interparty life will become much more demanding for the leadership, which in turn will make it more difficult for the party's internal homogeneity to be maintained at a level sufficient to ensure that the FPÖ will be able to function as a united actor externally.

CONCLUSION

This account of the recent development of Austrian right-wing radicalism is necessarily incomplete. In the first place, by focusing exclusively upon the FPÖ, it has neglected the various other (predominantly sociocultural) manifestations of right-wing radicalism. Secondly, its examination of the FPÖ has been organized with reference to analytical criteria that are regularly applied to more 'conventional' political parties, but which have to date not figured very prominently – if at all – in accounts of right-wing radical parties. Accordingly, it has devoted much less attention to the verbal '*faux pas*' of the FPÖ and of its leader, Jörg Haider, than most other publications on the party. Thirdly, it was written less than two years into the lifetime of the ÖVP/FPÖ government and so its assessment of the policy impact of the latter cannot be other than provisional.

In the light of such considerations, one might be tempted to conclude that the chapter underplays the more worrying, or extremist aspects of Austrian right-wing radicalism in general and of the FPÖ in particular. An alternative strategy would have been to place much greater emphasis upon the (verbal) radicalism and alleged peculiarity, or exceptional nature, of the FPÖ. One author who subscribes to this perspective is Anton Pelinka,[42] who insists that – compared to other European parties – the FPÖ really is an exceptional case (*Sonderfall*), the singularity of which results above all from its historical roots in the German-national *Lager*, its relationship to the Nazi regime in Austria and the biography of its first chairman (a titular SS general).

There is much to be said for this perspective. The electoral successes of the often unbridled populist protest employed by the FPÖ between 1986 and 1999 have not yet been matched elsewhere in Europe. Indeed, the verbally aggressive manner in which the FPÖ conducted itself was also one of the main reasons for the sanctions imposed by the EU-14, which justified them by asserting that the entry of a right-wing populist party into Austria's government posed a unique development in European politics and one that threatened European democracy. This would – they maintained – not only permit the other EU member-states to isolate Austria, but oblige them to do so.

On the other hand, analysing the FPÖ by means of the categories political scientists apply to more mainstream parties does provide useful insights. In the first place, it permits a fuller appreciation of the electoral strategy of Europe's electorally most successful right-wing radical party. Second, an empirical investigation of the three 'faces' of the FPÖ provides a more differentiated – and thus fuller – account of the party's internal life and how the 'dominant coalition'[43] has managed to assert itself. Third, it suggests that there are key respects in which the FPÖ might be considered to be markedly unexceptional. Above all, it is unable to avoid the party-strategic challenges brought about as a result of its assumption of governmental responsibility. Like all other parties that undergo this transition, it too is faced with the need to make 'hard choices' between policy, office or votes.[44] Indeed, this transition is likely to prove especially difficult for a party such as the FPÖ, which for so many years and so successfully pursued a strategy of populist agitation.

POSTSCRIPT

During the year between the completion of this chapter and the end of 2002, the FPÖ suffered a series of severe internal crises. They eventually caused Riess-Passer and key members of her team to resign, whereupon Schüssel terminated the coalition. In 1999, the FPÖ and ÖVP had each won 26.9 per cent of the vote and 52 seats. At the premature general election of 24 November, the FPÖ crashed to 10.1 per cent and 18 seats, whilst the ÖVP scored an historic victory, winning 42.3 per cent and 79 seats. Schüssel thereby became the pivotal player in the government formation game, hypothetically able to form a majority coalition with any one of the three other parliamentary parties. After unusually protracted coalition negotiations the ÖVP-FPÖ government was reconstituted, albeit with a much weaker FPÖ. A fuller account of the FPÖ's implosion and the subsequent general election has been provided elsewhere.[45] This postscript is limited to highlighting some of the main causes of the FPÖ's dramatic collapse and considering the party's likely future role.

The fundamental cause of the FPÖ's spectacular implosion was its failure to meet the challenges of the transition from populist protest to incumbency. As stated above, the leadership had expected incumbency to result in a worsening of the party's position in the electoral market. However, it proved unable to mitigate the ensuing intensification of candidate selection conflicts, inflammation of personal rivalries and accentuation of differences over policy priorities. One reason for this lay in the inadequacy of the personnel resources in the party central office, which could not meet the twin challenge of staffing and supporting the FPÖ government team, whilst simultaneously maintaining effective communication between the party in public office and the party on the ground. Second, the broader leadership team predominantly comprised persons of a more pragmatic or 'careerist' orientation. Whilst the under-representation of the more ideological group of 'believers' enhanced the party's capacity to co-operate with its coalition partner, and was thus consistent with the demands of incumbency, it exacerbated internal party divisions. The largely unincorporated ideological and territorial factions were thus vulnerable to the blandishments of internal counter-elites, who pursued their personal political animosities and ambitions within the increasingly fissiparous party.

Third, there was a marked unwillingness on the part of a significant proportion of party functionaries to accept the policy compromises of incumbency. Though adept at exercising the political roles appropriate for populist protest, they remained ill at ease justifying (unpopular) government decisions. Their disinclination to adopt roles consistent with the demands of incumbency might have been less serious for Riess-Passer's leadership had it not been for the unwillingness of her predecessor and mentor, Haider, to resist the temptation of playing to the gallery of local functionaries by conducting populist 'internal opposition' to the party's government team. Though he had negotiated the coalition agreement and as a member of the coalition committee still influenced government policy,[46] he persisted in publicly attacking many of those policies and frequently threatening to force early elections. In other words, he appears himself to have been unable to make the transition from the charismatic, polarizing leadership appropriate for a party of populist protest to a type of leadership more compatible with incumbency.

The beginning of the end came in August 2002, when in response to severe flooding, the government announced the postponement of tax cuts. This provoked a furious response from the fundamentalist wing of the party (including from Haider), which condemned this decision as signalling an abandonment of the party's commitment to the 'small man' (see above). Unable to reverse this decision within the highest party organs (in which they were under-represented), or via indirect media confrontations with Riess-Passer, Haider and his supporters turned to an obscure party statute clause requiring an extraordinary party conference to be held if a third of federal party conference delegates signed a petition to that effect. With the submission of that petition on 3 September, an already critical situation escalated out of control. Though Haider invited the signatories to an informal meeting in Knittelfeld on 7 September, to find a compromise solution, the delegates demonstratively tore up Haider and Riess-Passer's draft compromise agreement. The next day, Riess-Passer resigned, Schüssel ruled out cooperation with the 'Knittelfeld Rebels' and within days early elections had been called.

The FPÖ has been severely damaged. It has forfeited much of the political credibility it had started to gain under Riess-Passer's leadership. By losing two thirds of its voters, it is also destined to suffer a massive reduction in income from state party subsidies. This will have a profound impact upon the resources available to party central office, where redundancy notices were issued even before the election. Although the FPÖ has returned to government, the loss of two thirds of its parliamentary seats means the parliamentary 'party in office' will at a stroke lose the majority of its assistants and be deprived of its hitherto influential role on parliamentary committees. The position of the 'party on the ground' may not be quite as dramatic, though it is as yet too early to tell. Though there were reports of significant numbers of individual resignations and some cases of local branches dissolving, it would be premature to assume the party is finished. Unlike its counterparts elsewhere, the FPÖ is not a recent incarnation. It is a fully institutionalized party that retains a sizeable membership and strong local structures, and enjoys state funding at the provincial level. Though things could yet deteriorate, at present the likelihood is that the FPÖ will persist as an organization, albeit in a much weakened form.

The party's future political role will depend to a significant extent upon whether it remains in government, or returns to opposition. In the former eventuality, the FPÖ will continue to experience the challenges of incumbency highlighted in the main body of this chapter. Whether this will promote further de-radicalisation, or result in another major internal division is as yet unclear. By contrast, the opposition scenario would 'liberate' the party to resume a strategy of irresponsible outbidding. Yet even if the FPÖ were (prematurely) to leave Schüssel's second government it is unlikely to regain the strength it had achieved.

Some may wish to conclude that the Austrian experience suggests a strategy of isolating right-wing populist parties is likely to enhance their electoral potential, while incorporating them into governmental responsibility subjects them to the very demanding challenges of incumbency. In turn, these may well either de-radicalize such parties, or cause them to experience potentially critical internal tensions.

NOTES

1. See G. Falkner, 'The EU-14's "Sanctions" Against Austria: Sense and Nonsense', *ECSA Review*, 14, 1 (2001), pp. 14ff. and 20; M. Fleischhacker, *Wien, 4. Februar 2000 oder: Die Hysterie zur Wende* (Vienna: Czernin Verlag, 2001); and H.-H. Scharsach and K. Kuch, *Schatten über Europa* (Cologne: Kiepenheuer, Witsch, 2000).
2. See F. Karlhofer, J. Melichor and H. Sickinger (eds), *Anlassfal Österreich: Die Europäische Union auf dem Weg zu einer Wertegemeinschaft*, special issue of *Österreichische Zeitschrift für Politikwissenschaft* (Baden-Baden: Nomos, 2001); and M. Kopeinig and C. Kontakto, *Eine europäische Affäre: Der Weisen-Bericht und die Sanktionen gegen Österreich* (Vienna: Czernin Verlag, 2000).
3. For an earlier version of this chapter in German, see K.R. Luther, 'Parteistrategische Herausforderungen der Regierungsbeteiligung: Die FPÖ vor und nach ihrem Eintritt in die Bundesregierung', in Karlhofer, Melichor and Sickinger, *Analssfal Österreich*, pp. 61–79.
4. Though often rather emotive, there is a wide range of literature on these phenomena. See, for example, Dokumentationsarchiv des österreichischen Widerstandes (ed.), *Handbuch des Österreichischen Rechtsextremismus* (Vienna: Verlag Deuticke, 1994); W. Ötsch, *Haider light: Handbuch für Demogogie* (Vienna: Czernin Verlag, 2000); K. Ottomeyer, *Die Haider-Show: Zur Psychopolitik der FPÖ* (Klagenfurt-Celovec: Drava Verlag, 2000); S. Reinfeldt, *Nicht-wir und Die-da: Studien zum rechten Populismus* (Vienna: Braumüller, 2000); and H.-H. Scharsach, *Haiders Kampf* (Vienna: Orac im Verlag Kremayr Schierau, 1992).

5. See R. Michels, *Political Parties* (New York: Free Press, 1962) [first published in 1911].
6. See K.R. Luther, 'Die "Freiheitliche Partei Österreichs"', in H. Dachs, P. Gerlich and H. Gottweis (eds), *Handbuch des politischen Systens Österreichs* (Vienna: Manz Verlag, 1991), pp. 247–62, esp. p. 247.
7. During its first spell in government (with the SPÖ from 1983 until 1986/7) the FPÖ was an extremely weak coalition partner that was suffered or 'accepted'. The FPÖ's position in the Schüsel–Reiss–Passer government is very different, however. Because of its much greater electoral and parliamentary strength, but also in view of the portfolios it holds, the FPÖ is now very much an equal, and thus responsible, coalition partner.
8. We will return to the question of the FPÖ's 'singularity' in the closing remarks of this chapter. See also A. Pelinka, 'Sonderfall FPÖ: Sonderfall Österreich', in Karlhofer, Melichor and Sickinger, *Anlassfall Österreich*, pp. 61–7.
9. The modest increase in the party's share of the vote in the 1979 general election did not fulfil the expectations of the then leadership.
10. See K.R. Luther, 'The "Freiheitliche Partei Österreichs": Protest Party or Governing Party?', in E. Kirchner (ed.), *Liberal Parties in Western Europe* (Cambridge: Cambridge University Press, 1988), pp. 213–51, esp. pp. 213ff.
11. The following data derive from the relevant Fessel+GfK polls, the latest of which is reported in F. Plasser, P.A. Ulram and F. Sommer, *Analyse der Nationalratswahl 1999: Muster, Trends, und Entscheidungsmotive* (Vienna: Zentrum für Angewande Politikforschung, 1999).
12. The data for the other parties is as follows: SPÖ, 25 per cent; ÖVP, 17 per cent; Greens, 14 per cent; and LiF, 4 per cent.
13. In 1979, the SPÖ obtained 63 per cent of the blue-collar vote; but in 1999, it was supported by only 35 per cent of Austrian workers. See also K.R. Luther, 'Austria: A Democracy under Threat from the Freedom Party?', *Parliamentary Affairs*, 53, 3 (2000), pp. 426–62, esp. pp. 430ff.
14. See Plasser *et al.*, *Analyse der Nationalratswahl 1999*, p. 39.
15. The largest proportion is to be found in the electorate of the Greens (16 per cent); followed by that of the ÖVP (11 per cent).
16. Blue-collar voters: SPÖ, 16 per cent; ÖVP, 7 per cent; Greens, 5 per cent; and Liberal Forum, 4 per cent. White-collar voters: Greens, 64 per cent; Liberal Forum, 43 per cent; and SPÖ, 34 per cent.
17. See K.R. Luther, 'Die Freiheitlichen', in H. Dachs, P. Gerlich, H. Gottweis, *et al.* (eds), *Handbuch des politischen Systems Österreichs: Die Zweite Republik* (Vienna: Manz Verlag, 1997), pp. 286–303, esp. p. 301.
18. Interview with the author in Vienna on 18 February 1988.
19. On the political style of the FPÖ during this period, see the literature cited in Luther, 'Die Freiheitlichen'.
20. See K.R. Luther and K. Deschouwer (eds), *Party Elites in Divided Societies: Political Parties in Consociational Democracy* (London: Routledge, 1999), pp. 43ff. and 243ff.
21. Numerous interviews conducted by the author in recent years with party members and activists.
22. This paper has deliberately chosen not to discuss policy outputs. Nonetheless, it worth pointing out that FPÖ portfolios include ministries whose outputs may be rather unpopular in times of austerity such as these. These include above all the Ministry of Finance, but also the Ministry of Social Affairs.
23. In early 2001, one of the strongest (but not necessarily most influential) of intra-party voices supporting this line has been that of Rainer Gaugg, a Carinthian MP. It is worth noting that the party holds the relevant government portfolios, which should enable it to implement those measures, as well as to ensure that they can be 'sold' as FPÖ achievements.
24. The persons most usually identified by the Austrian media as being part of this wing are

Thomas Prinzhorn, a millionaire FPÖ industrialist and MP, who is currently the party's Second President of the national parliament, and Karl-Heinz Grasser, the FPÖ's youthful Finance Minister. The strategic and substantive reflections of this economic wing are similar in many respects to those held by Steger during the periods of his leadership. See Luther, 'Die Freiheitlichen', pp. 548ff.

25. One of the most prominent women to be promoted to a leading position in the FPÖ was Heide Schmidt, who in 1993 was to lead the group of FPÖ MPs who defected from the party and formed the Liberal Forum.

26. See R.S. Katz and P. Mair, 'The Evolution of Party Organizations in Europe: Three Faces of Party Organization', *American Review of Politics*, 14 (1993), pp. 593–617.

27. On the development and goals of the party's strategy, see Luther, 'Die "Freiheitliche Partei Österreichs"'; 'Friedrich Peter', in H. Dachs, P. Gerlich and W.C. Müller (eds), *Die Politiker: Karrieren und Wirken bedeutender Repräsentanten der zweiten Republik* (Vienna: Manz Verlag, 1995), pp. 435–44; 'Norbert Steger' in Dachs, Gerlich and Müller, *Die Politiker*, pp. 548–57; and 'Die Freiheitlichen'. The development and goals are predicted upon over 150 interviews that the author has conducted with party members, leaders and activists.

28. The M/V value at the general election of 1979 was 13 per cent; in 1983, when the party membership was stable but its share of the electorate declined, it stood at 15.4 per cent; the doubling of the party's share of the vote in 1986 reduced the M/V to 7.8 per cent and in 1999 it was only some 4.3 per cent. By way of comparison, the average value for the period 1966–1983, inclusive, was c. 12.5 per cent. On the relative utility of the different measures contained in Figure 8.3, see R.S. Katz and P. Mair, 'The Membership of Political Parties in European Democracies', *European Journal of Political Research*, 22 (1992), pp. 329–45.

29. See Luther, 'Die Freiheitlichen', pp. 291ff.

30. The average FPÖ value for 1966–1983, inclusive, was 0.63 per cent. In 1986, it was 0.68 per cent; and in 1999, it stood at 0.86 per cent. The M/E value of the SPÖ in 1986 was 12.3 per cent but had, by 1999, been halved.

31. See Michels, *Political Parties*.

32. The sources of the latest data are documents that were provided to the author on 12 October 2000 by the FPÖ Bundesparteizentrale (Central Party Office). The remaining data derive from internal party documents given to the author during recent years by party staff and office-holders.

33. See Katz and Mair, *Party Organization in Western Democracies*; and Katz and Mair (eds), *How Parties Organize: Change and Adaptation in Party Organizations in Western Democracies* (London: Sage, 1994).

34. This symbolic prioritization of female candidates occurred above all at the national and provincial levels and led to a modest increase in the proportion of female FPÖ office-holders. In 1999, for example, women comprised 19.6 per cent of office-holders at provincial and national levels. It must be noted, however, that this figure was still lower than the already low proportion of women in the FPÖ membership as a whole (in 2000, it was 26.4 per cent: see above and Table 8.1). At communal level, women made up merely 13.3 percent of FPÖ office-holders.

35. See A. Panebianco, *Political Parties: Organisation and Power* (Cambridge: Cambridge University Press, 1988).

36. Ibid., pp. 21ff.

37. This may, of course, have been related at least in part to the limited extent of these successes. On the problems of the Steger era, see Luther, 'Die "Freiheitliche Partei Österreichs"'; and Luther, 'Norbert Steger'.

38. See Luther, 'Die Freiheitlichen'.

39. According to Panebianco, *Political Parties*, the distribution of intra-party resources constitutes one of the 'zones of uncertainty', which the 'dominant coalition' of a party

needs to control in order to assert its dominance within the party.

40. Ibid., pp. 21ff.
41. Including, for example, his reference to the 'orderly employment policy' of the Third Reich, or his speech to an audience containing former members of the Waffen SS. See K.R. Luther, 'Zwischen unkritischer Selbstdarstellung und bedingungsloser externer Verurteilung: Nazivergangenheit, Anti-Semitismus und Holocaust im Schrifttum der Freiheitlichen Partei Österreichs', in W. Bergmann, R. Erb and A. Lichtblau (eds), *Schwieriges Erbe: Der Umgang mit Nationalsozialismus und Antisemitismus in Österreich, der DDR und der Bundesrepublik Deutschland* (Frankfurt: Campus Verlag, 1995), pp. 286–303.
42. Pelinka, 'Sonderfall FPÖ: Sonderfall Österreich', esp. pp.57ff.
43. Panebianco, *Political Parties*.
44. See W.C. Müller and K. Strøm (eds), *Policy, Office or Votes? How Political Parties in Western Europe Make Hard Decisions* (Cambridge: Cambridge University Press, 1999).
45. See K.R. Luther, 'Austria's 2002 Election: The Self-Destruction of Right-Wing Populism?', *West European Politics*, 26 (2003), forthcoming.
46. Following the major conflict over his trip to Iraq, Haider resigned from the Coalition Committee in February 2002.

CHAPTER NINE

Right-Wing Extremism and Xenophobia in Germany: Escalation, Exaggeration, or What?

Ekkart Zimmermann

IN JULY 2001 the European Council in its report on racism and intolerance said that Germany is in the same category as Croatia, Cyprus and Turkey: one of those countries where xenophobia and denial of rights to foreigners are widespread. Leading German newspapers[1] and politicians such as the Secretary of the Interior considered this to be a grossly distorted picture and reacted with indignation. Germany, for instance, is host to many Kurdish refugees, whereas Turkey, their nemesis, is treated with more clemency than Germany in the very same report. The Council later modified its statement as an overreaction.[2] Similar exaggerated accusations can be found throughout the history of united Germany and before 1990, for instance, in the analysis of American survey and mass media data.[3]

In this chapter, I will trace developments mainly from 1995 until 2000, and into the first half of the year of 2001, considering four indicators of right-wing extremism, namely violence, xenophobic attitudes, right-wing extremist organizations and voting for right-wing extremist parties. I will also compare developments in the 1980s and the first half of the 1990s. Since all four indicators testify to xenophobia in a more general sense, this term will be used in this broader sense as well. Ruud Koopmans[4] suggests that xenophobia is the main component of right-wing extremism, engagement in right-wing extremist activities and violence being largely a function of the huge influx of foreigners into Germany in the 1990s. Koopmans bolsters his argument with the close correlation between the influx of foreigners and violent aggression against foreigners,[5] while finding no similar correspondence between the immigration figures and voting for right-wing extremist parties. The full spectrum of right-wing extremist ideology is irrelevant compared to the xenophobic core component.

This chapter intends, first of all, to provide evidence as to the level and rate of change in the four indicators mentioned. Secondly, it aims to provide a representative overview and assessment of theoretical explanations that are found both in the scientific literature and in leading national newspapers. Both quantitative and qualitative evidence will be dealt with. Thirdly, emphasis is on clearing away a lot of the theoretical underbrush that can be found when dealing with right-wing extremism. Wilhelm Heitmeyer with his theses about social isolation and individualization in a capitalist world, for example, has great difficulties in explaining the formation and outbreak of massive forms of right-wing extremism in East Germany, an environment largely determined by socialist legacies.[6] The focus here is neither on the theoretical exposition of various explanations, nor on the degree of inter-elationship between theoretical statements and empirical indicators, but rather on the general theoretical empirical evidence that can be secured when studying the various forms of right-wing extremism in Germany from a broader perspective. Serious caveats remain. These comprise data limitations, for instance, when tracing acts of xenophobic aggression, and the general underrepresentation of extremist views in national surveys. Moreover, the work of journalists, often the initial sources for further scrutiny, frequently remains impressionistic. Thus the present assessment must be configurative in nature. It will, nevertheless, provide (at least partial) answers as to whether right-wing extremism in Germany has indeed escalated or whether these are mostly foreign exaggerations over the last half decade.

DATA TRENDS

The most general data source is the annual report of the BVS, which relies on local police reports and has been criticized for some time. Offences of youngsters under 14, for instance, are simply not reported. Non-*Staatsschutz-delikte* (i.e., offences not challenging the existence of the state) with right-wing extremist content are subsumed under categories other than right-wing extremist attacks[7] (in the meantime the Ministers of Interior in the German states have addressed this issue). Further, the Federal Office of Investigation (*Bundeskriminalamt*) has now begun to proceed with its own data collection. Initial comparisons lead one to suspect that serious underreporting has occurred. For the state of Mecklenburg-Pomerania, for example, 79 right-wing extremist criminal acts are reported over the year 2000, as compared to 1,142 in Thuringia, with about the same population size. A recounting of cases adds 11 more fatalities killed in right-wing extremist acts of violence.[8] Altogether, there are few systematic social-scientific data collections on the development of right-wing extremism. One of them deals with 'mobilization for ethnic relationships, citizenship and immigration',[9] another one with protest events in general from 1950 onwards.[10]

Acts of right-wing extremist violence

The trend is clear. After the decline from the peak in 1992 (2,639 *violent attacks*) to the lowest figure in 1998 (708), there has been a general increase over the years until 2000, with a huge increase in the year 2000. Thuringia and Mecklenburg-Pomerania experienced increases from 1999 to 2000, whereas for the other three East German states the figures decline. A large increase also occurs in the West, namely, in Northrhine-Westphalia (almost a doubling from 87 to 153) and Lower Saxony (from 80 to 129), and in the rich state of Baden-Württemberg (from 61 to 100). These figures may not be very reliable for the reasons stated above. Nevertheless, the trend of a 41 per cent increase over three years from 1998 (708 acts) to 2000 (998 acts) is alarming since it took place in spite of firmer measures on the part of the prosecuting authorities. Figures for the first half of 2001 are once again (slightly) increasing. Of 11,593 extremist acts (most of them propaganda offences, a third displaying xenophobic or anti-Semitic hatred), two-thirds (7,729) were attributed to a right-wing extremist background.[11] Some definitions have been changed and there is a marginal decline in anti-Semitic acts.

Further evidence of a growing right-wing extremist threat comes from the significant increase in *propaganda offences* (6,719 in 1999; 10,435 in 2000, an increase of 55.3 per cent) and in other criminal acts, in particular racist incitement (*Volksverhetzung*): an increase of 78 per cent from 1,932 in 1999 to 3,438 in 2000. These are alarming trends. The yearly rates of change have also accelerated from 5.4 per cent for acts of violence from 1998 to 1999 to 33.8 per cent from 1999 to 2000. The same holds for propaganda offences and for *Volksverhetzung*. A summary of all non-violent criminal acts of right-wing extremist background indicates a 61 per cent increase from 1999 (9,291) to 2000 (14,953). Again the rates of change have accelerated.

Some of this growth, paradoxically, may have to do with closer scrutiny by the police and prosecution offices, after the notable peak of right-wing extremist violence in the year of 1992. Also, an awareness on the part of the public may have contributed to more systematic reporting of such acts.

The evidence becomes even more dramatic when we trace the setting of these acts and relate them to the percentage of foreigners in the various states of Germany. First, in *absolute* numbers, Northrhine-Westphalia is in the lead, followed by Lower Saxony and Baden-Württemberg (see figures below), with nearly all other West German states ranking at the end. Second, with respect to the *population-deflated* figures, the East German states stand out even more: in the first seven ranks one finds only the West German city of Hamburg (ranked 4th with almost a doubling of the figures from 1999 to 2000) and Lower Saxony (ranked 6th with a 61 per cent increase). East German Thuringia is clearly leading and shows the most massive increase of per capita right-wing extremist violent acts of all the 16 states. Brandenburg and Mecklenburg-Pomerania rank second and third with about 25 per cent lower figures. Saxony ranks lowest amongst the five East German states (37 per cent of the level of Thuringia) and displays the greatest decline from 1999 to 2000 among any of the federal states.

These population-deflated figures reveal, of course, more about the incidence and trends than average East German percentage figures of the absolute values which rose from a share of 32.8 per cent in 1992 to 50.5 per cent in 1997, before declining again to 34.6 per cent in the year of 2000. With respect to *population-deflated figures* East German scores reach on average 2.25 times the magnitude of West German scores in the year 2000. All East German states share disproportionately in the violent right-wing extremist acts (from Thuringia with 3.74 to Saxony with 1.38) as do Hamburg (2.47), Lower Saxony (1.64), Schleswig-Holstein (1.27), and Berlin (1.15). The range from the lowest value in Bavaria (0.5) to the highest in Thuringia is by a factor of seven.

Third, when using population-deflated figures and relating them to the *percentage of foreigners* in respective German states, East German states clearly take the leading ranks. The range of variation in the resulting coefficients even spreads beyond the multiplier of seven, when we compare Bavaria with Thuringia. In 1996 (*Statistisches Bundesamt*) foreigners comprised between 2.4 per cent of the population in Brandenburg (highest value in the East) and 1.2 per cent in Thuringia. The highest values in the West were 16.9 per cent foreigners in Hamburg, 13.8 per cent in Hesse, 13.5 per cent in Berlin and 12.4 per cent in Baden-Württemberg; the lowest figure in the West is 5.1 per cent foreigners in Schleswig-Holstein.

With foreign population figures of 1991 and acts of violence per million inhabitants between 1992 and 1994, Koopmans (1995, p. 20; 1996) reported a negative correlation of −0.50 (N=16). For 2,000 acts of right-wing extremist violence and the foreign population share at the end of 1998 we find the same score (exactly −0.499). For West Germany there was no correlation between the 'levels and influx of foreigners … and substantial differences among … the levels of violence'.[12] In longitudinal perspective, though, a positive relationship emerges between right-wing extremist voting and violence.[13] Moreover, for eight West European countries at the national level, there is 'no evidence of any relation between levels of violence and the size of the foreign ... population'.[14]

Fourth, East Germans also favour restricting further immigration into the country as well as the (social welfare) rights of foreigners in the country.[15]

One hardly could argue that this is a case of overreporting on the part of the West German-dominated national press. Initially, local authorities are involved in reporting incidents and there has to be at least some reaction at the local level before the national press will pick up an item. According to these figures, there is no justification at all for the outcry of some East German politicians against the Secretary of the Interior, Otto Schily, that once again East Germans were presented in an unfavourable light when presenting these figures.

Xenophobic attitudes

Here the evidence is much less clear. There is no continuous reporting on the development of xenophobic attitudes and ideologies, for instance, comparable to the recurrent assessment of the popularity of political parties. There are few solid nationwide surveys on these questions. One finds highly specific studies among researchers using the biannual ALLBUS-data set.[16] Whatever methodological sophistication is employed, these studies are usually marred by sampling errors, by respondents understating their extremists' point of view, and, sometimes, by purely technical interests on the part of research analysts dealing with scant data. Several of the studies in Alba *et al.*[17] justify this verdict. They explain the low variances and great variations in the attitude patterns and that so far no powerful general theorizing is in sight.[18] Standard variables such as age, education, left/right political orientation and contact with foreign groups reappear in many studies, sometimes linked to Fishbein's general (and formal) attitude theory.[19] In one of those ALLBUS-nationwide surveys, left political ideology, religious tolerance and post-material priorities represent more positive preconditions for multicultural integration.[20]

Surveys on *anti-Semitism* are equally marred by sampling errors and sensitivity issues as far as the wording of questions is concerned. Kurthen *et al.*,[21] in an analysis of several nationwide studies during the 1980s and 1990s, report for instance that 'East Germans are clearly less anti-Semitic than West Germans, but more xenophobic' and that 'anti-Semitism has not gained significance in the population at large [after unification] but has, indeed, become more widespread and radicalized within a particular subpopulation: ultra-right-wing adolescents – particularly less educated, right-wing oriented male manual laborers'.[22] In terms of social structural variables, increased age, lower education and rural residence consistently point to stronger anti-

Semitic attitudes. Some studies report lower anti-Semitism scores in East Germany and explain this with the long-term socialization effects of the official anti-fascist ideology which left unaddressed the issues of German obligation to the Jews and the presence of Jews in Germany after the war. The issue of guilt was claimed to be an entirely West German one since the capitalist structures, allegedly associated with fascism, had been wiped out in East Germany.

Another explanation might be that anti-Semitism in East Germany was simply a non-issue. If this were the case one would be surprised by the swiftness with which anti-Semitism re-emerged in East Germany. Here one has to rely on estimates. The figures of Kurthen *et al.*[23] only go up to 1994. Also, resentment in East Germany always had an easy scapegoat in West German dominance. Interestingly, Schmidt and Heyder[24] find no great differences between the level of authoritarian political attitudes and the idealization of one's own nation in West and East Germany.

In a study of anti-Semitism up until 1996, Bergmann and Erb[25] suggest period effects as an explanation for the rise of anti-Semitism amongst East German youth groups. In terms of substance, one may add, a combination of socialization and breakdown variables is behind this period effect, as specified in the mass society theory of Kornhauser.[26] After a logistic regression for xenophobia, Bergmann and Erb sum up many of their results:

> Dissatisfaction with democracy is the central factor in West and East Germany. Actual politics is blamed for being unable to solve the immigration problem in the sense of xenophobes. They are anti-liberal, right-wing oriented, and authoritarian-nationalistic. They belong to the lower educational strata and assess today's economic situation in Germany as rather bad ... Whereas anti-Semitism is strongly caused by ideological prejudgments, in the case of xenophobia, situational crisis perceptions come into play as well.[27]

The number of attacks against Jewish public buildings and Jewish cemeteries has not decreased since 1995, but rather has been on the increase (in particular during the last two years). All this has occurred in spite of strict curbs on expressing anti-Semitism in public and forbidding national socialist (Nazi) symbols in German politics and cultural life. The speaker of the Organization of Jews in Germany, Paul Spiegel, thus raises the question: what else has to occur to make the public aware of the danger of increased anti-Semitism and xenophobia? Kurthen *et al.*,[28] however, state that the figures for expressed anti-Semitism in national surveys in Germany up until the middle of the 1990s do not differ from the scores in other West European countries.

Right-wing extremist organizations

Official figures indicate either the stagnation or decline of most of the right-wing extremist organizations. Thus, for example, the REP has lost over 2,000 members during the period 1998–2000 (13,000). The organizational base of the DVU has declined by 1,000 (2000: 17,000), whereas the NPD has gained 500 members (2000: 6,500). On the other hand, there is the massive restructuring and recruitment of militarized members on the part of the NPD in the state of Saxony. Stöss[29] argues that leading right-wing extremist organizations in West Germany aimed at institutional transfer into East Germany when unification came about, just as other intermediate West German structures were implemented in East Germany. Yet, the East German right-wing extremist scene, mostly consisting of young male skinheads as well as other anti-system adherents and drop-outs, did not want to be infiltrated by West German right-wing extremist organizations. Up until 1995, these Western organizations were considered irrelevant to the specific situation in East Germany and the shared anti-system grievances of these youth groups. The West German right-wing extremist functionaries were considered members of a grey political establishment and consequently failed to attract extremist youth in East Germany. After a series of failures[30] and more repressive reactions on the part of the state authorities (judiciary and police) and the media, however, the newly formed _Kameradschaften_ (comradeships) in East Germany became linked to Western resources and organizing staff. Saxony, with the JN hosts the strongest and apparently best-organized subgroup of the NPD in East Germany. Yet, in the federal election of 1998 the NPD mobilized only 7,000 voters in East Germany. They comprise the hard core of right-wing extremists in East Germany.[31] After eliminating double-memberships, the total right-wing extremist potential is estimated at 50,900 in the year of 2000 – a loss of 1,700 since 1998.

The newly constituted _Kameradschaften_ represent a new form of pre-political organization. Often they only serve the functions of a youth club at the local scene. Repression by the Ministry of the Interior and the judiciary has increased, as has public demand for such actions. To be safe from prosecution for neo-Nazi political propaganda and activities, right-wing extremist structures were and are being remodelled to care more for the needs of young recruits at the local scene. Activists are forming _Kameradschaften_ which have a positive connotation to many uninitiated youngsters. The military in Germany up to this point both in formal manuals and colloquially uses the word '_Kameradschaften_', even though it is rather tainted in West Germany. Apparently, the very same noun has never disappeared from political consciousness in the East German environment. After the NPD had failed to pass the 5 per cent hurdle in the national election in 1969 (with 4.3 per cent of the vote), its central organization broke down and was replaced by local *Kameradschaften*. Thus, there is a historical precedent of organizational readjustment.

All other right-wing extremist splinter organizations (the BVS mentions 78 in 2000) play a minor role (4,200 members altogether). They suffered, and still suffer, from enormous sectarian infighting and fragmentation, as is generally the case with right-wing extremism in Germany since World War II. The BVS draws special attention to skinhead music groups such as the 'WAW-Kampfkapelle' that make extremely loud techno music, coupled with outlawed nationalist political slogans. Some of these groups and movements (for example, 'Blood & Honour') have already been suppressed. It is through skinhead rock concerts and through the popularity of these bands that right-wing extremist strategists recruit new members and replenish their *Kameradschaften*. Also in many East German towns right-wing extremist youth functionaries organize local neighbourhoods along law-and-order issues much cherished by local inhabitants. These right-wing extremist groups protect children on their way to schools, organize play groups that are ideologically indoctrinated, and otherwise care for social needs in run-down neighbourhoods. These more long-term efforts can have a lasting socialization impact upon youngsters growing up into a political economic environment that does not look favourable to them.

Internet demagogy is another issue addressed by the very same report (the number of extreme right-wing home-pages has increased from 330 in 1999 to about 800 in 2000). Up until now no safeguard has been found against the spreading of extremist right-wing hate material and ideology, including anti-Semitism. The anarchic network structure of the internet allows for permanent trespassing of official standards of political and moral decency. Canons of human conduct can easily be lowered to an extremely dangerous level. On the other hand, the strength of the anarchic structure of the internet lends itself to the spreading and writing up of extremist ideological materials, for instance, by simply relocating hate sites into foreign countries. This is, most likely, also the central flaw in the efficient organization of right-wing extremist structures, both nationally and internationally. Monopolizing the information needed for effective organization, or not, is only one click away. Consequently, I would predict that the disorganizing qualities of the internet also undermine the probability of setting up a successful right-wing extremist organization. The internet is not only a bone of contention to right-wing extremist organization but could be counterproductive, due to a lack in language skills and grave ideological differences. This dialectical aspect has been overlooked so far. Still it holds true that with the internet, right-wing extremist challengers have many new opportunities to increase their repertoires of contention (for instance, McAdam[32]) that have not been met with equal resources and skills on the part of the prosecuting institutions.

Voting for right-wing extremist parties

The greatest electoral success from 1995 onwards was the DVU's 12.9 per cent share of the electorate in the election of Saxony-Anhalt in 1998. Among the 18–25 age group, this right-wing extremist party even scored up to 30 per cent of the votes. The party ended fourth after the SPD, the CDU and the PDS, but never converted its political resources in the subsequent parliamentary period. In January 2000 it split in two: the oppositional wing Freiheitliche Deutsche Volkspartei (FDVP) followed the Austrian example of Haider's FPÖ, but collapsed soon thereafter. The stronghold of that 'party' vanished just as quickly as it rose. It was financed mostly by the leader of the West German DVU, Gerhard Frey. Thousands of posters were placed in highly visible locations before the election. If a non-existent party with non-existent candidates and a bare political programme consisting of only a few political slogans could end up as number four in a state election, the threat to the liberal democratic public is anything but gone.

Other DVU electoral successes occurred in Baden-Württemberg in 1996 (9.1 per cent of the vote) and in 1992 (10.9 per cent, REP each), and in Schleswig-Holstein in 1992 (6.3 per cent). Altogether the number of successes and failures (defined as any result below the 5 per cent threshold) in state and national elections is anything but balanced. Failures dominate by a ratio of at least 5:1. The most recent tendency suggests an electoral decline of all three right-wing extremist parties. In the federal elections of 1998, the REP alone scored only 1.8 per cent of the vote and could not do any better than in 1994 (1.7 per cent). Even the well-established REP in Baden-Württemberg failed to pass the 5 per cent hurdle in the state election of 2000. The leading candidate, Schlierer, a skilful and 'moderate' nationalist politician, could not prevent this from happening. One of the reasons may lie in the greatly personalized contest between key figures of the CDU and the SPD. Also, the major public issue in that election was making the state fit for international economic competition and educational advancements, areas where the REP had little to offer in terms of the larger electorate.

AN INTERIM ASSESSMENT

Of the four indicators of right-wing extremism and xenophobia in a wider sense, only the first two dealing with violent acts and xenophobic attitudes point to developments that can be considered dangerous. This is not to deny the shock of some of the election results that have occurred. Long-term success at the electoral polls, however, requires organizational skills and persistence in organizational structures. At the present, neither can be found to such a degree that right-wing extremist gains at the polls constituted the most direct threat to the consensus and the functioning of a liberal democratic order. This verdict holds in particular, the more important the level of voting becomes (from local via state to national elections) with the notorious exception of the elections to the European parliament in 1989: the REP gained 7.1 per cent of the vote (3.9 per cent in 1994) which allowed some voters to express their protest against normal politics.

New forms of organization (*Kameradschaften*, penetrating the youth scene via musical preferences, subcultural devices and local services) are tried out, apparently with considerable success, especially in many East German towns and quarters. It is here where respective groups speak of 'nationally liberated zones' indicating both their national goals and where they want to control and dominate the content of public discourse, to give their own definition of law and order and, most important, to control who is 'in' and who is 'out'. Violence is used to implement this invasion and occupation of the minds and the territory, which is nothing but the traditional strategy of any guerrilla or terrorist group. Three clusters are to be intimidated at the same time: first, by increasing pressure on the extremist groups themselves, members of the very same core and fringe groups are intimidated and deterred from leaving their right-wing extremist *Kameradschaften*; second, the public is frightened into giving up control of communal places, areas and issues debated in local contexts; and, third, foreigners are outlawed and attacked, or at a minimum scared off. Theoretically the strategy of these right-wing extremist groups is a mixture of traditional terrorist techniques and Gramsci's idea of cultural and intellectual hegemony coupled with the administration and utilization of resources. In fact, the old Nazi movement in Germany in many regions followed a similar strategy.

It is in these forms of new local organizations and their violent strategies in economically deserted regions that a serious threat has emerged for German democracy. There are quite a few newspaper reports on how local communities adapt with great anxiety to those new challenges. Parents are still considering these youngsters as 'normal' kids, doing nothing bad, much as the local police and members of the judiciary used to think of them. More recently, however, at least in the intermediate structures and the organs of public prosecution, dramatic changes have taken place. Sentences passed upon the offenders have changed from mild or very moderate to rather harsh. There are reports that many local police chiefs are no longer following a policy of benign neglect. It seems as if at least these public authorities and figures at the local scene have learned about the grim impact violent activities have on foreign investment, if it occurs at all, in certain regions of East Germany. Even with the disappearance of such right-wing extremist activities, the newly awakened fears of foreign tourists, even West German tourists, and foreign investors will not disappear quickly.

Upon closer inspection, an 'all-clear' signal can be given only with respect to manifest forms of right-wing extremist organizational strength. Even the recent failures at the polls are not sufficient to overlook the electoral shock results in Saxony-Anhalt in 1998 and in Baden-Württemberg in 1996 and 1992. In terms of xenophobic acts, violent aggression, and the general persistence of xenophobic attitudes, a much more alarming overall assessment lies at hand. Before taking up this question again and putting it in both historical perspective within Germany and in balance with other West European countries, a look at several of the most prominent theoretical explanations is due.

THEORETICAL EXPLANATIONS

Here we follow the treatment of data in the preceding section and will start with explanations of extremist violence and attitudes and then concentrate briefly on assessing right-wing extremist electoral performance over the last decade. Later on, more general theories will be taken up to explain several features of right-wing extremism and the demand for such social and political forces. In all those instances, it is useful to distinguish between a perspective of *demand* and *supply*. Demand in general will imply the search of individuals or groups for certain ideological and political programmes. The search behaviour is largely influenced by personal attitudes, by social structural positioning and by local contexts. The latter aspect already points to characteristics of the political and societal opportunity structure occurring both at local and national levels. When the notion of political and societal opportunity structures comes into play, it generally is to be placed on the supply side. Without such a notion the distinction between the potential for right-wing extremism and its temporary forms of outlet, as in the three waves of right-wing extremism in West Germany during 1949–52, 1966–71 and 1986–90 could never be understood in a convincing way.[33] On the other hand, there is an inherent danger of circular explanation when invoking the theoretical notion of political opportunity structure (see the discussion by Koopmans[34]). *Ex ante* specification and a comparative perspective dealing with variations in the opportunity structure may help in avoiding this pitfall. This important theoretical approach is crucial when making conditioned predictions, as we will do in the final section of this chapter.

Explaining right-wing extremist and xenophobic violence

A lack of data about individual perpetrators makes this dependent variable the most difficult one to tackle. On the other hand, the most likely scenario for these acts is easily sketched.[35] 'The average racist offender is in fact a rather normal German youth, aged 18–20 years, still following an education for, or already working as a skilled laborer, with a normal family background, and living in a small town or in the countryside rather than in the anonymous, individualized big city'.[36] A group of youngsters, usually at evening times or during the night and usually in a state of (alcohol) intoxication, makes an impromptu decision and attacks a home of asylum-seekers or foreign workers. Usually it is not difficult to find out about those locations. Furthermore, they are not well protected, so they make for easy targets and victims. In some instances, the original site selected for attack is substituted by another, due to contingent factors. Also the risk of being detected seems to be lowest in medium-sized towns of between 10,000 and 50,000 inhabitants.[37] In small villages perpetrators may be supported by xenophobic public opinion, but may also easily be spotted. In large cities where multicultural tolerance is greater, the risk of being discovered while carrying out an attack may be greater than in small villages. This explanation squares with rational choice and also with the available evidence.

Intoxicated members of youth gangs are not to be confused with, or regarded as identical to, ideologues of political right-wing extremism. Nevertheless, there is an overlap between the ideological orientation of the latter and the willingness of the former to select objects of attack that meet this ideological distinction. Consequently, there is a lot to be said for the argument of Bergmann and Erb,[38] that there is a division of labour among these actors and that one may speak of a *social movement* of the right-wing extremist sector. This application of the term of social movement to right-wing extremism may seem an insult to the 'new' social movement analysts.[39] Many of the features of today's right-wing extremist activities in Germany differ profoundly from the left–libertarian movements, not just in terms of ideology but also of recruitment structure and support. The libertarian–left originated in the 1960s, spread during the 1970s and reached its peak in the early 1980s when environmental issues and issues of international peace were connected for a short period. Yet, these new developments on the right-wing extremist scene can just as fruitfully be captured with notions of social movement analysis. This holds for the division of labour between xenophobic acts against foreigners and voting for right-wing extremist parties, and also for the multitude of organizational forms that have sprung up, partly in response to pressures from the persecuting authorities and the public alike.

All these activities share a common ideological right-wing extremist background and usually meet with the sympathies of right-wing adherents.[40] As with the case of leftist movements, there is also room for the explanatory factor of political and societal opportunity structures when assessing the path of right-wing extremist activities.[41] Structural social movement analysis should be unaffected by the ideological content of various social and political movements.

Altogether there are three forms of organizational base models: namely a sect, a social movement and/or a political party. Sometimes, all three forms are used at the same time. Again the evolution of the strategic and tactical devices of national socialism supplies suggestive historical examples of blending different social and political audiences under a broad ideological umbrella. Features of an ample social and political movement were just as efficiently employed as the means and tactics of a highly effective mass party. Despite the problems involved in explaining many of these right-wing extremist violent acts, and despite the scarcity of data, the scenario above is the most general one to emerge. In some instances, local hegemony has led to these acts being committed even during the daytime and in public places. (For example, chasing a foreigner through the town of Magdeburg in 1994, or throwing a man out of a taxi and killing him, as happened in Dresden.) The social structural analysis of Eckert and Willems[42] – who have analysed police documents and acts of the judiciary – suggests that the perpetrators are not always hooligans and skinheads. Sometimes they come from established middle-class families. They are young males, aged up to their mid twenties, and usually have jobs.

The interesting question remains as to which factors will influence, or have influenced, the calculation of potential offenders regarding their deeds. Here, as with other acts of right-wing extremism, it seems as if a combination of diffusion effects, i.e. following the model acts displayed somewhere else, and decreasing (or increasing) costs of activity *per saldo* will explain to what extent and in what form violence against foreigners will continue, or increase, in Germany, in particular in East Germany. The *media* must be considered the most active of the diffusionist factors (even though a causal analysis has to face many interactions between the media, mass opinions and individual perpetrations).[43] There are many records of journalists making up their own pictures or stories (see the alleged right-wing extremist murder of a child in the Saxonian city of Sebnitz in 2000) and nourishing their own youthful clientèle, sometimes even through monetary incentives. Some youthful perpetrators boast of their 'success stories' making it into the news channels. Often reports of xenophobic acts on TV channels may have been an equal or even more serious catalyst than concrete local 'grievances'.[44]

Right-wing extremist and xenophobic attitudes

In terms of substantial explanations, usually economic competition draws more attention than the general fear of foreigners in the country. At least this holds for West Germany, while in East Germany the general absence or low presence of foreigners makes it simultaneously both understandable and yet not understandable as to why such xenophobic attitudes exist. A lack of knowledge, ignorance and lack of personal contact with foreigners easily contributes to the resentment and anxieties large portions of the East Germans associate with the presence of foreigners.[45]

The resentment is even stronger if these foreigners come from non-European backgrounds. This also holds true for West Germany. Here, as in other Western European countries, 'foreigners' are not associated with people coming from the member-states of the European Union. In France, the first association with 'foreigners' is people from North Africa; in Germany it is Turks. Also in Western European states, there is a strong correlation between the presence of foreigners in a country and the proportion of the population saying that there are too many foreigners in the country.[46] Both France and Germany score at the high end of the scale. A study of ten countries – Australia, Canada, Austria, Italy, Spain, the Netherlands, Sweden, the Czech Republic and Hungary[47] – reports a consistent increase of xenophobia with decreasing education. As to the degree of xenophobia, it places Germany in the middle category of the sample (see also the Eurobarometer 53 for related trends since 1988).

Altogether, experience with foreigners for over four decades in West Germany has led to a general acceptance of these people in the country, in particular if they come from EU member-states. The population overwhelmingly has learned the lesson that it profits from the economic activities of foreigners in the country.[48] All these economic analyses lead to unquestionably profitable and positive results for the underlying German population. As the liberal *Süedeutsche Zeitung* in Munich once put it ironically: 'Foreigners, spare us the German kitchen.' This also holds for foreigners contributing to taxes, pension funds and the welfare state in general.

It is only with the unforeseen and gigantic immigration wave of the years of 1991–93 (roughly one million migrants each year) that a significant increase in right-wing extremist attacks on foreigners, in particular asylum-seekers, took place. The peak of those activities was reached in 1992. In the very same year, Article 16 of the Basic Law was reformed so as to restrict unlimited (political and economic) asylum to political asylum only, namely to people prosecuted by state authorities in non-democratic states. The implementation of the Schengen Agreement in 1994–95 made it almost impossible for migrants and asylum-seekers to reach German territory without first entering the territory of a democratic neighbouring state. In line with the Schengen Agreement, they have to be sent back to these democratic neighbour states.

Both right-wing extremists and the population at large had their demands met to stem this wave of massive and uncontrolled immigration which had lasted for three years, and which in percentage terms (and most likely even in actual figures) was higher than immigration figures for the United States. The then dominant REP quickly lost its only issue of competence[49] among its right-wing extremist adherents, namely that of keeping foreigners out of the country.[50] With pooled time series data, Koopmans bolsters his assessment that it is the immigration issue of foreigners that feeds into anti-foreign sentiments and right-wing extremism. For Koopmans, right-wing extremism *per se* would have little or insignificant support, were it not for the immigration and xenophobic issues.[51]

Koopmans points out that the repatriation of German-speaking people or people of German ethnic origin from Eastern Europe and the former Soviet Union, with equally high annual figures between 1988 and 1996 (2.3 million repatriates vs. roughly two million asylum-seekers), led to completely different reactions by both the politicians who steered this issue and the public at large. Upon their arrival, these *Auslandsdeutsche* did not look different from many of the asylum-seekers, especially those from the Balkans.[52] These migrants were considered Germans by the German authorities throughout their lives. Thus at the moment these people entered Germany they enjoyed all the rights and benefits of the welfare state without ever being called 'bogus' economic asylum-seekers.[53] They were granted passports and social support in terms of housing, employment, clothing and other subsidies, and were spared almost without exception those attacks that asylum-seekers fear. Consequently, Koopmans[54] argues that the official definition of the status of immigrants, the protection and support given to these groups, clearly helps their integration and saves them from anti-foreign attacks.

Koopmans[55] pleads for making two crucial distinctions: one between the alleged content of right-wing extremist political ideology and resistance to large-scale foreign immigration that occurred without any steering concept or any public law, and the other being differentiation among the groups of immigrants. Those two components reappear in the current discussion of passing a progressive immigration law in Germany, i.e., actively defining who should come to the country, and at the same time giving those migrants support for the integration process and providing them with full political status and full citizens' protection. Liberal political elements and the government expert commission on immigration also want to convince the public and the population at large that by channelling the immigration process qualified and much-needed people could be attracted to Germany and integrated, with better results for both the migrants themselves and future German economic and social security needs.

On the other hand, it should not be overlooked that large parts of the population can easily be mobilized for anti-foreign issues in election campaigns (as with the CDU victory in Hesse in 1998). There is no easy solution as long as both major parties shy away from handling the immigration issue realistically and convincing the largely reserved elements of the public that a well-constructed immigration law with commensurate integration measures is the least costly response, and the most adequate one.

With respect to anti-Semitism, Kurthen *et al.* wrote:

> The German political culture is characterized by a sharp difference between the extent and expression of anti-Semitism and xenophobia. Xenophobic resentment can count on a much broader societal acceptance than anti-Semitism. Germany's attempts to distance itself from National Socialist ideology had a formative influence on the political culture and the German elite in postwar Germany ... In the case of hostility towards foreigners and ethno (cultural)-centrism, the picture is not so clear ... Among the indigenous population, immigrants are often associated with stereotypes and traits that are assigned conventionally to members of lower classes (dirty, lazy, noisy, promiscuous and deviant). This perception significantly differs from the Jewish stereotype, which has an upper-class profile.[56]

But tracing both features over time, they state that 'anti-Semitism clearly follows on the heels of xenophobia'.[57]

Organizational strength

The basic analysis has already been presented in the section 'Data trends' (p. 220) of this chapter. The impact of organizational fractionalization and infighting is discussed in the final section of this chapter (pp. 241–2).[58]

Elections

Estimates of the ideological core voters of German right-wing extremist parties speak of roughly 2 to 4 per cent at the maximum, depending on whichever of the three major parties, the NPD, the REP or the DVU is the strongest and whether a state election, a federal, or a European election is involved. Depending on the availability of an issue that is both highly salient and unaddressed by major parties, as was the case with uncontrolled immigration up till 1993, the protest vote could easily double or even triple the figures mentioned. Most of the voting analysts agree that about two-thirds of the protest voters come from the conservative political camp, whereas the rest mostly stems from the social democratic electorate. In terms of sociostructural analysis, it is mostly males with no more than eight years (*Hauptschule*) of education which make up the bulk of the electoral supporters of right-wing extremist parties. They fear becoming unemployed, or at least that their economic position is worsening. In an analysis of extremist groups, Falter demonstrates that there are mixed feelings, comprising relative deprivation, and the neglect of a dominant political and social issue.[59] A right-wing extremist party (in this case the REP) is credited among its party adherents, with competence beyond that of the major political parties. The result is xenophobia and the lower-class sociostructural syndrome typical of relatively unqualified workers (see also Edinger and Hallermann[60]). Roughly up to 1993, these factors in combination made for the typical REP voter.

The notion of the *modernization losers* has become prominent in this context, denoting those who, having missed out on education or modernization, either experience or fear a loss of economic and social status to foreign immigrants (already in the country or threatening to come) or, more generally, to foreign competitors. Koopmans makes an important distinction here: namely that it is the massive influx of foreigners that feeds into right-wing extremist sentiments, not the coherent presence of right-wing extremist sentiments by themselves.[61]

A theoretical treasury: forgotten or well-addressed?

Theories that draw on notions such as a *status frustrations, status politics*[62] and, even more pronounced, *status inconsistency* are hardly taken up any more by these voting researchers who embark on the usual sociostructural analyses without any broader theoretical perspective, for instance, with reductionist efforts as found in rational choice theory. Here, we criticize the reinvention, or, more often, neglect of important theories (for instance, the overview in Neureiter[63]) of right-wing extremism and national socialism (for instance, Larsen *et al.*,[64] or Zimmermann[65]). Prominent researchers of right-wing extremism at most refer to and quote the theoretical notion of a *normal pathology* of advanced industrial societies, as expressed by Scheuch and Klingemann).[66] These authors heavily draw on the Durkheimian framework and associate right-wing extremism with other normal pathologies in advanced industrial societies, such as drug consumption. Their assessment consequently is that there is nothing to worry about as long as the dimensions of the pathology stay within limits. Yet, even Durkheim did not have a clear criterion for deciding at what point a minor deviation may turn into an anomic majority situation. In their general assessment, Scheuch and Klingemann have other notable theoretical elements to offer, namely the contrast between the modernizing outside world and a local context that is perceived as threatened by these outside forces. Depending on the availability of mobilizing agents, this conflict between primary and secondary world could easily be exploited and aggravated by right-wing extremist organizations.

None of the other leading theoreticians of past manifestations of right-wing extremism in Germany and elsewhere, such as Parsons, Geiger, Lepsius, Ranulf and others has so far been rediscovered. Trow, for example, once argued that medium-sized businessmen, the *Mittelstand* (middle class) in particular, were opposed to the economic power of big companies and unions alike and inclined to support right-wing extremist middle-class parties.[67] We hold that, with certain changes, this theory still addresses the heart of much of the populist right-wing extremist protest in Western Europe better than the alleged 'winning formula' that Kitschelt believes to have found in a mixture of libertarian anti-statist economic ideology and xenophobia.[68] To a large extent, the key issue appears to be protest against an overextended welfare state in crisis, one that hands out money to foreigners and thus creates a crisis of legitimacy.[69] Native inhabitants should come first with their needs, since it is believed that only they funded the establishment of the welfare state. Such a view broadly shared over the last three decades is not to be confused with a generally critical attitude towards the state or favouring deregulation. Rather to the contrary, the state is seen as or demanded to be instrumental for one's own social group and social position.

Many fruitful theoretical suggestions could be derived from this older body of theoretical works. Rainer Lepsius,[70] with his analysis of extremist nationalism in Germany, provides another example in that the national state is still the most general frame of orientation for many groups in society, now in particular with globalization marching on. Depending on the location in respective milieux of social order (Lepsius speaks of *sozialmoralische Geltungsmilieus*, roughly: the order of social–moral values) and the 'protection' granted by the respective social positioning, different claims are raised towards the state and society at large. If such claims are not met, one may add, there are different vulnerabilities. A theoretical analysis along those lines of Lepsius would prove highly suggestive even in the present circumstances. Important and fruitful insights of Lepsius *mutatis mutandis* still hold: 'The stratum-specific nationalism of the middle class [*Mittelstand*] turns aggressive when its socio-cultural recognition within the national society is threatened; it turns extremist when at the same time its perception of the nation is shaken'.[71] Substitute (or include) parts of the lower classes for the stratum level and most likely you have a very powerful prediction in hand. A highly stimulating set of hypotheses, furthermore, deals with the more heterogeneously focused nationalism of the working classes and their claims for political equality of rights. Social and technological changes, international economic inter-dependency, increased competition, as well as massive immigration waves, all four clearly affect the perception, resources and responses of the social strata involved.[72] Their traditional frames of orientation break down, especially in East Germany, or are at least threatened (in West Germany as well). The fight over the fundamentals and the access to the benefits of the welfare state (in terms of Haider and Le Pen: 'natives come first') is only one manifest feature of the shifts addressed by Lepsius, though historically in a different context.[73]

There are also voters with right-wing extremist, anti-democratic senti-ments that nevertheless vote for the major democratic parties. It is not quite clear from standard voting analysis and attitudinal studies whether this group is smaller or larger than the protest voters emerging from time to time for right-wing extremist parties. There has been no theoretical debate as to which group presents a greater threat to liberal democracy. Is it the protest voters who according to the analysis of Pappi[74] and Roth[75] can often be considered rational individuals, or is it the *silent anti-democrats* who, under an appropriate political opportunity structure, might give much succour to charismatic leaders of right-wing extremist parties? When right-wing extremist political parties have a salient and unaddressed political and social issue, their chances of electoral success increase massively. Yet, with respect to a *general* theory of right-wing extremism, we now would argue that the most important underlying factor for any right-wing extremist success is the existence of an economic crisis or at least the perception of such a crisis by potential voters. Issues of a too massive presence of foreigners in the country are easily styled in terms of economic crisis.

There is a third factor in the supply-side model of Zimmermann and Saalfeld: the distribution of parties along the political left–right spectrum. We had attached primacy to this variable, by contrast, in our theoretical model (Zimmermann and Saalfeld[76]). What matters is which of the major parties of the left or right of the centre is in office or, even more, whether there is a grand coalition of these parties. Whenever a democratic mass party moves into the centre from the left of the centre or from the right, voters of more extremist political views will find their political aspirations frustrated. Consequently they will be inclined to move into oppositional direction rather than supporting their moderate 'ideological kin' in government. The overwhelming electoral success of Haider and his FPÖ in the national election in 1999 with 27.2 per cent of the vote (second only to the Austrian Social Democratic Party) could easily be explained with this theoretical model, just as much as the success of the DVU in the state election of Saxony-Anhalt (12.9 per cent of the vote in 1998) in Germany, or even the Swiss People's Party (23 per cent in 1999). Minkenberg argues, however, that this model would not fit, neither in the case of many state elections in Germany nor in France or the United States.[77] It would, however, account for the success of the REP in Baden-Württemberg in 1996 with 9.1 per cent of the vote, when the grand coalition was replaced (but not for the 10.9 per cent result in 1992). Yet, rigorous tests with alternative indicators have not been carried out. One could also argue, in part, that there are specific factors involved in several of the state elections that superimpose themselves on the basic theoretical logic. Broadly speaking, these three explanatory factors should carry some weight explaining right-wing extremist electoral support. Immerfall also adds a corollary hypothesis here:

> If the left side of the political continuum fragmentizes organizationally, the right side of the electorate feels less of a need to unite behind established, center-right parties. This in turn opens up the possibility for political entrepreneurs to create new parties as an alternative and also as a strategic instrument to keep center-right parties in line.[78]

We have not addressed *socialization* theories here, for example those expressed with respect to the alleged authoritarian personality, to models of rigid thinking, or to class patterns of socialization that Lipset has described as *lower-class authoritarianism*.[79] They may have more validity in East Germany due to the general socioeconomic backwardness and ideological isolation of that part of the country. As Richard Stoess wrote: 'State socialism has furthered the development of authoritarian, nationalistic and xenophobic orientations and, at the same time, was blind towards right-wing extremist developments on its own territory'.[80] For East Germany, Winkler (2000) also reported a negative correlation of the attitudes of workers towards foreigners, even after allowing for other factors.[81] In West Germany there was no such relationship. In a path model for a representative population sample in Thuringia in September 2000, Edinger and Hallermann demonstrate a rather strong impact of relative deprivation on 'system weariness' (*Systemverdrossenheit*), and less so on personal authoritarianism which in turn has by far the strongest effect on right-wing extremist attitudes.[82]

In a much-publicized, provocative and stereotypic analysis, Maaz pointed to deformations and deprivations in East German character formation. Feelings of inferiority were said to dominate a population with a limited response repertoire that feels overly challenged.[83] Within this setting, additional theoretical views appear in the literature. These comprise, for instance, rigid training patterns in state nursery schools, just as much as the isolationist policies toward foreigners and foreign ways of living. There was a guided authoritarianism, not only in politics but also in economic and social life, which may explain why East German tolerance for foreigners and deviating forms of lifestyle is limited. In essence, these entire explanations boil down to limited socialization skills and a lack of intercultural experiences, tied to a rigid anti-fascist official ideology that left no room for foreigners in personal contact or realistic assessments.

Social and political *grievances* by themselves do not explain the success of right-wing extremist organizations and parties. It is the theoretical element of *resources* that has to be added to grievances if there is to be a momentum that feeds into the political arena. Yet even with these two theoretical blocks, grievances and resources, the move from potential to actual discontent and to one of the four forms of right-wing extremist conduct can never be sufficiently explained. The notion of *political and societal opportunity structure* is a requirement for filling this theoretical vacuum. On the other hand, this notion is often invoked in a circular manner in that a certain outcome is explained by the widening or closing of the political and societal opportunity structure. What clearly is desirable is to separate resource variables from variables of the political and societal opportunity structure and also to further differentiate amongst these opportunity variables. Here the notion of *institutional structural factors*[84] and more *contingent factors of actors' behaviour* is crucial. The former institutional factors generally describe the openness or closedness of the area of political competition. The latter refer to the conditions under which the various actors take their steps within their course of political strategy and bargaining, either on the road to success or to failure. Since the latter set of variables strongly depends on human perceptions and (mis)calculations, a certain precariousness will always be with us when making predictions.

In the more narrow sense, there seems to be agreement on crucial factors invoked in the analysis of the political opportunity structure, namely dissent among incumbent political elites, and shifts in the agenda of public issues, in the media attention cycle, and in the strategic assessment of potential coalition-making and coalition partners. Reductions in the amount of political repression or an increase in the very same variable open up or close political opportunities, for example with the efforts of the federal government to have the NPD outlawed by the Supreme Court.[85] Applying this notion of political opportunity structure to the developments from 1995 onwards leads to the following assessment. The electoral success of the REP in Baden-Württemberg in 1996 (9.1 per cent of the vote) can be explained largely by counter-mobilization effects of the *de facto* grand coalition rule in that state. In 1998 the federal government changed from a conservative–liberal coalition to a red–green coalition with a chancellor highly skilled with the media. This has added several new topics to the agenda and contributed to unclear front-lines while at the same time underlining the basic tenets of the theoretical supply-side model: the conservatives in the political opposition are taking the ground from under the right-wing extremist political parties. At the same time, the issue of unrestrained immigration of foreigners into the country has to a great extent lost its importance. Right now it ranks far below the issues of unemployment (61 per cent) and the security of the pension schemes (12 per cent).[86] Also intermediate institutions such as the judiciary and the police force, as well as the media in general, have learned their lesson in self-restraint towards the acts of right-wing extremist offenders, while at the same time enforcing laws more strictly on those very same culprits.[87] In sum, this analysis of the political and societal opportunity structure clearly points to a narrowing of the opportunities for right-wing extremist parties and organizations.

Does this, on the other hand, imply that less conventional strategies and tactics, namely violent acts of aggression and perpetration may be pursued to make up for the loss of electoral influence? The empirical evidence of Koopmans seems to point in this direction at least in the German, Norwegian, French and Danish cases.[88] For the period from 1986 to 1994, right-wing extremist electoral success in these countries did *not* coincide with increases in right-wing extremist violence. Rather there is a decrease in the votes captured by right-wing extremist political parties. For Switzerland, Sweden and the Netherlands, though, there is some covariation. Koopmans suggests a rational choice explanation in that potential offenders may correctly assess their limited electoral chances. This may add to further frustrations or to acting them out directly in violent aggression. A simple grievance explanation, which Koopmans rejects, would not explain these inverse relationships between electoral gains and losses and peaks in violent right-wing extremist activities (see also the discussion in Minkenberg).[89]

There is also a stabilizing function of protest voting. As Decker summarizes in his comparison of new right-wing populist parties in Western democracies:

> Previous experiences have at least shown that there is no real threat from [right-wing extremism] for the democratic system. Getting used to the persistent success of new parties and the (theoretical) availability of alternative forms of protest rather lead one to conclude that there is

a stabilizing function involved. If parts of the electorate succumb to the charm of simple solutions displayed by the populists, this possibly bars the dissatisfied from mobilizing around the more extreme forces or from employing violent means.[90]

BEYOND ESCALATION AND EXAGGERATION: TOWARDS A SET OF CONDITIONED PREDICTIONS

The most likely factors for *containing* right-wing extremism in the future will be the very same ones as in the past: namely a high degree of fragmentation within the right-wing extremist camp and the absence of a charismatic political leader. The latter can, however, never be predicted. If one did appear, part of his immediate success would be a sizable decline in the fragmentation of the right-wing scene. In this respect, leaders like Le Pen in France or Schönhuber in Germany to some extent demonstrate their charismatic grip over their right-wing extremist clientèle. And the reverse applies: as soon as rivals appear, they lose their charismatic position. Haider, on the other hand, has kept his leadership position uncontested for almost two decades now. More than once it has been suggested that a 'German Haider' could easily score up to 15 per cent of the votes.

Returning to the three causal variables mentioned in the Zimmermann–Saalfeld model,[91] we would like to repeat our earlier assessment that the prime mover for any right-wing extremist success is to be sought with an intensive and persistent economic crisis. Since the Great Depression and after the two oil shocks, international economic cooperation has massively increased. Thus, there is some reason to be optimistic about avoiding an enduring, major economic crisis, not only nationally but also internationally. On the other hand, with intensifying globalization, the burden of economic adjustment will increase.

Even a modern immigration law as currently discussed in Germany will not reduce the complexity of the immigration issue. Moreover, there is the temptation on the part of the major political parties to cave in for short-term electoral gains by mobilizing the electorate against further immigration. The logic of competition along the left–right spectrum of political parties need not be repeated here. Leaders of the major political parties should, however, be aware that they facilitate the mobilization of a large part of the population for political extremism when they enter a grand coalition, and especially so if a persistent and salient political issue is left unaddressed.

Apart from the *self-constraining* factor of fragmentation in the right-wing extremist camp and, as we argue, the *necessary* factors of *economic crisis* and *issue neglect*, there is the battery of causal influences addressed under the heading of a widening political and societal opportunity structure. Our analysis thus far leads us to expect no further electoral gains for right-wing extremist parties in the near future, say up to about three years from now. What we would, however, expect is the possibility of a further increase in the amount of right-wing extremist violence. Here one could add a further factor, i.e. the almost equally high level of left-wing extremist political violence in the years of 1999 and 2000.[92] We would expect further increases in the general violence level, some of which will have to do with the active fighting between right- and left-wing extremist political groups.

Concerning the chances of right-wing extremist success within the political and societal opportunity structure, the most important factors seem to be *media restraint*, in particular avoiding the instigation to a further round of violent right-wing rallies, and effectiveness on the part of the *judiciary* and *local police authorities*. Here the evidence indicates that courts are acting more quickly and with tougher punishments than they did about five years ago. This also should have an effect on police control in distressed areas. In some East German communities, the police now warn known right-wing extremists before rallies and demonstrations take place and inform the parents when their offspring is taken into custody during right-wing extremist events. Some success of these measures has been reported.[93]

We are more sceptical as to the learning qualities and capacities of the media. Perhaps there is some hope if the media experience a sense of *déjà-vu* when the next wave of right-wing extremist violent attacks afflicts the country. Usually the media only act as a mirror of public demand. But there is a strong feedback effect between the two. Should, however, the repertoires of contention be creatively enlarged by the right-wing extremists, there may be another round of right-wing activities capturing the media. The public equally misses its critical part when it plays the unconcerned bystander and reacts with neglect, or, even more, when it silently sympathizes with right-wing offenders. In general, liberal values in political socialization and general socialization are lacking in those communities where violent attacks have become widespread. On the other hand, their presence is no guarantee for the absence of such acts, as many incidents in West Germany demonstrate.

Interestingly, Minkenberg[94] has argued that the growth of right-wing extremism in Western Europe can be understood in part as a value backlash against 'post-materialist' value change, as outlined by Ronald Inglehart. This theoretical argument sounds plausible for quite a few cultural and social domains. Nevertheless, we lack the theoretical and empirical specifications that would clarify, beyond the levels of rhetoric, how representatives of the individualistic, self-oriented liberalization perspective, with their outlook on life, react to the group-centred, corporatist and xenophobic view of the world (see Immerfall,[95] for some criticism of Minkenberg's conclusions).

The ease with which the extreme right is capturing 'liberated zones' is a consequence of the *near total collapse of intermediate structures* in East Germany. According to the theory of Kornhauser,[96] the lack of restraining intermediate structures contributes to the radicalization of social groups, in particular alienated ones such as youth groups which have no effective parental or other authoritative guidance. The appearance of extreme right, anti-statist youth groups in the last decade of the GDR underlines this aspect dramatically, even though harsh political repression was still present. With the collapse of that repression and all other intermediate structures alike, just as Kornhauser pointed out, the availability of social groups for extremist organization increased dramatically. In East Germany most of the social contacts were organized and mediated by the industrial *Kombinate*. There was no substitute after their economic collapse. Instead there was, and is, an exodus of the more talented individuals and thus a further lack of social control and societal demands.

These *anomic circumstances* are not present to a similar degree in West Germany. They explain to a very large extent the dramatic levels of xenophobic and right-wing extremist violence in East Germany. Thus in the five new states of Germany there is both a lack of socialization skills needed for adaptive behaviour in an interdependent world and at the same time no adequate guidance on the part of political and societal intermediate structures. For the elderly people the vacuum is filled by the PDS. For the younger generation, right-wing extremist organizations try to fill the gap. With at least even chances that East Germany might become another *mezzogiorno*, this triple negative aspect of lack of socialization skills, of non-existent or failing intermediate structures and of grim organizational alternatives makes for an alarming future scenario.[97]

If one wants to prevent or at least to reduce further right-wing extremist violence, there should be no toleration for liberated zones. Right-wing extremist votes in general have not reached dangerous levels in East Germany, levels where their zero-sum impact on the political scene would immediately be felt. Yet, the constant non-compliance with the state monopoly of violence and the use of latent and manifest terror both at night and during daylight in East German cities is a serious sign. Weimar Germany underwent this very same experience with the eventual collapse of democracy and human standards of conduct. This is no reason for complacency.

One of the fundamental weaknesses of the radical right in Germany and of other countries as well is the lack of qualified elite personnel. This would easily be overcome through a coalition with the established democratic political parties. Such a coalition would make available the skills of many elite members in numerous interest and pressure groups. Normal political bargaining between members of the system would replace the relationship of a smaller outgroup to a larger ingroup. There is no guarantee that the more conservative political parties would not make such a coalition offer, or at least would be open to some advances on the part of right-wing political extremist parties should they be needed to gain or to secure political power.

The early consensus of the FRG on fighting off political extremists both on the right and left extremes – militant democracy – seems to have broken down with the general success of the political, social and economic model of the Federal Republic and the (often tactical) moderation of most of the right-wing extremist political parties. The latter is a strategic must, given the catastrophe the National Socialist (Nazi) Party caused and the taboos this has led to. Thus it is a mixture of success, moderation and plain political bargaining that will hold the key to future coalitions. On the left side of the political spectrum it is the SPD which has opened the door to coalitions for the ex-communist PDS in Saxony-Anhalt and Mecklenburg-Pomerania. A new coalition has occurred also in Berlin as a result of the election of October 2001.

This raises the question whether such cooperative efforts will in the end be to the detriment or even death of the junior left-wing partner, or whether ideological outbidding[98] will occur which might lead to further ideological polarization and massive shifts in system legitimacy. The latter was the experience in the final phase of Weimar Germany. With his strategic genius, President Mitterrand in his day used the former strategy in dealing with his communist allies, or rivals. Right-wing extremist political leaders might claim credit for political measures that are passed.[99] Thus they might gain in the second round while losing out in the first. The extreme form of ideo-logical copying would be the accelerated version of outbidding. Even more likely, this could end in extremist leadership and victory.

The right-wing extremist scene is in flux, as is society. We also should reckon with the possibility that something entirely new, not just the redis-covery of *Kameradschaften*, will emerge. There is a growing sub-proletariat, a forgotten class that needs positive offers at societal reintegration. Immerfall[100] speaks of 'the political sidelining of the popular classes'. The recently discussed government programme to bail out right-wing extremists by providing job and existence subsidies of up to 100,000 DM to serious converts from right-wing extremism, at least will make the right-wing extremist scene insecure and affect the cost-benefit view of both followers and leaders. On the other hand, it could stir up massive vengeance. Dropouts from the *Kameradschaften* will have to be sufficiently protected by the state authorities.

In the end, the societal consensus at the local level will be decisive. The trade unions' insistence on maintaining high wages drives relatively unqualified youngsters out of the labour market and is a failing political and economic strategy. So is the tactic of benign neglect of racial youth crimes on the part of city notables. No society and no state can survive a permanent violation of the state monopoly of violence for a long time without losing effectiveness and, even more so, legitimacy.[101]

NOTES

1. For example, *Frankfurter Allgemeine Zeitung*, 4 July 2001, p. 12.
2. Quoted in *Süddeutsche Zeitung*, 9 July 2001, p. 6.
3. See H.A. Semetko and W. Gibowski, 'The Image of Germany in the News and US Public Opinion after Unification', in H. Kurthen, W. Bergmann and R. Erb (eds), *Antisemitism and Xenophobia in Germany after Unification* (New York: Oxford University Press, 1997), pp. 242–56, esp. pp. 255–6.
4. R. Koopmans, 'Rechtsextremismus und Fremdenfeindlichkeit als einwanderungs- und ausländerpolitisches Problem', *Zukunftsforum Jugend* (February 2000), pp. 3–10.
5. See also W.D. Chapin, 'Explaining the Electoral Success of the New Right: The German Case', *West European Politics*, 20, 2 (April), pp. 53–72.
6. W. Heitmeyer, H. Buhse and J. Liebe-Freunde (eds), *Die Bielefelder Rechtsextremismusstudie*, 5th edn (Weinheim/Berlin: Beltz, 1995).
7. See *Die Zeit*, 15 February 2001, p. 6.
8. See *Süddeutsche Zeitung*, 23 November 2000, p. 6.
9. See Koopmans, 'Rechtsextremismus und Fremdenfeindlichkeit'.
10. See D. Rucht, P. Hocke and T. Ohlemacher, *Dokumentation und Analyse von Protestereignissen in der Bundesrepublik Deutschland (Prodat) Codebuch*, Paper FS III (Berlin: Science Centre, 1992), pp. 92–103.
11. See *Süddeutsche Zeitung*, 18–19 August 2001, p. 5.
12. See R. Koopmans, *A Burning Question: Explaining the Rise of Racist and Extreme Right Violence in Western Europe*, mimeo, FS III (Berlin: Science Centre, 1995), pp. 95–101; esp. p. 21.
13. Ibid., p. 32.
14. Ibid., p. 19.
15. See the articles in R. Alba, P. Schmidt and M. Wasmer (eds), *Deutsche und Ausländer: Freunde, Fremde oder Feinde? Empirische Befunde und theoretische Erklärungen* (Opladen: Westdeutscher Verlag, 2000).
16. See, for example, ibid.
17. Ibid.
18. See also W. Bergmann and R. Erb, 'Kaderparteien, Bewegung, Szene: Kollektive Episode oder was?', *Forschungsjournal Neue Soziale Bewegungen*, 7, 4 (1994), pp. 26–34.
19. See, for instance, G. Lüdemann, 'Die Erklärung diskriminierender Einstellungen gegenüber Ausländern, Juden und Gastarbeitern in Deutschland: Ein Test der allgemeinen Attitüdentheorie von Fishbein', in Alba, Schmidt and Wasmer, *Deutsch und Ausländer*, pp. 375–99.
20. See M. Terwey, 'Ethnozentrismus in Deutschland: Seine weltanschaulichen Konnotationen im sozialen Kontext', in Alba, Schmidt and Wasmer, *Deutsch und Ausländer*, pp. 295–331.
21. Kurthen, Bergmann and Erb, *Antisemitism and Xenophobia in Germany after Unification*.

22. Ibid., pp. 22 and 27–8.

23. Ibid., pp. 21–8.

24. P. Schmidt and A. Heyder, 'Wer neigt eher zu autoritärer Einstellung und Ethno-zentrismus die Ost- oder die Westdeutschen?: Eine Analyse mit Strukturgleichungs-modellen', in Alba, Schmidt and Wasmer, *Deutsche und Ausländer*, pp. 439–83.

25. Bergmann and Erb, 'Kaderparteien, Bewegung, Szene: Kollektive Episode oder was?', pp. 410–11 and 423.

26. W. Kornhauser, *The Politics of Mass Society* (Glencoe, IL: Free Press, 1959).

27. Bergmann and Erb, 'Kaderparteien, Bewegung, Szene: Kollektive Episode oder was?', p. 431 [my translation].

28. Kurthen, Bergmann and Erb, *Antisemitism and Xenophobia in Germany after Unification*, pp. 235–62.

29. R. Stöss, 'Rechtsextremismuss im vereinten Duetschland: West–öst–Unterschiede und Institutionentransfer seit der deutschen Einheit', *Deutschland Archiv*, 2 (March/April 2000), pp. 181–92.

30. Ibid., pp. 190–1.

31. Ibid., p. 192.

32. D. McAdam, 'Conceptual Origins, Current Problems, Future Directions', in D. McAdam, J.D. McCarthy and M.N. Zald (eds), *Comparative Perspectives on Social Movements, Political Opportunities, Mobilizing Structures and Cultural Framings* (Cambridge: Cambridge University Press, 1996), pp.

33. See E. Zimmermann and T. Saalfeld, 'The Three Waves of West German Right-Wing Extremism', in P.H. Merkl and L. Weinberg (eds), *Encounters with the Contemporary Radical Right* (Boulder, CO: Westfield Press, 1993), pp. 50–74.

34. R. Koopmans, 'Political Opportunity Structure: Some Splitting to Balance the Lumping', *Sociological Forum*, 14, 1 (1999), pp. 93–105.

35. See H. Willems, *Fremdenfeindliche Gewalt: Einstellungen – Täter – Konflikteskalation* (Opladen: Leske and Budrich, 1993); and H. Willems, S. Würtz and R. Eckert, 'Erklärungsmuster fremdenfeindlicher Gewalt im empirischen Test', in W. Würtz and R. Eckert (eds), *Wiederkehr des 'Volksgeistes': Ethnizität, Konflikt und politische Bewältigung* (Opladen: Leske & Budrich, 1998), pp. 195–214.

36. See Koopmans, 'A Burning Question', p. 17: Koopmans draws upon Willems, *Fremdenfeindliche Gewalt*, pp. 16–29.

37. See Willems, 'A Burning Question'; and Willems, Würtz and Eckert, 'Erklärungsmuster fremdenfeindlicher Gewalt im empirischen Test', p. 201.

38. Bergmann and Erb, 'Kaderparteien, Bewegung, Szene: Kollektive Episode oder was?', pp. 27–8.

39. See H. Kriesi, 'Movements of the Left, Movements of the Right: Putting the Mobilization of the Two New Types of Social Movements into Political Context', in H. Kitschelt, P. Lange, G. Marks *et al.* (eds), *Continuity and Change in Contemporary Capitalism* (Cambridge: Cambridge University Press, 1999), pp. 398–423; and T. Ohlemacher, 'Schmerzhafte Episoden: Wider die Rede von einer rechten Bewegung im wieder-vereinigten Deutschland', *Forschungsjournal Neue Soziale Bewegungen*, 7, 4 (1994), pp. 16–25.

40. Bergmann and Erb, 'Kaderparteien, Bewegung, Szene: Kollektive Episode oder was?', p. 29.

41. R. Koopmans, 'Rechtsextremismus, fremdenfeindliche Mobilisierung und Ein-wanderungspolitik: Bewegungsanalyse unter dem Gesichtspunkt politischer Gelegen-heitstrukturen', in K.-U. Hellmann and R. Koopmans (eds), *Paradigmen der Bewegungsforschung: Entstehung und Entwicklung von Neuen sozialen Bewegungen und Rechtsextremismus* (Opladen: Westdeutscher Verlag, 1998), pp. 198–212.

42. See R. Eckert and H. Willems, 'Eskalationsmuster der Gewalt bei ausländerfeindlichen Jugendlichen', in K. Hilpert (ed.), *Die ganz alltägliche Gewalt: Eine interdisziplinäre*

248 Right-Wing Extremism

Annäherung (Opladen: Leske & Budrich), pp. 45–70 ; Willems, *Fremdenfeindliche Gewalt*; and Willems, Würtz and Eckert, 'Erklärungsmuster fremdenfeindlicher Gewalt im empirischen Test'.

43. See, for instance, T. Ohlemacher, 'Fremdenfeindlichkeit und Rechtsextremismus: Mediale Berichterstattung, Bevölkerungsmeinung und deren Wechselwirkung mit fremdenfeindlichen Gewalttaten, 1991–1997', *Sociale Welt*, 49 (1998), pp. 319–32); and H.-B. Brosius and F. Esser, *Eskalation durch Berichterstattung? Massenmedien und fremdenfeindliche Gewalt* (Opladen: Westdeutscher Verlag, 1995).

44. See H.-J. Weiss, 'Extreme Right-Wing Racial Violence: An Effect of the Mass Media?', *Communications*, 22, 1 (1993), pp. 57–68.

45. See Alba, Schmidt and Wasmer, *Deutsche und Ausländer*; and C. Kleinert, W. Krüger and H. Willems (eds), 'Einstellungen junger Deutscher gegenüber ausländischen Mitbürgern und ihre Bedeutung hinsichtlich politischer Orientierungen', *Aus Politik und Zeitgeschichte: Beilage zur Wochenzeitung das Parlament*, B 31/98 (24 July 1998), pp. 14–27.

46. See D. Fuchs, J. Gerhards and E. Roller, 'Wir und die anderen: Ethnozentrismus in den zwölf Ländern der europäischen Gemeinschaft', *Kölner Zeitschrift für Soziologie und Sozialpsychologie*, 45 (1993), pp. 238–54.

47. See M. Hjerm, 'Education, Xenophobia and Nationalism: A Comparative Analysis', *Journal of Ethnic and Migration Studies*, 27, 1 (2001), pp. 37–60.

48. See H.D. von Loeffelholz and G. Köpp, *Ökonomische Austvirkungen der Zuwanderungen nach Deutschland* (Berlin: Duncker and Humblot, 1998). However, see also the perceptual distortions reported by M. Fertig and G.M. Schmidt, *First- and Second-Generation Migrants in Germany: What Do We Know and What Do People Think?*, discussion paper no. 286 (Bonn: Institute for the Study of Labour, 2001).

49. See J.W. Falter, *Wer wählt rechts? Die Wähler und Anhänger rechtsextremistischer Parteien im vereinigten Deutschland* (Munich: C.H. Beck, 1994).

50. Koopmans, 'Rechtsextremismus und Fremdenfreindlichkeit'.

51. Ibid., p. 8.

52. Koopmans, 'Deutschland und seine Einwanderer: ein gespaltenes Verhältnis', in M. Kaase and G. Schmid (eds), *Eine lernende Demokratie: 50 Jahre Bundesrepublik Deutschland* (Berlin: Edition Sigma, 1999), pp. 165–99; esp. p. 190.

53. Ibid., p. 191.

54. Ibid., p. 197.

55. Ibid., pp. 189–97.

56. Kurthen, Bergmann and Erb, *Antisemitism and Xenophobia in Germany after Unification*, p. 260.

57. Ibid., p. 34.

58. M. Minkenberg, *Die Neue Radikale Rechte im Vergleich: USA, Frankreich, Deutschland* (Opladen: Westdeutscher Verlag, 1998); see p. 298.

59. Falter, *Wer wählt rechts?*, pp. 136–47.

60. M. Edinger and A. Hallermann, 'Rechtsextremismus in Ostdeutschland: Struktur und Ursachen rechtsextremer Einstellungen am Beispiel Thüringens', *Zeitschrift für Parlamentsfragen*, 32, 3 (2001), pp. 588–612.

61. Koopmans, 'Rechtsextremismus und Fremdenfeindlichkeit'.

62. See D. Bell (ed.), *The Radical Right* (New York: Doubleday/Anchor, 1964).

63. M. Neureiter, 'Rechtsextremismus im vereinten Deutschland', in *Eine Untersuchung sozialwissenschaftlicher Deutungsmuster und Erklärungsansätze* (Marburg: Tectum Verlag, 1996).

64. S.U. Larsen, B. Hagtvet and J.P. Myklebust, *Who were the Fascists?: Social Roots of European Fascism* (Bergen: Universitätsforlaget, 1980).

65. E. Zimmermann, 'Ein Vergleich von Theorien über den Rechtsradikalismus', unpublished Master's thesis, University of Cologne, 1970.

66. E.K. Scheuch and H.D. Klingemann, 'Theorie des Rechtsradikalismus in westlichen

Industriegesellschaften', *Hamburger Jahrbuch für Wirtschafts- und Gesellschaftspolitik* (1967), pp. 11–29.

67. M. Trow, 'Small Businessmen, Political Tolerance, and Support for McCarthy', *American Journal of Sociology*, 64 (1958), pp. 270–81.

68. H. Kitschelt, *The Radical Right in Western Europe: A Comparative Analysis* (Ann Arbor, MI: University of Michigan Press, 1995). See also R. Eatwell, 'The Rebirth of the "Extreme Right" in Western Europe?', *Parliamentary Affairs*, 53, 3 (2000), pp. 407–25.

69. See H.-G. Betz, *Radical Right-Wing Populism in Western Europe* (London: Macmillan, 1998).

70. M.R. Lepsius, *Extremer Nationalismus* (Stuttgart: Enke, 1966).

71. Ibid., p. 18 [my translation].

72. See also A.L. McCutcheon, 'Religion und Toleranz gegenüber Ausländer', in D. Pollack and P. Gert (eds), *Religiöser und kirchlicher Wandel in Ostdeutschland, 1989–1999* (Opladen: Leske and Budrich, 2000), pp. 87–104.

73. See Kitschelt, *The Radical Right in Western Europe*; Minkenberg, *Die Neue Radikale Rechte im Vergleich*; and Betz, *Radical Right-Wing Populism in Western Europe*.

74. F.U. Pappi, 'Die Republikaner im Parteiensystem der Bundersrepublik: Protesterscheinung oder politische Alternative?', *Aus Politik und Zeitgeschichte*, 21 (1990), pp. 37–44.

75. D. Roth, 'Sind die Republikaner die fünfte Partei?', *Aus Politik und Zeitgeschichte*, 41–2 (1989), pp. 10–20.

76. Zimmerman and Saalfeld, 'The Three Waves of West German Right-Wing Extremism', pp. 69–71.

77. Minkenberg, *Die Neue Radikale Rechte im Verglich*, p. 292.

78. S. Immerfall, 'The Neo-Populist Agenda', in H. Betz and S. Immerfall (eds), *The New Politics of the Right: Neo-Populist Parties and Movements in Established Democracies* (London: Macmillan, 1998), pp. 249–61.

79. S.M. Lipset, *Politcal Man* (New York: Doubleday, 1960).

80. Stöss, 'Rechtsextremismus im vereinten Deutschland', p. 183 [my translation].

81. J.W. Winkler, 'Ausländerfeindlichkeit im vereinigten Deutschland', in J.W. Falter, O.W. Gabriel and H. Rattinger (eds), *Wirklich ein Volk?: Die politischen Orientierungen von Ost- und Westdeutschen im Vergleich* (Opladen: Leske and Budrich, 2000), pp. 435–76.

82. Hallermann

83. H.-J. Maaz, *Der Gefuehlsstau: Ein Psychogramm der DDR* (Berlin: Argon Verlag, 1991). For further approaches linking deficits in socialization patterns and structural conditioning factors, see Neureiter, 'Rechtsextremismus im vereinten Deutschland', pp. 156ff.

84. See F. Decker, *Parteien unter Druck: Der Neue Rechtspopulismus in den westlichen Demokratien* (Opladen: Leske and Budrich, 2000), pp. 316ff.

85. See *Frankfurter Allgemeine Zeitung*, 1 February 2001, pp. 4 and 10, for excerpts from the proposal issued by the government.

86. See *Süddeutsche Zeitung*, 21–22 July 2001, p. 10.

87. See, for instance, *Frankfurter Allgemeine Zeitung*, 28 June 2001, p. 13.

88. Koopmans, 'A Burning Question', pp. 29–32; Koopmans, 'Explaining the Rise of Racist and Extreme Right Violence in Western Europe: Grievances or Opportunities', *European Journal of Political Research*, 20 (1996), pp. 185–216.

89. Minkenberg, *Die Neue Radikale Rechte im Vergleich*, pp. 308–9.

90. Decker, *Parteien unter Druck*, p. 336 [my own translation].

91. Zimmermann and Saalfeld, 'The Three Waves of West German Right-Wing Extremism'.

92. See Verfassungsschutzbericht (2000), *http://www.bmi.bund.de./Anlage6505/Verfassungsschutzbericht_2000_-_Pressefassung.pdf-*

93. See *Süddeutsche Zeitung*, 26 July 2001, p. 5.

94. Minkenberg, *Die Neue Radikale Rechte im Vergleich*, pp. 206–36.

95. Immerfall, 'The Neo-Populist Agenda', p. 256.

96. Kornhauser, *The Politics of Mass Society*.

97. See H.-W. Sinn and F. Westermann, 'Two Mezzogiornos', CESIFO working paper 378 (Munich).

98. See J. Linz, *The Breakdown of Democratic Regimes: Crisis, Breakdown and Reequilibration* (Baltimore, MD: Johns Hopkins University Press, 1978).

99. See Decker, *Parteien und Druck*, pp. 333–4; and Minkenberg, *Die Neue Radikale Rechte im Vergleich*, p. 67.

100. Immerfall, 'The Neo-Populist Agenda', pp. 252–4.

101. See Lipset, *Political Man*.

CHAPTER TEN

Right-Wing Extremism in Russia: The Dynamics of the 1990s

Vera Tolz

D URING THE early 1990s there were several indications that the far right was gaining ground in Russian politics. The success of Vladimir Zhirinovskii's ultra-nationalist Liberal Democratic Party (LDPR) in the 1993 Russian parliamentary elections; the active involvement of the Russian National Unity (RNU), led by a 'national socialist',[1] Aleksandr Barkashov, in the street violence against the troops supporting President Boris Yeltsin in the disbandment of the federal parliament in the autumn of 1993; the existence of some hundred or so violent and racist groups – all these led to speculation that a far-right government might come to power in Russia. So far, however, these predictions have not been fulfilled. Moreover, the electoral success of extreme right-wingers has been in decline since 1993. At the same time, the impact of right-wing extremism on Russian society remains visible. Although predictions of large-scale pogroms of the Jews did not materialize, assaults by right-wing extremists on people from the Caucasus, Central Asia and African countries, as well as the desecration of Jewish cemeteries and synagogues take place on a regular basis throughout the country. More importantly, this chapter argues that the main achievement of the far right is the contribution of its propaganda to the radicalization of political discourse in the country. This means that chauvinism, xenophobia, the idea that Russia is a victim of a conspiracy of external and internal enemies striving to weaken and even destroy her, are sometimes promoted by mainstream politicians in parliamentary debates and, on occasions, even inform government policies, particularly in the treatment of ethnic and/or religious minorities by local authorities. This chapter aims to analyse and explain the dynamics of the activities and the impact of the extreme right on Russian society. We will focus on the paradox of its relative unpopularity with the electorate, on the one hand, and its success nevertheless in 'legitimizing' the expression of a xenophobic and highly paranoid worldview, on the other.

This chapter starts with the discussion of the origins of the contemporary Russian extreme right in the late 1960s and the 1970s, their activities during *perestroika*, and a new situation in which extremists have found themselves after the demise of the Soviet Union. It then defines who can be classified as an extremist in contemporary Russia and offers profiles of some of the most well-known radical organizations. It estimates the impact of the extreme right on Russian society at large by looking at opinion polls, assessing the levels of xenophobia among the Russian population, and at the results of elections to the Duma (the lower chamber of the federal parliament). Finally, it analyses the relationship between extremism and the mainstream Russian political establishment.[2]

THE ORIGINS OF THE CONTEMPORARY RUSSIAN RIGHT

It was at the beginning of Mikhail Gorbachev's *perestroika* that the extreme right-wing groups started openly to hold their meetings, which received coverage in the official press. By the late 1980s these groups began to distribute publicly their own newspapers and journals. They resurrected the heritage of Russia's 'Black Hundred' – a conglomerate of extreme nationalist and anti-Semitic organizations formed in the early twentieth century and best known for organizing Jewish pogroms. Other sources of inspiration were the writings of reactionary Russian émigrés who promoted the idea that the February and October Revolutions of 1917 were the result of a Judeo-Masonic plot to destroy Russia.[3] Some of the extremists of the *perestroika* period utilized the terminology of the highly anti-Semitic campaign against 'rootless cosmopolitans', launched by the Soviet government in the last years of Stalin's rule.

However, the most direct link between the extremism of the late 1980s was not with these earlier periods but with the formation of a very specific Russian nationalist discourse in the early 1970s. This is the time when the New Right also emerged in France and Germany. There are clear parallels between the Russian and the West European phenomena. Michael Minkenberg has argued that the New Right emerged in the post-1968 Western Europe, as Western capitalism entered the 'post-industrial' phase. This was marked by the exhaustion of the welfare state and major cultural and social shifts, which challenged established social values and institutions. New social movements and parties (a 'New Left') emerged, which promoted egalitarianism, multiculturalism with the defence of rights of minorities, feminism and grass-roots democracy. Many parts of the New Left's agenda were concerned with the question of identity, so important in postmodern societies. It was in response to this post-materialism of the New Left that some members of the elite and the public turned to the right.

> The New Right was not 'simply the revival of traditional conservatism' in the Old Politics sense – that is, opposition to the welfare state and to the redistribution of income, or the return of church-based religious traditionalism – but a new coalition of forces which see their common enemy in the post-materialist New Left and its political agenda.[4]

Therefore, the New Right attempted to address the same issues as the New Left. This countering agenda included the promotion of an organic ethnic identity, based on blood and cultural purity, the so-called ethnopluralism, entailing the rejection of any mix of races through marriage or immigration, rejection of liberal, participatory democracy in favour of an elitist political order. The New Right combined anti-communism with anti-Americanism and spoke about the 'colonization' of Europe by the United States. Appealing to those threatened to be marginalized by the weakening of the welfare state, new right-wing groups used populist, anti-establishment slogans. The promotion of the idea of a strong state above society and individual rights indicated the influence of the Old Right of pre-World War I France and Weimar Germany.

The New Right in Russia emerged in the same period – i.e. in the early 1970s. It was not simply a 'revival' of the early twentieth-century right-wing ultra-nationalism. Instead, it was an attempt on the part of some intellectuals, whose ideas found support among the leadership of the Communist Party, to 'reinvent' Russia in response to fundamental political, social and cultural changes occurring in the Soviet Union. The main element of the change was the crystallization of ethnic (often anti-Russian) nationalism among the non-Russian nationalities of the Soviet Union. A result of the contradictory nationalities policies of the Communist Party of the Soviet Union (CPSU) which both suppressed but also effectively encouraged the construction of exclusive ethnic identities among non-Russian people, by the late 1960s ethnic nationalism began to inform the policies of political leaders in the non-Russian Union republics. The result was that Russians residing in those republics began to lose their hitherto privileged access to higher education and the best jobs. For the first time in Soviet history, immigration into the Russian Federation began to surpass emigration from it.[5] These non-Russian ethnic nationalisms posed a threat to the territorial integrity of the USSR and challenged the traditional Russian imperial identity.

It is to this period that many of the ideas of the contemporary New Right in Russia should be traced. Consisting of intellectuals (writers, journalists and scholars) as well as some members of the party establishment, the Russian

New Right was far from a homogenous group, as reactions to the challenge of non-Russian nationalisms varied. Some ideologists of the new Russian nationalism only sharpened the defence of the Russian-dominated multi-ethnic empire. Others, in contrast, for the first time in history, formulated the premises of anti-imperial ethnic Russian nationalism by urging the creation of a purely ethnic Russian state.[6] They felt that particularly such non-Russian areas as Central Asia, Transcaucasus and the Baltics should become independent. Both groups however argued that the Russians were discriminated against in the Soviet Union and government measures were needed to protect them. At the extreme side of the spectrum, representatives of the New Right proposed the biological definition of a nation, based on blood; they also professed anti-Semitism and xenophobia. In this period, peoples from the Caucausus and Central Asia rather than the Jews started to be seen by some nationalists as the main 'enemies of the Russian people'. In addition, the ideology of the New Right was anti-Western, particularly anti-American.[7]

In constructing the ideology of new Russian nationalism in response to the growing non-Russian nationalism, intellectuals borrowed from conservative Russian thinkers of the nineteenth century, the extremists of the early twentieth century, and official writings of the late Stalin period, as well as the New Right in France and Germany. Thus, leaders of the far right of the *perestroika* and post-communist periods also began their activities in the 1970s and the early 1980s. Among them is journalist Aleksandr Dugin, who began to propagate ideas of the radical right-wing French intellectual, Alain de Benoist, in Russian *samizdat* in the 1970s. In 1979 another ideologist of Russian extremism, a specialist in Oriental studies, Valerii Emelianov, published a book in the Paris-based Free Palestine Press that claimed that the Jewish conspiracy against the Russians began with the Christianization of Kievan Rus in 988, when paganism was abandoned in favour of a religion which was under a strong Judaic influence.[8] The extremist group Pamiat (Memory), whose activities were intensively discussed in the Soviet and Western media in the late 1980s, was, in fact, founded at the very beginning of the decade as a literary and historical society attached to the Soviet Ministry of Aviation.

In sum, the leaders of the extreme Russian nationalist right were ideologically well prepared to use the relaxation of state control over the media in the late 1980s, their views having largely been formed prior to the advent of *glasnost*. The period of liberalization under Gorbachev witnessed the proliferation of the extremist groups and periodicals, as organizations and media outlets not controlled by the state began to be initially tolerated and then were formally legalized. Indeed, some of the best-known radical groups of today, including Zhirinovsky's LDPR and Barkashov's RNU were set up in 1989 and 1990 respectively. Another important development of the late *perestroika* period was the emergence of a bloc, uniting reactionary members and officials of the Communist Party with nationalists. These two seemingly different groups were drawn together by the desire to preserve the Soviet Union as the only legitimate state of the Russians. Whereas a few nationalists argued that Russia no longer had the resources to maintain the empire, the majority of nationalists were imperialists. Even those nationalists who were willing to see the Central Asian or Transcaucasian republics go were still hoping for a tightly knit union of the three Slavic republics: Russia, Ukraine and Belarus, as they believed that the three peoples belonged to one pan-Russian nation. Extreme nationalists and unreformed communists also were united by radical anti-Westernism, as both viewed Gorbachev, Yeltsin and other reformers as agents of Western powers, carrying out their plans of dismantling the USSR. The liberal Soviet and Western press published reports that the KGB was closely involved in the far-right groups, as had been the case with the tsarist Okhrana (police) and the Black Hundred. Thus, the media alleged close ties between the LDPR, Pamiat and the security organs.[9]

However, despite the fact that meetings of Pamiat and other similar organizations were very vocal and attracted much attention in the media, that a number of party and KGB officials apparently sympathized with and supported the extremists, that the most extreme publications were sold in public places in major cities and a number of such periodicals were available on subscription, the impact of the far right on mainstream politics and on the population at large during *perestroika* was marginal. Opinion polls demonstrated that liberal, pro-reformist periodicals were far more widely read by Russian citizens than the nationalist ones.[10] In the 1989 and 1990 parliamentary elections, candidates of nationalistic groups were largely defeated.[11]

The reasons for the lack of electoral success of radical right-wing groups in the last years of the Soviet Union were (1) the absence of charismatic leaders; (2) the right-wing radicals' concentration on plots and conspiracies which sounded rather implausible to average Russians; and (3) their simultaneous neglect of the country's real problems – for instance, in the economy. The final blow to nationalists seemed to be made by their alliance with the reactionary communists, whose public prestige was at rock bottom in 1989–90.

THE NEW SITUATION AFTER THE DEMISE OF THE SOVIET UNION

In 1992 the now independent Russian Federation (RF) entered the phase of radical systemic change. Discreditation of the communist regime produced an ideological void, and economic reforms that were initiated by the Russian government in January 1992 turned out to be socially disruptive. They resulted in a dramatic weakening, if not a complete destruction, of a welfare state in its communist mode, and the deterioration of living standards of large groups of the population, whereas the small group of people who benefited from reforms included many of the old Communist Party personnel. Widespread corruption of the political and economic élites also have stirred up discontent among the population. In the course of the 1990s, many young Russians have fought in wars in Chechnia, Tadjikistan and Moldova, where their views and behaviour have often been radicalized. All in all, in the period of transition many people have found themselves in extreme situations, which have provoked extreme behaviour. Crime and political extremism are the most common manifestations of such behaviour in post-communist Eastern Europe. Both left- and right-wing radicals exploit economic hardships, corruption of new governments and their seeming powerlessness in the face of rising crime.

Studies of the impact of economic reforms on societies in transition show that there is no direct correlation between poverty and extremism.[12] For instance, it is not so much the unemployed, but rather those who fear possible social and economic marginalization that become particularly receptive to the propaganda of extremist groups looking for easily identifiable scapegoats, particularly ethnic minorities, refugees and economic migrants. Post-communist Russia has experienced an influx of migrants and refugees. After the collapse of the Soviet Union, an estimated 30 million Russians and Russian-speakers[13] found themselves outside the borders of the RF, in the new states, where they were overnight transformed from a privileged group into an ethnic minority. In some of the newly independent states, such as Moldova, Georgia and Tadjikistan, armed conflicts erupted. So it is not surprising that a significant number of Russians from these states are trying to resettle in the RF. Thus, a flood of forced migrants has been created, which presents a major problem for the Russian government. The Russian forced migrants are, moreover, resented by the population of the RF as newcomers who compete with local people for housing, employment and government social care.[14] (Until the end of the year 2000, these migrants were entitled to receive Russian citizenship automatically.) In addition, after the disintegration of the Soviet Union, Russia started to experience an influx of refugees – people from the developing countries. The reason was the relaxation of border controls within Russia and other countries of the former Soviet Union. These refugees do not enjoy the privileges allotted to forced Russian migrants, but they often provoke racist feelings on the part of the native Russians. Like their counterparts in Western Europe, Russian ultra-nationalists effectively exploit tensions created by the influx of refugees and forced migrants. Barkashov, for instance, states: 'The central regions of Russia are full of emigrants from the Caucasus and Central Asia who are committing acts of violence against Russian people. There will come a time when it will no longer be possible to put up with this and we will have to defend ourselves and our people.'[15]

The collapse of the communist bloc also reopened the question of redefining national identities of the people in post-communist countries. The complexity of the issue is exacerbated by the existence of many ethnic minority groups in the area. In the course of debates over national identities, some representatives of dominant nationalities have put forward extreme ideas, based on racial, highly exclusive, definitions of national identity. Russia finds itself in an arguably unique position in its attempts to forge a new national identity. Whereas non-Russian Soviet successor states realize that they have gained something important as a result of the USSR's disintegration, that is, independence (although they have been divided over what to do with it), the Russians found that they had lost the empire at whose centre Russia had traditionally stood. (Russia's territorial losses after the break-up of the USSR were far more significant than those of Germany following the Versailles Treaty or of France in the 1950s, when it had to withdraw from Algeria – the two countries with which Russia is often compared.) There are different reactions to this new situation in Russia. Many have come to terms with a new reality, trying to get on with nation- and state-building within the borders of the RF.[16] However, not everybody among the élites and broader public accept the new borders as legitimate. Those questioning the legitimacy of the RF borders argue that they do not include all the territories that were historically populated by members of the Russian nation. There is no agreement either between the extremists or between more moderate Russian nationalists over how the membership of the Russian nation should be defined. For some extremists, '*Russiannes*' should be determined by blood (how the purity of blood is to be assessed, they do not say). Therefore, representatives of ethnic minorities should be expelled from Russia or deprived of their rights as citizens if they decide to stay. For others, Russians are those who regard themselves as belonging to 'the Russian civilization'. The extremists believe that all Soviet citizens belong to 'the Russian civilization', and therefore the Soviet Union should be recreated, even by force, if need be. Finally, some extremists as well as more moderate nationalists include Ukrainians and Belarusians into the Russian nation, and therefore deny the Ukraine's and Belarus's right to independence.

Last but not least, the emergence of radical groups is encouraged by the fluid nature of Russia's political institutions and by the use of populist methods (that is, disregard for the political, constitutional and judicial constraints that democracies impose) even by mainstream politicians. Part of today's Russian political culture, which has deep historical roots, fosters a more radical political atmosphere stemming from the distrust of any form of opposition to authority – making it harder for moderate parties, critical of policies of a president, to put their case, leaving the opposition in the hands of extreme groups and leaders.

CLASSIFICATION AND PROFILES OF EXTREMIST GROUPS

The fact that some mainstream parties and politicians at times use extremist rhetoric or are known to support actions of extreme groups complicates the question of whether or not a group can be classified as extremist. Often the definition is situational. In defining extremism within the context of today's Russian politics, two main criteria will be applied – an anti-systemic nature of a group or movement and a particular ideology. The anti-systemic nature of a group or movement is reflected in a goal to overthrow the existing regime, usually, by means which include political violence and a consistent refusal to play by the established political rules. An extremist right-wing ideology, above all, includes national chauvinism, i.e. complete substitution of rights of individuals to the interests of the 'constructed' nation, propaganda of discrimination of individuals on the grounds of nationality, religion, sexual preferences, etc., and complete rejection of democratic institutions and practices. Most extremist groups have rigid hierarchical structures with a strong leader at the helm and strive to set up paramilitary organizations to practise violence against those whom they perceive as enemies of the nation.

Most groups discussed below clearly fit the criteria (ideology and methods) of an extremist organization. The problem is with those parties whose members adhere to extremist ideologies but at the same time effectively operate within the existing political system, as they have been represented in the parliaments elected in 1993, 1995 and 1999. In this connection, we will look at the three parties: the LDPR, Sergei Baburin's Russian Public Union (ROS in Russian abbreviation) and Gennadii Ziuganov's CPRF.

The LDPR is often cited as an example of the largest extremist organization in Russia. Political rhetoric of the LDPR is unquestionably extremist. The party leader and members call for Russia's territorial expansion, which will include not only the newly independent states of the former Soviet Union, but also Poland. They accept the use of violence for achieving Russia's enlargement. They profess anti-Semitism, xenophobia, religious and other forms of intolerance. However, since 1993, when the LDPR received the plurality (22.9 per cent) of the vote in the Duma elections, the party has been functioning within the existing political system. Its members have headed and been represented in various parliamentary committees and held ministerial posts in the government;[17] the LDPR faction in the Duma also has been consistently voting in support of government policies.

At the same time the LDPR also demonstrates anti-systemic patterns of behaviour. The Russian media have reported the involvement in illegal activities of members of many political parties, but the LDPR is being portrayed as the only parliamentary party which is virtually 'completely criminalized'. Its members, particularly outside Moscow, have been allegedly involved in racketeering and the illegal trade of arms and narcotics.[18] This makes the LDPR similar to other extremist groups, such as Barkashov's RNU, which enjoy very close links with the criminal underworld. As is the case with other extremist organizations, the LDPR is highly centralized, and its leader has dictatorial powers, granted by the party statute adopted in 1994.[19]

The ROS (*Rossiiskii*) was set up in September 1991 as a movement whose stated goal was to preserve the Soviet Union from disintegration. The group is led by Sergei Baburin, a member of the Russian Federation of Socialist Republics (RSFSR) and Deputy in the Congress of People, who began his career as a democrat. In the early 1990s Baburin and his followers from the ROS decided to limit their territorial claims to Ukraine, Belarus and north Kazakhstan, whose unification with the RF they desired. Baburin denies that Ukrainians and Belarusians have a separate national identity from Russians and speaks about 'one history, one nation, one state' in relation to the three Slavic peoples. Baburin does not refrain from employing extreme rhetoric. Thus, speaking about the danger of possible disintegration of Russia, he claims that 'Any person who supports Chechen sovereignty or the sovereignty of any other republic at Russia's expense is an ideological and/or practical successor of Hitler.'[20] Moreover, the ROS includes a subgroup led by Nikolai Pavlov, which defines the Russian nation in racial terms and calls for discriminatory measures against ethnic minorities in the RF. In 1994–97, Pavlov was a member of the National Republican Party of Russia, an unquestionably extremist group, whose main aim is to fight against people from the Caucasus and Central Asia.

Although the ROS failed to win elections to the federal parliament, its individual members were elected to the 1993, 1995 and 1999 Dumas in single-candidate constituencies. Baburin himself won elections in 1993 and 1995, but lost in 1999. In his capacity as deputy, he took some radical steps, as for instance when he urged his colleagues to re-examine Ukraine's jurisdiction over the Crimea.[21] In 1999 the leader of the ROS, together with representatives of other nationalist organizations, including the extremist ones, signed an appeal to the Council of Federation not to ratify a treaty on friendship and cooperation with Ukraine.[22] Yet, particularly during his tenure in the Duma, Baburin was trying to make the position of the ROS more moderate and to act according to existing political rules.[23] Thus, the extremism of the ROS is situational and it can be regarded as a nationalist, but not an extremist organization.

The same can be said about the CPRF. Although this party (set up in 1990) still preserves some elements of left-wing, anti-capitalist, rhetoric in its platform, its programme is strongly influenced by right-wing ideologies. The CPRF leaders, including the chairman Gennadii Ziuganov, call for the recreation of the Soviet Union, deny Ukrainians and Belarusians separate identity from the Russians, speak about external and internal enemies of Russia who have been trying to destroy the country for centuries, and regard *perestroika* and post-communist reforms as a plot of US intelligence services. It is noteworthy that Ziuganov's statements in the Duma, where his party obtained a plurality of the vote in 1995 and 1999, are usually considerably more moderate than the position outlined in his books (*Derzhava, Za gorizontom* and *Rossiia i sovremennyi mir*). The CPRF also includes extremists among its members. Thus, General Albert Makashov, who suggested that the Movement in Support of the Army (DPA), of which he is a leader, should be renamed the Movement Against the Yids (*Dvizhenie protiv zhidov*), was elected to the 1995 Duma on the party list of the CPRF. However, overall, the CPRF acts as a within-system party and its top leaders rarely make extremist statements in public. So, the CPRF's extremism is occasional and the party cannot be seen as an extremist organization.

The groups, which unquestionably can be classified as extremist, can be divided into aggressive imperialist, ethnic chauvinist and racist, as well as religious fundamentalist, according to the ideology which they profess.

1. In the early post-communist period, the extremist camp was dominated by aggressive 'imperialists'. One of the leading ideologists of this camp was the above-mentioned Aleksandr Dugin, who in 1992 began to publish the periodical, *Elementy*, named after the extreme right-wing French magazine *Elements*. Since 1992 Dugin has been expressing the hope that the Russians will create a continental empire from Dublin to Vladivostok.[24] In the early 1990s, 'imperialists', who preferred to call themselves neo-Eurasians after the 1920 Russian émigré movement of Eurasians, were grouped around the major opposition newspaper *Den* (renamed *Zavtra* in 1993), edited by the military writer Aleksander Prokhanov. Neo-Eurasians are like their predecessors of the 1920s, anti-Western and especially anti-Anglo-Saxon. They tend to view the world as 'an arena of perennial struggle between two global forces: maritime (Atlanticist) and continental (Eurasian). Atlanticist forces are represented, above all, by the Anglo-Saxon civilization. It is assumed that the

Roman–Germanic world is part of the continental bloc.'[25] Thus the whole concept is, in effect, anti–American. This interpretation of East–West confrontation helps the Russian right to justify close contact with their counterparts in France and Germany. According to this scheme of history, Russia plays a key role in the perennial struggle between the two blocs of power.[26]

Among parties and movements who profess similar ideologies, one should mention the LDPR and a more radical National Bolshevik Party (NBP), some of whose members initially had belonged to the LDPR. The NBP was set up in 1992 under the leadership of the writer Eduard Limonov. The party publishes the newspaper *Limonka* (a play on the editor's name but the word also means a hand-grenade in Russian), which appeals (particularly to the youth) to use violence and terror to overthrow the existing regime.

2. After the demise of the Soviet Union, Russia has witnessed a proliferation of racist groups, which focus their propaganda on the need to 'cleanse' Russia of members of ethnic minorities. People from the Caucasus and Central Asia attract these groups' main attention, but the groups' members also desecrate Jewish cemeteries and plant bombs near synagogues. Attacks on people from Africa by members of these groups have been reported by the press.

The largest racist group is Barkashov's RNU, which was founded in 1990 by former members of Pamiat. The party leader openly claims to be a 'national socialist' and one of the party symbols is the swastika. According to Barkashov the choice of symbols indicates 'our unwillingness to compromise in the battle for the Russian cause'.[27] According to the programme adopted by the organization in 1997 the main goal is to 'restore justice in the treatment of the Russian people', which members of the organization should do by 'using their own power and their own weapons, without turning to law enforcement and other official bodies'.[28] Only members of the 'Russian Nation' are allowed to enrol in the RNU, and the membership of Jews, Gypsies, peoples of the Caucasus and Central Asia is explicitly forbidden. According to the RNU, the only mistake made by Hitler was to start a war against the Soviet Union. The RNU is reportedly the most criminalized political organization in Russia, whose members illegally possess arms and are involved in crimes on a regular basis, including murders, some of which, though not all, are racially motivated.[29]

Other organizations which practise racially motivated violence, particularly against the people from the Caucasus and Central Asia, are Iurii Beliaev's National Republican Party of Russia, which split in 1994 from another extremist organization of the same name, headed by Nikolai Lysenko; the Russian National Socialist Party of Konstantin Kasimovskii; and Aleksandr Shtilmark's Black Hundred. Racially motivated violence also marks the activities of some of the armed units of the Cossacks. Thus, in the autumn of 1995 local Cossacks together with members of the RNU attacked Meskhetian-Turks in the village of Armianskoe in the Krasnodar Krai. The majority of men and some women from the Meskhetian community were severely beaten up. The organizers of the pogrom warned their victims that they would be attacked again unless they left the Krai.[30]

An exotic variation of racism is to be found in a neo-pagan movement, which first received publicity in the press in the late 1980s. The best known among pagan groups is the Union of the Veneds (*Soiuz venedov*), set up in 1990 by a lecturer at a military academy in Leningrad, Viktor Bezverkhii. Rejecting Christianity as a 'Judaic religion', these people have created their own religion which is a mixture of poorly understood Indian Vedic culture and arbitrarily reconstructed pre-Christian Slavic paganism. Explicitly emphasizing a connection with the 'Aryan race' conceptions of the Third Reich, Bezverkhii proclaims a 'victory of fascism' in Russia as a goal of his movement.[31]

3. Xenophobic nationalism is fairly widespread throughout the Russian Orthodox Church. Among the Church hierarchs, the key role in articulating the position of religious fundamentalism with its image of Russia, the only true Christian state in the world, under threat of destruction by external and internal enemies, particularly Jews and Catholics, was played by the Metropolitan of St Petersburg and Ladoga, Ioann. Fundamentalists in the Church publish their own periodicals, the best known of which are *Pravoslavnaia Rus* and *Rus derzhavnaia*. The Union of Christian Revival and the Brotherhood of St Sergei of Radonezh can serve as examples of religious fundamentalist organizations. A leader of the former, Viacheslav Demin, identifies himself as 'monarcho-fascist'. The Union and the Brotherhood see as their goal the fight against 'Western, Zionist, Ecumenist, Masonic and Judaic influences within the Church'. In 1994 the hierarchy of the Church demanded that both the Union and the Brotherhood be expelled from the Union of Orthodox Brotherhoods, which has existed under the auspices of the Moscow Patriarchate since 1990. However, the Orthodox hierarchy has been unable consistently to fight the expression of xenophobic nationalism and religious fundamentalism which exists within the Church.[32]

THE LEVEL OF PUBLIC SUPPORT

As mentioned earlier, experts in Moscow estimate that up to a hundred extremist groups, most of which are right-wing, and 200 extremist publications exist in Russia today.[33] Yet, most of these groups are small. The LDPR with over 10,000 members is the largest extremist party. The second largest is the RNU. This organization claims to have 200,000 members in its ranks, but this figure is believed to be exaggerated. In 1995 the then head of the Federal Security Service, Sergei Stepashin, estimated the RNU membership at 2,000. Experts from the Moscow-based Panorama Centre for the study of political extremism in Russia suggest 5,000 as the most plausible figure.[34] Denied registration at the federal level by the Ministry of Justice, the RNU has managed to register a hundred out of its 350 regional branches with local authorities. Other organizations with memberships of over a thousand are the Union of Officers, whose members combine extreme nationalism with elements of communist ideology (5,000 members), and Lysenko's and Beliaev's National Republic Parties (1,000–2,000 members each). There are several thousand 'skinheads' in major Russian cities, although some of them have accepted only external attributes of the movement without the 'White Power' ideology. Ten organizations, including the National Patriot Front Pamiat of Dmitrii Vasil'ev and the Russian Party of Vladimir Miloserdov, have between 100 and 1,000 members. All other extremist groups enjoy the membership of only a few dozen people.[35]

The electoral support of all extremist organizations, apart from the LDPR, is extremely low. In the absence of competition from other nationalist organizations, most of which were not allowed by the government to participate in elections, and because the image of the Communist Party was still undermined by the criticism of the Soviet regime during *perestroika*, the LDPR won the plurality of votes (22.92 per cent) in the 1993 parliamentary elections. However, the LDPR did not manage to sustain its electoral triumph. In the 1995 elections, its popular support was reduced by half (11.8 per cent) and in the 1999 elections it further declined to reach 5.98 per cent. Thus in the 1995 and 1999 elections, those dissatisfied with the current political situation tended to vote for the CPRF. (In the early 1990s the CPRF managed to regain public support by reinventing itself as a party representing losers in the reform process, particularly among older people.)

A study of the LDPR's electorate, conducted by the All-Russian Centre for the Study of Public Opinion (VTsIOM) in the wake of the party's success in the 1993 elections, reveals a profile of voters which is similar to that of the electorate of extreme nationalist parties elsewhere in Europe. A half of the people were workers at small and medium-size factories and enterprises, which were threatened by heavy cuts in personnel; 56 per cent lived in small towns; educational level was considerably lower than average in the country, i.e. the majority had only incomplete secondary education. In other words, these were not so much unemployed, but those in fear of economic and social marginalization, and with lower levels of education. Significantly, 25 per cent mentioned that a vote for Zhirinovskii was an emotional act to demonstrate the protest against either the Communists or the new government. Reference to the impact of the coverage of the electoral campaign on television was mentioned twice as much by the supporters of the LDPR than was average for the electorate as a whole. (Among all the parties, the LDPR managed to buy one of the largest amount of broadcasting time to publicize its campaign in 1993.)[36]

Thus the LDPR and the CPRF were the only nationalist organizations to get elected in the parliament in the 1990s. Other organizations failed to cross the 5 per cent threshold to get parliamentary representation. In the 1999 Duma elections, the five nationalist groups which participated in addition to the LDPR and the CPRF all received less than 1 per cent of the vote. The most extremist groups even failed to collect enough signatures to be eligible to take part in elections. Until 1999 the RNU had not shown any interest in elections. Its attempt to try chances with the voters in 1999 failed, as the authorities refused to register the electoral bloc 'Spas' which Barkashov helped to set up.[37]

However, the electoral failure of most of the extremists is not the only measure of their influence. Opinion polls assessing the level of xenophobia, particularly the resentment against the groups singled out by extremists as 'enemies' of the Russian people, is another area to be looked at. Thus, in 1992, an opinion poll conducted by the VTsIOM at the Moscow State University on the question 'Towards which of the following nationalities do you have a negative attitude?' revealed that 46 per cent did not like Azeris; 40 per cent disliked Chechens; 34 per cent disliked Armenians; 33 per cent disliked Georgians and Gypsies; 11 per cent disliked Tatars; and 8 per cent did not like Jews.[38] (It should be noted that both Chechens and Tatars are citizens of the RF, having national autonomies within Russia.) This showed that in targeting the peoples from the Caucasus and Central Asia as the main object of their hatred, the extremists were in line with the general mood in society. According to the experts from Panorama, by the late 1990s the level of xenophobia had not risen significantly.[39] The only change is the increase in a negative attitude towards Chechens and Islam. If in 1992, 17 per cent thought that Islam 'was a bad thing', in early 2000, 80 per cent subscribed to this view.[40]

A group which is always targeted by extremist organizations is the youth, i.e. people under twenty-five. Particularly active in this regard is the RNU, which has set up a 'National Club' for its young activists and a 'Junkers' Group' for teenagers in the Krasnodar Krai.[41] The youth is also attracted to the RNU by the fact that it has several training centres, where it is possible to learn shooting and hand-to-hand fighting. There are also extremist youth organizations, all of whose members are under twenty-five. Apart from the organizations of 'skinheads', the best known right-wing extremist youth group is the RNU of Aleksei Vdovin and Konstantin Kasimovskii. However, the membership of such groups is very low, the Union having no more than 60 members. It is not surprising that these young people are overwhelmingly male and so is the electorate of the LDPR. The majority of the latter are men in the 25–40 age-group.[42]

EXTREMISTS AND THE RUSSIAN POLITICAL ESTABLISHMENT

The post-Communist Russian government has been making attempts to curb the activities of extremist groups and publications. The 1993 Russian Constitution, the media law and the law on public organizations all forbid activities which incite inter-ethnic strife and organizations which propagate racism, xenophobia and religious intolerance, call for the overthrow of the constitutional regime and set up paramilitary formations. The Criminal Code, in turn, stipulates criminal responsibility for the violation of national equality, instigation of inter-ethnic strife and disseminating propaganda on the practice and ideology of fascism (Article 74). In 1995 President Yeltsin issued a decree against fascism and other forms of extremism. The decree called on government agencies better to coordinate their measures aimed at curbing extremist activities. However, neither before nor after the decree has much been done to take even the most aggressive extremists to task. The reasons seem to lie in the chaotic nature of government measures, the vagueness of the law and the sympathy on the part of a number of representatives of law-enforcement organs and government officials towards the ideas expressed by the extremists.

The chaotic nature of government measures was particularly visible in the autumn of 1993, when in the wake of the September–October clashes between the government forces and the opposition, the Ministry of Justice and Moscow city authorities banned a number of extremist groups and publications. However, this ban was illegal, as the relevant legislation allows the ban to be imposed only after a court hearing. After the state of emergency had been lifted in Moscow, most organizations and periodicals resumed their activities.

The vagueness of the legislation and the complexity of the procedures that it stipulates make it difficult to ban extremist activities. The legislation does not clearly define terms such as extremism or fascism, and Article 74 of the Criminal Code also limits criminal responsibility for actions, which are done intentionally (*umyshlenno*). Those charged under the article often manage to argue effectively that they have had no intention to offend anybody, let alone instigate inter-ethnic strife.

In the 1990s several dozen cases were initiated under Article 74. However, with the exception of one case in 1990, not a single person served a prison sentence. At most, a defendant gets a suspended sentence. In most cases, defendants are acquitted, even in the presence of seemingly clear-cut evidence against them (for instance, if they have published and disseminated publications calling for the extermination of Jews or people from the Caucasus and Central Asia). In a number of cases, a clear sympathy on the part of judges and prosecutors as well as local authorities towards the extremists is reported in the press. Thus in 1994 a prosecutor in a Moscow city court suggested that charges be dropped against the leader of an extremist Russian party, Viktor Korchagin, as he did not find any offence in the fact that the defendant had produced and distributed 100,000 copies of a highly anti-Semitic brochure 'The Catechism of a Jew' – a forgery similar to the 'Protocols of the Elders of Zion'.[43] The press reported instances of patronage offered to local extremists by the governor of the Krasnodar Krai, Nikolai Kondratenko, and to activists of RNU by the former member of the upper chamber of the parliament, the Council of Federation, Petr Romanov.[44] However, no data is available on the number of sympathizers of extremist causes, particularly in the law-enforcement organs. But even if they are in a minority, as far as it is known, those openly protecting extremists have not been taken to task.

Such a situation contributes to the feeling of impunity on the part of extremists. Therefore radical right-wing activists have been continuing to disseminate their propaganda openly, and one can see its effect even on the mainstream political discourse, particularly parliamentary debates. Indeed, the most racist and xenophobic periodicals and brochures, whose print-runs sometimes reach 100,000 copies, are openly available on sale throughout the country. In 1994 liberal deputies raised the issue that in the building of the Duma itself there was a stand to sell extremist literature, including a collection of Hitler's speeches.[45]

It is not particularly surprising that extremist rhetoric has often been employed in the parliamentary debates by deputies from the LDPR. However, anti-Semitic, xenophobic and ultra-nationalistic statements have also been made on occasions by deputies from the CPRF as well as the Agrarian and 'Power to the People' (*Narodovlastie*) factions, both close to the CPRF. Thus, after the Chechen terrorists took hostages in a hospital in the town of Budennovsk close to the border with Chechnia in June 1995, the LDPR proposed to deport from Russia 'all citizens from the southern foreign countries'.[46] On 20 February 1997 Zhirinovskii delivered a long speech about how people from the Caucasus and Central Asia 'have brutally raped tens of thousands of our women'. In contrast, a similar act could be committed by a Russian 'once in a hundred years'.[47] Zhirinovskii and other members of his faction often portray a picture of Russia on the verge of disintegration and being taken over by foreigners. Anti-Semitic statements are also made. It is fairly common to question the nationality of a government official or a deputy, if his or her actions are not to the liking of a parliamentarian. Thus, on 10 February 1995, in a speech at the Council of Federation, Kondratenko expressed hope that at some point in time, Russia would finally have as a president (instead of Yeltsin) 'a normal Russian by origin' (*po rodu i plemeni*). He was genuinely surprised when his statement was questioned by the deputy speaker of the Council, Romadan Abdulatipov. In response, Kondratenko argued that he did not mean to offend non-Russians who traditionally have had ethnic autonomies within the RF. Instead, his statement was aimed against those 'who call themselves Russian citizens, Russian speakers, but whose roots are not in Russia, those who are today, I am sorry to say, the enemies of Russia'.[48] In the language of ultra-nationalists this was a clear reference to the Jews. In the 1995 Duma, the radical General Makashov, elected from the CPRF, often claimed that his opponents in parliament were Jews and that they should go to live in Israel. But, even those deputies who are considered moderates are not immune from similar behaviour. Thus, on 5 July 1995, the head of the parliamentary Committee on Agrarian Policy, Viacheslav Zvolinskii, said that he would like to remind his audience who it was in the executive branch of the Russian government who criticized the Committee's programme on the stabilization of the agro-industrial complex: 'I would have liked, my dear friends, to mention the name of our opponent – Urinson Iakov Moiseevich. I think there is no need to say more. I will not evoke the names of either Golda Meyer or Moshe Dayan. I think I have said enough.' This outburst did not occasion any rebuke from a chairman of the session.[49]

Finally, even moderate deputies (particularly from the CPRF) tend to subscribe to the idea, so popular among extremists, that all Russia's problems are a result of the deliberate conspiracy of the West. A debate in the Duma on 29 November 1996 over a peace treaty signed by Yeltsin's government with Chechnia was characterized by such views. Among other things, Ziuganov mentioned that he himself possessed documents which demonstrated that Western governments in conjunction with their agents inside the country had been planning and effectively carrying out the destruction of Russia: 'the first stage ended with the demise of the Union; the second stage ... ended with the destruction of the Russian economy, the genocide of the Russian people, the bankruptcy of the state apparatus and the degradation of the army. Everyone can see: this has already happened, *de facto* ...'[50] Ziuganov's ideas, repeated by other deputies at this and other sessions, indicate that the extremists and the moderates often share the same views on the causes of Russia's contemporary problems – they are blamed on the conspiratorial acts of some external and internal enemies. In effect, the moderate nationalist opposition has failed to develop either analytical tools or even a language for a balanced analysis of Russia's situation.

The legislative branch of government is not the only one to be criticized for employing radical language. Particularly in defending its actions in Chechnia, the executive branch has been using inflammatory rhetoric as well. Thus, the Russian domestic intelligence chief, General Nikolai Baruskov, said in defence of Moscow's decision at the beginning of the first wave of Russian military operations in 1994: '[O]ne local man told me that a Chechen can only be a robber or a killer, and if not this, then he will be prepared for some other kind of crime.'[51] In defending the renewal of military operations against Chechnia in 1999, President Vladimir Putin maintained that the Chechens 'would not be content with remaining inside' the borders of their republic and, if Chechen 'extremists' were not stopped, 'we will have the Islamization of Russia'.[52] The coverage of the Russian–Chechen relations by the main government newspaper *Rossiiskaia gazeta* has often been racist, as the newspaper has called the Chechens 'treacherous predators' and 'a nation of bandits'.

CONCLUSION

There are similarities and differences in the conditions which give rise to right-wing extremism in Western Europe and post-communist Russia. Some of the roots are the same in the East and in the West. Social and cultural changes, the challenging of established identities, values and institutions in post-1968 Western Europe – the weakening of the welfare state, political scandals involving opposition and government parties – also mark the process of transition in post-communist Russia. As is the case in Western Europe, in Russia most extremist organizations (with the notable exception of the LDPR) operate on the margins of political and social life. Not only did ultra-nationalists fail to come to power in Russia in the 1990s, but their fortunes in parliamentary elections had been declining since 1993. Extremist groups are not very large and they constantly split and quarrel with each other. Despite support among some military officers for ultra-nationalist ideas, there are no explicit links between the army and paramilitary formations of extremist parties. Some extremists are present in the ranks of mainstream opposition parties, such as the CPRF. However, mainstream nationalist leaders have not forged strong links with extremists.

At the same time, social, economic and political changes in Russia are much more drastic, affecting more people and in more dramatic ways than is the case in Western Europe. Challenges to long-accepted identities, particularly national ones, are also much greater in Russia. As a result, in Russia extremist propaganda exercises a greater impact on society. Thus, the main difference between the unstable Russia in transition and established Western democracies lies not so much in the number of extremist organizations or their electoral success but in the fact that the expression of racial intolerance and of a paranoid worldview is much more acceptable in Russia, both among members of the mainstream political establishment and the public at large.

NOTES

1. A 'national socialist' is Barkashov's self-definition, which he proudly emphasizes in interviews with the media. See A. Verkhovskii, E. Mikhailovskaia and V. Pribylovskii, *Politicheskaia ksenofobiia. Radikalnye gruppy, predstavleniia liderov, rol' tserkvi* (Moscow: Panorama, 1999), p. 40.
2. This chapter does not analyse the activities of extremist organizations in non-Russian ethnic autonomies of the Russian Federation.
3. W. Laqueur, *Russia and Germany. A Century of Conflict* (Boston, MD: Little, Brown & Co., 1965) demonstrated that the ideas of the Russian extreme right, which were initially formed under the influence of German and French ultra-nationalist ideologists of the 1880s, would later have an impact on Adolf Hitler and other Nazi leaders. For the discussion of the history of right-wing extremism in Russia see W. Laqueur, *Black Hundred. The Rise of the Extreme Right in Russia* (New York: HarperCollins, 1993) and J. Devlin, *Slavophiles and Commissars: Enemies of Democracy in Modern Russia* (New York: St Martin's Press, 1999).
4. M. Minkenberg, 'The New Right in France and Germany. Nouvelle Droite, Neue Rechte, and the New Right Radical Parties', in P.H. Merkl and L. Weinberg, *The Revival of Right-Wing Extremism in the Nineties* (London: Frank Cass, 1997), pp. 65–90.
5. See T. Rakowska-Harmstone, 'The Dialectics of Nationalism in the USSR', *Problems of Communism*, 23.3 (1974), pp. 1–22 and R.G. Suny, *The Revenge of the Past. Nationalism, Revolution, and the Collapse of the Soviet Union* (Stanford, CA: Stanford University Press, 1993).
6. However, many of those speaking about the need to create an ethnic Russian state without the Baltics, Central Asia and the Caucasus, were in favour of preserving the union with Ukraine and Belarus, as they saw Ukrainians and Belarusians as part of the Russian nation.
7. For a detailed description of the ideology of the Russian New Right in the late Soviet period, see Y.M. Brudny, *Reinventing Russia. Russian Nationalism and the Soviet State 1953–1991* (Cambridge, MA: Harvard University Press, 1998). See also J. Dunlop, *The Faces of Contemporary Russian Nationalism* (Princeton, NJ: Princeton University Press, 1983); *The New Russian Nationalism* (New York: Praeger, 1985); and A. Yanov, *The Russian New Right: Right-Wing Ideologies in the Contemporary USSR* (Berkeley, CA: Institute of International Studies, University of California, 1978).
8. Emelianov's book was published by an extreme Palestinian group in Paris and Damascus: V. Emelianov, *Desionizatsiia* (Paris: Free Palestine Press, 1979).
9. *Moskovskie novosti*, 45 (1991). See also J. Wishnevsky, 'The Origins of Pamyat', *Survey*, 3 (1988), p. 91.

10. See V. Tolz, 'The Impact of *Glasnost'*, in V. Tolz and I. Elliot (eds), *The Demise of the USSR: From Communism to Independence* (London: Macmillan, 1995), p. 98.

11. J. Wishnevsky, 'Patriots Urge Annulment of RSFSR Elections', *Report on the USSR*, 2.14 (1990), pp. 18–21.

12. See P.H. Merkl, 'Why Are They So Strong Now? Comparative Reflections on the Revival of the Radical Right in Europe', in Merkl and Weinberg (eds), *The Revival of Right-Wing Extremism*, p. 26.

13. Roughly, Russians are those who were classified as such in entry number 5 (nationality) of Soviet passports; Russian speakers were those who had another nationality (Ukrainian, Armenian, Kazakh, etc.) in their passports, but for whom Russian was the main and often the only language they could speak.

14. S. Marnie and W. Slater, 'Russia's Refugees', *RFE/RL Research Report*, 5.37 (1993), pp. 51–3.

15. *Moskovskii komsomolets* (4 August 1993).

16. For the analysis of views of the Russian political élites as well as the general public on the 'just' borders of Russian national homeland, see V. Tolz, 'Conflicting "Homeland Myths" and Nation-State Building in Postcommunist Russia', *Slavic Review*, 57.2 (1998), pp. 274–9.

17. In 1998 S. Kalashnikov, a member of the LDPR, was appointed as Minister of Labour in Evegenii Primakov's government. He retained this post after Primakov had been replaced by Sergei Stepashin as prime minister in May 1999.

18. A. Verkhovskii, 'Finansirovanie i sviazi s prestupnym mirom', in A. Verkhovskii, E. Mikhailovskaia and V. Pribylovskii, *Politicheskii ekstremizm v Rossii* (Moscow: Panorama, 1996–99) (see *http://www.panorama.ru*).

19. Verkhovskii, *et al.*, *Politicheskaia ksenofobiia*, p. 26.

20. *Moskovskii literator*, 2 (March 1995), p. 3.

21. *Ekho Moskvy* (26 April 1995). His motion was voted down by the Duma.

22. Verkhovskii, *et al.*, *Politicheskaia ksenofobiia*, p. 16.

23. See, L. Belin, 'Ultranationalist Parties Follow Disparate Paths', *Transition*, 1.10 (1995), pp. 10–12.

24. *Den*, 2 (1992).

25. I. Tarbakov, 'The "Statists" and the Ideology of Russian Imperial Nationalism', *RFE/RL Research Report*, 49 (1992), p. 14.

26. *Den* (21–27 June 1992).

27. *Russkaia pravda*, 3 (1995), p. 2.

28. Quoted in Verkhovskii, *et al.*, *Politicheskaia ksenofobiia*, p. 39.

29. Ibid., pp. 55–6.

30. See A.G. Osipov and O.I. Cherepova, *Narushenie prav vynuzhdennykh migrantov i etnicheskaia diskriminatsiia v Krasnodarskom krae. Polozhenie meskhetinskikh turok* (Moscow: Pravozashchitnyi tsentr 'Memorial', 1996).

31. E.L. Moroz, 'Vedism i fashizm', in *Bar'er. Antifashistskii zhurnal*, 4 (1994), pp. 4–8.

32. K.N. Kostiuk, 'Pravoslavnyi fundamentalizm', *Polis*, 5 (2000), pp. 133–54 and Verkhovskii, *et al.*, *Politicheskaia ksenofobiia*, pp. 44 and 46.

33. *Interfax* (14 April 1995).

34. Verkhovskii, *et al.*, *Politicheskii ekstremizm v Rossii*. See the section 'Spravki na organizatsii'.

35. See *Politicheskii ekstremizm v Rossii*, the sections 'Chislennost' i vliianie' and 'Spravki na organizatsii'.

36. *Segodnia* (11 December 1993).

37. E. Mikhailovskaia, *Itogi parlamentskikh vyborov 1999 goda dlia natsional-patriotov (v tom chisle imperskoi napravlennosti)* (*http://www.panorama.ru*).

38. *Moskovskii komsomolets*, 12 March 1992, quoted in Verkhovskii *et al.*, *Politicheskii ekstremizm v Rossii*, the section 'Uroven' ksenofobii i uroven' revoliutsionnosti'.

39. Ibid.

40. P. Goble, 'Idel-Ural and the Future of Russia', *RFE/RL NewsLine*, 17 May 2000.
41. *Izvestiia* (15 January 1994) and *Vechernii Krasnodar* (30 August 1994).
42. *Segodnia* (11 December 1993).
43. Verkhovskii *et al.*, *Politicheskii ekstremizm v Rossii*.
44. Verkhovskii *et al.*, *Politicheskaia ksenofobiia*, p. 54.
45. A. Verkhovskii, E. Mikhailovskaia and V. Pribylovskii, *Nationalizm i ksenofobiia v rossiiskom obshchestve* (Moscow: Panorama, 1996–99) (*http://www.panorama.ru*), the section 'Spory o fashizme'.
46. Quoted in Verkhovskii, *et al.*, *Politicheskii ekstremism v Rossii*, esp. the section 'Liberalno-demokraticheskaia partiia Rossii'.
47. *Gosudarstvennaiia Duma. Stenogramma zasedanii. 1997 god. Vesenniia sessiia*, 79, pp. 22–3.
48. *Federal'noe Sobraniie Rossiiskoi Federatsii. Sovet Federatsii. Zasedaniie shestnadtsatoe* (10 February 1995), *stenograficheskii otchet*, pp. 34–5.
49. *Federal'noe Sobraniie Rossiiskoi Federatsii. Sovet Federatsii. Zasedaniie dvatsat' tret'e* (5 July 1995), *stenografichekii otchet*, pp. 17–19.
50. *Gosudarstvennaia Duma. Stenogramma zasedanii 1996 goda. Osenniia sessiia*, 59, pp. 22–3.
51. Quoted in A. Lieven, *Chechnya. Tombstone of Russian Power* (New Haven, CT: Yale University Press, 1998), p. 350.
52. *The Times* (21 March 2000).

CHAPTER ELEVEN

Patterns of Response to the Extreme Right in Western Europe

Jaap van Donselaar

INTRODUCTION

OVER THE last two decades the extreme right in Western Europe has taken on renewed importance. This is evident not only in election results but also in public demonstrations and racist and political violence. Further, extreme right groups exert influence on established political movements, and established political movements have reacted in definable ways to that influence. Governments have devised a number of responses to confront problems of racism and right extremism, and amongst these, three primary strategies can be observed[1]:

(1) *Efforts to influence public opinion.* Governments seek to combat racism and right extremism by educating and informing citizens on inter-ethnic relations, World War II, the Holocaust and related subjects. These actions encourage people to avoid racism/right extremism in the first place or to turn away from them.

(2) *Remedying causes of attraction to racism/right extremism.* Governments act to combat unemployment and increase confidence in the existing political order, and devise policies towards minorities and urban workers that have the same effect. Those who adopt this strategy claim the value of removing a breeding ground in which racism and right-wing extremism can flourish. Like the effort to influence public opinion, the effort to remedy causes is an indirect approach to controlling racism and the extreme right.

(3) *Influencing racist and/or right extremist expression.* This strategy involves repressive measures such as bans on extreme right demonstrations and criminal prosecution for distribution of racist propaganda. In addition to undertaking repressive measures, governments may construct barriers to

right-wing expression within political systems. How seats are distributed in elections – whether via a Dutch system of proportional representation or a French/British majority system – makes a big difference in the management of extremist expression.

This chapter will focus on the last strategy: barriers to the extreme right within political systems and the repressive response of governments to the extreme right in five Western European countries: the Federal Republic of Germany, Belgium, Britain, France and the Netherlands.[2] We consider in detail the following forms of expression: distribution of (racist) propaganda, public meetings and demonstrations, participation in elections and involvement in political and racist violence.

RACIST PROPAGANDA

All five countries are parties to the UN Convention on the Elimination of all Forms of Racial Discrimination (1966).[3] The Convention has been an important source of statutory measures against racist propaganda in the Netherlands (1971), France (1972) and Germany (1973). The Netherlands ratified the UN Convention without reservation.[4] In Germany specific legislation was already in place to prevent the revival of national socialism ('the distribution of propaganda material by unconstitutional organizations', and 'the use of symbols by unconstitutional organizations').[5] In Britain the UN Convention played a more minor role in suppressing propaganda than in other countries, since longstanding statutory provisions were already in place against racist propaganda when the UN Convention was enacted (the Public Order Act of 1936 and the Race Relations Act of 1965). In Belgium, the UN Convention resulted in an anti-racism act, but not until 1981. This act was weak in comparison with provisions enacted in the other four countries.

Amendments to statutory schemes have been made in all five countries over the years, removing loopholes in statutory schemes, broadening scope, toughening sanctions, enacting technical improvements and so on.[6] The most dramatic modifications took place in France, where the French instruments were changed in 1990 to provide for the possibility of removing the passive voting right as an additional punishment for racism. The tightening of statutory provisions in France has generally been seen as a response to the ascendancy of the FN.

Revisionism, in particular Holocaust denial, was classified as an offence in French criminal law in 1972 (and improved in 1990). A similar criminal law dates from 1996 in Belgium; while in Germany, legislation against denial of the Holocaust, enacted as a part of the postwar constitution, was improved in the 1990s.

Neither Britain nor the Netherlands have specific statutory provisions on Holocaust denial; both governments assume that the existing legal framework is sufficient. In Belgium and France, certain anti-racist organizations can appear as plaintiffs in criminal law disputes. This procedural arrangement means that such organizations can institute prosecutions, so relieving governments of the responsibility.

Judging by their armoury of legal measures, the Netherlands, Germany, Britain and France are, in principle, well placed to stop the spread of racist propaganda.[7] Belgium is less well equipped, but recent developments may change this. Belgium's Anti-Racism Act (1981) has to date not been an appreciable obstacle to the spread of racist propaganda by the VB, nor has it had a significant moderating influence on the propaganda itself. Belgium stands in contrast, therefore, to the capacity for deterrence evident in the other four countries.[8]

We turn now to application of statutory instruments available in the five countries and obstacles to their application. Racist propaganda is often packaged in such a way that, at least from a criminal law point of view, prosecutors cannot always act. Extreme right leaders are adept at *impressing management*, finding a balance between recognizability for supporters and protection from judicial or legal intervention.

Successful application of instruments designed to control right-wing extremist expression depends on prosecution policy. Here too, Belgium is an exception. Shortly after Belgium's anti-racism act became effective, it was found that the Belgian judiciary did not consider it desirable to prevent the dissemination of Hitler's *Mein Kampf*. In the 1990s an attempt was made to intensify Belgium's prosecution policy, at the same time tightening the anti-racism act mentioned above.

In France, Germany and the Netherlands, particularly in recent years, attempts to implement a more intensive prosecution policy have appeared. In Germany and the Netherlands those efforts seem to have been more successful than in France. In Britain, extreme right activists have been convicted on many occasions. Nevertheless, the number of convictions for racism is generally regarded as low in all five countries under discussion.

Prosecution policy regarding racist propaganda is not an independent matter in any of the five countries, but rather forms part of broader prosecution policy. Depending on time and place, it may be aimed at expressions of racism, right extremism or both. In all five countries prosecution policy seems to be 'vote-sensitive', influenced by shock effects, particularly as far as violence and elections are concerned. Below we offer many examples of trigger events found to have a catalytic effect on the application of available prosecution instruments.[9] Any decline in the power of the extreme right – Britain in the early 1980s and the late 1980s in the Netherlands – seems to temper prosecutions. Another important curb on prosecutions, it seems, is a clear preference for an alternative approach. Alternatives may include disregard of racist or extreme acts, for example. Not infrequently societies seem to fear that criminal prosecution will make an extreme right leader an attractive underdog or martyr, or, even worse, cause that leader to profit from unsuccessful legal proceedings. In short, fear of reverse effects may inhibit efforts to prosecute. This fear may apply not only to the control of propaganda but in principle to any other repressive measure a government may choose to undertake/impose.

DEMONSTRATIONS

All five countries under discussion can use repressive instruments to take action against public demonstrations by the extreme right: public demonstrations may be banned as a precautionary measure if serious riots are anticipated. In the Netherlands, Belgium, Britain and France the reason for the ban has a *neutral value*: the content of the demonstrations has nothing to do with the government's choice to act. Nor may threat of a disturbance of the peace by third parties play a part in the decision to ban public demonstrations. In such instances the police must protect the demonstrations. Only if there is a question of a situation being beyond the administration's control can a precautionary ban be issued in any of these four countries. Germany permits additional grounds for imposing restrictions on public demonstrations, including anticipation that certain offences will be committed. This broadening implies that governments can identify justifiable grounds for a ban on extreme right demonstrations. Hence, Germany's reasons for imposition of bans are *non-neutral*.[10]

Statutory frameworks for dealing with riots do not differ greatly in the Netherlands, Britain, France, Belgium and Germany, but practical application of those statutory frameworks does differ.[11] However, practice in the Netherlands, Britain, France and Belgium differs significantly from practice in Germany with respect to the question of how strictly potential risks to public order are weighed. The first four countries strictly judge the danger of extreme right demonstrations to public order. Powerful arguments are necessary if the freedom to demonstrate and assemble is to be overridden in order to protect public order, even where counter-demonstrations have been announced. (Occurrence of counter-demonstrations are more the rule than the exception.) All four countries place emphasis on the question of how public order can be maintained *in spite of* demonstrations and counter-demonstrations. As a consequence, a number of extreme right demonstrations have taken place in Britain, Germany, France and Belgium, protected by heavily equipped police forces. Often such demonstrations have been accompanied by violent confrontations among the parties involved: extreme right demonstrators, opponents of the extreme right and the police. Attempts by the police to keep extreme right demonstrators and their opponents apart have often resulted in serious confrontations between the police and anti-fascist demonstrators.

In Belgium, precautionary bans on demonstrations are rare. So far as France is concerned, two periods can be mentioned during which precautionary bans occurred frequently: (1) in 1990 after the shocking desecration of the Carpentras Jewish cemetery and (2) during the election period of 1992. Although in France banning is usually resorted to in the event of fear of disturbance of the peace, political considerations have also played a part in the decision to impose a ban. It seems that reluctance to ban demonstration both in Belgium and France is linked with the fear of possible reverse effects.

In Germany, the precautionary ban on extreme right demonstrations was rarely used until the 1990s. Because violence has increased, especially the shock of violent attacks in Möln (1992) and Solingen (1993), the climate of opinion and governmental decision-making has changed. Since 1993 the imposition of precautionary bans on public demonstrations has become the rule rather than the exception. If right-wing extremists demonstrate on the streets now, they do so without prior announcement and thus by definition without consent.

The authorities in Britain often make public gatherings dependent on the maintenance of public order. Election meetings and other public gatherings cannot be banned as a precaution. Only the threat of a serious disturbance of the peace is grounds for a ban. In other words, the law concerning precautionary bans is politically neutral (a situation which is often discussed).

In France in the 1970s the rising FN habitually demonstrated on the streets on a large scale. Application of the precautionary ban in France was fairly rare until about 1980. Then serious riots became the rule, characterized by mass confrontations between the police and opponents of the extreme right, and resulting in death and serious injuries. Deteriorating relations between ethnic minority groups and the police were often involved, deterioration precipitated by extreme right provocations. The fact that police were protecting extreme right marches but were not in a position to curb explosive growth in racist violence created bad blood between the police and minority communities. More recently the precautionary ban on extreme right demonstrations has been applied, but infrequently.

In the Netherlands since the end of the 1970s virtually any attempt by the extreme right to call a demonstration has been regarded as an unacceptable public order risk. The precautionary ban is therefore the rule in the Netherlands, with only a few exceptions. Decisions by certain mayors to ban extreme right demonstrations have been upheld by administrative judges. In the first ten years of its existence (1984–94) the extreme right Centrumpartij (CP) has never succeeded in calling a public meeting. The calling of closed meetings has also often proved to be a problem for the extreme right. Current practice (frequent imposition of the precautionary ban) and the government's clear intention to continue on the present course is at loggerheads with the law and jurisprudence, which are by nature neutral. The fact that the law and jurisprudence are neutral has occasionally led to pleas that automatic bans on extreme right demonstrations no longer take place in the Netherlands.

Clearly then, regulations allowing bans on public demonstrations differ with respect to their 'neutrality'. In the Netherlands, Belgium, Britain and France those regulations are *neutral*.[12] In Germany those regulations are *non-neutral*. '*Neutral systems*' contradict deeply rooted social resistance to right-wing extremism, especially in Britain and France.[13]

Even in the Netherlands, disputes about the neutral character of regulations concerning bans have become at times intense; in practice a neutral application of a neutral law does not always take place.

In addition we note differences in the application of repressive legal means. Belgium and the Netherlands form the extremes in this regard. Perhaps the steady successes of the VB in Belgium and the FN in France in the 1980s and 1990s can partly be explained by the liberal climates in Belgium and France with regard to demonstrations. Given this liberal climate, both the VB and the FN have been able to build up longstanding traditions of demonstrations large and small. Such traditions have developed to a much lesser degree in Britain and Germany, and have been almost altogether excluded in the Netherlands.

INVOLVEMENT IN VIOLENCE

In 1962 leaders of the extreme right British group called Spearhead were prosecuted for planning violent action. Members of the group were convicted and Spearhead was banned as a 'paramilitary organization'. (Spearhead's intended violent action was not carried out, only prepared.) When the phenomenon of 'racist violence' in Britain greatly increased towards the end of the 1970s, many people held that extreme right organizations were responsible for this.[14] By contrast, the British government thought these organizations played no primary role in racist violence, and did not prosecute groups as they had done in the case of Spearhead. The government was, strictly speaking, correct, but its position did not alter the fact that far-right extremists had on a large scale been guilty of violent racist crimes. Given the government's 'no primary role' attitude, policy regarding control of racist violence was therefore not aimed at the extreme right, even though extreme right demonstrations were drastically limited by government intervention.[15]

Things were quite different in Germany. When racist violence increased dramatically at the beginning of the 1990s, the government responded with a broad package of measures aimed at the extreme right: bans on gatherings, restriction of demonstrations, tightening up and extension of legislation, intensification of attention paid to the extreme right by police, the judiciary and the information services, and threat of the application of the 'Radicals' resolution (*Radikalenerlass*, 1972).[16] Germany thus greatly limited the scope of extreme right activity. The REP were depicted as 'psychological arsonists' and stigmatized. By officially labelling the REP as 'unconstitutional', Germany took a major step towards banning the organization altogether.

In France, supposed involvement in racist and anti-Semitic violence brought the FN into a perilous position on several occasions, particularly in 1990 at the time of the Carpentras incident.[17] France limited the scope of extreme right activity, though not to the same extent as Germany had done. In France, as in Britain, limitations primarily involved restrictions on demonstrations.

'Supposed involvement' and 'psychological wrongdoing' also became accepted terminology in the Dutch case, though during a period preceding the 1990s. In 1976 a neo-Nazi party was suspected of being responsible for a race riot, and in the early 1980s the racist CP implicated itself in circumstances not dissimilar to those of the desecration at Carpentras and the 1994 attack on a Turkish family in Möln, Germany. In the Netherlands, too, there was restriction of the freedom of movement of the extreme right, in particular by threat of a party ban.[18] In Belgium, the supposed involvement of the extreme right in violent acts led to the establishment of a parliamentary commission.[19]

We turn now to problems of perception and actuality. How far is the extreme right involved in political and racist violence? What precisely constitutes 'involvement'? How must governments respond and when? These questions have caused governments considerable thought, and have elicited various responses, including criminal prosecution of individual perpetrators, restrictions upon the movement of right extremists (through bans on demonstrations and meetings) and even bans on organizations themselves.[20] If a society associates violence with the extreme right, then some form of action is generally taken against the extreme right. This is so in all five countries under discussion. The association does not in itself have to be factually based or even proven before punitive action takes place. Sometimes powerful action is taken in response to 'supposed' or 'psychological' involvement by the extreme right in violence. In other cases, actual participation in violence leads to little or no response. In other words, in serious cases a mild response has sometimes taken place, whereas in non-serious cases there have been instances of harsh responses. We might ask how well proven must the link be between the extreme right and violence which takes place. Countries differ greatly in this matter and Britain and Germany seem to represent two extremes of the spectrum.

In my opinion, remarkable differences in the behaviour of these two countries cannot be explained by differences in the extent of racist violence in them; behavioural differences can only partly be explained by the size of the extreme right in each country. In short, 'involvement' of the extreme right in racist violence cannot always be objectively defined, nor is it objectively judged. We can suggest certain reasons for this state of affairs. (1) The leaders of extreme right parties often cannot afford to propagate political violence openly, since this would lead to confrontation with the government and leaders might lose part of their electorate. (2) On the other hand, maintaining too rigorous a distance from militant activism also poses risks. Radical supporters may be alienated or repelled by silence or the denial of ideological principles and membership in right extreme groups may suffer as a result. Extreme right organizations often exert a power of attraction on persons who are more radical or more militant than the image the organization wishes to give itself *front-stage*. The behaviour of a radical fringe can discredit the organization as a whole when publicly acknowledged.

But *back-stage* affiliation is different. Often organizations respect 'radicals' for their services and their nerve. Back-stage radicals translate the ideas shared by many into action, ideas few dare publicly admit for fear of confrontation with the judiciary or other authorities.

Because many racist incidents are not described in detail, one can often only speculate about the role of extreme right organizations in them. Even where there seems to be a measure of clarity, a link can often only be *inferred* between racist offences and the extreme right. What is demonstrable is usually an indirect link: the offence cannot be attributed to a particular organization, but rather to persons who in some way form part of that organization. In short, the involvement of extreme right organizations in the phenomenon of 'racist violence' is complex, and this applies in each of the cases of the five countries under discussion.[21]

An alternative analytical strategy is less difficult to pursue: starting not from racist violence and trying to determine the extreme right's involvement in it, but starting rather from extreme right formations and trying to determine the degree to which each exhibits violent behaviour. In each of the five countries links can be seen between violent incidents and extreme right organizations. In Belgium, links between violent incidents and extreme right organizations are open, hence noticeable. Members of the VB often participate in militant action or even political violence. By contrast, in Germany, the Netherlands and France, extreme right activists see their positions in the REP, the CP or the FN as endangered, if not made impossible, by open association with militant actions. In Belgium, the extreme right is faced to a much lesser degree with a repressive climate than is the extreme right in either Germany or the Netherlands.

BANNING EXTREME RIGHT ORGANIZATIONS

Belgium and Britain differ from the three other countries, both in the means they employ against right-wing extremism and in the application of those means. Both countries enacted legislation between the two world wars regarding the identification of an organization as a 'militia': in Belgium a 'private militia' (1934) and in Britain a 'paramilitary organization' (1936). In both countries competence to define a defendant's status lies with the judge and involves the criminal prosecution of individual 'militia' members. In Britain since World War II the 1936 measure has been applied only once against the extreme right, namely against Spearhead in 1962. Since then no further extreme right paramilitary organization has been banned, not even any extreme right groups with an explicitly violent record, such as Combat 18. The reticence which the British government has shown in dealing with racist organizations contrasts, in the eyes of some, with the energy of its repression of military and political groups in Northern Ireland. This energetic repression of Irish groups can also be regarded as a demonstration of potential power. Because Britain does not have a written constitution, far-reaching measures can be taken very rapidly. There have been no discussion about bans in Britain, as there have been in the Netherlands and Germany, at least not on the issue of whether racist and extreme right organizations should exist. When discussion of bans takes place, it asks whether extreme right demonstrations pose a threat to public order.

In Belgium it is not possible to ban a political party.[22] Only if a political party can be regarded as a private militia is it possible to bring a criminal prosecution against its members. Organizations as such cannot be disbanded, at least not officially. The basic right of association is quite firmly anchored in the Belgian Constitution. Thus a Belgian criminal judge cannot accomplish anything against associations which overstep the mark. One must also consider the reservations of the Belgian government when it implemented the UN Convention on the Elimination of all Forms of Racial Discrimination. The reservations related, among other things, to a country's obligation to deal with racist organizations. (Britain also had the same reservations.) The 1934 Act on Private Militias was applied in Belgium during 1980 against members of the Flemish Militant Order (VMO) and the Front de la jeunesse, which had been guilty of violence on a big scale. The absence of a ban system in Belgium only became a subject of political discussion in 1981, at the time of the Wijninckx Commission. Otherwise the ban on parties has not been a matter of political consequence, and this issue is not really relevant to the VB.

France too maintains a militia act enacted during the prewar years: the Act of 10 January 1936 on Armed Groups and Private Militias.[23] This Act provides for the disbandment of military and/or violent organizations. It places competence to decide not with the judge but with the Council of Ministers. The Armed Group and Private Militias Act is, as regards its origin and development, strongly tailored to right extremist organizations. Over the years the Act has been extended and revised to include racism, discrimination and terrorism as grounds for a ban.[24] However, if we look at application of the Act, then we see that in practice only a hybrid of explicit violence and Nazism has caused the French Council of Ministers to pass a disbandment resolution. In two cases such a disbandment resolution involved the FN. In the early 1970s the threat of a ban was distinctly present for the FN, but Le Pen and his associates succeeded in manœuvring the party out of the danger zone. In the mid 1980s the likelihood of a ban also diminished when the political influence of the FN in parliament largely disappeared. For the FN, threat of a ban is not a manifest but a latent danger. The organization's supposed involvement in racist and anti-Semitic violence has, however, brought it into a perilous position on a number of occasions, particularly in 1990 at the time of the incident at Carpentras. The circumstances self-evident as this time could potentially occur again should there be intermittent electoral growth. But for the time being even the shocking electoral scores of 1995 did not bring about a debate on a ban. Just as in Britain, discussions on bans in France have been aimed primarily at the question of how far it is or is not desirable to ban demonstrations by the party. Discussions of this nature took place in 1992.

In the Netherlands, actual application of the party ban is a rare occurrence; nevertheless the threat of a ban has been important for the development of the extreme right.[25] The power to decide whether to impose a ban on an organization rests with the judge. In 1953 a small neo-Nazi party was banned; by contrast, an attempt to ban a neo-Nazi party, the Nedelandse Volksunie (NVU), failed. This failure resulted a change to the statutory framework in the Netherlands. Events felt to be shocking made the latent threat of a ban manifest. In 1953 news that former Dutch SS and Nazi party members had formed a new party and wanted to take part in elections precipitated a ban. There was no question of any discussion of a ban – the need for it was self-evident. In the 1970s participation in the elections by the racist and neo-Nazi NVU initiated discussion of a ban. Further concerns were raised by the NVU's involvement in violence and international criticism of the UN Convention on the Elimination of all Forms of Racial Discrimination. In the 1980s and 1990s extreme right parties were often confronted with the threat of being banned. In 1998 the neo-Nazi Centreparty '86 was banned by the Amsterdam Court. The leaders of other parties are certainly aware of this possibility.

Of the five countries, Germany is the most likely to ban extreme right organizations. It has both the statutory means and the political will and competence to enforce them.[26] Unconstitutional parties – parties that are contrary to the existing free and democratic order – may thus be banned.[27] Taken together with Germany's ban on association and the government's ability to restrict basic political rights, the party ban forms the third measure with which German democracy can defend itself. The decision to enact a party ban rests in Germany with the Constitutional Court; the decision to impose a ban on association rests with the (Federal) Minister of the Interior. Unlike the association ban, the party ban is rarely imposed: in 1952 a neo-Nazi party, the Socialist Reich Party (SRP), was banned, and in 1956 a communist party, the KDP, was banned. As in the Netherlands, the threat of a party ban is a significant deterrent for extreme right groups. Threat of a ban can be stimulated by catalytic events. International public opinion seems to carry more weight in Germany than in other countries. In other words, an outcry abroad causes German authorities to take action. Because of the anti-Semitic 'Schmierwelle' in 1960, the fate of the German Rightist Party (DRP) hung by a thread and the threat of its entry in the Bundestag brought the NPD perilously close to a ban. Since 1992 application of the association ban has expanded enormously. From the point of view of the authorities, the existing instruments offer sufficient means of dealing effectively with extreme right groups.

In the early 1990s the REP also reluctantly came into the firing line and has remained there to this day. At this point it does not appear that the party will be banned, given its electoral decline; as with the NPD in 1969 a political solution thus presents itself. For the REP, pressure from outside has not been without consequences. The party has tried to find a balance between protection from repressive measures and recognition for supporters. Under pressure the balance has been disturbed and as a result the REP has lost its position as a 'bridge' between the extreme right and established political parties. The fate of the REP in the 1990s is an appropriate illustration of the link that may exist between division in extreme right ranks and pressure exerted from the outside. Here there are also parallels between the Netherlands and Germany.

Another banned organization, the Free Workers' Party (FAP), has, since the middle of the 1980s, also shown itself to be a violent organization. The FAP was, however, not banned until 1995. In 1999 and 2000 the German government and parliament sent an *Antrag* (proposal) to the Constitutional Court in Karlsruhe to have the party banned.

BARRIERS IN POLITICAL SYSTEMS

The political influence of the extreme right is determined not only by the degree to which it is able to attract voters but also, and primarily, by the *method of seat allocation*. A vital distinction for the extreme right is evident when we contrast *majority systems* with systems of *proportionate representation*. The first is unfavourable and the second favourable to small political parties. Extreme right parties are as a rule relatively small. The bigger the group, the less disadvantageous a majority system, as the British and French cases show.

In France, specific disadvantages for the extreme right are linked with the election system, or at least elections where the 'two-round' majority system is used. The disadvantage lies in the political isolation of the extreme right, which is found to be an obstacle to the formation of coalitions in the second round. The French case shows how crucial has been the effect of a change in the system: 9.9 per cent of the votes in 1986 produced 35 parliamentary seats; 9.6 per cent of the votes in 1998 produced only one. In France the method of seat distribution depends on the type of election. Thus, in 1993 the FN received 12.5 per cent of the vote but did not get into the national parliament. One year later, 10.5 per cent of the vote obtained 11 seats in the European Parliament. This example illustrates the difference between the effects of a majority system as opposed to a system of proportionate representation.

In Britain only the (relative) majority system has been used, and this has proved fatal to the electoral prospects of the extreme right. Extreme right parties in Britain have, certainly in view of their relatively small electoral size, virtually no chance of breaking through the majority system. However, this situation could potentially change in two ways. The first would be a relative growth of the electorate devoted to extreme right parties, while the second would entail a change in the electoral system itself, with the introduction of proportionate representation. (The second seems a more likely prospect than the first.)

Use of the majority system in France and Britain means that, in relative terms, political power is less accessible in these two countries than in the other three countries under discussion. Political power is potentially most accessible in the Dutch and Belgian democracies. In the Netherlands and Belgium, elections are based on proportionate representation. Nevertheless, in Belgium the beneficial effects of proportional representation have been somewhat tempered for the VB by the federal structure of the parliamentary democracy where proportionate representation is '*indirect*' (because of differences between French- and Dutch-speaking electoral districts). Democracy in the Netherlands is, relatively speaking, the most accessible because of *direct* proportionate representation. The CD would, in view of their voting percentage, have not a glimmer of a chance in British or French parliamentary elections, but they achieve measurable results in the Netherlands.

In Germany, the Centre Democrats would also not have achieved admission to the national parliament. The German election threshold of 5 per cent is an obstacle which has never been beaten by an extreme right party, at least in Bundestag elections. But the REP did obtain over 7 per cent in the European elections of 1989. In terms of accessibility, the Federal Republic of Germany falls between Belgium and the Netherlands, on the one hand, and Britain and France on the other.[28]

Extreme right parties must overcome certain hurdles if they are to participate in elections, hurdles both financial and personal. *Financial barriers* are real. Parties must deposit funds to participate in elections and must reach certain vote levels or thresholds if those funds are to be returned. The threshold for return of a deposit in the Netherlands is conspicuously low.[29] A party need only achieve 75 per cent of the quota to get the deposit back; for parliamentary elections in the Netherlands that amounts to a mere 0.5 per cent of the votes. Thresholds are higher in France and also in Britain, where the financial return rule seems to have an inhibiting effect on electoral participation of extreme right candidates.[30] In Germany, election participation offers more financial advantages than disadvantages (the '*Wahlkampf-kostenvorauszahlung*'). But in Germany *personal* barriers are strong.[31] The German signatures requirement is very high in comparison with requirements in

Belgium and the Netherlands. Indeed, the Dutch election system is most accessible, and least characterized by the personal and financial barriers which prevail elsewhere.

In Britain the threshold for receiving *political broadcasting time* is derived from yet another criterion, namely, participation in a minimum of 50 electoral districts. (In France the threshold is 75 electoral districts.) Because of the financial risks associated with broad electoral participation, a high threshold for securing broadcast time exists in practice. The opposite applies for the Netherlands: because electoral participation is easily obtained, the threshold for receiving broadcast time is correspondingly low.

In the political system of the Federal Republic of Germany the notion of '*defensible democracy*' has a firm foundation not only in the electoral system but also in other ways. The German Constitution determines that parties must have an 'internal democratic order' and must not conflict with the established free and democratic order of the state. The French Constitution also requires political parties 'to respect the principles of national sovereignty and democracy'. But the French Constitution does not include a ban on parties as a constitutional provision, nor does France elaborate the position of parties in a special 'parties act'.

In Germany, the 'internal democratic order' is indeed elaborated in the Parties Act of 1967, which provides that members of any party must demonstrably influence the decision-making process, and that members are free to enter and leave parties at will. Many extreme right organizations in Germany do not, or only partly, meet this requirement. In accord with the Parties Act, political parties must formulate a manifesto which does not conflict with the established free and democratic order of the German state. For extreme right parties this means balancing membership and ideology on the boundaries of what is permissible.[32] The German political system includes many safeguards to prevent the problem of 'hostility to the system'. Hostility to the system is explicitly mentioned in non-neutral terms, as the phrase 'conflict with the established free and democratic order' illustrates. In none of the other four countries are these safeguards explicit or present to the same degree, nor are they given the same value.

DEGREE OF POLITICAL ISOLATION

The question of how far the extreme right is surrounded by a cordon sanitaire in the various countries is not easy to answer. The cordon sanitaire is a stubborn, morally charged issue which lends itself to both divergent and arbitrary approaches. Though we cannot analyse this complex topic in detail here, we can offer preliminary observations. We are concerned primarily with cordons sanitaires in political systems, not in social life. Based on the cases we have reviewed, an overall difference between '*physical*' and '*ideological*' cordons sanitaires becomes evident. The first term alludes to the political isolation of extreme right groups and their representatives; the second alludes to the political isolation of the conceptual world within which extreme right groups operate.

In none of the five countries does a *physical* cordon sanitaire exist.[33] But it is true that in all five countries interpretation of political messages coming from the extreme right by politicians in established movements almost always goes hand in hand with 'physical' separation from the extreme right origin of the messages.[34] In other words, established politicians almost never express support or approval for colleagues from the extreme right. Nevertheless, established politicians may speak in ways that resonate with extreme right sections of their audiences. The politician expressing such views is as a rule the last person to link him or herself with racism or extreme right groups; expression of the kind described here is often unconscious on the speaker's part, though ideologically recognizable. Further, if confronted with the sympathies evident in utterance of this kind, the politician from an established group is likely to defend him or herself. Even where the cordon sanitaire we have associated with political expression begins to crumble (in Britain during the 1970s, more recently in the Netherlands), certain subjects are clearly taboo within established political orders – revisionism and anti-Semitism in particular.

Analysis of the cordon sanitaire by country is problematic because it is often difficult to compare events distant from one another in date and time.[35] Description is easier than comparison. Indeed, how can one compare the response to a coup by thousands of FN members today with responses by two councillors in Blackburn in 1976? But despite these obvious difficulties a few principles present themselves. The isolation of extreme right parties from others seems relatively strong in the Netherlands. This also seems true of Germany where, since 1992, the REP has become considerably more remote from other groups. By contrast, in Britain, particularly in the early 1980s, there was a good deal of overlap between extreme right groups and the Conservative Party. Indeed, many right extremists defected to the Conservatives and were tolerated to a certain degree. By contrast, in Belgium representatives of the VB have to date been kept out of municipal executives. In Belgium, the standard is that there may not be any political cooperation with the VB, but the cordon is less solid where informal contacts are concerned. Orientation toward Flemish nationalism seems to carry more weight in defining the cordon than political discrepancies otherwise defined.

In France, the cordon has a specific significance in relation to the majority system. Is a pact signed with the FN during the second round of election, or is it not? Agreements between the 'established right' in France and the FN have become increasingly rare, but they have also become less necessary, given the weakened position of socialism. Nevertheless, each established political movement in France has attempted now and then to use the FN as a political factor in seeking its own ends.

STATE RESPONSES: FACILITATING AND INHIBITING FACTORS

How prepared are the various countries to cope with the problem of right-wing extremism? The Federal Republic of Germany scores highly in all areas, especially during the late 1990s. German democracy is the most heavily protected among the five countries under analysis. In the Netherlands an 'imbalance' between firmly repressive instruments and an extremely accessible political system is striking. Again, manifest repression dates, as it does in Germany, to the 1990s. By contrast, French preparedness to deal with extremism is defined primarily by barriers within the political system. In Britain this is even more clearly the case: the political system includes many obstacles to the extreme right, but because a system of banning is absent, Britain scores relatively low in an analysis of latent repressive measures. Finally, Belgium is striking because it scores low in all areas. Belgium's system of latent instruments of repression is relatively weak, as is its application of that system. Belgium's democracy is, we believe, the most vulnerable of the five.

All governments face what we might call a *dilemma of repression*. On the one hand, all recognize the threat of right extremism. Recognition prompts governments to aim repressive measures at extreme right activists and their organizations. On the other hand, it is the task of governments to protect basic political rights such as freedom of expression, the right to meet and demonstrate, and the right of association. Governments must consider and decide on each occasion what should be given greater weight: control of extremist right-wing expression or protection of basic political freedom.

We have already discussed the factors, latent or manifest, which have stimulated repressive action by governments. We have also looked at those factors which appear to inhibit repressive governmental action. We now turn to the most important factors which appear to operate within both categories.

The most powerful stimulating factors include: (1) *trigger events*; (2) *international forces* (including international prestige); (3) *the protection of minorities and inter-ethnic relations*; (4) *social organizations and their lobbies*.[36]

Trigger events have shock effects as a result of which governments are mobilized. Usually trigger events involve violence, riots or the recording of an electoral success by the extreme right. A television broadcast in which an extreme right leader makes statements regarded as shocking may also constitute a trigger event. (An example of this is Jean-Marie Le Pen's statement that the Holocaust was a mere detail in the history of World War II.) The link between the seriousness or actual power of a specific event and the shock created by it is not necessarily proportionate. Sometimes not much is needed to cause a considerable shock reaction and sometimes there is little reaction despite a powerful cause. There are significant differences between the various countries with respect to their reactions. For example, the Netherlands reacts with shock to events in Germany. Indeed, racist violence in Germany always gets far more of a reaction than, say, racist violence in Britain.

International forces and events can be stimulating factors.[37] *International prestige* can play a part, such as the reaction by governments to criticism from abroad or anticipation of international criticism. This is particularly apparent in the Federal Republic of Germany which is especially sensitive to criticism regarding the control of racism and right-wing extremism, and which is also more readily criticized than other countries. As Boris Becker once said, 'As a German you have to act twice as nice abroad.' Anti-Semitic incidents during the 1960s in Germany and elsewhere were one of the major reasons why the UN Convention on the Elimination of all Forms of Racial Discrimination was enacted.

Protection of minorities and inter-ethnic relations can also be termed a factor precipitating repressive governmental action.[38] In Britain the repressive measures against the NF in the early 1980s were largely the result of concerns about the deterioration of inter-ethnic relations and particularly relations between ethnic minorities and the authorities.

Often governments are unwilling to act but are induced to do so by other agencies. *Social organizations and their lobbies* (political parties, pressure groups, minority organizations, anti-racist and anti-fascist organizations and the media) play an important part in stimulating such action.[39] Such organizations act in three ways: as conscience, watchdog and adviser. In Germany, representatives of the Jewish community have a considerable influence on governmental response. In France, Britain and the Netherlands, authorities have invested in a variety of ways in the lobby infrastructure, while in Belgium this has taken place on an much more modest scale.

In the above discussion we have focused on factors which stimulate governmental repression of extremism. Some of those factors can, however, have a reverse effect; hence they act as *inhibiting factors*. Several factors can be mentioned which both influence governmental action and also have an inhibiting effect, such as enhanced protection of basic political rights. Instead of repression, governments may prefer to use *alternative strategies*. These may be either *passive* (ignoring a situation) or *active* (using alternative methods of control). Rather than repression, governments may choose to emphasize more general control of prejudice, information campaigns, enactment of policies to improve the position of minorities or even restrictive immigration policies. Above all, attempts to restrict immigration are preferred by governments as an alternative strategy against the extreme right. Also, governments may seek explanations for rising right extremism in economic conditions, in particular recession and unemployment. Endeavouring to improve these conditions also can serve as a strategy to control right-wing extremism.

Another curb on repression is the *fear of failure*: the fear that a confrontation in court will be lost, whether in cases concerning control of racist propaganda, bans on demonstrations or ban procedures themselves. Sometimes fear of loss weighs so heavily on governments that they do not even begin proceedings. The decision not to proceed rests on the assumption that a lost cause is harmful to the control of racism and right extremism. (However, research shows little empirical basis for this assumption.[40] In fact latent repression and even lost causes are as a rule detrimental to the stability of extreme right groups.)

Fear of failure often goes hand in hand with a governmental preference for alternative strategies and *fear of reverse effects*. The assumption that repressive measures may have counterproductive effects is an argument often raised against government action. The argument appears in all five countries; usually it includes the presumption that repressive action will encourage underground violent acts. Prosecuting extreme right leaders, it is feared, may cast those leaders in the role of *underdog*, as a result of which their popularity will increase. *The fear of reverse effects* – and lost causes – cannot be refuted on a rigorous empirical basis, but events in the five countries under discussion put the question in perspective. Violence as a rule is the *cause* of repressive governmental action, not the *consequence*.[41] The same is true for arguments about organizations 'going underground'.

As for the question of *underdogs*, it seems that in both Germany and the Netherlands the electoral tide turned before the extreme right could advance any further. The pursuit of extreme right leaders did not in fact turn them into attractive underdogs. Instead repressive governmental action turned them into panicky shepherds with no power to keep their routed flocks together.

The leaders of extreme right groups are compelled to keep their organizations in the firing line. They have to face two existential dangers: the danger of criminalization – which can lead to repression – and the loss of the right to exist if they maintain too vague a political profile. The second largely determines the distinction between 'established' political movements and non-established political movements. Reacting against established political movements is one of the pillars of extreme right behaviour. Extreme right leaders draw boundaries, but so do politicians of established parties. Here the cordon sanitaire is significant. The shift of established politicians to the extreme right means meddling with the political profile of the extreme right. In itself this does not have to cause problems for extreme right politicians. Indeed, the shift can be beneficial to them should the taboo on extreme right approaches to immigration crumble. Still, in order to partici-pate successfully in elections, extreme right leaders may need to restore the balance disturbed by a shift to the right by established politicians. They may need to restore their political exclusivity in some way. They do this by opposing the 'ordinary' politicians fiercely, mainly by cursing and blaming them.

An alternative situation occurs when established politicians jump to the right where ideas about ethnic minorities are concerned. Le Pen did this subtly with his well-known statement 'the voters prefer the original to the copy'. Perhaps Le Pen was right, but we still need to ask if his statement is generally valid. It may be that voters prefer the copy when, in their eyes, the original is crumpled, torn or otherwise damaged. Under governmental repression the 'original' racist message of a Le Pen, by definition, is also under attack and a 'jump to the right' by moderate politicians and voters involved great risks.

In short, the ideological interaction between extreme right politicians and 'established' politicians is influenced by more or less repressive conditions. And the response of the extreme right to a crumbling cordon sanitaire is considerably limited by threat of repression. The German and Dutch cases illustrate this well. On the other hand, the extreme right has more freedom of choice where there is less chance of repressive government action. This is the case in Belgium.

The dilemma of adaptation thus involves interaction between the extreme right and more or less repressive governments.[42] The five countries under discussion can be divided into three categories in this regard: Germany and the Netherlands initiate fairly strong repressive responses. Belgium stands at the opposite extreme. France and Britain form the middle ground. The need for the extreme right to adapt in Germany and the Netherlands is far more apparent than the need to adapt in Belgium. Hence the Belgian VB needs to worry less about what is or is not permissible than the German Centre Democrat or the REP parties. Similarly, the VB needs to worry less about how to stand up to pressure from the outside than do the Centre Democrat or the REP parties. The pressure on right-wing extremist parties has a great effect on their internal cohesion, especially when it takes the form of the threat of governmental action. The leader who adapts too much to repressive conditions runs the risk of being regarded as 'lax' and 'weak', and hence runs the risk of endangering his own position. A leader who adapts too little and who holds on to too radical a profile can be just as controversial, just as endangered; for with him his fellow group members are criminalized. Leaders are also vulnerable who have an insufficient moderating effect on party members who have been discredited because of extreme ideas or behaviour.

The greater the pressure on an extreme right organization, the greater the need to adapt.[43] And with increased adaptation, the greater the difference between the ways in which such an organization manifests itself to the outside world (*front-stage behaviour*) and goings on behind the scene (*back-stage behaviour*). Leaders stringently undertake and control *impression management*. The organization becomes unstable. This scenario applies in particular to the extreme right in Germany and the Netherlands. By contrast, we may define the Belgian situation as follows: less pressure from the outside on the extreme right means a reduced need to adapt. In Belgium the difference between what happens front-stage and what happens back-stage is less obvious. As a result, the VB is more stable than other extreme right organizations operating under more repressive conditions. From all of the above it is apparent that repressive government action, threatened or actual, has a profound effect on the phenomenon of right extremism.[44]

NOTES

1. See J. van Donselaar, *De staat paraat?: De bestrijding van extreem-rechts in West Europa* (Amsterdam: Babylon de Geus Bakker, 1995), pp. 14–16.
2. This chapter is mainly based on a comparative analysis of state responses to the extreme right in Western Europe in the 1990s (see van Donselaar, *De staat paraat?*).
3. See N. Lerner, *The UN Convention on the Elimination of all Forms of Racial Discrimination* (Alphen a.R.: Sijthoff and Noordhoff, 1980); and S. Coliver, K. Boyle and F. D'Souza (eds), *Striking A Balance: Hate Speech, Freedom of Expression and Non-Discrimination*, Article 19 (London/Colchester: International Centre against Censorship/Human Rights Centre, University of Essex, 1992).
4. See van Donselaar, *De staat paraat?*, pp. 19 and 24.
5. See H.-G. Jaschke, *Streitbare Demokratie und innere Sicherheit: Grundlagen, Praxis und Kritik* (Opladen: Westdeutscher Verlag, 1991); and H.H. Kalinowsky, *Kampfplatz Justiz: Politische Justiz und Rechtsextremismus in der Bundesrepublik Deutschland 1949–1990* (Pfaffenweiler: Centaurus, 1993).
6. See the case studies in van Donselaar, *De staat paraat?*
7. Ibid., pp. 267–94.
8. Ibid.

9. Ibid., pp. 269–72.
10. See H.J. Schwagerl, *Verfassungsschutz in der Bundesrepublik Deutschland* (Heidelberg: C.F. Müller Juristischer Verlag, 1985); and *Schwargerl, Rechsextremes Denken: Merkmale und Methoden* (Frankfurt-am-Main: Fischer Taschenbuch Verlag, 1993).
11. See van Donselaar, *De staat paraat?*, pp. 269–72.
12. Ibid.
13. Ibid.
14. See P. Gordon, *Racial Violence and Harassment* (London: Runnymede Trust, 1990); and Gordon, 'The Police and Racist Violence in Britain', in T. Björgo and R. Witte (eds), *Racist Violence in Europe* (New York: St Martin's Press, 1993), pp. 167–78.
15. Ibid.
16. See van Donselaar, *De staat paraat?*, pp. 107–16.
17. See C. Lloyd, 'Racist Violence and Anti-Racist Reactions: A View of France', in Björgo and Witte, *Racist Violence in Europe*, pp. 207–20.
18. See van Donselaar, *De staat paraat?*, pp. 57–65.
19. Ibid., pp. 164–8.
20. Ibid., pp. 272–6.
21. Ibid.
22. See J. Valaers, 'Verdraagzaamheid ook t.a.v. onverdraagzamen? Enkele beschouwingen over de beteugeling van racistische en xenoobe uitingen in een democratische samenleving', in *Recht en verdraagzaamheid in de multiculturele samenleving* (Antwerpen: Maklu, 1993), pp. 303–47).
23. See van Donselaar, *De staat paraat?*, pp. 254–62.
24. Ibid., pp. 255–6.
25. See J. van Donselaar, *Fout na de oorlog: fascistische en racistische organisaties in Nederland 1950–1990* (Amsterdam: Bert Bakker, 1991).
26. See van Donselaar, *De staat paraat?*, p. 279.
27. See U. Backes and J. Eckhard, *Politishcer Extremismus in der Bundersrepublik Deutschland: Band I: Literatur* (Cologne: Verlag Wissenschaft und Politik, 1989); and Backes and Eckhard, *Politischer Extremismus in der Bundersrepublik Deutschland: Band II: Analyse* (Cologne: Verlag Wissenschaft und Politik, 1989); Jaschke, *Streitbare Demokratie und innere Sicherheit; and Schwargl, Rechsextremes Denken*.
28. See van Donselaar, *De staat paraat?*, pp. 281–2.
29. Ibid. pp. 45–57.
30. Ibid., p. 282.
31. Ibid., p. 283.
32. See the portrait of the REP in H.-G. Jaschke, *Die 'Republikaner': Profile einer Rechtsaussenpartei* (Bonn: J.H.W. Dietz Nachf, 1993).
33. See van Donselaar, *De staat paraat?*, pp. 283–5.
34. Ibid.
35. Ibid.
36. Ibid., p. 287.
37. Ibid., p. 288.
38. Ibid., p. 289.
39. Ibid.
40. Ibid., p. 290.
41. Ibid., pp. 290–1.
42. Ibid., p. 292.
43. Ibid., p. 293.
44. Ibid., p. 294.

Conclusion

Leonard Weinberg

ONE OF the benefits of writing the conclusions to a collection of essays is that it permits the author to step back and examine the issues raised by the other contributors. I intend to take advantage of this opportunity by placing the previous discussions of right-wing extremism in Europe within a somewhat wider perspective.

Readers who have made their way through the chapters of this book will be aware that the authors, taken collectively, have sought to identify the defining attributes both theoretical and behavioural of the contemporary far right. Once they have defined their terms, they have then sought to explain why the far right enjoys the support it does. Why and where are they strong? Who votes for the various far-right parties and why do they do so? When and under what circumstances do young people join right-wing, racist groups, chant 'Foreigners Out' and then launch physical assaults on passersby belonging to racial and religious minorities? How widespread are racist and xenophobic attitudes among members of the general public? Are these attitudes waxing or waning? And what, if anything, can state agencies, non-governmental organizations and local communities do about these distressing developments?

In an era in which 'globalization' has become a term common to peoples on virtually all the continents, we will perhaps benefit by viewing Europe's far right from a wider perspective. In this regard it is well worth calling to the reader's attention Timothy Garton Ash's recent observation about the very idea of 'Europe'.[1] In writing about the responses of the EU and the major Western European governments to the events of 11 September 2001, Ash notes that 'Europe' as both geographic location and a particular political identity began to replace 'Christendom' in the wake of the Crusades and in relationship to the advances of Islam at the edges of this geopolitical entity.

Even earlier, Ash writes: 'The first political usage of the term [Europe] comes in the eighth and ninth centuries as the descendants of the Prophet ... are thrusting by force of arms linked to a faith ... into the underbelly of

Europe.'[2] Or, to quote Norman Davies along the same lines: 'To talk of Muhammad and Charlemagne, however, is not enough. Islam affected Eastern Europe even more directly than it affected Western Europe. Its appearance set the bounds of a new, compact entity called "Christendom" ... Above all, it created the cultural bulwark against which European identity could be defined. Europe, let alone Charlemagne, is inconceivable without Muhammad.'[3] In other words, 'Europe' to a large extent became Europe because of the prolonged tension between Christendom and Islam. Today, are we witnessing a renaissance of this historic intercivilizational tension? And, if so, what is its relevance so far as Europe's far right is concerned?

Around the periphery of the Muslim world today there are small groups of the most extreme Islamists engaged in armed conflicts aimed, among other things, at expelling Western influences – political, cultural, economic – from the House of Islam.[4] These extremist bands may be found from East Asia to Sub-Saharan Africa. Europe has not been exempt from their operations, as recent events in Albania (a centre for Al Qaeda's European operations), Chechnya and Macedonia suggest.[5] In addition, a number of European countries have not been merely the venue for the planning of terrorist assaults on American targets but the targets themselves, as in the case of France because of its government's support for the Algerian regime's largely successful struggle with the Armed Islamic Group.[6] Commentators have gone out of their way to stress that these radical Islamist organizations hardly represent the mainstream of the Muslim population either in the Middle East or on a world wide basis.[7] Approximately the same may be said with respect to Europe's general population.

The majority of respondents to the 1997 Eurobarometer survey and other polling instruments appear relatively tolerant and supportive of democratic values. Nevertheless, as Charles Westin's analysis indicates, a significant segment of the public in various Western European countries defines itself as racist (even while asserting their support for democratic principles) and resents the presence of so many extra-European immigrants in these previously far more homogenous societies. Clearly, not all the extra-European immigrants and their native-born offspring are from the Muslim world. Yet at least according to one reasonable estimate, over 11 million of these new Europeans are of such origin.[8] What are the political consequences of this presence?

One answer is that Europe, Western Europe in particular, now abounds with far-right groups whose followers define themselves as militant opponents of the growing Muslim presence. For instance, the Norwegian right-wing activist Arne Myrdal argues that immigrants and asylum-seekers are really pioneers in a Muslim army of conquest. 'According to this theory, the so-called refugees have come to establish "bridgeheads" for Islam in Norway. This is part of an evil Muslim conspiracy to establish global Islamic rule.'[9]

In many cases the violent attacks directed against Muslim residents of Norway, Sweden, Germany, France, Britain, etc. are perpetrated by loosely organized and frequently inebriated teenage gang members without any coherent set of political ideas to justify their assaults.[10] Ingo Hasselbach, the former German neo-Nazi figure, who certainly had coherent political ideas, nonetheless captures their sensibility: 'There's a unique thrill to being in the middle of a violent dangerous crowd and slugging, slamming and kicking your way to victory.'[11] In addition to these anomic action-seekers, at least some of the anti-Muslim violence is committed by xenophobic, right-wing bands.

Eastern Europe has hardly been exempt from the newly revived anti-Muslim sensibility. In at least one horrific instance the latter achieved the status of state policy. The 'ethnic cleansing' campaigns in both Bosnia and Kosovo undertaken by the Yugoslav government in Belgrade and its client Bosnian Serb mini-state were frequently justified by Slobodan Milosevic, Radovan Kasradzic and their spokesmen as a defence of European civilization under threat by a new Muslim attack on the Balkans. Similar sentiments have been at work in Croatia as well.[12]

A second answer to the question about the political consequences of the growing Muslim presence in the countries of Western and Central Europe concerns party politics. As readers of this and other volumes on far-right European political parties are aware, the relationship between the latter's success at the polls and the magnitude of the North African, South Asian and Turkish populations is complicated. In his book *The Radical Right in Western Europe* Herbert Kitschelt reports 'the virtual absence of any systematic relationship between the success of the Extreme Right in the 1980s and objective or subjective measures of societal "stress" imposed by immigration and ethnocultural pluralization.'[13]

Kitschelt's observation certainly may be true when we consider the relationship between voter support for far-right parties and the presence of immigrants from Muslim and other countries at the national level. And the same may be said about the linkage between the size of the immigrant population and the magnitude of xenophobic responses on national opinion surveys. But there are other factors to consider (see Roger Eatwell's observations earlier in this volume). What may be true at the national level, for example, may not hold at the local or regional levels. Consider, for example anti-immigrant feelings in Eastern Germany, Northern Italy and Flanders. Also, the British and German cases are illustrative. The leaders of conventional parties of the right, Margaret Thatcher and Helmut Kohl for example, may contest the electoral space the far-right parties are attempting to occupy by making speeches and subsequently by taking the lead in enacting anti-immigrant legislation. Just as the extreme right parties are not 'single-issue' parties, so too they have no monopoly over the immigration issue.

If we pay attention to the rhetoric of such far-right leaders as Jean-Marie Le Pen, Filip Dewinter, Jörg Haider, Gerhard Frei, Christoph Blocher, and indeed the entire leadership of Western Europe's more successful far-right parties, the anti-immigrant sentiments are hard to ignore – as are the calls for repatriation, voluntary or otherwise, contained in their campaign appeals to the voters.[14] According to Minkenberg and other analysts, the 'new racism' is not biological but cultural. That is, each of the world's cultures has its own natural geographic space. From this perspective, Muslim culture and its bearers are certainly valuable but neither belongs nor should be part of the European landscape.[15]

The European far right's campaign against the growing Muslim population is only part of the story, however. In this regard we should not forget that at the beginning of 'Operation Desert Shield' in 1990, the American-led drive to expel Saddam Hussein's forces from Kuwait, the FN's leader, Jean-Marie Le Pen, visited Baghdad in order to express his sympathies. For some French and German neo-Nazis the affinity went beyond the sentiment. The former German neo-Nazi figure Ingo Hasselbach reports:

> As international preparations for the war progressed that fall, many neo-Nazis saw it as their great chance to get involved in a fight against Israel. Michael Kuhnen and Michel Faci, the French Fascist, founded an 'Anti-Zionist Legion' of German neo-Nazis to fight in the Gulf on the Iraqi side … Faci went to Baghdad at Saddam Hussein's invitation to set things up. They signed a contract to provide German volunteers … to support Iraq against the 'present aggression of Zionist and US imperialist forces …'[16]

The Gulf War ended too abruptly for this foreign neo-Nazi legion to have had any impact on the 'Zionist and US imperialist forces' arrayed against Saddam's Republican Guards. But the avidity with which Faci, Kuhnen and other neo-Nazis came forward to participate in the fight against the American-led alliance and Israel (obviously not a direct belligerent) draws our attention to the fact that the coin has another side.

From the interwar period onwards, certain European fascists and neo-fascists have expressed an affinity for the Arab world, what they understood to be its Islamic values in particular. For instance, the Italian fascist philosopher Julius Cesare Evola, whose writings condemned the materialism of modern industrial civilization, expressed admiration for the values of self-sacrifice and heroism expressed in the concept of *Jihad*.[17] Many of Evola's admirers in Italy and elsewhere in Europe followed his lead. Beyond these philosophical expressions there is the matter of anti-Semitism and hostility to the state of Israel. Both these sentiments are widely shared by the public in the various Arab countries and the European far right, at least certain segments of it. To ask the proverbial question then, what about the Jews?

What about the Jews? As with America's radical right, is there something of a division of labour at work? In his book *The Racist Mind* the psychologist Raphael Ezekiel reports on a series of interviews he had with far-right leaders and followers in the United States. Ezekiel discovered that the followers, the white working-class members of the Detroit area Death's Head Strike Group for example, directed their hatred at African-American and Hispanic people in their immediate surroundings. They perceived 'the Jews', to the extent they perceived them at all, as an abstraction. For the radical right leaders, on the other hand, 'the Jews' were an obsession.[18] For Tom Metzger, founder of the White Aryan Resistance, and other far-right leaders, the masses of African-American, Asian and Hispanic peoples populating Los Angeles and America's other major cities were a source of racial contamination, etc., but they were not the real villains. They reserved the latter role for Jews. As Metzger and the others saw it, the Zionist Occupation Government (ZOG) controls developments in Washington, including the Federal Reserve System. Israel directs American foreign policy. Jews run the entertainment industry and own the major channels of mass communication. Jews promote abortion and birth-control for whites while encouraging interracial marriage. Jews were responsible for the September 11th attacks on the World Trade Center.[19] In short, for America's radical right leaders, 'the Jews' represent an *idée fixe*, an omnipresent source of evil.

Do we find a similar division of labour within Europe's far-right: racism and xenophobia for the foot-soldiers and obsessive anti-Semitism for the elite? If we judge the situation from the point of view of the family of far-right political parties active in Western Europe and base our evaluation on the same kinds of public interviews Ezekiel and others conducted in the United States, the answer is probably not. From time to time Le Pen, Haider, Frei and the other party leaders make relatively circumspect references to Holocaust exaggerations, the inordinate power of certain bankers on the East Coast of the United States and excessive claims Israel and various Jewish organizations have made on the Swiss banks or the German treasury. But these statements do not seem to exhibit the obsessive quality of the American Klu Klux Klan and neo-Nazi types Ezekiel interviewed. The situation in Eastern Europe and Russia is somewhat different, however, as Vera Tolz notes in Chapter 10 the leaders of three Russian parties, the LDPR, NBP and

RNU are willing to make public statements attacking the insidious role of 'the Jews' in Russian national life. As bearers of both communism and international capitalism, they are out to destroy the country's traditional culture.

In the countries of the former Soviet bloc the Jewish communities have shrunk to minuscule size. This fact, however, has not meant that right-wing party leaders in Romania, Hungary, Slovakia and a few other countries have ignored 'the Jews', even when there are few living ones on hand to attack. For instance, deputies representing the Party of Romanian National Unity (PUNR) in that impoverished country's national parliament 'initiated a letter of protest addressed to the US Senate, protesting the appointment of Alfred Moses, the president of the American Jewish Committee, as the next US ambassador to Bucharest. The move was backed by the entire PUNR leadership ...'[20] Likewise, the American Jewish philanthropist George Soros has proven to be a godsend for far-right party leaders. His efforts to promote democratic institutions in Eastern Europe through, inter alia the European University in Budapest, have provided these leaders with an irresistible opportunity to denounce his work as an effort to destroy national cultures and replace them with American- and Zionist-inspired globally focused cosmopolitan societies. So even in the virtual absence of a local Jewish community, the simple appearance of Soros in Prague, Budapest, Bucharest, etc., permits far-right spokesmen to depict their countries as under attack by 'the Jews'.

As in the United States so too in Europe, and on both sides of the former 'iron curtain', it is the small far-right-wing extraparliamentary groups which articulate obsessional Jewish conspiracy theories with the least inhibitions. These organizations, some paramilitarized and almost all now with their own websites, are usually not trying to attract electoral support so much as they hope to win followers drawn from a small race-conscious subculture.[21] Is it possible for them to be both fiercely hostile to 'the Jews' and the 'Islamic invasion' of Europe at the same time? The answer is yes. The underlying principle is race and, specifically, the threat to the 'nordic' race posed by both 'the Jews' and Muslim immigrants to Europe. For instance, Yaron Svoray, an Israeli journalist posing as an American TV reporter, became familiar with the German neo-Nazi 'scene' some years ago. Svoray discovered that the neo-Nazi figures he got to know hated Jews but were also bitterly hostile to Germany's Turkish residents.[22] And according to Ingo Hasselbach's account, Gottfried Kussel, the Austrian neo-Nazi leader, felt the same way. He would lead his band of 'storm-troopers' in attacks on the quarters of asylum-seekers while simultaneously filling his Vienna apartment with the worst forms of anti-Semitic propaganda left over from the Third Reich.

Is there then a division of labour involving racism and anti-Semitism in Europe along the lines suggested by Ezekiel's account of the American radical right in *The Racist Mind*? To the extent that a meaningful division does exist, it tends to occur not within the far-right parties so much as between most of these parties, with their anti-immigrant rhetoric and occasional veiled anti-Semitic references, and the extra-parliamentary right-wing organizations with their anti-Semitic conspiracy theories and often violent attacks on largely Muslim immigrant communities.

The other civilization with which Europe's right-wing extremists are in conflict is really an offshoot of their own. For many on the right, American civilization exemplifies recent developments in their own countries they have come to despise. Trends towards multicultural and ethnically diverse societies come to mind immediately. So does 'globalization'. For the collection of far-right extra-parliamentary groups and political parties discussed in this volume, America stands for the seemingly irresistible trend towards economic and cultural 'globalization'.

The latter term, though not the phenomenon itself, came into widespread usage during the 1980s and was first associated with an enormous surge in direct foreign investments undertaken by multinational corporations.[23] Some of the multinationals involved were of Japanese and European origins, but many of the most visible ones were, and are, based in the United States. And many of the investments flowed from America to Europe, giving those on the right the impression their national economies were being absorbed by the American economy. Some of the multinationals' foreign investments were directed at the world's industrializing countries where labour costs were relatively low. The 'off-shore' manufacture of such products as clothing and steel led to dislocations in Europe's labour markets. Jobs declined in the traditional manufacturing sector. The EU could be blamed, but America seemed an especially attractive target.

The attraction was not based simply on economic considerations. The other element was cultural. The reference here is to fears about the Americanization of European culture. In this context, the European right's opposition to 'globalization' takes the form of opposition to the 'McDonald-ization of society'.[24] The spread of American fast food restaurants and the diffusion of American films, American television shows and such American-based TV networks as CNN have produced a backlash. As is true for the reaction against extra-European immigration, the backlash has hardly been confined to the far right. Nonetheless, in view of the far right's outlook, its party leaders and spokesmen have been quick to exploit the sentiments aroused.

Today the family of European far-right parties and extra-parliamentary organizations represent a politics of backlash, resentment and xenophobia. The appeal, to quote Minkenberg and Schain, is based upon the fact that 'In all fast-growing modernizing countries there are people who cannot cope with cultural and economic dislocation, and who react to the pressures of readjustment with rigidity and close-mindedness.'[25] The curiosity is that in seeking to mobilize support among such individuals, the European far right has come into conflict with not one but two cultures: Muslim and American. The irony is that the various militant Islamist groups operating at the fringes of the Muslim world share the same enemy as the Europe's right-wing extremists – the United States, defined as both a civilization and sponsor of a new world order.

NOTES

1. T. G. Ash, 'Europe at War', *The New York Review of Books* (20 December 2001), pp. 66–8.
2. Ibid., p. 67. Ash cites D. Hay, *Europe: The Emergence of an Idea* (Edinburgh: Edinburgh University Press, 1957) as presenting a particularly cogent analysis of the origins of 'Europe'.
3. N. Davies, *Europe: A History* (New York: Oxford University Press, 1996), p. 258.
4. M. S. Doran, 'Somebody Else's Civil War', *Foreign Affairs*, 81.1 (January/February 2002), pp. 22–42.
5. See, for example, *The New York Times* (9 December 2001), p. A4.
6. See, for example, *The New York Times* (11 December 2001), p. B2; and N. Simon, 'Alarm Bells Along the Champs Elysées', *The Jerusalem Report* (22 October 2001), pp. 36–7.
7. See, for example, J. Esposito, *The Islamic Threat* (New York: Oxford University Press, 1992).
8. J. Cesari, 'Passport Photo with a Headscarf', *Equal Voices*, EUMC, 6 (July 2001), pp. 28–31. For an introduction to the problem of immigration in Western Europe, see especially, M. Baldwin-Wallace and M. Schain (eds), *The Politics of Immigration in Western Europe*, special issue of *West European Politics*, 17.2 (April 1994).
9. T. Bjorgo, 'Extreme Nationalism and Violent Discourses in Scandinavia', in Bjorgo (ed.), *Terror from the Far Right* (London: Frank Cass, 1995), p. 191.
10. See, for example, H. Willems, 'Development, Patterns and Causes of Violence Against Foreigners in Germany', in Bjorgo (ed.), *Terror from the Far Right*, pp. 162–81.
11. I. Hasslebach, *Führer-Ex: Memoirs of a Former Neo-Nazi* (New York: Random House, 1996), p. 21.
12. I. Grdesic, 'The Radical Right in Croatia', in S. Ramet (ed.), *The Radical Right in Central and Eastern Europe since 1989* (University Park, PA: Pennsylvania State University Press, 1999), p. 178.
13. H. Kitschelt, *The Radical Right in Western Europe* (Ann Arbor, MI: University of Michigan Press, 1995), p. 61.
14. See, for example, P. Davies, *The National Front in France* (London: Routledge, 1999), pp. 161–3.
15. For a discussion see, for example, M. Minkenberg, 'The New Right in France and Germany', in P.H. Merkl and L. Weinberg (eds), *The Revival of Right-Wing Extremism in the Nineties* (London: Frank Cass, 1997), pp. 65–90.
16. Hasselbach, *Führer-Ex*, p. 206.
17. See, for example, N. Goodrick-Clarke, *Black Sun* (New York: New York University Press, 2002), pp. 52–71.

18. R. Ezekiel, *The Racist Mind* (New York: Viking, 1995), pp. 61–146.

19. See, for example, 'Reaping the Whirlwind', *Southern Poverty Law Center's Intelligence Report* (Winter 2001), pp. 16–20.

20. M. Shafir, 'The Mind of Romania's Radical Right', in S. Ramet (ed.), *The Radical Right in Central and Eastern Europe since 1989* (University Park, PA: Pennsylvania State University Press, 1999), p. 216.

21. See, for example, J. Y. Camus (ed.), *Extremism in Europe* (Paris: CERA, 1998), *passim.*

22. Y. Svoray, *In Hitler's Shadow* (New York: Doubleday, 1994), *passim.*

23. R. Gilpin, *The Challenge of Global Capitalism* (Princeton, NJ: Princeton University Press, 2000), pp. 22–3.

24. R. Holton, *Globalization and the Nation-State* (New York: St. Martin's, 1998), pp. 166–72.

25. M. Minkenberg and M. Schain, Chapter 7 this volume (p. 163).

Index

aborticide, 82
Adenauer, Konrad, 63
Adorno, Theodore W., 163
Adreatine Caves massacre (Italy), 31
Al Qaeda, 294
al-Islam, Saif (Gadafy's son), 26
Algeria, 294
All Russian Centre for the Study of Public
    Opinion (VTsIOM), 263, 264
ALLBUS survey (Germany), 224
Alleanza Nazionale, Italy (AN) *see* AN (Alleanza
    Nazionale)
Almond, G., 152
Amnesty International, 2
Amsterdam Treaty (1997), 111, 112, 118, 123
AN (Alleanza Nazionale), 25, 74, 154, 155;
    economic interest thesis, 57; elections, 47, 52;
    and immigration, 27, 50, 110; mediatization
    thesis, 61; national traditions thesis, 62; political
    opportunity structure thesis, 59; post-
    industrialism, 146; programmatic thesis, 64; *see
    also* MSI (Italian Social Movement)
Anders Lange Party (*later* Norwegian Progress
    Party FRPn) *see* FRPn (Norwegian Progress
    Party, formerly Anders Lange Party)
Anglo-American New Right, 55
Anti-Islamic Front, 28
Anti-Nazi League, 2–3
Anti-Racism Act, Belgium (1981), 274
anti-Semitism: Arab countries, 297; Austria, 106;
    Eastern Europe, 7, 37; EUMC, purpose, 98;
    France, 30; Germany, 224, 225, 235, 282;
    internet, 227–8; and liberal ideology supporters,
    99; Russia, 251, 252, 266, 267; synagogues,
    attacks on, 16, 30, 41; *see also* Holocaust; Jewish
    people
Antonio, Robert J., 77
Appeal of the 250 (France), 177
Armed Groups and Private Militias Act, France
    (1936), 281
Armed Islamic Group (Algeria), 294
Asians, violence by, 1–3
assimilation theory, 10, 107, 108
asylum-seekers, bogus, 2, 234
Aussiedler, 107
Australia, ONP (One Nation Party), 9, 79–80, 88
Austria: anti-Semitism, 106; economic interest
    thesis, 56, 57; electorate, socioeconomic
    background, 186; EU sanctions, 75, 105–6;
    Eurobarometer survey (2000), 112; extreme
    right, political impact, 144; Federal Party
    Congress, 205; Greens, 196; immigration, 13, 30,
49, 51, 105, 106; *Länder*, 196; *Lager*, 13, 196; *Land*
    government, 196, 197, 205, 206, 207, 211, 212;
    Landtag elections, 197, 198; Liberal Forum, 196;
    Libya, aid from, 26; on minority groups, 120;
    protest thesis, 51; revival of extremism, 74; right-
    wing voters, 11; rise of extreme right,
    explanations, 149, 151, 152; Second Republic,
    196; self-declared racism, 102; single-issue thesis,
    49; social breakdown thesis, 53, 54; SORA
    (Institute for Social Research and Analysis), 9,
    111, 112, 113, 119, 122; Upper, FPÖ
    membership composition, 204, 205; Waldheim
    affair, 13; *see also* FPÖ (Austrian Freedom Party);
    LIF (Liberales Forum), Austria; NDP (Austrian
    party); ÖVP (Austrian People's Party); SPÖ
    (Austrian Social Democratic Party); VdU
    (Austrian far-right party)
authoritarianism, 153, 239; FN, 169
Automobilist Party, Switzerland, 130
Aylesbury, violence in, 1

Baburin, Sergei, 16, 259
Baden-Württemberg: acts of violence, 37, 222,
    223; REP, electoral successes, 228, 239, 241
Balladur, Edouard, 183
Barkashov, Aleksandr, 15, 251
Baruskov, General Nikolai, 268
Bauböck, R., 118
Belgium: Austria and, 25; cordon sanitaire, 286;
    demonstrations, ban on, 275; economic interest
    thesis, 57; electorate, socioeconomic
    background, 186; extreme right, political
    impact, 144; FNB (Front Nouveau de
    Belgique), 154; football violence, 33, 34;
    immigration, 27, 30–1, 51–2, 106; institutions/
    political establishment, distrust, 104; KP (Belgian
    Trotskyist party), 145; on minority groups, 120;
    Private Militias Act (1934), 281; protest thesis,
    51; racist propaganda, 274; right of association,
    281; right-wing voters, 11; rise of extreme right,
    explanations, 149, 151, 152; self-declared racism,
    102; social breakdown thesis, 54; VB (Vlaams
    Block) *see* VB (Vlaams Block), Belgium; VMO
    (Flemish militant order), 281
Beliaev, Iurii, 261
Berlin, acts of violence, 223
Berlin Holocaust Memorial, demonstrations
    against, 37
Berlusconi, Silvio, 47, 59, 74
Betz, Hans-Georg, 8–9, 74–93, 127
Bezverkhii, Viktor, 262
Bjorgo, Tore, 43

BKA (German Federal Criminal Office), 35
Black Hundreds (anti-Semitic bands), 15, 252, 255, 261
Blackburn, 56
Blair, Tony, 2, 3
Blocher, Christoph, 27, 78–9
BNP (British National Party), 1, 2, 3, 8, 9, 154; economic nationalism, 81; elections, 48, 68; immigration, 27, 64; mediatization thesis, 61; national traditions thesis, 62; political opportunity structure thesis, 58; post-industrialism, 146; post-material thesis, 56; programmatic thesis, 64; soccer hooliganism, 34; and White Resistance movement, 82, 83
Bosnia, 295
Bossi, Umberto, 31, 66, 67, 83, 84, 127, 130
Bradford, violence in, 1–3, 6
Brandenburg, East Germany, 14, 37
Britain: Austria and, 25; Combat 18 group, 34, 76; demonstrations, ban on, 275; economic interest thesis, 57; governmental responses, 288; Holocaust denial, 274; immigration, 9, 27, 64, 108, 118; majority system, 3, 284; marginality of extreme right, 144; National Crime Intelligence Service (NCIS), 32; National Front (NF) see NF (National Front), UK; political broadcasting time, 285; post-material thesis, 56; Public Order Act (1936), 273; Race Relations Act (1965), 18, 273; racist propaganda, 274; rise of extreme right, explanations, 149; soccer hooliganism, 2, 3, 31–4; Spearhead group, 277–8, 280; violence in, 1–3, 6; see also BNP (British National Party); United Kingdom
British National Party (BNP) see BNP (British National Party)
Brox, Ottar, 121
Bundesrat (territorial chamber, FPÖ), 207
Burgenland elections (Austria), 197, 206
Burger, Norbert, 143
Bush, President George (Senior), 12
BVS (Office for the Protection of the Constitution, Germany), 8, 36, 38, 59, 150, 221, 227

Cable, Vincent, 85
Canadian Reform Party, 78
Canovan, Margaret, 78, 79
Carinthia: FPÖ membership composition, 204, 205; Jörg Haider, governor of, 207, 211
CD (Centre Democrats, Netherlands), 153, 154, 284
CDU (Christian Democrat Party, Germany), 25, 35, 36, 43, 89; elections, 228, 235; 'Grand Coalition' with Social Democrats, 130; political opportunity structure thesis, 58; protest thesis, 52; social breakdown thesis, 53
Ceaușescu, Nicolae, 24, 26
Central Council of Jews (Germany), 37
Centreparty '86 (neo-Nazi), 282
Cerny, Philip, 86
Chambers of Labour and Commerce (Austria), 208
charismatic leader thesis, 65–7
Charleroi, soccer violence at, 33
Chechnya, war against, 16, 256
Chirac, President Jacques, 30, 58, 184
Christian Democrat Party, Germany (CDU) see

CDU (Christian Democrat Party, Germany)
Christian Democrats, Italy (DC), 59
Christianization of Kievan Rus (988), 254
Churchill, Sir Winston, 26
CNN TV network, 299
Cold War, 167
Combat 18 group (UK), 34, 76
Commonwealth Immigration Act (1968), 108
Comparing Democracies: Elections and Voting in Global Perspective (L. LeDuc), 133
'competition state', 86
Convention on the Elimination of all Forms of Racial Discrimination (1966), UN (United Nations), 273, 281, 282
cordon sanitaire, 285–7
Cossacks, 261
Cossiga, President (Italy), 59
CP (Centre Party, Netherlands), 153, 277, 278, 280
CPRF (Communist Party of the Russian Federation), 16, 258, 260, 268; public support, 263, 264; Russian establishment, 266, 267
CPSU (Communist Party of the Soviet Union), 253
Creil incident (1989), 63
Crimea, Ukraine jurisdiction over, 259
Criminal Code, Article 74 (Russia), 265
CSU (Christian Social Union, Bavaria), 35; protest thesis, 52; social breakdown thesis, 53
Czech Republic, 17

D'Alema, Massimo, 25
Dalton, Russell, 130
Davies, Norman, 294
DC (Christian Democrats, Italy), 59
de Vries, Claas, 28
Death's Head Strike Group (Detroit), 297
demand-side theories, 48, 49–58, 67; economic interest thesis, 56–8; post-material thesis (reverse), 56; protest thesis, 51–2; single-issue thesis, 49–51; social breakdown thesis, 52–4
Demin, Viacheslav, 262
Democracies: Patterns of Majoritarian and Consensus Government in Twenty-One Countries (Lijphart), 133
democracy: 'defensible', 285; and globalization, 70; and radical right, 77, 162
demonstrations, 31, 37, 275–7; neutral/non-neutral regulations, 275, 277
Den (Russian newspaper), 260
Denmark: Austria and, 25; DF (Danish People's Party), 27, 88; DFP party, 154; Eurobarometer survey (2002), attitude dimensions, 115, 117; FRPd (Danish Progress Party), 79, 109, 143, 145, 149, 150, 154; immigration, 9; integration, 101; on minority groups, 120; rise of extreme right, explanations, 149, 150, 151, 152
Dewinter, Filip, 30
DF (Danish People's Party), 27, 88
DFP (Danish party), 154
discourse analysis, 61
discursive opportunity structure, 62
DPA (Movement in Support of the Army), Russia, 260
Dreux, FN success, 177, 184
DRP (German Rightist Party), 282
Düsseldorf, bomb attack in, 43

Dugin, Aleksandr, 16, 254, 260
Duke, David (Ku Klux Klan leader), 82
Duma (federal parliament chamber, Russia), 252, 258
Durkheim, Emile, 237
Dutch People's Union (NVU), 282
Dutch Popular Militia, 28
DVU (German People's Union), 8, 9, 35, 36, 154;
    economic nationalism, 81, 82; elections, 48, 228,
    235, 239; national traditions thesis, 62; political
    opportunity structure thesis, 58; post-
    industrialism, 146; post-material thesis, 55

Eastern Europe: on democracy, 17; racism in, 7; *see
    also* Western Europe
Eatwell, Roger, 8, 47–73, 295
Eckert, R., 232
economic interest thesis, 56–8
economic nationalism, 81
Edinger, M., 236
education, Eurobarometer surveys, 119–20
efficacy, 69
Eichmann, Adolf, 31
Electoral Systems and Party Systems (A. Lijphart), 133
electorate *see* voting behaviour
Elementy (Russian periodical), 260
Emelianov, Valerii, 254
employment status, racism/xenophobia, 120–1
encadrement, 181
ENEP (Effective Number of Electoral Parties),
    Greece, 145
EPEN (National Political Union), Greece, 145
equal opportunities, 118
Erfurt, 41
Ersson, S.O., 133
Esping-Andersen, G., 132
ETA (terrorist group), 123
ethnic cleansing, 295
ethnic nationalism, 52–3
ethnocentrism, 153, 177
ethnopluralism, 84
EU (European Union): age composition, member-
    states, 119; Amsterdam Treaty (1997), 111, 112,
    118, 123; Austria, sanctions against, 75, 105–6;
    Eurobarometer survey (1997), 99–100;
    Eurobarometer survey (2000), 113, 114; extreme
    right, strength of, 25–6, 29
Eubank, William, 10–11
EUMC (European Monitoring Centre on Racism
    and Xenophobia), 98, 111, 112–13, 119
Eurobarometer surveys: in 1997, 98–105, 294; in
    2000, 10, 101, 111–22; attitude dimensions,
    115–19; attitudinal differences, explaining,
    119–22; education, 119–20; gender differences,
    119; methodological obstacles, 112–13
Eurocup riots (2000), 2, 3, 32
European Council, on racism, 220
European Court of Human Rights, 25
European Monitoring Centre on Racism and
    Xenophobia (EUMC), 98, 111, 112–13, 119
European Union (EU) *see* European Union (EU)
Evola, Julius Cesare, 296, 297
Evreux, 48
exclusionary populism, 77–80, 82, 84, 88
exclusionary welfarism, 9
extreme-right groups: banning of, 280–3;
    comparison, rationale, 39–43; development of
    (twentieth century), 143–58; Germany, 226–8;

growing threat, 74–93; ideology, 146, 162–3,
    166–9, 234; origins, 4; parties, characteristics,
    5–6, 11; rise of, factors explaining, 149–53, 154;
    social movements, 5, 6; subcultures, 5, 6, 15, 54;
    theories, 47–73; values, 53; *see also* far-right
    support, national variations (1990–2000);
    political parties
Ezekiel, Raphael, 297, 299

Fabius, Laurent, 184
FANE (Federation of National European Action),
    165
FAP (Free Workers' Party), Germany, 283
far-right support, national variations (1990–2000),
    126–42; findings, 133–8; methodology, 131–3;
    theories, 128–31
fascism, 76–7, 110–11; structural, 121
Fassman, H., 132
FDP party (Switzerland), 154
FDVP (Freiheitliche Deutsche Volkspartei),
    Germany, 228
Federal Office of Investigation (Germany), 221
Federal Party Congress, Austria, 205
Federal Republic of Germany (FRG), 107, 245, 285
Federation of National European Action (FANE), 165
Fini, Gianfranco, 25, 31, 62, 127
Finland: Eurobarometer survey (2002), attitude
    dimensions, 117; immigration, 109–10;
    integration, 101; on minority groups, 120;
    proto-fascist re-emergence, 143–4; self-declared
    racism, 102
first-past-the-post electoral system, 3, 283–4
FN (Front National), France, 10, 11, 25, 151, 152,
    153, 154, 161–89; action against, 273, 278, 281;
    charismatic leader thesis, 66; coalition
    formation, 181–3; collective action, 176–7;
    creation, 165, 169; demonstrations and, 276, 277;
    economic interest thesis, 57; elections, 47, 48,
    57, 123, 126, 153, 170; exclusionary populism,
    79; hegemon, party as, 164–71; ideology, 166–9;
    immigration, 12, 27, 29–30, 49–50, 53, 110,
    171–5; interaction, impact of, 176–85; issue
    priorities, 178–81; Languedoc-Roussillon,
    'Programme of Action' with, 182; local power,
    185; National Assembly (1997), 168, 183–4;
    national traditions thesis, 62; new radical right,
    concept, 162–71; parliamentary representation,
    144; party 'families', 163; policy agenda
    formation, 183–5; political isolation, 286, 287;
    political opportunity structure thesis, 58, 59, 60;
    post-industrialism, 145, 148; post-material thesis,
    55; programmatic thesis, 64, 65; protest thesis,
    52; racism, 101; single-issue thesis, 49–50, 51;
    social breakdown thesis, 53; social movement
    research, 176; split (2000), 12; structures, 163–4;
    subcultures, 54; xenophobia, 50
FNB (Front Nouveau de Belgique), 154
FNJ (Front national de jeunesse), France, 177
football hooliganism, 2, 3, 7–8, 31–4
Football Offences and Disorder Act (1999), 32
Fortuyn, Pim, 54
Forza Italia, 47, 59
FPÖ (Austrian Freedom Party), 7, 9, 10, 13, 14, 25,
    26, 27, 74, 80, 153, 154, 191–219; charismatic
    leader thesis, 66; economic interest thesis, 56, 57;
    elections, 47, 48, 57, 74, 126, 127, 153, 193–201,
    238–9; elite recruitment, 206; exclusionary

populism, 79; extent of membership, 202–4;
ghetto period, 192, 193, 202, 203; governmental
responsibility, 192; immigration, 30, 49, 51, 105;
internal organization, 201–12; mediatization
thesis, 61; membership composition, 204–7;
normalization period, 192, 202, 203;
parliamentary representation, 143, 144; party
central office, 209–12; party on the ground,
202–7; party in public office, 207–9; political
opportunity structure thesis, 59; populist protest,
192, 199, 202, 203, 210–11; post-industrialism,
148; programmatic thesis, 64; protest thesis, 52;
racism, 101; single-issue thesis, 51; 'singularity',
192; social breakdown thesis, 53
Fraf, Jürgen, 83
France: Appeal of the 250, 177; Armed Groups and
Private Militias Act (1936), 281; Austria and, 25;
cordon sanitaire, 287; demonstrations, ban on,
275; economic interest thesis, 57; equal
opportunities, 118; Eurobarometer survey
(2000), 112; governmental responses, 288;
immigration, 12, 27, 29–30, 49–50, 51, 63,
106–7, 110, 118, 171–5; integration, 101;
majority system, 284; post-material thesis, 56;
Poujadist movement (1956–58), 143; protest
thesis, 51; racism, 7, 274; right-wing voters, 11;
rise of extreme right, explanations, 149, 151,
152; self-declared racism, 102; single-issue thesis,
49; Sofres survey (2000), 30; xenophobia, 30, 49,
51; see also FN (Front National), France; FNJ
(Front national de jeunesse), France; GRECE
(Groupement de recherche et d'études pour la
civilisation européenne); MNR (Mouvement
National Républicain), France; PCF (Parti
Communiste Française); PS (Parti Socialiste),
France; RPR (French Gaullist party); SCALP
(anti-fascist movement), France; UDF (French
right-wing party)
Franco, General Francisco, 5
Frankfurt School, 150
Free Palestine Press, 254
Free Workers' Party, Germany (FAP), 283
Freiheitliche Deutsche Volkspartei (FDVP),
Germany, 228
Frey, Gerhard, 36, 228
FRG (Federal Republic of Germany), 107, 245, 285
Fritsche, Klaus-Dieter, 36
Front National Party see FN (Front National), France
FRPd (Danish Progress Party), 79, 109, 143, 145,
149, 150, 154
FRPn (Norwegian Progress Party, formerly Anders
Lange Party), 9, 27, 79, 143, 145, 154, 155;
elections, 74; post-industrialism, 145, 149;
programmatic thesis, 65; rise of extreme right,
explanations, 150; single-issue thesis, 50
Fukuyama, Francis, 70

Gadafy, Muammar, 24
Galinski, Heinz, 37
Garland, Jon, 34
Garton Ash, Timothy, 293
GDR (German Democratic Republic), 39, 42, 107
Geertz, Clifford, 6
gender differences, Eurobarometer surveys, 119
Geneva Convention (1951), 28
Gera, 41
German Basic Law (Constitution), 43, 233

German Democratic Republic (GDR), 39, 42, 107
German Law on Political Parties, 18
German Office of Constitutional Protection
(BVS), 8, 36, 38, 59, 221, 227
Germany, 220–50; anti-Semitism, 224, 225, 235,
282; 'decriminalization' of history, 78;
demonstrations, dealing with, 275; electorate,
socioeconomic background, 186; extremist
organizations, 226–8; Federal Office of
Investigation, 221; football violence, 33–4;
governmental responses, 288; immigration, 50,
107, 118, 234; institutions/political
establishment, distrust, 104; integration, 101;
Kurdish refugees, 220; Länder, 62; on minority
groups, 120; Parties Act (1967), 285; protest
thesis, 52; racism and, 7, 274, 278; Red Army
Fraktion (RAF), 81; RFB (Rotfront, communist
youth of Weimar republic); rise of extreme right,
explanations, 149, 150, 151; SA (Nazi storm-
troopers), 298; Saxony-Anhalt, success of
extreme right, 8, 14, 36; self-declared racism,
102; single-issue thesis, 50; violence, acts of,
35–9, 222–4; Völkisch socialism, 9, 81, 84; voting
behaviour, 228; Weimer Berlin, right-wing
activity, 6, 15; xenophobia, 35–42, 224–5; see also
BKA (German Federal Criminal Office); BVS
(Office for the Protection of the Constitution,
Germany); CDU (Christian Democrat Party,
Germany); CSU (Christian Social Union,
Bavaria); DRP (German Rightist Party); DVU
(German People's Union); FDVP (Freiheitliche
Deutsche Volkspartei), Germany; Free Workers'
Party, Germany (FAP); FRG (Federal Republic
of Germany); GDR (German Democratic
Republic); JN (Young National Democrats),
Germany; NPD (National Democratic Party),
Germany; PDS (Party of Democratic Socialism),
East Germany; REP (Republican Party),
Germany; SED (Socialist Unity Party); SPD
(Social Democrat Party), Germany; SRP
(Socialist Reich Party)
glasnost (transparency), 15
globalization, 12, 57, 70, 85–8, 161, 299;
demonstration against, 31
Goldthorpe, J.H., 132
Gorbachev, Mikhail, 15, 252, 254, 255
Graf, Jürgen, 83–4
Greater Romania Party (PRM), 6–7, 24
GRECE (Groupement de recherche et d'études
pour la civilisation européenne), 169
Greece: assimilation, 10; Austria and, 25; Effective
Number of Electoral Parties (ENEP), 145;
immigration, 106, 111; institutions/political
establishment, distrust, 104; National Political
Union (EPEN), 145; rise of extreme right,
explanations, 149
Green, Michael, 34
Griffin, Roger, 77, 85
GUD (Union Defence Group), 177
Gulf War (1991), 12, 166, 167, 296

Hague, William, 2
Haider, Jörg, 7, 13, 14, 24, 26, 74, 127, 192, 198,
207, 210, 213, 215, 238, 242, 297; charismatic
leader thesis, 66; elections, 47, 48, 105, 148, 191,
193–4; on immigration, 27, 31, 49, 61; on Islam,
84; see also Austria; FPÖ (Austrian Freedom Party)

Hallermann, A., 236
Hamburg, acts of violence, 223
Hammar, T., 118
Hanson, Pauline, 79–80, 88
Hasselbach, Ingo, 295, 296, 298
Heimatschutz website (East Germany), 40
Heitmeyer, Wilhelm, 42–3, 221
Heyder, A., 225
Hill, M., 132
Hillsborough Stadium tragedy (1989), 32
Hitler, Adolf, 5, 13, 26, 106, 259, 274
Holmes, Douglas, 81
Holocaust, 7, 31, 75, 83, 288; denial of, 273, 274, 297
'Holy War' website (Italy), 31
Huber, E., 131
Human Development Index, 132
Hunt, W.B., 133
Hussein, Saddam, 166, 167, 296

Ignazi, Piero, 11, 130, 143–58
Iliescu, Ion, 24
Immerfall, S., 239
immigration: attitudes to immigrants (France), 175;
    Austria, 13, 30, 49, 51, 105, 106; Belgium, 27,
    30–1, 51–2, 106; Britain, 9, 27, 64, 108, 118;
    concentrations of immigrants (France), 171–4;
    Denmark, 9; Finland, 109–10; France, 12, 27,
    29–30, 49–50, 51, 63, 106–7, 110, 118, 171–5;
    Germany, 50, 107, 118, 234; Greece, 106, 111;
    Ireland, 28, 111; Italy, 27, 31, 50, 106, 110, 118;
    Netherlands, 9, 108; Norway, 50–1; Portugal,
    110, 118; Scandinavia, 9; single-issue thesis,
    49–51; Spain, 28–9, 106, 110, 118; strength of
    extreme right, 27–31; Sweden, 108–9;
    Switzerland, 29; United Kingdom, 9, 27; *see also*
    racism; xenophobia
Immigration Control Platform (Ireland), 28
immigration/incorporation policies, 105–11; EU
    core states, 105–7; northern cluster, 100–1,
    108–10; southern cluster, 101, 110–11; *see also*
    assimilation; immigration; integration
Index of Social Progress, 132
individualism, 162
Inglehart, Ronald, 130, 131, 243
institutions/political establishments, trust in, 103–4
integration policy, 9–10, 100–1, 108, 180–1
intermarriage, 82
Ireland: assimilation, 10; extreme right, political
    impact, 144; immigration, 111; on minority
    groups, 120; right-wing reactions, 28
Islam, 84
Italy: assimilation, 10; economic interest thesis, 56,
    57; immigration, 27, 31, 50, 106, 110, 118;
    revival of extremism, 74; right-wing voters, 11;
    rise of extreme right, explanations, 149, 151;
    social breakdown thesis, 53; *see also* Alleanza
    Nazionale (AN); DC (Christian Democrats,
    Italy); Forza Italia; LN (Lega Nord), Italy; MSI
    (Italian Social Movement); MSIFT (neo-fascist
    Italian party); NA (Italian post-fascist group)

Jena, 41
Jewish people: cemeteries, desecration of, 225, 251,
    276; Italian violence, 31; pogroms, Russia, 251;
    public buildings, attacks on, 225; *see also* anti-
    Semitism; Holocaust; Judaism; Judeo-Masonic
    conspiracy; synagogues, attacks on

Jewish World Congress, 79
Jihad (Holy War), 84, 297
JN (Young National Democrats), Germany, 226
John Paul II (Pope), 26
Jospin, Lionel Robert, 184
Judaism, status in Russia, 16
Judeo-Masonic conspiracy, 15, 252

Kameradschaften (comradeships), 226, 227, 229, 245
Karelians, 110
Kasimovskii, Konstantin, 261, 265
Kasradzic, Radovan, 295
Katz, R.S., 201, 202, 209
KGB (Russian secret police), 255
Kitschelt, Herbert, 80, 130, 148, 237, 295
Kjaersgaard, Pia (Denmark), 88, 149
Klestil, Thomas (Austrian President), 26
Klingemann, Hans-Dieter, 129, 130, 163
Klink, Manfred, 35
Klu Klux Klan, 297
Knigge, Pia, 151
Knutsen, O., 133
Kohl, Helmut, 63, 295
Kondratenko, Nikolai, 266, 267
Koopmans, Ruud, 10, 123, 220, 234, 236, 241
Korchagin, Viktor, 266
Kornhauser, William, 14, 225, 244
Kosovo crisis, 84, 295
KP (Belgian Trotskyist party), 145
Krasnodar Krai (Russia), 262, 264, 266
Kurdish refugees, Germany, 220
Kussel, Gottfried, 298
Kymlicka, W., 118

Länder, Austria, 196
Lager (Austria), 13, 196
Land government (Austria), 196, 197, 205, 206,
    207, 211, 212
Landtag elections (Austria), 197, 198
Landtagsabgeordnete (provincial parliamentarians), 207
Lane, J.E., 133
Laucks, Gary, 35
Laver, M., 133
LDPR (Liberal Democratic Party of Russia), 251,
    254, 255, 258–9, 261, 268, 297; public support,
    262, 263, 264, 265; Russian establishment, 266
Le Pen, Jean-Marie, 12, 14, 29–30, 152, 165, 238,
    242, 281, 290, 297; Baghdad visit (1990), 296;
    charismatic leader thesis, 65, 67; as danger to
    democracy, 177; elections, 47, 148, 170; ideology
    of FN, 166, 168; immigration, 110; national
    traditions thesis, 62; street language, 130; trigger
    events, 288; *see also* FN (Front National), France;
    France
lebensunwert (unworthy of life), 83
LeDuc, L., 133
Leeds United, 32
Leeds, violence in, 1
Lega Nord, Italy (LN) *see* LN (Lega Nord), Italy
legitimacy, 68–9, 79; crisis of, 150
Lehmbruch, G., 132
Lepsius, Rainer, 237, 238
LET (legitimacy, efficacy and trust) hypothesis, 49,
    68–70
Libya, 26
LIF (Liberales Forum), Austria,
Lijphart, A., 133

Limonka (Russian newspaper), 261
Limonov, Eduard, 261
Lipset, Seymour Martin, 14, 163, 239
LN (Lega Nord), Italy, 31, 47, 74, 80, 154;
  charismatic leader thesis, 66; economic interest
  thesis, 56; elections, 126, 130; exclusionary
  populism, 78, 79; mediatization thesis, 60; post-
  industrialism, 149; programmatic thesis, 65;
  protest thesis, 52; single-issue thesis, 50; social
  breakdown thesis, 53; and White Resistance
  movement, 83, 84
Lower Saxony, acts of violence, 222, 223
Luther, Richard, 13, 24, 191–219
Luxembourg, 102, 107
Lysenko, Nikolai, 261

Maastricht Referendum (1992), 12, 167, 168
Maaz, H.J., 239
Magnette, P., 106
Mahler, Horst, 81
Mair, P., 133, 201, 202, 209
majority systems, 283–4
Makashov, General Albert, 260, 267
Manchester United, 32
Marignane, FN success, 182, 185
Marseilles, FN success, 184
Marsiglia, Luis, 31
Martin, Pierre, 172, 173
Marx, Karl, 113
mass society theory (Kornhauser), 225
Mayer, Nonna, 151, 173
Megrét, Bruno, 12, 30, 166, 168, 183
Mecklenburg-Pomerania, criminal acts, 14, 221,
  222, 245
media/mediatization thesis, 60–2
Mein Kampf (Adolf Hitler), 274
Merkl, Peter H., 6–8, 23–46
Meskhetian-Turks, attacks on, 262
Metzger, Tom, 297
Michels, Robert, 192, 204
Miloserdov, Vladimir, 263
Milosevic, Siobodan, 83, 295
Minkenberg, Michael, 12, 37, 75, 239, 241, 243,
  252, 296, 300; on Front National (FN), 161–90
MIRN (Portuguese Party), 145
Mittelstand (middle class), 237
Mitterrand, François Maurice Marie, 59, 245
MNR (Mouvement National Républicain),
  France, 12, 30, 154, 155, 166
Möln, violence in (1992), 276
modernization losers, 236
modernization theory, 163, 200
Moiseevich, Urinson Iakov, 267
Moldova, war in, 256
Money, Jeanette, 174
moral traditionalism, 153
Moran, Richie, 33
Moscow Choral Synagogue, 16
Moscow Patriarchate, 262
MSI (Italian Social Movement), 11, 25, 127, 145,
  154; economic interest thesis, 57; elections, 153;
  and immigration, 31, 110; mediatization thesis,
  60, 61; parliamentary representation, 143, 144;
  political opportunity structure thesis, 59; post-
  industrialism, 145; *see also* AN (Alleanza
  Nazionale)
MSIFT (neo-fascist Italian Social Movement), 9, 81

multiculturalism, 83, 99, 101, 108
Munz, R., 132
Mussolini, Benito Amilcare Andrea, 5, 62, 66
Myrdal, Arne, 294
Myrdal, Gunnar, 99

NA (Italian post-fascist group), 126, 127
National Bolshevik Party, Russia (NBP), 261, 297
National Crime Intelligence Service (NCIS), 32
National Democratic Party, Germany (NPD) *see*
  NPD (National Democratic Party), Germany
National Front, UK (NF) *see* NF (National Front),
  UK
National Political Union, Greece (EPEN), 145
National Republican Party, Russia, 259, 261
national settings, changing, 12–18
National Socialism *see* Nazism/Nazi activity
National Socialist Party, Russia, 261
national traditions thesis, 62–3
nationalism: economic, 81; ethnic, 52–3
Nationalrat (lower chamber, FPÖ), 207
NATO (North Atlantic Treaty Organization), 83,
  84, 167
Nazism/Nazi activity, 6, 15, 229; growing threat of
  radical right, 75, 83; racism, 97, 106; theories of
  extreme right, 60, 63; *see also* Holocaust; neo-
  Nazi groups
NBP (National Bolshevik Party), Russia, 261, 297
NCIS (National Crime Intelligence Service), 32
NDP (Austrian party), 143
neo-fascist groups, 75, 76, 154
neo-liberalism, 80, 89
neo-Nazi groups, 1, 37–41, 75, 76, 278, 282, 296
Netherlands: Centre Democrats (CD), 153, 154,
  284; Centre Party (CP), 153, 277, 278, 280;
  demonstrations, ban on, 275, 277; Dutch
  Popular Militia, 28; Eurobarometer survey
  (2000), 112; extreme right, political impact, 144;
  football violence, 34; governmental responses,
  288; Holocaust denial, 274; immigration, 9, 108;
  integration, 101; NVU (Dutch People's Union),
  282; POS theory, 59; proportional
  representation, 284; racist propaganda, 274; rise
  of extreme right, explanations, 149, 151, 152;
  self-declared racism, 102; social breakdown
  thesis, 53, 54; UN Convention (racism), 273;
  VVD (Dutch right-wing party), 52
New Left, 11, 15, 23, 252, 253
New Politics, 176, 177
New Right, 11, 15, 166, 252, 253, 254; Anglo-
  American, 55
New York, terrorist attacks, 15–16, 65, 297
Newton, Judith, 87
NF (National Front), UK, 1, 3, 8; action against,
  288; national traditions thesis, 62; post-material
  thesis, 56; racism, 97; soccer hooliganism, 34
North Atlantic Treaty Organization (NATO), 83,
  84, 167
Northrhine-Westphalia, acts of violence, 222
Norway: immigration, 50–1; revival of extreme
  right, 74; right-wing voters, 11; rise of extreme
  right, explanations, 149, 151, 152
Norwegian Progress Party (FRPn) *see* FRPn
  (Norwegian Progress Party, formerly Anders
  Lange Party)
NPD (National Democratic Party), Germany, 9,
  14, 35, 36, 42, 43, 154, 240; economic

nationalism, 81; elections, 130, 235; membership recruitment, 226–7; national traditions thesis, 62; parliamentary representation, 143; post-industrialism, 146; responses to, 283

NVU (Dutch People's Union), 282

NyD (New Democracy), Sweden, 27, 154

OECD (Organization for Economic Cooperation and Development), 86, 133

Oldham, 56, 58, 61, 68; riots in, 1, 2

ONP (One Nation Party), Australia, 9, 79–80, 88

'Operation Desert Shield', 296

Orange, FN success, 182, 185

Order and Conflict in Contemporary Capitalism (J.H. Goldthorpe), 132

Ordre nouveau, 165, 169

Organization for Economic Cooperation and Development (OECD), 86, 133

origins of extreme-right groups, 4

ÖVP (Austrian People's Party), 13, 24, 191; elections, 47; and FPÖ, 196, 197, 198, 199, 201, 212, 213, 214

Pamiat (Russian far-right movement), 254, 261, 263

Panorama Centre, Moscow, 263

paramilitary organizations, 277, 280

Parteiverdrossenheit (disaffection with party), 152

Parties Act (1967), Germany, 285

Party System Change: Approaches and Interpretations (P. Mair), 133

Pasqua, Charles, 58, 88–9

Pavlov, Nikolai, 259

PCF (Parti Communiste Française), 169, 174

PDC (Portuguese party), 145

PDS (Party of Democratic Socialism), East Germany, 31, 37, 52, 228, 244, 245

Pétain, Marshall, 50

Pelinka, Anton, 192, 213

perestroika (restructuring), 15, 252, 255, 263

Perger, Werner, 24

pluralism/anti-pluralism, 152

polarization, 11, 113, 149

Policy and Party Competition (M. Laver and W.B. Hunt), 133

Political Data Handbook, 131, 132

political opportunity structure thesis (POS), 58–60, 240

political parties, 5–6, 191–2; banning, 280–3; electorate, sociodemographic profile, 155, 170, 186, 206; explanations of rise, 149–53; far-right support, national variations (1990–2000), 126–42; ideal-types (extreme right), 146; right-wing party, meaning, 5; *see also* extreme-right groups; *individual parties*

Politikverdrossenheit (alienation from politics), 152

Pontic Greek Diaspora, 111

populism, 9, 64; exclusionary, 77–80, 82, 84, 88

populist nativism, 88

Portugal: assimilation, 10; Austria and, 25; immigration, 110, 118; on minority groups, 120; PDC party, 145; POS theory, 59–60; rise of extreme right, explanations, 149

POS (political opportunity structure) thesis, 58–60, 240

'positive nationalism', 85

post-industrialism, impact, 11, 145–9; alienation, 147; atomization process, 146, 147; displacement, 147; individualization, 146; parties, development, 154; self-affirmation, 146; self-defence, 147

post-material thesis (reverse), 54–6

postmodernization, 85, 87

Poujade, Pierre, 126

Poujadist movement (1956–58), France, 143, 165

PR (proportional representation) *see* proportional representation (PR)

Private Militias Act, Belgium (1934), 281

PRM (Greater Romania Party), 6–7, 24

programmatic thesis, 63–5

Prohibition on Incitement to Hatred Act (Ireland), 28

Prokhanov, Aleksander, 260

proletarianization, 11

proportional representation (PR), 59–60, 283, 284; Austria, 196

Proporz (political patronage), 199

protest thesis, 51–2

PS (Parti Socialiste), France, 169

public opinion indicators, comparing, 9–11

Public Order Act (1936), 273

PUNR (Party of Romanian National Unity), 298

Putin, President Vladimir, 268

Race Relations Act (UK, 1965), 18, 273

racism, 93–125; Belgium, 274; Britain, 274; employment status, 120–1; Eurobarometer survey (1997), 98–105; Eurobarometer survey (2000), 10, 111–12; European Council report, 220; as European problem, 123; France, 274; Germany, 7, 274, 278; immigration/incorporation policies, 105–11; Netherlands, 274; propaganda, 273–5; self-declared, 101–2; soccer hooliganism, 2, 3, 31–4; UN Convention (1966), 273, 281, 282; *Volksverhetzung* (racist incitement), 222; *see also* immigration; xenophobia

radicalism/radicalization, 11, 74–93, 149, 154, 163

RAF (Red Army Fraktion), Germany, 81

rational choice theory, 236

reactionary tribalism, 77

Reagan, Ronald, 12, 167

REP (Republican Party), Germany, 35, 36, 37, 151, 153, 154, 155; action against, 278, 282–3; adaptation, 290; economic interest thesis, 56; elections, 228, 235, 236, 239, 240–1, 284; immigration, 50, 234; militant actions, 280; political isolation, 286; political opportunity structure thesis, 59; social breakdown thesis, 53

response patterns (Western Europe), 272–301; back-stage behaviour, 279, 291; banning of extreme-right organizations, 280–3; barriers, political systems, 283–5; dilemma of adaptation, 290–1; dilemma of repression, 287; fear of failure, 289; fear of reverse effects, 289; front-stage behaviour, 279, 291; impression management, 291; inhibiting factors, 288; international forces, 287, 288; minority protection, 287, 288; political isolation, 285–7; prosecution policy, 274; public opinion, efforts to influence, 272; racism, dealing with, 272; social organizations, 287, 288; state responses, 287–91; trigger events, 287, 288; underdogs, 289

ressentiments, 78, 79

revisionism, 273
Rex, John, 117
RF (Russian Federation), 255, 257, 259
Riess-Passer, Susanne, 25, 200, 214, 215
right-wing party, meaning, 5
riots, 1–3, 6, 275
RNU (Russian National Unity Party), 15, 16, 251, 254, 259, 261; anti-Semitism, 298; public support, 262, 263, 264, 265; Russian establishment, 266
Rodrik, Dani, 86
Romania: PRM (Greater Romania Party), 6–7, 24; PUNR (Party of Romanian National Unity), 298
Romanov, Petr, 266
ROS (Russian Public Union), 16, 258, 259, 260
Rossiiskaia gazeta (Russian newspaper), 268
Rowe, M., 34
RPR (French Gaullist party), 25, 30, 168, 169, 174, 178, 182, 183
RSFSR (Russian Federation of Socialist Republics), 259
Rucht, Dieter, 162
rule of law, 77
Russia: in 1990s, 251–71; anti-Semitism, 251, 252, 266, 267; Black Hundreds, 15, 252, 255, 261; classification/profiles of extremist groups, 258–62; DPA (Movement in Support of the Army), 260; National Republican Party, 259, 261; National Socialist Party, 261; origins of contemporary right, 15, 252–5; political establishment, and extremists, 265–8; public support, level, 262–5; racist activity, 7; *see also* CPRF (Communist Party of the Russian Federation); LDPR (Liberal Democratic Party of Russia); NBP (National Bolshevik Party), Russia; Pamiat (Russian far-right movement); RNU (Russian National Unity Party); ROS (Russian Public Union); RSFSR (Russian Federation of Socialist Republics); Russian Federation (RF); Soviet Union (former); VTsIOM (All-Russian Centre for the Study of Public Opinion)
Russian Federation (RF), 255, 257, 259
Russian Federation of Socialist Republics (RSFSR), 259
Russian Orthodox Church, xenophobia, 262
Russian Revolution (1917), 15, 252

SA (Nazi storm-troopers), 298
Saltzburg, FPÖ membership composition, 204
Sartori, Giovanni, 84
Saxony-Anhalt, success of extreme right, 8, 14, 36, 245
SCALP (anti-fascist movement), France, 177
Scandinavia, immigration, 9
Schain, Martin, 12, 161–90, 300
Scheler, Max, 78
Schengen Accord/Agreement, 32, 168, 233–4
Scheuch, Erwin, 129, 130, 163
Schleswig-Holstein, acts of violence, 223
Schmidt, P., 225
Schönhuber, Franz, 37
Schroeder, Gerhard (German Chancellor), 43
Schüssel, Wolfgang, 24, 25, 216
Schwarzenbach Initiative (1970), 29
SD (Swiss Democratic Party), 154

SED (Socialist Unity Party), 37
self-declared racism, 101–2
September 11 2001 attacks, 15–16, 65, 297
Shtilmark, Aleksandr, 261
single-issue thesis, 49–51
skinheads, 1, 8, 14, 38–9, 40, 165, 176–7, 264–5
soccer hooliganism, 2, 3, 7–8, 31–4
social breakdown thesis, 52–4
Social Democrat Party, Germany (SPD), 35, 36, 43, 228, 245
social movements, 5, 6, 147; FN, (France), 176; Germany, 231
Social Policy: A Comparative Analysis (M. Hill), 132
Socialist Reich Party (SRP), 282
Socialist Unity Party (SED), 37
socialization theories, 239
Solingen, violence in (1993), 276
SORA (Institute for Social Research and Analysis), Austria, 9, 111, 112, 113, 119, 122
Soros, George, 298
Soviet Ministry of Aviation, 254
Soviet Union (former): Communist Party (CPSU), 253; defectors to Finland, 110; demise, 15, 256, 257; following demise, 255–8; POWs in, 26–7
Spain: assimilation, 10; immigration, 28–9, 106, 110, 118; on minority groups, 120; POS theory, 59–60; rise of extreme right, explanations, 149
SPD (Social Democrat Party), Germany, 35, 36, 43, 228, 245
Spearhead (extreme-right British group), 277–8, 280
Spiegel, Paul, 225
SPÖ (Austrian Social Democratic Party), 13, 130; and FPÖ, 196, 197, 198, 199, 204
SRP (Socialist Reich Party), 282
Steger, Norbert, 13, 193, 199, 210
Stöss, R., 226, 239
Stoke-on-Trent, riot in, 3
Stolpe, President Manfred, 36
structural fascism, 121
Styria, FPÖ membership composition, 204, 205
subcultures, 5, 6, 15, 54
supply-side theories, 48, 58–67; charismatic leader thesis, 65–7; mediatization thesis, 60–2; national traditions thesis, 62–3; political opportunity structure thesis (POS), 58–60; programmatic thesis, 63–5
Svoray, Yaron, 298
SVP (Swiss People's Party), 9, 27, 29, 78, 79
Sweden: Eurobarometer survey (2002), attitude dimensions, 117, 121; extreme right, political impact, 144; integration, 108–9; integration, 101; NyD (New Democracy), 27, 154; POS theory, 60; right-wing voters, 11; rise of extreme right, explanations, 149, 151, 152
Switzerland: Automobilist Party, 130; FDP party, 154; immigration, 29; right-wing voters, 11; SD (Swiss Democratic Party), 154; social breakdown thesis, 54; SVP (Swiss People's Party), 9, 27, 29, 78, 79; Tessin League, 154; World War II, role in, 78–9
synagogues, attacks on, 16, 30, 41

Tadjikistan, war in, 256
Tamás, G.M., 77
Tessin League (Swiss), 154
Thatcher, Margaret, 12, 167, 295

theories, extreme right, 47–73; demand-side, 49–58; LET (legitimacy, efficacy and trust) hypothesis, 49, 68; macro–meso–micro approach, 48, 68; supply side, 58–67
Thierse, Wolfgang, 42
'Third Way' economics, 65
Third World immigration, 175
Three Worlds of Welfare Capitalism (G. Esping-Andersen), 132
Thuringia, acts of violence, 14, 40, 221, 222, 223
Tixiérism, 165
Tolz, Vera, 7, 15, 16, 251–71, 297–8
Toulon, FN success, 182, 185
Townend, John, 2
Trow, M., 237
trust, 69, 103–4
Tudor, Corneliu Vadim, 7, 24
Turkey, football violence, 34
Twin Towers attacks (11 September), 15–16, 65, 297
Tyndall, John, 62

UDF (French right-wing party), 168, 169, 174, 178, 182, 183
UK *see* United Kingdom
Ukraine, Crimea, jurisdiction over, 259
UN (United Nations): Convention on the Elimination of all Forms of Racial Discrimination (1966), 273, 281, 282; Gulf War, intervention in, 167; World Conference against Racism) 2001, 2
Union of Christian Revival (Russia), 262
Union Defence Group (GUD), 177
Union of Orthodox Brotherhoods (Russia), 262
Union of the Veneds, 262
United Kingdom: equal opportunities, 118; immigration, 118; integration, 101, 108; on racism, 98; *see also* Britain
United Nations *see* UN (United Nations)
United States: anti-Americanism (FN doctrine), 167, 168; male role, destablization of, 87; New World Order, 12, 167, 168
universalism, 162
US *see* United States
USSR (Union of Soviet Socialist Republics) *see* Soviet Union (former)

Vadim *see* Tudor, Corneliu Vadim
van Donselaar, Jaap, 17, 27, 272–91
Vasil'ev, Dmitrii, 263
VB (Vlaams Block), Belgium, 10, 18, 88, 153, 154; adaptation, 290–1; demonstrations and, 277; economic interest thesis, 57; elections, 47, 123, 126; exclusionary populism, 78; immigration, 27, 30–1, 51–2, 106; political isolation, 286; post-industrialism, 146, 149; post-material thesis, 55; proportional representation, 284; racism, 101, 274; stability, 291; violence, 280
Vdovin, Aleksei, 265
VdU (Austrian far-right party), 143
Verba, S., 152
violence, 277–80; Belgium, 280; in Britain, 1–3, 6; by Asians, 1–3; as cause of repressive governmental action, 289; football, 33, 34;

Germany *see* violence, extremist/xenophobic (Germany); Italy, 31; nature of extreme right activities, 6
violence, extremist/xenophobic (Germany): acts of, 14, 35–9, 40, 222–4; assessment, 228–30; attitudes, 224–5; data trends, 221–8; demand and supply, 230; elections, 228, 235–6; explaining, 230–5; organizational strength, 235; organizations, 226–8; preconditions, 242–6
Vitrolles, FN success, 182, 185
VMO (Flemish militant order), 281
Völkisch socialism, 9, 81, 84
Voigt, Udo, 81
Volksverhetzung (racist incitement), 222
Vorarlberg group (Austria), 211–12
voting behaviour: apathy, 51; extreme-right theories, 47–73; FN electorate, 170–1; in 1990s, 137; right-wing voters, 10–11; sociodemographic profile, 155, 170, 186, 206
VTsIOM (All Russian Centre for the Study of Public Opinion), 263, 264
VVD (Dutch right-wing party), 52

Waldheim, Kurt, 106
War of Annihilation: Wehrmacht Crimes (travelling exhibit, bombing of), 37–8
Wasmund, Klaus, 38
Weber, Max, 14, 66
Weinberg, Leonard, 10–11, 126–42, 293–301
Western Europe: national variations, far-right support (1990–2000), 126–42; racism, 7; response patterns, 272–301; *see also* Eastern Europe
Westin, Charles, 9–10, 294
White Aryan Resistance, 37, 297
White Power, 28
White Resistance movement, 9, 75, 82–5, 88
Wilcox, Allen, 10–11, 126–42
Willems, H., 232
Winkler, J.W., 239
World Trade Centre, attacks on, 15–16, 65, 297
World Value Survey, 10, 131, 132

xenophobia, 220–50; Britain, 3; comparison of right-wing movements, 39–43; employment status, 120–1; Eurobarometer survey (1997), 98–111; as European problem, 123; France, 30, 49, 51; Germany, 35–42, 224–5; radicalism, extreme right, 76; Russian Orthodox Church, 262; soccer hooligans, 7–8; *see also* EUMC (European Monitoring Centre on Racism and Xenophobia); immigration; racism

Yeltsin, Boris (Russian President), 15, 251, 255, 265, 267
Young National Democrats (JN), Germany, 226
Yugoslavia, former, 83, 295

Zhirinovskii, Vladimir, 15, 16, 263, 266–7
Zimmermann, Ekkart, 14, 220–50
Zionist Occupation Government (ZOG), 297
Ziuganov, Gennadii, 260, 267
Zvolinskii, Viacheslav, 267

DISCARD